Myungkyu Park, Bernhard Seliger.
Sung-Jo Park (Eds.)

Europe – North Korea

Global Cultural and Economic Research

editor-in-chief:

Prof. em. Dr. Dr. h.c. Sung-Jo Park
(Free University Berlin/
Seoul National University/
Yanbian University
of Science and Technology)

in cooperation with

Prof. Dr. Mica Jovanovic
(Megatrend University
of Applied Sciences, Belgrade)

Volume 6

LIT

Europe – North Korea

Between Humanitarism and Business?

edited by

Myungkyu Park, Bernhard Seliger
and Sung-Jo Park

LIT

Bibliographic information published by the Deutsche Nationalbibliothek
The Deutsche Nationalbibliothek lists this publication in the Deutsche Nationalbibliografie; detailed bibliographic data are available in the Internet at http://dnb.d-nb.de.

ISBN 978-3-643-10351-2

A catalogue record for this book is available from the British Library

Fresnostr. 2 D-48159 Münster
Tel. +49 (0) 2 51-620 320 Fax +49 (0) 2 51-922 60 99
e-Mail: lit@lit-verlag.de http://www.lit-verlag.de

Distribution:
In Germany: LIT Verlag Fresnostr. 2, D-48159 Münster
Tel. +49 (0) 2 51-620 32 22, Fax +49 (0) 2 51-922 60 99, e-Mail: vertrieb@lit-verlag.de

In Austria: Medienlogistik Pichler-ÖBZ, e-mail: mlo@medien-logistik.at

In Switzerland: B + M Buch- und Medienvertrieb, e-mail: order@buch-medien.ch

In the UK: Global Book Marketing, e-mail: mo@centralbooks.com

In North America by:

Transaction Publishers
New Brunswick (U.S.A.) and London (U.K.)

Transaction Publishers
Rutgers University
35 Berrue Circle
Piscataway, NJ 08854

Phone: +1 (732) 445 - 2280
Fax: + 1 (732) 445 - 3138
for orders (U. S. only):
toll free (888) 999 - 6778
e-mail: orders@transactionpub.com

Table of contents

Figures and Tables
List of contributors

Introduction *13*
Myoung-Kyu Park, Sung-Jo Park and Bernhard Seliger

Part I. Human Rights, Humanitarianism 19

1. The EU and Inter-Korean Relation: Agency, Method and Theory *21*
Myoung-Kyu Park

2. Training for Economic Reform: The Role of European and Other Actors and NGOs *43*
Peter M. Beck and Nicolas Reader

3. Instrumental versus Solidaric Rationality: European NGOs in North Korea.. *59*
Sung-Jo Park

4. Human Rights Crisis in North Korea: Basic Understanding from the Perspective of International Law *77*
Dae-Soon Kim

Part II. Economic, Political and Ideological Relations between East/West Germany and North Korea, and their legacies 99

5. Reunification in a Constitutional State *101*
Kolja Naumann

6. Differences in Self-Confidence: East Germany, North Korea and Concepts of the Nation *141*

Bernd Schaefer

7. Aspects of North Korean Defectors' Integration in South Korea: Reflection and Application of the German Unification Experience on North Korean Defectors with Cultural Homogeneity *149*

Soon-Hyung Yi

Part III. Capacity-Building and Development 173

8. Capacity Building for Economic Change in North Korea: The Experience of Hanns Seidel Foundation *175*

Bernhard Seliger

9. Specific Structural Features and Future Development Perspectives of the South Korean Province Gangwon *195*

Peter Jurczek

10. Building Up North Korean Foreign Trade Institutions from the Scratch: Lessons from New EU States and the Role of Capacity Building *211*

Ralph M. Wrobel

11. Creating a Good Bank for North Korea (and a bad bank within) – Creative Capacity-Building as a Domain for Asian-European Cooperation *225*

Bernhard Seliger

Part IV. Investment, Business and Business Schools 247

12. The Nampo-Pyongyang Corridor: a Strategic Area for European Investment in DPRK *249*

Stanislas Roussin and César Ducruet

13. The North-Korean IT-sector: "a hidden diamond" Some Observations from a Dutch Consultant.. *269*

Paul Tjia

14. Software and Animation in North Korea: EU Firms' Activities, Korea Computer Centre Europe and Nosotek JV Company and EU's 'Route to DPRK' *277*

Sung-Jo Park

15. From Communist Cadres into Capitalistic Managers?: The Case of Western Business Schools - Pyongyang and Rajin-Sonbong *307*

Joon-Young Hur

Figures and Tables

Figures

Figure 2.1 Relation between instrumental and solidaric rationality 64
Figure 2.2 South and North Hamkyung Province 66
Figure 11.1 The North Korean transport system and truck accessibility of main cities 258
Figure 11.2 Evolution of traffic at Nampo port, 1985-2005 260
Figure 11.3 Overview of the Nampo-Pyongyang corridor 261
Figure 11.4 Direct maritime linkages of Nampo port 265
Figure 13.1 IT outsourcing services and IT enabling services 295
Figure 14.1 Outline of Rajin Business Institute 315

Tables

Table 2.1. Habermasian type of behaviour 63
Table 2.2 Details of German Agro Action Proposal 2002 68
Table 6.1 Demographic information of North Korean defectors 154
Table 6.2 Demographic Information of East Germans 155
Table 8.1 Level and development of population in the cities and the districts in the South Korean Gangwon province (2005 – 2007) 196
Table 10.1 A comparison of four regional development banks 234
Table 10.2 North Korea's Outstanding Debt with the Paris Club of official lenders 241
Table 11.1 Overview of economic activities in main economic areas of North Korea 252
Table 11.2 Benchmarking main economic areas of North Korea 255
Table 11.3 Estimated modal split in 1989 and 2005 257
Table 13.1 Labour Productivity Gap between West and East Germany 279
Table 13.2 Computer programmes developed by East Germans 280

Table 13.3 International Comparison of software engineers (annual, unit: US $) 296
Table 13.4 List of North Korean IT firms for matchmaking for EU-DPRK workshop March 28-29, 2007 298
Table 14.1 ECDP Projects by year 1997 – 2006........ 314

Contributors

Beck, Peter M., Pantech Fellow, Asia-Pacific Research Centre, Stanford University, is a leading expert on Korean peninsula affairs

Ducruet, César, PhD, senior researcher, UMR 8504 Géographie-cités (Paris), specializes in urban and transport economics

Hur, Joon-Young, Ph.D. Candidate of Faculty of Political and Social Sciences, Free University, Berlin; the topic of his dissertation is the "integration of East Germans into the West German economy by means of qualification and occupation

Jurczek, Peter, Dr, Professor, Department of Geography, Technical University of Chemnitz, has considerable experience on research in the inner-Korean border area, where he consulted a project by Hanns Seidel Foundation and Gangwon province

Kim, Dae-Soon, PhD, Professor, Department of Law, Yonsei University, Seoul, Korea; author of many publications on International Law and European Law; formerly Chairman, Korean Association of Contemporary European Studies

Naumann, Kolja, Dr., Institute for International Law, Faculty of Law, University of Cologne, Cologne, Germany

Park, Myoung-Kyu, PhD, Professor, Department of Sociology, Seoul National University /Director, Institute for Peace and Unification Studies (IPUS), Seoul, Korea

Park, Sung-Jo, Professor em. Dr. h.c. Free University, Berlin, Germany; currently Chair professor, Dong-A University, Busan, Korea; formerly Chairman, Euro Asia Management Studies Association (EAMSA); most recent publications include 'System Transformation in Comparative Perspective' (LIT 2007)

Reader, Nicholas, a former researcher with the International Crisis Group

Roussin, Stanislas, General Manager, Korea Strategic Data, has extended experience in business consulting in North and South Korea

Schaefer, Bernd, Dr., Cold War International History Project Senior Scholar, Woodrow Wilson Centre for Scholars,

Seliger, Bernhard Johannes, Dr., representative of Hanns Seidel Foundation, Korea office Senior lecturer (Privatdozent), University of Witten-Herdecke; most recent publications include 'System Transformation in Comparative Perspective' (LIT 2007)

Tjia, Paul, Chairman of GPI Consultancy, the Netherlands; Co-author of the famous book “Offshoring Information Technology: Sourcing and Outsourcing to a Global Workforce” (Cambridge University Press 2005)

Wrobel, Ralph M., Professor of University of Applied Sciences Zwickau, specializes in economic systems and economic transformation and lectured in Eastern Europe and North Korea

Yi, Soon-Hyung, PhD, Professor, Department of Child Development and Family Studies, Seoul National University; Head of the Research Project “Integration of North Korean Defectors in South Korea”, Seoul National University; profound empirical research works on the integration of North Korean refugees into occupation of South Korea

Introduction

Myoung-Kyu Park, Sung-Jo Park and Bernhard Seliger

To write a book about the relations of Europe and North Korea requires some explanation. Europe is not a member of the six-party-talks and it has no intention to be one. Also, its trade with North Korea is negligible by European standards. No wonder then, that, while North Korea figures prominently mainly due to the nuclear crisis in European media, European relations with North Korea are rarely mentioned, if not at all. However, there is an imbalance in this view: while being not involved in official political talks about denuclearisation, Europe has been an important partner for North Korea in terms of humanitarian assistance, as well as capacity-building and cultural exchanges. According to the OECD development assistance database (www.oecd.org/dac/stats/idsonline) the European Union (EU) and some of its member states, notably Sweden and Germany, have been together one of the most important donors of aid to North Korea, on par or exceeding that of the US (depending on the year and that means on the state of political relations of North Korea and the US), and surpassed only, though strongly, by South Korea (before 2008) and China.[1] However, the political role of Europe seems to be underexposed. This role has been described as that of an "honest advisor", based on the particular European and German experiences of division, by Hartmut Koschyk, Chairman of the German-Korean Parliamentary Group in the German Parliament and one of the most active contributors to European-North Korean political exchanges.

Given the imbalance of relatively dense relations (by North Korean standards for relations with the Western world) and relative underexposure of these rela-

1 For an overview of the last years see Nanto/ Chanlett-Avery (2009), p. 41.

tions in the media and in academic discussions the aim of this book, to review the many facets of European – North Korean relations, becomes more understandable. And indeed, the relations between Europe and North Korea have many facets. From a macro-perspective, though the relations have a short history, there can be seen ups and downs. Starting with the influx of European NGOs, when North Korea opened up to humanitarian assistance in the midst of the catastrophic famine of the 1990s, relations had a first peak with the establishment of diplomatic relations with the EU and most member states in 2001. However, this honeymoon phase ended relatively soon, with the revelation of the continuation of North Korea's nuclear programme. The freezing of the planned comprehensive technical assistance programme on the EU level was a logical consequence. Relations had a clear down with the threat to expel all NGOs of the EU in 2005 and the subsequent trimming and reorganisation of European NGOs in so-called "European Union Project Support" units or EUPS. Afterwards, relations were growing again from this much lower level. However, the two nuclear tests of 2006 and 2009 precluded any substantial increase of assistance to North Korea. Looking more closely into the different phases of relations, it is interesting to see that sometimes they are in unison with North Korea's relations to the other members of the six-party-talks, but sometimes they seem to be "counter-cyclical", with European involvement relatively stronger, when relations to the US and to South Korea were on a freeze.

Looking at the multifaceted European – North Korean relations means first of all, to review different fields of interaction, in particular political, humanitarian and business interaction, as well as cultural interaction. Also, it means looking at different actor perspectives, with political actors, NGOs and business actors as well as academic and cultural actors. This perspective is obviously closely intertwined, though not necessarily congruent with the aforementioned perspective. Besides active involvement in relations with North Korea, Europe also serves as a blueprint. Here, in particular the German experience with division and unification has to be mentioned. This also means that the European relations with North Korea never can be seen isolated from those with South Korea. South Korea is a much stronger partner for relations with European countries in terms of the density of political, economic, and cultural exchanges. It has a strong interest in analyzing potential developments in North Korea based on European experiences of transformation and unification. Last, but not least it should be mentioned that European – North Korean relations are not limited to the European Union, but that among the few outsiders of the EU in Europe there are two rela-

tively active in relations to North Korea, namely Norway and, in particular, Switzerland.

This book looks into various perspectives mentioned above, though, given the quite varied experiences in Europe, it cannot be a really exhaustive guide to European – North Korean relations. The experience of NGOs and businesses as well as the comparative analysis of North Korean development perspectives based on the experience of Europe, and in particular Germany, with division, transformation and unification, take precedence in this book. The book is the outcome of multi-annual research cooperation between Hanns Seidel Foundation in Korea and the Institute of Peace and Unification Studies, Seoul National University. In particular, papers of a conference in SNU on European – North Korean relations in June 2007 have been included in the book. The coordinating activities of Prof. Sung-Jo Park, Prof. Emeritus of Free University Berlin, have been pivotal for the publication of this volume. The particular German-Korean connection in this research project is also reflected in the authorship of many, though not all, articles in this volume.

The first section of the book reviews human rights and humanitarian issues in European- North Korean relations from an NGO and legal perspective. The first chapter by Myoung-Kyu Park director of the Institute of Peace and Unification Studies at Seoul National University, co-editor of this volume, not only assesses the European experience of cooperation with North Korea, but also uses Europe's history of integration to analyse possible trajectories of Korea's future integration. The next two chapters discuss the NGO experiences in dealing with North Korea. Peter M. Beck, at the time of writing was working at the U.S. Committee for Human Rights in North Korea, and Nicholas Reader, International Crisis Group, review the experience of European and other actors in training for economic reform. Sung-Jo Park of Free University Berlin (Germany) discusses instrumental rationality versus humanitarian considerations in the work of European NGOs in North Korea. The last paper of Part I, the paper of Dae-Soon Kim of Yonsei University (Korea) reviews the human rights crisis in North Korea from an international law perspective.

The second part includes three papers dealing with economic, political and ideological relations between East and West Germany and North Korea and their legacies. Kolja Naumann of the University of Muenster (Germany) compares the Korean and German case of reunification in a constitutional state.

Bernhard Schaefer discusses differences in self-perception between East Germany and North Korea with regard to the concept of the nation. Soon-Hyung Yi of Seoul National University (Korea) takes up the topic of integration of North Korea defectors into the South Korean society and considers the German model of vocational training as a possible means for integration. This paper is written against the background of an unprecedented inflow of several thousand defectors each year in the last couple of years and the problems of these defectors to integrate into the South Korean society.

Part III looks at European development and capacity-building experiences in North Korea. Bernhard Seliger, resident representative of Hanns Seidel Foundation in Korea, reviews the experience of capacity-building for economic change in North Korea, in particular of the EU-DPRK Trade Capacity Project, one of the first capacity-building project carried out for the European Union as part of the Asia Invest II initiative from 2006-2009. Based on the German experience with the development of the inner-German border area, Peter Jurczek of Technical University Chemnitz (Germany) discusses the development perspectives of the Southern part of the inner-Korean border area, (South) Gangwon province. His research is part of a cooperation project of Hanns Seidel Foundation Korea and Gangwon province on sustainable development in the inner-Korean border area. Ralph M. Wrobel, Professor at the West Saxon University of Applied Sciences (Germany) reviews the lessons from new EU states in building foreign trade institutions from the scratch. Finally, Bernhard Seliger of Hanns Seidel Foundation Korea reviews the problems of defaulted debt and the lack of access to the legitimate financial system of North Korea and the possibility to remedy these problems by the foundation of a Northeast Asian Development Bank, based on the experiences of similar development banks for Eastern Europe and Central Asia

Part IV deals with business activities and training for business for North Korea. Stanislas Roussin of SERIC COREE and César Ducruet, working at the time of writing at the University of Rotterdam, analyze the Nampo-Pyongyang economic corridor as a strategic area for European investment in DPRK. Paul Tjia, a Dutch business consultant with extensive experience in North Korea, views the North Korean IT sector as a “hidden diamond”. Sung-Jo Park of Free University Berlin (Germany) ponders the potential of North Korea to become a centre for software and animation production, based on the experience of two European companies active in North Korea. Finally, Hur-Joon Young of Free

University Berlin (Germany) analyses the chances of converting communist cadres into capitalistic managers by newly emerging institutions in Pyongyang and Rajin-Sonbong (recently merged to Rason).

The two nuclear tests of 2006 and 2009 as well as the hardened North Korean stance throughout 2008 was not foreboding well for improved relations with Europe. However, the history of North Korea has been one where the invariable and the unpredictable always have been in a curious relationship. And this means also that relations between Europe and North Korea are less fixed than pessimists might think and that signs of opening, like those at the time of writing this introduction (February 2010), might lead to new life for European-North Korean relations.

This book would not have been possible without the work of a number of collaborators. First of all, this includes the contributors to the volume. The work would not have been possible without the encouragement from Dr. Hopf, publisher at the LIT Verlag. Also, staff at the Institute for Peace and Unification Studies of Seoul National University and staff at Hanns Seidel Foundation Seoul were important in the collaborative research project, in particular, Hyun-Woo Noh and Chris Antonette Pugay at HSS Korea as editorial assistants. Thanks go to Nari Kim, Seoul National University, for language checking. We hope, this volume can stimulate academic discussion but also exchange activities between Europe and North Korea and help to make relations, cumbersome as they are under the strains of North Korea's political and economic system and nuclear ambitions, a success story.

References

Nanto, Dirk, and Emma, Chanlet-Avery (2009). North Korea – Economic Leverage and Policy Analysis, CRS Report for Congress, August 14, 2009, Washington, D.C.: Congressional Report Service.

PART I

Human Rights, Humanitarianism

1

The EU and Inter-Korean Relation: Agency, Method and Theory

Myoung-Kyu Park

Introduction

Since the mid 1990s, the EU has tried to increase its relationship with Pyongyang with the expressed aim "to support the inter-Korean reconciliation process and to increase assistance to the DPRK in response to progress by North Korea in addressing the concerns of the EU and the international community with respect to human rights, non-proliferation and security issues, progress in inter-Korean reconciliation, economic structural reform and social development."(European Commission 2002) In 1995, when North Korea was experiencing severe economic difficulties, it asked the international community for aid, and in response, the EU launched a programme of humanitarian assistance and economic aid. In addition, the EU participated in the KEDO project, a project based on the Geneva Agreement between the US and North Korea, which focused on resolving North Korea's nuclear problem. After the first inter-Korean summit in 2000, several member states of the EU supported reconciliation in the Korean peninsula and normalised diplomatic relations with Pyongyang. The EU continued to have good relations with North Korea, relations that were strong enough to hold political dialogues on issues such as human rights. Many EU-based NGOs could work within the DPRK, thanks to Pyongyang's positive attitude towards the EU.

In that context, there were frequent discussions around expectations for the role of Europe in resolving the North Korean problem. Topics including denuclearisation and system transformation of North Korea, applicability of the Helsinki process in inter-Korean reconciliation, and mode of integration and unification were discussed among the scholars. (Park, C. 2003; Lee 2009; Smith 2007; Koo n.y.; Park, Y 2009). During the first period of the Bush administration, there was even an expectation of "a more independent international policy of the EU as a reaction to growing concerns about US unilateralism, especially, but not exclusively, after September 11." (Frank 2002). As Frank mentioned, however, the EU wanted to remain in a cooperative role with the US rather than as an independent global player, and since 2003, when the EU initiated the adoption of a Resolution on the North Korean human rights in UN Human Rights Commission, further development of the relationship between North Korea and the EU has been hindered. In terms of the denuclearisation of North Korea, the EU could not find a seat within the six-party talks framework.

As far as denuclearisation issues are concerned, it seems that the EU is not considered to be an independent global player like the US and China. Nevertheless, EU-North Korean relations are still worthy of attention when developing ideas about inter-Korean relations on practical as well as theoretical basis. This paper will focus on three aspects of the EU's experience regarding inter-Korean relation. Firstly, the idea of the EU as an agent in North Korea-related issues needs to be explored. It is clear that the EU, as a powerful polity in the 21th century, could play an important role in inviting North Korea into the international community as well as in establishing a peace regime on the Korean peninsula. Secondly, the EU has shown unique measures in successfully implementing political ideas, and these experiences could provide useful lessons for inter-Korean policy making. Finally, this paper argues that ideas and discourse in developing EU integration are also very important in thinking about a future inter-Korean reconciliation and unification. In this respect, the EU can be a theoretical reference.

The EU as an Agent

The EU has played several roles in relation to North Korea; as a donor of humanitarian aid and technical assistance, as a critic on the human rights issue, and as a partner in international endeavours for North Korea's denuclearisation. It is interesting that the EU's main motivation to help North Korea was not one of self-interest, but of implementing its common policy toward world affairs and international relations. Since the 1995, the EU has undertaken "various actions in support of international efforts to promote peace and stability on the Peninsula, mainly through food aid, humanitarian assistance and contribution to KEDO" (European Commission 2002).

(1) Donor and helper

The EU was really the top donor in sending humanitarian assistance and economic aid toward North Korea during Pyongyang's most difficult period. As of October 2009, humanitarian aid provided by the European Commission totaled 380 million Euro (Wissenbach 2009). After sending supplies of emergency equipment to deal with the devastating effects of natural disasters since 1995, the EU began to provide large amounts of food aid. Assistance had been provided bilaterally via the WFP and via European NGOs. Since 2000, the Food Security Programme for agricultural rehabilitation and production was introduced. At present, ECHO (Humanitarian Aid Department), the directorate general (DG) of the Commission in charge of humanitarian and food aid closed its office in May 2008 after evaluating the current situation in the country and concluding that its mandate of supplying relief to natural disasters and providing food in times of crisis no longer apply as the situation has improved. Instead, "Europeaid, the DG managing the delivery of aid but also active in the development field tackling universal issues such as good governance, human and social development, security and migration and works with six NGOs present on the ground in the DPRK providing technical aid." (Human Rights without Frontiers 2008)

The EU also planned to support technical assistance to the DPRK. The EC-DPRK Country Strategy Paper (CSP) and the EU's National Indicative Programme (NIP) for the DPRK set out the framework and objectives for technical assistance projects in North Korea. North Korea's priority needs were defined as: 1) Training with regard to institutional building; 2) Basic technical advice on the energy system; 3) Rural development; and 4) Transport. (European Commission 2002) The key ministers in the North Korea such as Foreign Affairs, Finance, and Foreign Trade were expected to participate in the training programme of the officials (Frank 2002). It was known that North Korean leaders wanted to do an initiative in IT and software development. These projects, if implemented, could have provided for training in market economic principles and promoting capacity-building for sustainable management in North Korea. However, due to the second nuclear crisis, the EU decided to freeze its technical assistance projects.

Another very important role was the EU's political dialogue with Pyongyang. The EU asked North Korea to hold a political dialogue covering diverse issues, including human rights. The first human rights dialogue took place in Brussels in June 2001. "The ministry officials acknowledged the importance of human rights, but argued that they had their own standards and that their priority concerns were the right to subsistence, right to development, and equality." (Berkofsky 2003) A second round of talks were held in June 2002 with the EU voicing concern "at the lack of access by UN human rights rapporteurs and NGOs, as well as the absence of any official statistics on human rights issues." EU Troika delegations have visited Pyongyang in 2003, 2004, 2007, 2008 and twice in 2009 for talks with the North Korean authorities on a number of issues including human rights and the nuclear programme. It is difficult to say that those dialogues have brought about what the EU had expected. Nevertheless, such an endeavour for enhancing mutual trust and communication by supporting political dialogue has provided a unique experience in a persuasive approach toward North Korea-related issues.

(2) Critic

The EU has been very critical of North Korea due to human rights concern. The EU has taken the initiative since 2003 in the Commission on Human Rights to table a draft resolution on the situation of human rights in North Korea. Thanks to the EU's initiative, the resolution on North Korean Human Rights was adopted by the Commission on 16 April 2003, and a similar resolution has been adopted at the General Assembly since 2005 every year. EU also initiated the creating of the position of the UN Special Rapporteur on North Korean Human Rights. The EU has continuously expressed its serious concern on human rights violation in the North Korea including: torture, public execution, extrajudicial and arbitrary detention, the absence of rule of law and an independent judiciary, severe restrictions on freedom of thoughts and speech, the refugees and asylum-seekers expelled or returned to the North Korea, violations of the economic, social rights of the people, etc.

It is said that the motivation for the EU to play such a critical role derives from the high priority of the promotion and protection of human rights within the EU's common policies. Indeed, human rights have been an important part of Europe's political values and strategic principles for a long time. The Council of Europe, founded in 1949, stated that "every member of the council of Europe must accept the principles of the rule of law and of the enjoyment obey all persons within its jurisdiction of human rights and fundamental freedoms" (Kim, S. 2007). Two multilateral treaties were formed, namely the European Convention for the Protection of Human Rights and Fundamental Freedoms (European Convention for Human Rights) and the European Social Charter. The former guarantees basic civil and political rights, while the latter focuses on economic and social rights. Human rights were also the main issues of the Helsinki Process, which is widely regarded as one of the main factors that brought East and West together during the Cold War, and that was very instrumental in putting an end to the socialist systems in the former Soviet Union and Eastern Europe. The Helsinki Final Act (HFA) is composed of three main sections informally known as "baskets," each of which deals with broad range of measures. Basket I contains a Declaration of Principles Guiding Relations between the participating states, including the all-important Principle VII on human rights and fundamental freedoms. Basket III is devoted to cooperation in humanitarian and other fields, freer movement of people, human contacts including family reunification and visits; freedom of information including working conditions for journalists; and cultural and educational exchanges. Principle VII and Basket III together have come to be known as "The Human Dimension." (Park, Y. 2009)

The EU welcomed the role "in promoting human rights and democratisation in third countries, which represents an invaluable contribution towards strengthening the coherence and consistency of the EU's policy on human rights and democratisation." (European Commission 2001) The EC Country Strategy Paper mentioned that the EU commitment was supporting "the inter-Korean reconciliation process and to increase assistance to the DPRK in response to progress by North Korea in addressing the concerns of the EU and the international community with respect to human rights, non-proliferation and security as well as the progress in inter-Korean reconciliation, economic structural reform and social development." (European Commission 2002) Ambassador Brian McDonald (2007) said that "resolutions on this issue at the UN are not intended as political attacks on the DPRK. Rather they serve as constructive roadmaps to help the overall economic and social development of the country."

(3) Cooperative global player

To support peace and security on the Korean peninsula is one of the main objectives for the EU to engage in the Korean issue. The EU participated in KEDO, recognizing "the importance of maintaining regional security in North-East Asia and also of upholding the international nuclear non-proliferation regime" (European Commission 2002). The EU was a full member of KEDO Executive Board, making regular financial contributions.

According to a resolution on the agreement between EURATOM and KEDO, adopted by the European Parliament in 2001, the KEDO was regarded as 'a major industrial constituting a vital contribution of nuclear non-proliferation and peace and stability on the Korean Peninsula.' The aims and expectations regarding the KEDO project were described as follows: "Recalling the fact that an important element in the policy of the EU on the Korean peninsula is the political dialogue with the DPRK which started in 1998 and in which the EP has played an important role, and that since July 1999 the EU has followed an approach of constructive engagement in its relation with the DPRK; Recognizing that KEDO is but one element of EU-DPRK cooperation, albeit a very important one, as it is a cornerstone of tension reduction in the region' stressing that human rights in the DPRK continue to be an area of major concern to the EU and that it will need to see evidence of improvements." (European Parliament 2001) After North Korea's nuclear test in 2006, the fundamental position of the EU is strongly against North Korea's nuclear possession with the urging that North Korea must not develop nuclear weapons and keep the international norms of the non-proliferation treaty. After North Korea's nuclear test, the EU condemned it and asked North Korea to take immediate steps to dismantle the programme in a verifiable manner and comply with its international commitments. The EU has supported the six party talk framework and the United Nations Security Council, stating that "The European Union expresses its satisfaction with the results of the most recent Six-Party talks which took place in Beijing from 10 to 12 July 2008, and hopes that those talks will continue with the aim of achieving the complete, verifiable and irreversible dismantling of the whole of North Korea's nuclear programme, in accordance with the objectives of United Nations Security Council Resolution 1718." (Declaration by the Presidency on behalf of the European Union on the Six-Party talks, 22 July 2008.)

It seems clear that the EU was disappointed by North Korea's nuclear policy. The EU might have been optimistic in that being a 'distant power' with no strategic interests and colonial legacy on the Korean Peninsula would be advantageous in mediating the political conflicts between the US and North Korea. However, the engagement policy based on the union's Common Foreign and Security Policy (CFSP) could not bring about positive effect in resolving North Korean problem. Regarding the weakening of the relationship, the EU clarified that "the EU clearly puts the responsibility for the freeze on the shoulders of the North Korean government," stating that it "remains open to resume further contacts when DPRK makes concrete and committed steps implementing phase II of the Six Party Talks and moves into phase III." (Human Rights Without Frontiers 2008) Nevertheless, the EU has revealed the importance of dialogue and assistance along with the sanction and condemnation. European Commission president Barroso was quoted in Reuters as saying that "We consider [the recent nuclear and missile tests] a provocation and we strongly condemn them. At the same time, I think we should be ready to come back to the six-party talks and to try to work for a peaceful development in the Korean peninsula."

EU as a Method

Alongside the role of the EU as an agent, the EU has revealed practical methods in implementing a policy of engagement in a concrete context. As a region where two World Wars have been instigated, the European nations have shared a strong fear about the hostility among the states within and without the region. In addition, with the successful transition of the Helsinki Process, which finally led the dissolution of the socialist bloc and the achievement of European integration, the political practicability of dialogue and diplomacy have been widely accepted. The EU's experience needs to be explored and used as a good reference in the practical implementation of political ideas.

(1) Engagement with Principles

The EU's relationship with North Korea has changed since its early stage when, in 1995, it was characterized as 'the encounter by accident'. Haknoh Kim (2006) categorized the relationship by dividing it into three periods: the limited engagement policy during 1995-1998; active and constructive engagement policy during 1998-2002; and a standstill policy since 2002. However, there have been some principles that have continued to underpin the EU's approach toward North Korea. Even in humanitarian assistance, the EU has always tried to abide by certain principles. For example, the EU Council reaffirmed its commitment to the principles of coherence and consistency, integration of human rights into all of its actions, and openness of its policies and identification of priority areas. Two basic principles were mentioned: to intensify the process of integrating human rights and democratisation objectives into all aspects of its external policies, and to maintain the degree of pragmatism and flexibility in initiating a human rights-specific dialogue with a particular third country. The DG ECHO report, which provided an extensive overview of the operations in various countries and regions funded by the Commission in 2007, focuses heavily on the adherence to the principles and guidelines, and states that all assistance provided by the EU must be in line with internationally agreed humanitarian principles in a neutral, impartial and non-discriminatory manner. In addition, it also mentions that "the decisions and actions taken by the service are solely determined by the assessment of humanitarian needs and are not guided by or subject to political considerations other than the affirmation of the European Union's solidarity with people in need." In the area of human rights, the EU produced guidelines on Human Rights Dialogues with third world countries that aimed at "strengthening the coherence and consistency of the EU's policy on human rights and democratisation."

Political conditionality is another characteristic in the EU's policy principles. It has been stated that all EU policy must be interlocked with certain conditions. For example, the document "Promotion of Human Rights and Democratization in the EU's external relations" said that "the principles of liberty, democracy, respect for human rights and fundamental freedoms and the rule of law are inherent to the European integration process. Adherence to these principles constitutes the prerequisite for peace, development and security in any society." "The EU has made human rights a central aspect of its external relations in the political dialogues it holds with third countries; through its development policy and assistance; or through its action in multilateral for a such as the United Nations." (http://ec.europa.eu/exteranl_relations/human_rights) Several trade agreements with the third world countries include these articles on human rights and democracy (Oh, S. 2003).

Hazel Smith suggests that all economic transactions from the outset should be based on internationally recognized principles arguing "the institutionalization of the principles of transparency, openness, accountability, and efficiency helps to create the conditions for a successful liberal market economy [and].....also helps to build a foundation for the future introduction into DPRK society of individual liberal political freedoms." (Smith 2007) Transparency is possible when both the goal and the procedure of the policy are clearly understood among the people. For the EU, North Korea was regarded as a good case for implementing its common policy beyond individual member states' interests. Thus, the EU could approach its complex dealings and relations with North Korea with high transparency. The principle of openness is the same. There is no reason for the EU to carry out their relationship with North Korea in secrecy. The principle of accountability and efficiency is related to the expectation and demand of transparency from the North Korean side. The EU has always asked North Korea to allow EU personnel to monitor how economic aid and humanitarian assistance were distributed. Even though such a principle of clear monitoring became a big hurdle in developing the EU-North Korea relations, the EU has kept strictly to its stance.

(2) Institutional Cooperation:

The EU, as a very special transnational polity, has to proceed with policies that are based on the principles fully agreed upon among the member states. In the case of security issues, the EU has developed the common Foreign and Security Policy (CFSP), which must be respected with regards to every related individual polity, including North Korea. In this respect, the treaties, agreements and resolutions are very important in making policies which are expected to be accepted by every member state. Also, special governance structures and intergovernmental dialogue need to be institutionalized in order to bring about effective decision-making within the EU.

There are three major institutions involved in the decision-making in the EU: the European Council, the European Commission and the European Parliament. The institutional structure for cooperation is complex but well-organized in dealing with North Korea. For example, there have been coordinated activities by each EU institution to effectively implement policy. In 2001, the European Commission decided to establish diplomatic relations with North Korea "to facilitate the European Community's efforts in support of reconciliation on the Korean Peninsula, and in particular in support of economic reform and easing of the act food and health problems in the DPRK." In this context, talks between the EU and North Korea on human rights began on June 13th 2001. The European Parliament also set up a Korean Peninsula Delegation in charge of the relations with both the north and south in 2004. The EP has passed numerous resolutions concerning human rights in North Korea. In 2006, Human Rights without Frontiers and Freedom House organized a two-day conference about human rights in North Korea at the European Parliament in Brussels. The event was chaired by the vice chair of the EP Delegation for Relations with the Korean Peninsula. In the aftermath of the event, HRWF contributed to the adoption of two resolutions by the EP. (Human Rights without Frontiers 2008)

As Hazel Smith has suggested, a regional institutional cooperation mechanism is a good policy option. In Europe, thanks to the institutional frameworks, which the EU and NATO have provided, many Eastern Europe countries in transition from communism to a capitalist democracy have been supported in implementing market principles, the rule of law and participation in a collective defence institution involving states that had been enemies for long time. Smith also introduced three lessons from the EU experience: firstly, the process of economic aid should be implemented through continuing inter-governmental dialogue based on support for economic and legal and juridical institution-building in the context of the creation of a stable intra-regional institutional framework of collaboration; secondly, economic institution-building should be complemented by a policy of regional military deterrence with the possibility left open for eventually creating an intergovernmental Northeast Asian organisation institutional cooperation; thirdly, the promotion of peace and freedom is more likely to succeed as a spillover process from the support for economic transformation rather than from the application of the threat of force, the pursuit of diplomatic isolation and the application of megaphone diplomacy as a substitute for diplomatic dialogue (Smith 2007). Moreover, Smith mentioned that such institution-building process could be achieved through the development of "a light intergovernmental multilateral framework built around an intergovernmental institution whose demonstrable objectives were technical and 'non-political.'" According to her, "such an institution could generate the confidence-building routines of cooperation" and "provide routinized channels for conflict resolution-both on the technical and economic issues."

Bernhard Seliger (2003) has also mentioned that 'institutions matter' as an important lesson from Europe, when writing with regards to North Korea. According to him, 'institutions matter' means that time is necessary for institution-building, especially to create the capacity to effectively support institutions. In regards to this, he has stressed the lesson of 'good governance,' which states that a government guaranteeing the enforcement of institutions, acting impartially with a low degree of corruption, and following a policy sending clear signals to market participants respectively is important for a functioning polity.

(3) Capacity Building

According to the Country Strategy Paper 2001-2004, the EU's main position regarding economic assistance toward North Korea is not just for supporting immediate humanitarian problems, but for helping them to increase their own capacity to get food security and sustainable rural development by themselves. According to the EU, it is desirable to help North Korea acquire a basic capability to manage the key infrastructural systems of energy and transport in order to achieve immediate savings in energy inputs, ensure sustainable energy and transport services and thus support North Korea's long-run social and economic development.(European Commission 2002)

For that, three areas were specifically mentioned: institutional support and capacity building, sustainable management and use of natural resources, and reliable and sustainable transport sector. Capacity-building means making every endeavour "to provide North Korea with the necessary capacity to prepare a policy blueprint on its future development. It entails the need to strengthen the capacity of key institutions and human resources, in particular as regards their ability to define a path of economic and democratic development and to implement poverty reduction policies." Along with these capacity-building policies, technical assistance and extensive training programmes to help North Korea integrate into the international trade system were also suggested. It was expected that through the training activities, the transfer of knowledge to key ministries and institutions, focusing primarily on international finance and trade, economic relations and economic development principles, could take place. (European Commission 2002)

Uwe Wissenbach (2009) reviewed the different forms of assistance provided by the EU over the last 14 years since 1995. In the beginning, emergency assistance seemed enough, but gradually it changed into wider measures to assist North Korea in its efforts to grow its own food. Initially, large amount of fertilizer were given to North Korean agricultural organisations. Nowadays, upon adoption of the EU's 2007-2010 Food Security Thematic Programme (FSTP), EU-funded aid to North Korea has shifted towards an approach which aims at Linking Relief, Rehabilitation and Development (LRRD). According to Wissenbach, under the LRRD component, "the FSTP is therefore particularly looking into – among others- a community-based approach, self-reliant production facilities, introducing innovative resource-efficient technologies on farms, training and promoting diversified crops and crop systems, post-harvest treatment and primary agricultural products processing, creating sustainable employment possibilities and promoting the development of diversified sources of income at household level in rural and urban areas, enhancing the resilience of social groups most affected by natural disasters and the economic hardship, and into environmental protection if food production." (Wissenbach 2009) In short, capacity-building aims to equip the North Korean experts with sufficient knowledge and skills to enable them to lead the transitional period successfully.

EU as a Theory

The EU has revealed the importance of the idea and discourse in designing a new community without oppressing diverse identities and customs. In the theoretical area, constructivism which focuses on the role of ideas and discourses in defining the situation has enjoyed a great influence since 1990s (Wiener and Diez 2009). Social constructivist theory explains that social reality does not exist through tangible things but that human agents construct and reproduce the social reality through their daily communication and cultural representations. The concept of discursive analysis is used for stressing the role of communicative dialogue in framing problematique and constructing reality. According to constructivism, 'things' only become meaningful in social discourse as a practice in the semantic as well as socio-political context. "Neither things nor subjects and their intentions are given by themselves. We therefore, have to cult into the discursive webs that provide meaning to such concepts." (Waever 2009)

It seems that discursive aspects cannot have significant influence in the period of nuclear crisis in the Korean peninsula. However, the way of defining the situation itself is very important in setting the political agenda, which frames the measures and approaches to resolve them. Political discourse produced by major agents is critical in this sense, and this discourse is influenced by the intellectual framing of the situation. New concepts and theoretical perspectives could play an important role in constructing reality in the continually changing the situation. As Koselleck, a famous conceptual historian, once mentioned, the basic concept is not only a word expressing the past collective experience, but also one including the collective expectation for the future. In that sense, he mentioned the 'future past' in analyzing a historical concept. (Koselleck 1985)

In that sense, the experience of EU integration can be regarded as a discursive reference for thinking inter-Korean future relation. The EU community might not be able to exist without the discursive consensus that helps people think of themselves as the same members of a community. In practice, as a unique transnational polity in the 21th century in the world, intellectuals and politicians expect the EU to act as a significant role model for the future political community. Intellectual discourses on European integration could provide a good conceptual resource that will act as a significant reference in thinking about the future inter-Korean integration. That is what I mean by the 'EU as a theory.'

(1) Mode of integration and Federal ideas

With the activation of the Lisbon Treaty, the EU became a more integrated political unit which includes complex institutions, structures, procedures and identities. As Michael Burgess (2009) mentioned, the EU as "a union that currently includes intergovernmental, supranational, federal, confederal, and functional elements" was able to be integrated mainly thanks to federal ideas, which are something rooted in the value of equality, partnership, reciprocity, mutuality, the very elements of the modern civilization that had developed in Europe over a long period of time. (Burgess 2009) Federal ideas are very broad and can encompass a wide spectrum of political regime. According to Burgess, the core of the federal idea is the principle of association, which in the context of European integration is based on "the notion of a voluntary union of states and people – the result of a bargain, treaty, contract or covenant freely entered into- that is binding upon its members and rooted in mutual respect, recognition, reciprocity, tolerance, consent, and equality" (Burgess 2009).

During and after 1990s, the concept of multi-level governance is used to explain the process of emerging transnational authorities with diverse interrelations among transnational institutions, member states, and autonomous civil subjects. Based on the Maastricht Treaty, common policies could be developed and implemented at the level of the EU instead of intergovernmental discussion. For example, the Common Foreign and Security Policy established in 1993 was an important motivation for developing the European governance in the world security affairs. It could give a stable institutional frame through which the conventional level of bargaining between the individual states could be overcome in the security issues. In the economic sphere, the European Union's Commercial Policy and the multi-national committees has played a similar role.

The formal unification theory of the Republic of Korea is the "three states unification based on national community" formula in which the unification process is considered as a process toward a complete one nation-state via inter-Korean Commonwealth. A very important and contentious stage is the second one, the inter-Korean Commonwealth stage. The 2000 summit between the South Korean president Kim Dae-Jung and North Korean leader Kim Jung-Il made a communiqué where "the idea of South Korea's inter-Korean Commonwealth and North Korea's idea of lower level of Koryo Federation are similar enough to try a common approach towards Korean unification." There are many disputes on the idea of an 'inter-Korean Commonwealth', not least whether it is federation or confederation, what conditions should be made, and whether two

Koreas really agreed on the idea. Aside from the theoretical problems, there are practical issues such as what kind of institutions should be constructed for a successful inter-Korean confederation. Nevertheless, there is a wide consensus that in order to escape from the possible difficulties caused by rapid unification between two fundamentally different systems, a confederation-like integration formula has to be invented. In that respect, the experience and theoretical discussions on the EU could be good intellectual reference for preparing Korea's mode of unification.

(2) Spillover effect and system transformation

European integration is a long historical process that emerged over decades. Thus, figuring out the elements and forces that supported the integration process has been one of the main tasks of integration theory. Neo-functionalists focus on the spillover function in the socio-economic realm and supranational institutions rather than the role of nation-states. The concept of 'spillover' was first used in relation to the economy, but then used in relation to political and social spheres for explaining a gradual spread of commonality, an essential condition for the community-building. The idea of 'unintended consequences' was coined to explain the process of institution-building that became increasingly irreversible. (Diez and Wiener 2009) There has been a lot of discussion on the role and agents of the 'spillover effect' particularly between the neo-functionalism school and the intergovernmentalist school. While the former focuses on functional spillover and unintended consequences from one sector to another, the latter stresses that the role of the individual nation states has always been important in establishing the common policy.

While there are disputes regarding the idea of the spillover effect, there was no doubt that socio-economic relations gradually deepened within Western Europe, as well as between Western and Eastern Europe, and that these ties played a great role in integrating Europe into a functioning community. In that regard, the concept of system transformation is indispensible in thinking about the gradual process of integration. As Hazel Smith (2007) argues, Europe experienced very unique changes moving many nations from socialist economies to the market economies as the regional integration continued. System transformation was a particularly important concept in relation to the former socialist countries following the collapse of the socialist bloc and their integration into the EU. During the 1990s, there were several journals and institutions that focused on the ideas of 'system transformation', for example, the Centre for Economic Policy Research's Programme "transition economics". The journal, titled "Communist Economies," then changed its title to "Communist Economies and Economic Transformation" and eventually was renamed "Post-Communist Economics." Unlike transformation, which does not have end-state, transition has a clear end-state – that is, a transition to a market economy. Transformation is usually defined as the state-directed change of institutional regimes in a historically short period of time (Seliger 2007).

Another related issue is the link between economic integration and political integration. Margaret McCown (2006) tried to explain the linkages between economic integration and security cooperation in the European integration process in order to garner lessons for future regional cooperation in East Asia. According to her, there is a wide agreement on the linkages between economic integration and security cooperation in the region as well as on some internal issues such as migration and terrorism. However, she argues that the existence of a relationship does not necessarily suggest the possibility of creating of regional policy solutions on security matters (McCown 2006). She summarizes that "the linkages between economic integration and security cooperation does, indeed, have to do with confidence building between member states and that what builds that confidence is shared trust in and experience with a large number of rules, both formal and informal, that implement economic integration project." With regards to East Asian regionalism, she suggests the importance of construction of shared, trusted and enforced norms.

Diversity, identity and normative power

One of the big issues in the European integration is how to make a common European identity without oppressing the socio-cultural diversities between and within member states. Europe is a loose category within which many political, cultural, and social differences coexisted and has had to face the dilemma of managing political stability in a multicultural society. In the EU context, integration needed to be interpreted as a social process, involving multiple aspects, such as "institution-building, European reunification, and its demographic implications, the creation of Europe-wide interest representation, the emergence of transnational product and labour markets, and inter-European migration." (Klausen and Tilly 1997) Jytte Klausen and Louise Tilly (1997) explained European integration as a response to the transborder movements of the people, trade, jobs, and investment, and only indirectly in response to the international conventions." They focus on the micro-foundation of the European integration process which could not be understood without understanding the concepts such as citizenship, migration, multiple identities and forms of representation.

Thomas Diez and Antje Wiener (2009) mentioned three main functions of the theory. Firstly, theory can provide an explanation and understanding of a situation where people can share a common purpose, and it can help explain why or how an event has come about. Secondly, theory can be a description or analysis and can help in the development of definitions and concepts with which to grasp particular developments, practices, and institutions. Thirdly, theory can be used in critical and normative interventions (Diaz and Wiener 2009). In this respect the theory can problematize a given situation or provide normative alternatives. Thomas Risse (2009) also summarizes three contributions of the approach of social constructivism regarding European integration: First, accepting the mutual constitutiveness of agency and structure allows for a deeper understanding of Europeanization, including its impact on the statehood in Europe; Second, and related, emphasizing the constitutive effects of the European law, rules, and policies enables us to study how European integration shapes social identities and interests of actors; Third, focusing on communicative practices permits us to examine more closely how Europe and the EU are constructed discursively and how actors try to come to grips with the meaning of the European integration and how they develop a European public sphere (Risse 2009). In addition, the contested nature of the European identity and the socially constructed image on the 'Europeanness' is discussed from the theoretical and practical perspective. Ole Waever (2009) explains the discursive approach, which focuses on "the indicators for perceptions, thoughts, and beliefs, raising all kinds of problems, regarding the validity of discourse as a source of knowledge about people's minds." (Waever 2009) This explains that the construction of integrated unity is dependent upon our capacity to think about the common bases and principles in real life as well as theoretical concepts. In that sense, the EU is said to approach international affairs with the idea of 'normative power,' in other words "the power of making the idea of the normative and capacity of controlling and regulating others according to this standards." (Kim, N. 2007) It is a 'principled idea' with a strong normative element. For the EU, the most important of these normative elements are, for example: human rights, democracy, rule of law, and good governance. In the arena of diplomacy, the EU has used the human rights issue alongside other policy issues to leverage changes in policy within the third world nations.

There are diverse disputes in the Korean society regarding issues relating to North Korea. In addition, there are significant gaps among different disciplines and perspectives on the idea of integration and unification. In order to get a more appropriate, synthetic approach that can move beyond confrontation, it will be necessary to explore the concepts and discourses that we have discussed with a perspective of reflection. Constructivism can be used not only as a theoretical alternative, but also as an intellectual lesson for enhancing the capacity of mutual understanding and for arriving at a discursive consensus through communication.

Conclusion

The past and future relationship between the EU and the Korean peninsula should not limit the role of the EU to a political agent or economic donor. As events on the Korean peninsula continue to develop, there are many more elements from the EU-Korean relationship that should be focused upon and utilized. The EU's practical methods for approaching problems, as well as the EU's intellectual discourses on integration, are very informative and constructive in inventing creative policies and measures for use in other regions. Rosella Ideo (2009) argues that "Europe with its success story of economic integration and confidence building practices could help bridge the differences and help US and North Korea to forge a new relationship cleared of suspicion and prejudices." She argues that the EU example provides some lessons: Firstly, Europe has been able to "invent" and practice among its member states peace, democracy, human rights, and a sustainable development that were able to spread out amongst its members. Next, Europe is the world's largest donor of international aid and cooperation, as well as the most engaged in alleviating the suffering in poor countries. Thirdly, Europe, the continent that once created imperialism and colonialism, has acquired a deep consciousness of the need to understand cultural differences and now pays a lot of attention in developing its policies using the knowledge of historical and political realities of other countries.

With deepening globalization and economic integration in the East Asian region, the previously used conventional ways of thinking about reconciliation and unification of the Korean peninsula need to be reformulated. Even though the conditions might be different from Europe, similar phenomena, such as international migration, cultural diversities, multiple governance, regional integration, and negative aspects of nationalism are also relevant to today's Korean problems. The increasing asymmetric confrontation between the two Koreas requires new ideas and concepts for a peaceful integration. Based on the EU experience,

Koreans need to invent a constructive role as an agency, to look for new methods for implementing policies of reconciliation, and conceptualize a process that will be appropriate for the complex task of integration in the Korean peninsula.

References

Berkofsky (2003). Axel, EU's North Korea Policy a Non-starter, *Asia Times On Line* 2003. Retrieved from http://www.atimes.com/atimes/Korea/EG10Dg01.html

Burgess, Michael (2009). Federalism, in Antje Wiener and Thomas Diez, *European Integration Theory*, Oxford University Press, 25-44.

European Commission (2001). EU Guidelines on Human Rights Dialogue with Third Countries. Retrieved from http://www.eu-in-china.com/download/political/human_rights/guidelines3_en.pdf

European Commission (2008). North Korea-Food Security Programme 2007 (LRRD Component), http://ec.europa.eu/europeaid/tender/data/d26/AOF80926.pdf

European Commission. *The EC-DPRK Country Strategy Paper 2001-2004*. Retrieved from http://ec.europa.eu/external_relations/korea_north/docs/01_04_en.pdf.

European Parliament, EAEC/KEDO agreement Minutes of 12/12/2001 Final Edition. Retrieved from http://www.europarl.europa.eu/pv2/pv2?PRG=DOCPV&APP=PV2&SDOCTA=6&TXTLST=1&TPV=DEF&POS=1&Type_Doc=RESOL&DATE=121201&DATEF=011212&TYPEF=A5&PrgPrev=TYPEF@A5%7CPRG@QUERY%7CAPP@PV2%7CFILE@BIBLIO01%7CNUMERO@448%7CYEAR@01%7CPLAGE@1&LANGUE=EN

Frank, Roedinger (2002). EU-North Korean Relations: No Effort Without Reason, *International Journal of Korean Unification Studies*, 11(2), KINU, 87-119.

Han, Jong-Soo (2003). European Integration and Korean Integration in View of Integration Theories, *Yureop yeonku*, 17, 1-18.

Heo, Man-ho (2004). EU Policy on North Korean Human Rights and Adoption of Resolutions by UN Commission on Human Rights. *Daehanjeongchihakhoebo,* 12(2), 1-29.

Human Rights Without Frontiers International (2008), The Role of the European Union in North Korea. Retrieved from http://hrwf.net/uploads/1016%20%20EU-DPRK%20Paper.doc

Ideo, Rosella (2009). A Paradigm Shift on Economic Assistance in North Korea: What Can EU Do to End an Endless Game?, The Future of North Korea and Global Cooperation, proceedings of the international conference organized by the IPUS Seoul National University and the Embassy of Canada on March 13, 2009.

Kim, Hak-noh (2006). The EU-North Korea Relations and the Peace-Building Process between South and North Koreas, *Deahanjeongchihakhoebo*, 14(2),

Kim, Jun-seok (2008). Historical Review on Confederation, *Hangukjeongchinonchong*, 48(1)

Kim, Nam-Kook (2007). Human Rights Policy of the European Union: War, Refugee and Identity. *EUhakyeongu,* 12, 2-39.

Kim, Soo-Am (2009). Significance and Characteristic of Helsinki Final Act: Focusing on Human Rights Issues. *Peace Studies,* 17(1).

Kim, Sung-jin (2007). A New Approach to Human Rights in North Korea from a Perspective of International Human Rights Law. in Kie-Duck Park and Sang-Jin Han (Ed.). *Human Rights in North Korea*, (pp.281-305), The Sejong Institute.

Kim, Sung-Jin (2007). A New Approch to Human Rights in North Korea from a Perspective of International Human Rights Law. In Kie-Duck Park & Sang-Jin Han (Ed.). *Human Rights in North Korea*, (pp.281-305). The Sejong Institute.

Klausen, Jytte and Louise A.Tilly (1997), *European Integration in Social and Historical Perspective*, Oxford, Rowman & Littlefield Publishers Inc.

Ko, Sang-tu, (2008). Vanguard of European Politics: The Role of Member States in the EU's Foreign Policy Toward North Korea. *Journal of International and Area Studies,* 15 (1).

Kodama, Masami (2005). The EU's Relation with the DPRK: Involvement of the EU and Its Implications on the International Politics over the Korean Peninsula, *Yureop yeonku (Journal of European Studies*), 22.

Koo, Chun-kwon (2001). Changes in Modes of European Integration and the Challenge of Critical Integration Theory, *Hangukjeongchihakhoebo*, 35(3), 417-436.

Koo, Gap-U. Theories of Regional Integration Revisited: State-Centric Versus Non-State-centric Views, *Hangukkwagukjejeongchi*, 153-181.

Koselleck, Reinhar (1985). *Futures Past: On the Semantics of Historical Time*, The MIT Press.

Lee, Jong-Sue (2008). A Study on the EU Policy's Feature with the DPRK and the Possibility of a. Stabilizer for the Korean Peninsula, *Yureop yeonku*, 26,

187-216.

Lee, Moo-sung (2006). The EU's North Korean Policy: A Study based on Integration Theories. *Yureop yeonku*, 24, 165-185.

Lee, Son-Phil (2009). The Role of the EU's Human Rights Policy toward North Korea. *Gukjejiyeokyeongu*,13(2).

Ljunggren, Borje (2003). The Korean Peninsula: recent developments from an EU perspective. In E.Kwan Choi, E.Han Kim and Yesook Merill (Ed.), *North Korea in the World Economy*. 9-15. RoutledgeCurzon.

McCown, Margaret (2006, June 4). Lessons from European Regionalism: Linkages between Economic Integration and Security Cooperation. *Political Economy of the Northeast Asian Regionalism, KINU International Colloquium Collection*

McDonald, Brian (2007). Perspectives on EU Relations with North Korea after the February 13th Agreement, in IUS-HSS International Conference, Recent Developments in North Korea and the Role of the European Union.

Meinardus, Ronald (2003). Europe's New Role in Korea. in E.Kwan Choi, E.Han Kim & Yesook Merill (Ed.), *North Korea in the World Economy*, (pp.219-223). RoutledgeCurzon.

Niemann, Arne, Phillippe C.Schmitter (2009). Neofunctionalism. In Antje Wiener and Thomas Diez (Ed.). *European Integration Theory* (pp.45-66). Oxford University Press.

Park, Chae-bok (2003). North Korea's Nuclear Weapons Programme and the EU, *Bukhanyeonguhakhoebo*, 7(2), 165-183.

Park, Young-ho (2009). The Helsinki Process in Comparative Perspective: Implications for the Korean Peninsula. *Bigyominjujueuiyeungu*, 5(1).

Risse, Thomas (2009). Social Constructivism and European Integration. In Antje Wiener and Thomas Diez (Ed.). *European Integration Theory*, (pp.144-160).Oxford University Press.

Seliger, Bernhard (2003). Economic Transformation of North Korea: lessons and "non-lessons" from Germany and Europe. In E.Kwan Choi, E.Han Kim and Yesook Merill (Ed.), *North Korea in the World Economy,* (pp.119-150). RoutledgeCurzon.

Seliger, Bernhard (2007). Economic Transformation after 15 years – A Reassessment. In Mica Jovanovic, Lee Dalgon, Oh Yeon-Chean, Sung-Jo Park and Bernhard Seliger (Ed.), *System Transformation in Comparative Perspective*, (pp.45-80). LIT.

Smith, Hazel (2007). Regional Dialogue and Institutional Building: The Necessary Foundation for Human Rights Reform in the DPRK. In Kie-Duck Park &

Sang-Jin Han (Ed.), *Human Rights in North Korea*, (pp.307-336).The Sejong Institute.

Suh, Bo-hyuk (2009). A Study of the Formation of Helsinki Framework: Focusing on the Strategic Triangular Relationship between the United States, Soviet Union, and West Empire. *Hangukkwagukjejeongchi*, 25(2), 61-88.

Waever, Ole (2009). Discoursive Approaches. In Antje Wiener and Thomas Diez, *European Integration Theory*, (pp.163-180), Oxford University Press.

Wiener A. and Diez,T. (2009). *European Integration Theory*. Oxford University Press.

Wissenbach, Uwe (2009, November 24). Proceeding of 2009 International Conference on Humanitarian Assistance to the DPRK – Current Humanitarian Situation and International Cooperation: EU Position on the Humanitarian Situation in the DPRK. Korean Sharing Movement, Friedrich Ebert Stiftung, Gyeonggi Province and KINU.

Yang, Oh-Suk, (2003). 'Political Conditionality' in the Framework Agreements between the European Union and Non-Member States: Politics of Dual Ideas. *Yureopyeongu*, 18, 309-330.

2

Training for Economic Reform: The Role of European and Other Actors and NGOs

Peter M. Beck and Nicolas Reader

Abstract

Despite the continuing nuclear confrontation between North Korea and the world, the North is undergoing the most profound economic changes since the founding of the state. The international community can improve North Korea's chances of making a successful transition by first taking advantage of the new opportunities to train North Koreans in financial, technical and market economic skills. Additionally, the international community can address infrastructural constraints, and undertake comprehensive needs assessments. North Korea will not and should not receive significant international development assistance until it gives up its nuclear weapons, but increasing knowledge about the economy will improve the prospect that any deal reached on the nuclear issue will lead to transformation of the economy.

Introduction[1]

North Korea's provocative behaviour makes it difficult for countries seeking engagement to facilitate reform. It is difficult to argue anything but that most direct international assistance should remain unavailable until the nuclear crisis is resolved. Moreover, if that crisis grows worse, it may well become necessary to move in the opposite direction -- to sanctions -- as the only measure short of force

[1]A previous version of this paper was published in Asian Perspective, 2006. A longer version of this article can be found in Crisis Group Asia Report N°96, *North Korea: Can the Iron Fist Accept the Invisible Hand?*, Seoul/Brussels 25 April 2005.

available to persuade Pyongyang to reverse course.[2] However, resolving that crisis is only the first step. For North Korea eventually to become a more stable and normal country, it also needs to complete the transition from a command economy to a market economy. It is unclear if the present regime is up to the task. The country's population, isolated for 60 years, also faces immense challenges to adapt. Yet, it is in the best interest of the international community to help North Korea make that transition as smoothly as possible.

North Korea has relaxed its Stalinist economic model, authorized some markets and entrepreneurship, and sought foreign trade and investment. These changes have been overshadowed by the crisis over Pyongyang's nuclear weapons programmes, but they have created unprecedented opportunities for engaging one of the world's most repressive and opaque regimes. To help policy makers put them in context, this article evaluates what contributions the international community can make to move the reform process forward.

North Korea does not lend itself to comprehensive reporting. It frequently ranks at the bottom of human rights indexes for restricting almost all freedoms, not the least of which are information flows and foreign interaction with its citizens. Moreover, it has not published any statistics since 1965. Nevertheless, the economy is not a complete mystery, and analysis using a range of sources is possible.

Anecdotal evidence from the hundreds of foreign aid workers, diplomats and government officials who have been granted access to the North allows for corroboration of many details provided by North Korean officials and the state-run media. North Korea has also allowed international agencies and experts to conduct detailed in-country studies ranging from the state of the environment to nutritional standards and management techniques. Interviews with refugees and defectors have been documented. The Bank of (South) Korea and the Korea Trade Promotion Agency (KOTRA) both produce data on the economy, and trade statistics can be extracted from those of North Korea's trade partners.[3] Yet, our scope of knowledge about the North Korean economy is far from complete, making economic assistance to the North problematic under the best of circumstances.

---

[2] This is the position taken in Crisis Group Asia Report N°87, *North Korea: Where Next for the Nuclear Talks?*, Seoul/Brussels, 15 November 2004.

[3] The Bank of Korea inputs raw data provided by the National Intelligence Service into a model to arrive at its growth estimates for North Korea. A combination of satellite imagery and eyewitness accounts are used to measure agricultural activity and factory utilisation rates. Nevertheless, some analysts question the accuracy of the statistics. Crisis Group interviews, Bank of Korea and South Korean government officials, Seoul, December 2004.

Facilitating Reform

While direct technical and especially financial assistance is impossible without resolution of the nuclear standoff and a deeper commitment to reform by the regime, there are important opportunities to provide assistance that would do little to support the regime now but would help considerably in strengthening the nascent market mechanism. The growth of the private sector and the legitimacy afforded to it since 2002 mean for the first time that there are opportunities to direct support to individuals and groups outside the elite, including to pro-reform constituencies.

Build a vanguard for change

While the decision for deeper reform will have to come from Kim Jong-il himself and the ossified inner circle surrounding him, and North Korea experts see little political space for a bottom-up reform much less a popular revolution,[4] experience in other potential transition countries shows that building pro-change constituencies contributes directly to the speed and success of reforms when the decision to change is eventually made.[5]

Since 2002, North Korean bureaucrats and officials have been authorized to receive training from abroad in some economic-related subjects. This is an important difference. Previously, the regime encouraged foreign financial and technical engagement only in areas expected to enhance its legitimacy and the stabilisation of the ruling system. Social sciences training (including finance and business management) was permitted only in politically friendly countries.[6] As a Western diplomat noted:

The approach before was that Kim Il-sung had created the perfect society, and change was politically suspect. You could not talk about change with North Koreans because they were not allowed to be interested in change. Also, there was nothing that could be taught to North Koreans, as they knew it all already and had

---

[4] John Feffer, "The Forgotten Lessons of Helsinki", *World Policy Journal*, Fall (2004).

[5] Many of the thousands of Soviet cultural, academic and scientific exchange candidates during the Cold War played critical behind-the-scenes roles in advocating for and supporting change, and filled key positions after the Soviet Union dissolved. Yale Richmond, *Cultural Exchange and the Cold War: Raising the Iron Curtain* (Penn State Press, 2003). China's Deng Xiaoping spent the early 1920s -- his formative years -- in France.

[6] Kyung-Ae Park, "North Korea's Non-Governmental Foreign Contacts", *The Korean Journal of Defence Analysis* 12, no. 2, Winter (2000).

the perfect system. By mid-2002, suddenly everyone was talking about change, and it was quite acceptable to learn from other countries.[7]

Anecdotal evidence from regular visitors to and residents of Pyongyang suggests that many exchange candidates return as firm advocates for deeper systemic change.[8] Among groups that have studied, travelled or conducted business in China and Russia, have had access to foreign media, or live close to the Chinese border, knowledge and appreciation of alternative systems, the world, and news outside North Korea is growing.[9]

NGO Programmes

Significant programmes and exchanges have been successfully implemented by non-governmental organisations (NGOs) to boost this growing tend. One such example is that the California-based and Congressionally-funded Asia Foundation held training seminars for approximately 50 North Koreans in Beijing and Shanghai between 1999 and 2002. Moreover, the Asia Foundation has expressed an interest in continuing this type of programme in the future.[10] Another example is that the California-based Nautilus Institute hosted delegations of North Korean energy specialists for conferences and training courses in the U.S. and China between 1997 and 2001.[11] Additionally, the German Friedrich Naumann Foundation ran a five-day workshop on economic reform in cooperation with the EU in July 2004. It was attended by a delegation of European economists who had worked in transition economies in Europe and Asia, business representatives already active in North Korea, European diplomats, and over 70 North Korean officials from a range of ministries and institutions handling economic affairs. The foundation has also run smaller, short training courses in accountancy and banking.[12] Finally, the Centre for Applied Studies in International Negotiations (CASIN) in Geneva hosted fourteen mid-career and senior diplomats from the ministry of foreign affairs, the ministry of procurement, the ministry of foreign trade, and the ministry of light industry in 2004, a much wider range of participants than in the seven pre-

---

[7] Crisis Group interview, diplomat, Seoul, November 2004.

[8] Crisis Group interviews, cooperation program organisers, diplomats, NGO staff and academics, Seoul and Beijing, October 2004-March 2005.

[9] Crisis Group interview, South Korean businessperson, Seoul, December 2004.

[10] Asia Foundation President Doug Bereuter says the Foundation is prepared to restart training if it is invited by North Korea."Continue Supporting Training Programs for North Korean Scholars in the U.S." (in Korean), *Joongang Ilbo*, 29 March 2005.

[11] http://www.nautilus.org.

[12] Crisis Group interview, Ulrich Niemann, Friedrich Naumann Foundation, Seoul, 15 October 2004.

vious years.[13] CASIN included for the first time training in commercial diplomacy, the UN, the principles of market economics, international trade and sustainable development, bilateral and multilateral trading systems and regional trade agreements, and conditions attached to development assistance from international financial institutions.[14]

Academic Exchanges

In addition to NGO activities, many universities have opted to expand their engagement and exchanges with the DPRK. North Koreans have studied short courses and degree programmes at the University of Essex, the University of Warwick, the University of Sydney, and the Australian National University, as well as at other Western institutions, in subjects ranging from human rights to MBA programmes. One specific example is that since 2002, the German Academic Exchange Service (DAAD) has sponsored exchanges between German universities and several institutions in Pyongyang.[15] Additionally, North Korean bureaucrats and academics have been trained in the principles of economics in Pyongyang, Hanoi and Stockholm by Stockholm School of Economics scholars and transition economics experts.[16] Furthermore, in 2003 an exchange programme with Kim Il-sung University was launched by the Far Eastern National University (Vladivostok), which includes both North and South Korean students.[17]

American institutions have also been getting into the act. Syracuse University in the U.S. and Kim Chaek University of Technology in Pyongyang are engaged in joint research, and North Korean students are studying in New York. The project is funded by the Henry Luce Foundation and the Ford Foundation.[18]

North Korea's receptivity to training programmes is not always positive, despite its more open attitude. Some institutions offering training have found their North Korean counterparts unwilling to provide enough commitment or transparency, and naive about the opportunities available. English language educa-

---

[13] Crisis Group interview, Jung Seung-ho, Korea Development Institute Knowledge Cooperation Program, Seoul, 7 December 2004.

[14] Centre for Applied Studies in International Negotiations, http://www.casin.ch/news/cds/presentationdprk04.html.

[15] Richard Stone, "A Wary Pas de Deux", *Science* 315, 17 September (2004): 1,703.

[16] Crisis Group interviews, Swedish diplomats and Stockholm School of Economics officials, Beijing/Seoul, October/ November, 2004.

[17] Stone, "A Wary Pas de Deux", op. cit.

[18] "The KUT/SU Research Collaboration Project Status Report: July 2004", http://www.nautilus.org/DPRKBriefing Book/economy/30-KoreaSociety.html.

tion is still the most requested programme.[19] North Korea has funded students to follow architecture courses in Italy but is still reluctant to sponsor economics-related programmes.[20] Even when programmes are successfully arranged, North Koreans travelling abroad are required to be accompanied at all times by a minder and to be housed apart from other students. Attendance at programmes ranges from perfect, to not at all, and "disappearances" of students recalled to Pyongyang and never heard from again are not uncommon.[21] Despite the obstacles, this is an important avenue into the heart of North Korean decision making, and it should not be overlooked.

Support the market economy

Building the market system adds momentum for deeper reform. A Hanoi-based economist noted of the early stages of Vietnamese transition: "The key later was opening up to get the market access and technology, the big things that had a big impact. But a lot can also be achieved just by making it easier for the household enterprise sector to work properly."[22] North Korea achieved much higher centralisation and authoritarianism than Vietnam and has a much smaller agricultural sector. However, the two share large workforces prepared to work for subsistence wages in low-skilled industries and pre-reform outputs far below their productive potentials.

Foreign investment in North Korea is also important for diminishing the government's ability to restrict the flow of news and information, expanding interactions with foreigners, and highlighting the shortfalls of the current system. The clearest example of this corrosion is the introduction of mobile phones by Chinese traders, which they use in the absence of reliable landline communications to conduct business. As many as 20,000 North Koreans -- including the officials supposed to be keeping them out -- are believed to have access now to these phones.[23] In 2003, Chinese cell phone companies began building relay-stations along the North Korean border, meaning penetration now extends deep inside the country, and unregulated, unmonitored calls are frequently made to Japan, China, and South Korea.[24]

---

[19] "Report on a visit to the Democratic People's Republic of Korea", part of the University of Cambridge East Asia Institute's constructing confidence project on economic and academic engagement with the DPRK, 22-29 May 2004.

[20] Crisis Group interview, European academic, Seoul, 26 January 2005.

[21] Crisis Group interview, Christopher Hughes, University of Warwick, Coventry, 21 December 2005.

[22] Crisis Group interview, IFI consultant, Hanoi, 16 March 2005.

[23] Rebecca MacKinnon, "Chinese Cell Phone Breaches North Korean Hermit Kingdom", *YaleGlobal Online*, 17 January 2005, http://yaleglobal.yale.edu.

[24] Donald Kirk, "New Agent of Change in N. Korea: Cell Phones", *Christian Science Monitor,* 15 December (2004).

Supporting the economy does not necessarily mean delivering ready-made enterprises to run vocational training schemes, as several South Korean charities and companies have already done. If investment seemingly arrives from the sky, it risks creating a "cargo cult" mentality -- a lack of appreciation for how goods and value are actually made. A more practical short-term contribution could be made by concentrating on resolving the major infrastructure obstacles to industrial output: energy and transport.

First, refurbishment must be considered. North Korean power plants were mostly built in the 1950s and 1960s and are reaching the end of their natural life cycle. The problems of aging facilities are exacerbated by the use of low-quality fuels and the lack of spare parts to replace broken equipment. New power plants, both thermal and hydroelectric, are desperately needed. Additionally, North Korea's power distribution system has suffered from decades of neglect, and scavenging for spare parts, and thus will need to be rebuilt almost in its entirety, from transmission lines to relay stations.

Efficiency is a second avenue of change. Electricity has traditionally been provided by the state free of charge. Installing metering equipment and requiring customers to pay for energy used would go a long way toward discouraging waste. Other low cost efficiency measures include better insulation and providing modern, more efficient end-use equipment.[25]

Additionally, renewable energy sources are an important consideration. North Korea has significant potential for renewable energy, including hydro, wind, thermal, and tidal energy. Other than hydropower, very little of this potential is utilized. Renewable energy sources also have the advantage of being difficult to divert to military uses.[26]

Finally, the important aspect of training needs to be addressed. As already noted, an EU survey in 2001 estimated that training in modern energy and transport network management could potentially yield a 25 to 30 per cent efficiency savings.[27]

Begin comprehensive needs assessments

In other countries where commitment to reform was weak, support for change and for foreign assistance has been built by focusing on developing domestic capacity to undertake substantive analysis of the economy and institutional con-

---

[25] David von Hippel, Peter Hayes, Masami Nakata, Timothy Savage, and Chris Greacen, "Modernising the Agreed Framework", Nautilus Institute, 16 February 2001, http://nautilus.org/archives/papers/energy/ModernizingAF.PDF.

[26] David Von Hippel and Peter Hayes, "North Korea and Renewable Energy", *Science* 307, 14 January (2005): 207.

[27] See Section III D and fn. 26 above.

straints on growth.[28] In Vietnam this approach meant that by the time international inputs into capacity building were politically possible, officials had in many cases already achieved a good appreciation of their needs and of which institution would be best able to provide assistance.[29]

North Korea's long-term need is for a comprehensive economic assessment to be completed collaboratively with international financial institutions. [30] To prepare for that, it should conduct detailed surveys at the national, sectoral and household levels. These would be of significant value in helping the regime understand the condition of the economy and investment priorities.

The experience of humanitarian agencies in North Korea since 1995 indicates the problems of dealing with a government that has "viewed all data through a national security prism, which considered that even basic micro socio-economic statistics could be useful to its adversaries."[31] The humanitarian experience also shows that improved working relationships can be achieved through long-term, patient engagement.[32] Since 2002, the World Food Programme (WFP), the United Nations Food and Agriculture Organisation (FAO), and the United Nations Children's Fund (UNICEF) have gained unprecedented access for household surveys. As early as 1997, the United Nations Development Programme (UNDP) was able to work with the North Korean authorities to gather basic macro-economic data that could be presented to the International Monetary Fund (IMF).

Preparing for the Future

Despite the obstacles, there are compelling reasons for the main UN agencies, international financial institutions, and bilateral donors to start preparing now for the tasks ahead. The extent of North Korea's institutional weakness and its officials' poor appreciation of international standards mean even the most basic assistance will go a long way to making future cooperation easier. Recent development agency visitors report that their interlocutors had very little understanding of the processes involved in economic transitions and development, suggesting consider-

[28] Raymond Mallon, "Managing Investment Climate Reforms: Viet Nam Case Study", draft case study prepared as input for the World Bank's World Development Report 2005 on Investment Climate, Growth and Poverty, 17 January 2005.

[29] Crisis Group interview, IFI consultant, Hanoi, 16 March 2005.

[30] Bradley Babson, "The International Financial Institutions and the DPRK: Prospects and Constraints", Institute of Asian Research, University of British Columbia, (2002): 22.

[31] Hazel Smith, "Overcoming Humanitarian Dilemmas in the DPRK (North Korea)", United States Institute of Peace Special Report, Washington DC, July 2002.

[32] Ibid.

able familiarization will be required before on-the-ground assistance is possible.[33] Insecure North Korean elites are very unlikely to make decisions about deeper systemic change without assurance of meaningful support afterwards. Demonstrating that the international community is serious about supporting a long-term transition once the nuclear issue is settled, will be an important step to achieving progress.

United Nations

There are important parallels between the role played by the UN in Vietnam and its potential role in North Korea. Since 1986, Vietnam has made the institutional transition from a centrally planned to a market economy, while remaining a one-party, communist state. Like North Korea, it was initially dependent on "learning by doing" and incremental change rather than following a long-term structured programme; and it was also barred from wider interaction with the international financial institutions by U.S. sanctions. Between 1975 and 1993 the UN, through UNDP, was the main source of technical assistance, training, and capacity building for the Vietnamese government.

Until 1990, UNDP in Vietnam concentrated on economic rehabilitation. In that year it embarked on a "Strengthening Economic Management" project, to support economic reform by familiarizing senior policy makers with the functioning of a market economy. This was followed by projects on education sector review, gender, public administration reform, and industrial strategy.[34] UNDP, with the Vietnamese government, produced 28 economy-wide and structural reports before 1993 and spent over $700 million on training and capacity building between 1985 and 1997. These contributions laid the groundwork for a relatively fast and successful stabilisation and transition of Vietnam's economy once wider multilateral engagement became possible in the early 1990s.[35]

UNDP has had a presence in North Korea since 1979. When North Korea joined the UN in 1991, it opened the door for the involvement of other agencies, including the United Nations Educational, Scientific and Cultural Organisation (UNESCO), the United Nations Industrial Development Organisation (UNIDO) and, since 1995, WFP and FAO. In 1993 UNDP and UNIDO launched together a Management Development Programme. However, momentum was lost during

[33] Crisis Group interview, Department for International Development (DfID) official, London, 15 December 2004.

[34] Gus Edgren and Dharam Ghai, "Capacity Building for Eradicating Poverty in Vietnam: An Impact Evaluation of UN System Activities in 1985-1997" (Hanoi:UNDP, February 2001)

[35] Crisis Group interview, IFI consultant, Hanoi, 16 March 2005.

the famine, and since that time donors have focused on emergency aid and relief work, with UNDP working mostly on agriculture projects.[36]

In early 2005, UNDP started negotiations with the government to implement initial stages of a $20 million transition programme. If the agency is to influence North Korea's potential for more stable transition directly, it will need to first build a close relationship with the government and bureaucracy. The Resident Representative should become a trusted advisor to key North Korean decision makers, and UNDP should be the "go to" organisation for technical assistance, training, and consultations. It could also be the facilitator for high-level training programmes, for example visits to Pyongyang by leaders from the corporate sector and other Asian governments.[37] Additionally, UNDP will need to build capacities for preparing the documentation, surveys and planning necessary for basic sectoral programmes at the ministry of finance, central planning bureau, and statistical bureau. Once this is in place, they must complete a census and quality of life report for North Korea, and use in-country workshops as well as generate opportunities for overseas training. The United Nations Institute for Training and Research (UNITAR) in Hiroshima could have an important part in this process.[38] Finally, UNDP must focus assistance on how to use trade to further reform and the role of sustainable and renewable energy production.

International Financial Institutions

Direct contact between the international financial institutions (IFIs) and North Korea started in 1997 when the IMF sent a fact-finding mission to Pyongyang. This was followed in February 1998 by an introductory mission from the World Bank. Contact since then has been sporadic and informal.

In the short to medium term, the Asian Development Bank (ADB), IMF, and World Bank all have the potential to play important non-lending roles in North Korea. These include economic evaluation, policy advice, and technical assistance. IFIs also advise on specific industry issues and adoption of international standards and codes of good business practice and provide grants for technical assistance and training.[39]

---

[36] Crisis Group interview, former UN official, 8 December 2004.

[37] In Vietnam in the late 1980s, UNDP successfully organised visits to Hanoi by prominent reformers from Singapore and South Korea and by the CEOs of multinational companies.

[38] UNITAR is a training, capacity building, and research institute that provides education in international affairs management and economic and social development through programs, seminars and workshops for participants from developing countries and countries in transition, http://www.unitar.org/hiroshima.

[39] Babson, "The International Financial Institutions and the DPRK", op. cit., p. 22.

There are legal and political obstacles to the direct development of IFI activities with North Korea. The U.S. does not support IFI efforts to help North Korea improve its economy before there has been satisfactory progress on the nuclear issue. The U.S. Treasury is precluded by domestic law from supporting any IFI actions that could assist North Korea until the country has been removed from the U.S. list of state sponsors of terrorism. The worsening nuclear crisis has meant direct IFI involvement has been relegated to the list of incentives on offer.[40]

These obstacles do not preclude informal discussions between IFI and North Korean officials, informal studies of North Korea's economy, and the provision of information and training on market economics.[41] Efforts in all these areas could be improved.

Staffing on North Korea is inadequate at all the IFIs. At the ADB the official in charge estimates he spends ten minutes each month on the country and says he has never communicated with a North Korean.[42] The World Bank position covering North Korea has been vacant since 2003. Even if there is no immediate potential for collaboration, there should be greater institutional understanding of the country and its problems and consideration of the IFIs' eventual role.

North Korea needs to be made aware of the benefits of IFI memberships and given realistic expectations about the demands these will involve. This can be achieved by inviting North Korean officials to IFI events (although IFIs will not be able to pay) and working with UNDP to provide training on IFI policies and programmes and preliminary economic surveys.

IFIs should take the lead on discussions of international economic engagement policy, drawing in perspectives from elsewhere in the region and promoting the potential of multilateral and regional economic cooperation.

South Korea

South Korea's direct contribution to technical assistance and capacity building in North Korea is made problematic by the political and historical dynamic of North-South relations. The most sensitive stages of transition may be better handled by the UN and IFIs. South Korea has, however, been a core source of much of the economic and political engagement that has taken place with North Korea in recent years, creating new opportunities for interaction and reducing tensions on the Peninsula. Continuing this will be essential to building an enabling environment for change. In the context of movement toward resolving the nuclear stand-off, South

---

[40] Crisis Group Report, *North Korea: Where Next for the Nuclear Talks?*, op. cit.
[41] Babson, "The International Financial Institutions and the DPRK", op. cit.
[42] Crisis Group interview, ADB official, 17 March 2005.

Korea could improve its contribution by first continuing to support expansion of the Kaesong Special Economic Zone (SEZ), while encouraging more profit-oriented direct investment in North Korea by South Korean companies, for example, by offering incentives for investing in the North instead of China. Making a profit in North Korea is not impossible, but so long as engagement by loss-leading NGOs and South Korea's major conglomerates (the *chaebol*) provide the best-known examples of what is possible, there will be little chance of North Korean growth, or generation of wider international interest. Secondly, South Korea should emphasize transparency in financial transactions with North Korea, to support the growth of effective institutions. Finally, South Korea can coordinate more closely with the U.S., China, Japan and Russia on the technical assistance it could deliver as part of a schedule leading to North Korea's denuclearisation.

Japan

While two-way trade has fallen dramatically, Japan could have considerable scope for exerting economic leverage over North Korea. It is likely to become North Korea's biggest aid donor when the two countries normalize relations, with reparations payments alone of up to $10 billion.[43] Resolving the abductions issue and the nuclear crisis are the two biggest obstacles to this. However, there is urgent need for more advanced planning as to where and how Japanese economic input can best be made when normalization is achieved. Steps that should be taken now include sending Japan External Trade Organisation (JETRO) researchers to study the North Korean economy. The Japanese government will likely have to offer significant incentives to lure Japanese private sector investments away from China and South Korea to North Korea. It needs more information about available opportunities.[44] Additionally, Japan can start to research North Korea's infrastructure and industry. Possibly more than half the reparations would be paid "in kind" through contracts to Japanese infrastructure contractors to work in North Korea but there is still no planning about how this money could best be spent and little awareness of the areas of the economy most in need of assistance.[45] Finally, Japan should initiate discussions at the ministry of foreign affairs on how best to clear North Korea's debts. Options include either total forgiveness, or transfer of the debt to an IFI.

---

[43] For more on the obstacles to normalization, see, Crisis Group Asia Report No. 100, *Japan and North Korea: Bones of Contention*, Seoul/Brussels, 27 June 2005.
[44] Crisis Group interview, JETRO officials, Tokyo, 24 January 2005.
[45] Ibid.

Others

United States. The Bush Administration has made it known that it will not stand in the way of aid by others if a deal on denuclearisation can be reached but limits imposed by the legislative branch severely restrict the technical and financial assistance the U.S. itself could provide.[46] Nevertheless, the U.S. could still promote and help facilitate economic reform in North Korea, assuming a nuclear deal, by channelling assistance through the National Committee for North Korea (NCNK), which is administered by the American NGO Mercy Corps and acts as a clearing-house for information on facilitating training and exchange Programmes.[47]

China. As its leverage grows, it is already using business people to nudge Pyongyang toward further reform. "They are compassionate to the North's position, as they were there themselves once, but are still quite harsh", said the representative of a Chinese agency who has worked in North Korea. "They will not just give them money for anything. They want North Korea to put money in too, to contribute and learn them".[48]

EU. Although many North Koreans still study in China, when its officials speak of needing modern skills, languages and experience to help with their reforms, they are obviously also interested in Western experiences.[49] North Korea's diplomats are now proactively pursuing new avenues for training overseas, and Europe is among their preferred destinations.[50] "Europeans are seen as non-threatening", explained a South Korean analyst involved in knowledge cooperation projects.[51] In the short term, this makes European countries best suited to provide more opportunities for latent capacity building. Long-term, the EU will be well placed to implement a major training and capacity building programme inside North Korea, as it was set to do before the nuclear crisis began in 2002.[52]

Coordination of all these actors is essential to ensure their policies are complementary. One way could be by creating a Consultative Group or Roundtable, as has been done to coordinate donor assistance to Vietnam, Sri Lanka, Indonesia, and elsewhere. Typically, this is chaired by the World Bank and/or the UNDP. Representatives of all the IFIs, the six parties to the nuclear talks, the Korean Peninsula Energy Organisation (KEDO), which manages the half-finished light water reactor project that resulted from the 1994 Agreed Framework, and the EU, as well,

[46] Crisis Group Report, *North Korea: Where Next for the Nuclear Talks?*, op. cit., pp. 15-16.
[47] http://www.mercycorps.org.
[48] Crisis Group interview, Kosimu Weber Liu, Environmental Education Media Project, Beijing, 20 October 2004. China-North Korea relations is also the subject of a forthcoming Crisis Group report.
[49] Crisis Group interview, North Korean official, 15 December 2004.
[50] Ibid.
[51] Crisis Group interview, Jung Seung-ho, Korea Development Institute, Seoul, 7 December 2004.
[52] "EC-DPRK Country Strategy Paper, 2001-2004", op. cit.

possibly, as second-tier actors like Australia, Germany, the UK, Sweden, Italy, New Zealand, and Canada, should also participate.

Conclusion

Economic reform in North Korea is real -- too real for most people in that country. Most enterprises have already been removed from the state planning system and land has been de-collectivized. Markets stocked with consumer goods and burgeoning foreign investment are changing how the country looks and the way its people think. South Korea is still North Korea's enemy, but also its second largest trade partner. South Koreans can catch a bus from downtown Seoul to manage their North Korean employees working at a special economic zone north of the DMZ. The time of shared hardships is long gone: North Koreans doing best now are the ones who are quickest to adapt to the new system, but most people inside and outside the bureaucracy are struggling to keep up.

Although much has changed, North Korea's leadership, aware of the economic rationale for reform but personally dependent on the old system, is still obstructing deeper change. It no longer believes the command system is the best way to run a country but neither does it yet believe it can exist without it. It has accepted some of the ideological and social repercussions necessary to move the economy back to growth, but has stopped short of reforming the institutions needed to manage and sustain a market. So long as deeper institutional reform is ignored, North Korea will experience worsening economic instability and stay dependent on handouts from China and South Korea.

Even while the nuclear crisis is ongoing, some preparatory work should begin both to bring the North Korean bureaucracy to a better appreciation of international standards and the tasks ahead and to prepare the organisations that will be called on to respond to change if and when a nuclear deal is struck. So long as North Koreans lack the analytical skills, experience, and knowledge to make the changes their country needs, and the international community is too disorganized and unprepared to respond meaningfully, North Korea's economy will remain fragile and dysfunctional, and the chances of successful transition will be limited. The regime has proven since 2002 that gradual and cumulative change is possible. Given all that is at stake, the time to react is not at that indefinite point when the regime falls -- a week, a year, a decade, a generation hence -- but now.

References

Babson, Bradley (2002). *The International Financial Institutions and the DPRK: Prospects and Constraints*. Institute of Asian Research, University of British Columbia.

Centre for Applied Studies in International Negotiations, http://www.casin.ch/news/cds/presentationdprk04.html.

Continue Supporting Training Programmes for North Korean Scholars in the U.S. (in Korean) (2005, March 29). *Joongang Ilbo*.

Crisis Group Asia Report N° 87 (2004, November 15). *North Korea: Where Next for the Nuclear Talks?*, Seoul/Brussels

Crisis Group Asia Report N°100 (2005, June 27). *Japan and North Korea: Bones of Contention*, Seoul/Brussels.

Crisis Group Report N° 96 (2005, April 25). *North Korea: Can the Iron Fist Accept the Invisible Hand?*, Seoul/Brussels.

Edgren, Gus and Dharam Ghai (2001, February). *Capacity Building for Eradicating Poverty in Vietnam: An Impact Evaluation of UN System Activities in 1985-1997*. UNDP, Hanoi.

Feffer, John (2004, Fall). The Forgotten Lessons of Helsinki. *World Policy Journal*,

Kirk, Donald (2004, December 15). New Agent of Change in N. Korea: Cell Phones. *Christian Science Monitor*

MacKinnon, Rebecca (2005, January 17). Chinese Cell Phone Breaches North Korean Hermit Kingdom. YaleGlobal Online. Retrieved from http://yaleglobal.yale.edu.

Mallon, Raymond (2005, January 17). Managing Investment Climate Reforms: Viet Nam Case Study, *draft case study prepared as input for the World Bank's World Development Report 2005 on Investment Climate, Growth and Poverty*.

Park, Kyung-Ae (2000, winter). North Korea's Non-Governmental Foreign Contacts. *The Korean Journal of Defence Analysis*, 12 (2).

Report on a visit to the Democratic People's Republic of Korea (2004, May 22-29). part of the University of Cambridge East Asia Institute's constructing confidence project on economic and academic engagement with the DPRK.

Richmond, Yale (2003). *Cultural Exchange and the Cold War: Raising the Iron Curtain*. Phillidelphia: Penn State Press.

Smith, Hazel (2002, July). Overcoming Humanitarian Dilemmas in the DPRK (North Korea). *United States Institute of Peace Special Report*, Washington DC.

Stone, Richard (2004, September 17). A Wary Pas de Deux. *Science,* 315, 1,703.

The KUT/SU Research Collaboration Project Status Report (2004, July). Retrieved from http://www.nautilus.org/DPRKBriefing Book/economy/30-KoreaSociety.html.

Von Hippel, David and Peter Hayes (2005, January 14). North Korea and Renewable Energy, *Science*, 307, 14, 207.

Von Hippel, David and Peter Hayes, Masami Nakata, Timothy Savage, and Chris Greacen (2001, February 16).*Modernising the Agreed Framework*, Nautilus Institute, http://nautilus.org/archives/papers/energy/ModernizingAF.PDF.

3

Instrumental versus Solidaric Rationality: European NGOs in North Korea

Sung-Jo Park

Introduction

Alteri vivas oportet, si vis tibi vivere
(Seneca, Ep.48/2)

"The Collapse of the Korean Peninsula" (Park 2006) was originally intended to be named, "Does Kim Jong Il like God?" This book attempted to shed light on Christian European NGOs' activities in North Korea. The NGOs' activities in North Korea show that the North Korean government makes a clear distinction between *specific* European NGOs and others. The latter were forced to cease their operation in North Korea and withdraw roughly at the end of 2005. Why are the Christian European NGOs granted such gracious tolerance from the North Korean government and thus allowed to continue their operation? The author's *hypothesis* is that there *is* no conflict, but rather, a large degree of compliance between the North Korean government's policies towards NGOs and the activities of the Christian European NGOs'. It is common knowledge that Kim Jong il's strategy aims at maintaining and strengthening his political legitimacy which he systematically and consequently pursues. This could be termed as *instrumental rationality* which works ideologically, morally, and ethically free. However, Christian NGOs' are interested in extending humanitarian aid to the people of North Korea which is epitomizing the principle of *solidaric rationality.* We have already established that there is no noteworthy conflict between the North Korean government and Christian European NGOs. Thus, one could infer that the relation between instrumental rationality (of the North Korean government) and solidaric rationality (of NGOs) are *complementary* by nature. If NGOs would place more emphasis on rapidly gaining *social reputation and political influence* in North Korea with their (short-term) projects this would do nothing but enhance instrumental rationality, as has been the case with human rights-centred NGOs and some South Korean NGOs). In this case, however, the North Korean government does not seem to conform to initiatives and actions by those NGOs. Conflicts often occurred between both sides, such as the case of Cap Anamur, MSF, OXFAM, etc. Why? Obviously, the North Korean government as well as these NGOs aimed at the same goal of *instrumental rationality* which resulted in a concurrent situation. Specifically, in the *first* case, an NGO aiming at *political influence* in the human rights issue in North Korea desires to achieve it *par tout* within a *short* period, and in the *second* case, an NGO (from South Korea) helping North Koreans is 'enthusiastic' about implementing projects with ostensible success. These NGOs are primarily concerned with gaining high *reputation* within an extremely short period.

The above-mentioned discrepancies between the North Korean government and NGOs resulted in the NGOs being required to cease their operations allegedly for the reason of political intervention in North Korea for the first case, and for the second case the North Korean government showed little interest to be 'victimized' for enhancing the reputation of any NGO.

This paper will try to show how European NGOs of primarily Christian associations manoeuvre through conflicting situations between the North Korean government's policy and their solidaric strategy.

Comparative Advantages of European NGOs

Since 1995 a large number of NGOs from different countries have been operating in North Korea and, about two years ago, most of them ceased their operation or had to quit North Korea. However, quite a number of European, especially Christian NGOs are still in operation. In the following, I will show the differences of the European NGOs from American, Japanese, and especially Korean NGOs.

The Kantian Dilemma and Survival Strategies:

There is no doubt that most western European countries have a high capability of handling communistic dictatorship due to the experience they gained from the Cold War. This experience was about how to handle communistic dictatorship which could be interpreted in the Kantian notion. Kant mentioned in his famous article "Zum ewigen Frieden" (Kant 1795) about three tactics of wartime dictatorship.

fac et excusa: dictator seizes power and the people's sovereignty suppresses people and tries to legitimize his behaviour, further seeking God's blessing for his legitimacy. He regards himself as *deux ex machina.*

si fecisti nega: dissatisfaction by my subordinates (people) and their misfortune is not my fault (*mea culpa*), but the people's fault.

divide et impera: dictator divides elites (leaders) into various fighting groups under pretence of 'bigger freedom'. Also, taking advantage of the split between elites and commoners, by which the latter is said to need more protection from *deus ex machina* (Kant 1795).

Reflecting on the Kantian notion, it seems there is no substantial difference between the dictatorship à la kant and that of Kim Jongil, one who abides with the attributes such as socialism, social justice, proletarian revolution, etc.

Germans have been through a long period of dictatorship, right and left-isms, and arduously succeeded in developing western democracy after the Second World War. West Germans were especially well prepared considering how they dealt with East Germany during the long period of division. Thus, it is no coincidence that West German NGOs such as Caritas, Diakonie, German Agro Action etc. have been quite successful in establishing their operations in North Korea. Furthermore, the government of United Germany having diplomatic relations with North Korea has benefited German NGOs, and last but not least the German Cultural Institute was opened in Pyongyang three years ago.

In addition, most European countries allow for the existence of communist parties, of which a few are sometimes even allowed some form of political power. Also, these countries have shared common experiences through the ECSC (European Conference for Security and Cooperation) and other East-West cooperation schemes (such as Eureka) in order to alleviate tensions and to facilitate dialogue between Western Europe and communistic regimes in Eastern Europe. Based on these experiences the European Union has been confident to carry out a two-wing policy, to, on the one hand, claim human rights (cf. EU-initiated UN Resolution on North Korea this year) and on the other hand extend humanitarian aid by eventually anchoring the NGOs' activities in North Korea. One could name this double-head strategy 'Zuckerbrot und Peitsche'-strategy (*stick and carrot-strategy*), in which West Germany was extremely successful in dealing with East Germany before the unification.

Satisfactio Operis:

German (protestant) churches had to observe three creeds by ushering in a new postwar era in regards to all kinds of misconduct for fascist regimes in the past: *contritio cordis* (heart of remorse), *confessio oris* (readiness of confession) and *satisfactio operis* (compensation by concrete action). European NGOs were greatly driven by the desire of cleansing 'the suppression of the past and exploitation through dictatorship, colonialism and war'. The principle of *satisfactio operas* in particular inculcated the mind of the young generation culminating in the unlimited support for the Third World and for reform and opening process of transformation economies since 1990. There was no dissent among social groups, clerical circles and cultural elites over this. This was conducive to public and private support as well as aid at international and EU levels. What's particularly striking is that European NGOs placed more priority to long term, sustainable projects instead of short term-return oriented performance, not to mention populistic, actionist prestige-projects. In other words, European NGOs preferred contribution to structural changes and development from the ground up in countries and regions that the NGOs were involved in.

Instrumental versus solidaric rationality

The juxtaposition of instrumental rationality and solidaric rationality is somewhat venturesome because of the term 'solidarity'. The notion of solidaric rationality leans on the combination of high degrees of reciprocity in altruism (altruistic punishment and altruistic reward) --- which goes beyond reciprocal altruism of the 70ties --- and social prestige-oriented altruism of the 80/90ties. It is common sense that the new ideal of human-beings in future are to be oriented increasingly toward this new type of altruism instead of sticking to egoistic rationalistic profit-driven behaviour (instrumental rationality) (Fehr 2004).

In regards to the question of how to handle the North Korean regime, to help it carry out reform and opening, to alleviate food shortage (by humanitarian aid) and to promote development, different ideas concur. Nevertheless, these different positions converge towards the question of how the principle of solidaric rationality can be put into reality.

Habermas (Habermas 1981) argues that the forced modernization and industrialization entailed power concentration and plutocracy having repercussion on daily life, formalized sphere and communicative behaviour of human-beings. In order to overcome the negative impacts of industrialization and modernization, human-beings need a new communicative culture (communicative rationality). Looking at the Habermasian typology as follows, we miss what is needed *in concret*

Table 2.1. Habermasian type of behaviour

goal of action individual or collective	performance-orientation	Mutual understanding-orientation
individual	behaviour with instru-mental rationality	
collective (societal)	strategic behaviour	behaviour with collective rationality

For mutual understanding-orientation at the individual level it is necessary to make the principle of communicative rationality a maxim of human-beings' behaviours for constructing a new communicative culture, especially in a society providing very little or no room for communication. The question is how? For instance, experts in the united Germany perceived 'new kinds of communications' between East and West Germans as necessary for enriching the substance of the unification and further for creating a new identity of the unified Germany: in brief, *a new communicative culture*. I think this kind of new approach is unavoidable in getting along with North Koreans. The concept of solidaric rationality goes beyond the principle of Habermasian communicative rationality in a more practical, concrete sense in that, in the case of North Korea, one should embark on *forming ambiance* of communication by planning, implementing and evaluating projects together with local people. To help the North Korean locals should not be a matter of cost-benefit analysis, nor a question of selfish social reputation, but a matter of mind the 'strength of mind' (in German 'Willenskraft'), that Antonio Damasio (2005) describes as an essential condition for altruism. He further argues that the strength of mind is symbolic of the readiness of human-beings to perceive the results of their action in the long run, not in a short period, as is the case of instrumental rationality. I would propose solidaric rationality as a method of realizing communicative rationality.

We classify NGOs into three categories: first, those who were attempting to exercise political influence by prioritizing the human rights issue in North Korea within a short period to reach a high degree of instrumental rationality. These (type ***a*** of the following graph) are e.g. Médicins sans Frontières, Cap Anamur which could be dubbed 'radical approach'; second, christian NGOs such as Campus für Christus (Caritas), Diakonie (Protestants), ADRA (Adventist)

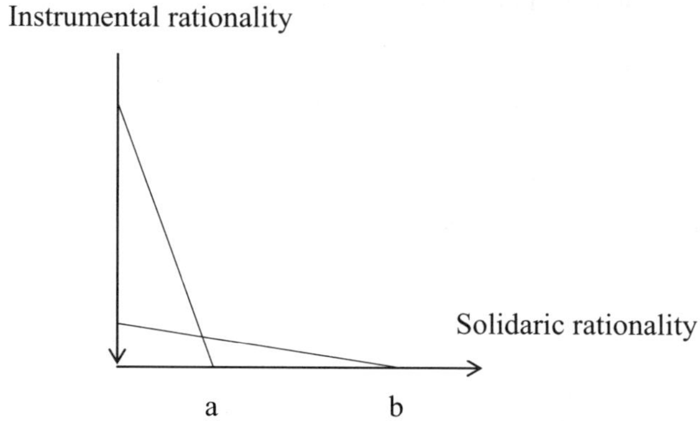

Figure 2.1 Relation between instrumental and solidaric rationality

Development and Relief Agency and some others such as German Agro Action (Deutsche Welthungerhilfe), etc are of type *b* aiming at long term solidarity for providing self-help for North Korean people with less emphasis on instrumental rationality. This typology should not mean that type *a* is solely for reaching instrumental rationality, however, considering to a certain degree solidaric rationality, as has been the case with Cap Anamur, Médicins sans Frontières, etc. NGOs of type *a* are *sui generis* human rights issue-oriented, while those of type *b* strongly based on humanitarianism are closely associated to a large extent with Christian organisations and prefer a 'calm', 'moderate', and 'integrative' approach instead of a radical one. Nevertheless, one can admit that a kind of fundamental tension between instrumental rationality and solidaric rationality is inherent in handling poverty-stricken dictatorship such as the case of North Korea (Park 2006; Schloms 2004).

Characteristics of NGOs' Operations: a Shift from Humanitarian Aid to Development Projects?

There is a wide consensus on how to solve food shortage in North Korea: the food aid offers no solution for a long-term sustainable food supply. European NGOs placed more importance on local initiative-based self-help projects in principle, reminding one of the 'basic needs approach' in the Third World. On the other hand, some American experts argued for necessity of industry policy. A prominent supporter of the industry policy concept, Marcus Noland premised that "aid is not a viable long-term solution" and emphasized the urgency of revitalizing of the industrial policy which could ascertain an expansion of industrial exports that would allow North Korea to import a huge volume of grains

(Noland 2003). His argument *per se* would be logical and plausible if the abolition of domestic and external impediments (which is quite improbable in the near future) combined with huge infrastructure investments would entail an efficient allocation of resources for the industrial policy. The industry policy argument seems to be an illusion, however, as seen from current perspective of investments and insurmountable political, institutional and other impediments.

In contrast, the arguments by McCarthy are aligning with the position represented by European NGOs in efforts of enhancing local food production share for food supply in North Korea (McCarthy 2000). It is obvious that the local development approach will necessitate not only an investment but also primarily an engagement of human capital for a longer period. In this case, a greater identity of local people with their own project results compare with any other efforts induced from the outside. Pursuing this approach, not only are classical concepts of community development intensely linked to a full-fletched agricultural extension service, but also visible physical and emotional engagement of 'foreign helpers' as 'true, reliable and sacrificing friends' are necessary. It must be assured that local people in North Korea perceive these helpers not as 'flying experts', but accept them as their own comrades. They should be resident on the spot with local people. This approach contributes to cultivating reliable relations between both sides. The importance and necessity of the engagement of these helpers has been described regularly in internet-available reports of those NGOs such as Caritas, Diakonie, Campus für Christus, German Agro Action, ADRA (Adventist Development and Relief Agency), ASB (Der Arbeiter Samariter Bund), CARE Germany, Johanniter Unfallhilfe, World Vision Germany, Maltheser Hilfsdienst, Medico International, and others.

Case Two

Campus für Christus:

Campus fuer Christus is a Swiss-Christian NGO operating in the rural areas of the North Korean provinces (cf. the map, not in remote, backward provinces such as South and North Hamkyung Province) since 1995.

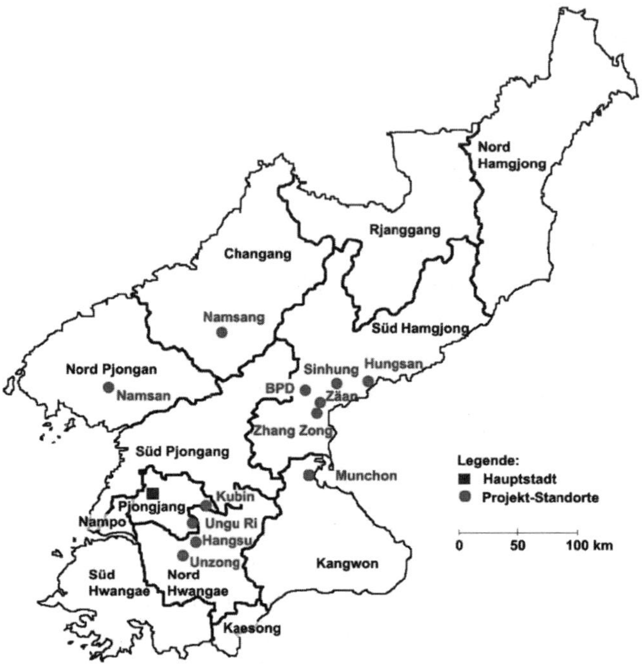

Figure 2.2 South and North Hamkyung Province

The basic principle of its operation is to recognize the principle of *self-help* in promoting agricultural production, rural development and capacity-building. To be more precise, the operation of Campus für Christus has been focusing on the following fields:

-food aid

-aid with pharmaceutical products, medical facilities and instruments for working small hospitals in rural areas

-agricultural development combining three aspects: local food production, food import (only to a limited degree) and food aid

-supply of clothes, food, stationery, etc. to children

-provide education and training programmes

The orientation of Campus für Christus was primarily humanitarian-aid centred. Nevertheless, Kaethi Zellweger, refers to possibilities of 'political intervention' in North Korea. To what extent and in which spheres the mentioned political intervention is possible is not clear. Zellweger pointed to the fact that 'politics is different from humanitarian aid, but this has great impact on politics' (Park 2006, p. 145).

The problem Campus für Christus its operation is faced with is an obscurity of political and administrative process, and lack of understanding about the culture and mentality of North Korean people (Zellweger 2006).

In her report of July 2006 for Caritas she referred to Caritas' new projects in the field of agricultural cooperatives and medical care near the city of Hamheung. She reported about 6 farms showing quite an optimistic picture of the future with the help of Caritas which enabled farms to purchase agricultural machines and transportation tools. Also in the medical field 3 hospitals having received Caritas' donations were brought into the situation to provide essential medical services. In both cases of 'success stories' she stressed cooperation between Caritas and local government agencies. What was striking for her was the fact that North Korea has increasingly moved from humanitarian aid to development projects, for which especially the capacity building was highly appreciated and financial and technical assistance for that is greatly demanded for (Zellweger 2006).

German Agro Action:

Activities since 1997 by *Deutsche Welthungerhilfe* are also noteworthy. In the meantime 27 Million Euro was granted to different projects in North Korea by the German Agro Action. The focus of their operations is based on a build-up of institutional infrastructures (production cooperatives) for agricultural and rural development frequently flanked by humanitarian first-aid in the field of medical care (www.welthungerhilfe.de/nordkorea-ernaehrungslage.html).

A significant performance of German Agro Action project was to teach local people how the rural and agricultural development should be planned. The principle of the project was 'learning by the local people for their own development'. In 1999, the German Agro Action worked out the project framework and finalized all relevant preparations for a concrete planning which was presented in February 2002 in Pyongyang, as follows.

Table 2.2 Details of German Agro Action Proposal 2002

<table>
<tr><td colspan="5">goals:
- help for self-help (aimed at securing food by own efforts the local people)
- development-oriented public relations in Germany
target group:
- disadvantaged people in rural areas
portfolio (specific targets):
- agriculture and securing food
- handicraft and small scale shops
- set-up and promotion of social infrastructure
- support of traeger
- support for children and youth
- emergency aid and rehabilitation
current status of projects:</td></tr>
<tr><th>food</th><th colspan="2">urgent demand</th><th>agriculture</th><th>water/hygiene</th></tr>
<tr><td rowspan="2">1997-2002 5 projects in South Hwanghae province target groups : children, pupils, the aged</td><th>coal</th><th>winter clothes</th><td rowspan="2">1997-2000 6 projects South Hwanghae cooperatives, social institutions</td><td rowspan="2">2000-2002 1 project finished in North Pyongan: project ongoing in North Pyongan kindergartens, cooperatives</td></tr>
<tr><td>1997-2000 4 projects South Hwanghae kindergartens</td><td>1997-2000 3 projects South Hwanghae; 3 projects in North Pyongan kindergartens</td></tr>
<tr><td colspan="5">comments by North Korean partners</td></tr>
<tr><td colspan="3">still demand for short-term emergency aid</td><td rowspan="2">middle-term concepts needed with regional and sectoral integration</td><td rowspan="2">volume of the planned project unclear</td></tr>
<tr><td colspan="3">demand for coal in South Hwanghae province</td></tr>
<tr><td colspan="5">A continuous joint planning and perspective is accentuated.</td></tr>
</table>

(*translated by the author*)

The German experts Thomas Magura and Michael Schloms were very instrumental for putting the refined *learning programme* by German Agro Action into use jointly with rural and agricultural development planners as the following phases show. First of all, they started with a set-up as a basis for mutual communication between 7 resident experts of German Agro Action and local leaders as well as central civil servants (Park 2006).

1. Step: The details are as follows:
2. Step : project basis for mutual communication
3. Step: project definition
4. Step: project conceptualization
5. Step: project financing definition
6. Step: project implementation
7. Step: project monitoring begins
8. Step: project evaluation : project final result report

The above-mentioned scheme indicates that in the first *phase* local people in North Korea begin to grasp their own needs and learn to formulate publicly their needs which are systematized in a catalogue of local needs according to urgency, forming the groundwork for the project (project conceptualization). After clearing the financial burden (financing definition) and the project financing is secured the implementation plan is worked out. Upon progression of the project implementation, the monitoring automatically begins. After this monitoring, the *evaluation* is carried out, followed by the final project result. This is the cycle of conceptualization, financing, monitoring and evaluation.

The problem is to judging the efficiency of this learning cycle. Experts, including the German Institute for Development Policy (Deutsches Institut für Entwicklungspolitik), argue that due to lack of civic society's elements (people's participation and transparency) frank opinions and judgment by the local people cannot be expected. However, at least one positive effect of this learning project is that 'reliable relations' between foreigners and North Korean locals can be established, and furthermore, the latter have gradually drifted away from an extremely reserved attitude toward German Agro Action projects. Michael Schloms very carefully formulates a critical remark on the concrete outcome of the project (Schloms 2000, p.15). If one considers the 'official goal' of German Agro Action to convince North Korean authorities of locally adapted production forms, which is to satisfy the needs of the locals one may say that this project received a certain level of acceptance (op. cit. p.31). More significant is the fact that this project could provide momentum to the local people to bring their learning intensity into this comprehensive multipurpose agricultural extension project.

It is really deserving for German Agro Action to note that "only when the consensus between concepts and possibilities of grantors, grantees and of implementing Organisations can be realized is it meaningful to execute joint projects" (translated by the author, Deutsche Welthungerhilfe 2005). One can presume that communications between the North Koreans and the German side were possible, or tolerated to a certain degree, given further that the latter was prepared to participate in the project and was motivated to learn.

The German Agro Action has reached noteworthy results with 10 experts from Germany and with more than a 7 Million Euro investment. Their activities have become quite broad in scope, including food supplies for school children, seed expansion culture, drinking water supplies, vegetable cultivation in vinyl greenhouses, cold storage isolation for 150 schools, etc. (Deutsche Welthungerhilfe 2003).

'North Korean Personality'

To create reliable relations with North Koreans, especially with government agencies, is extremely difficult. It seems that European NGOs have seemingly more readiness and capability to understand the mentality and culture of North Koreans than any other NGOs. The question is how the European NGOs grasp North Korean mentalities better and more realistically. Besides their virtual experiences with socialistic regimes there are other constellations which bring NGOs together with local people.

According to assessments made by those NGOs based on their on-the-spot experiences described in their reports (German Agro Action 2004;medico international 2004; Caritas et al 2005;Campus für Christus 2002, 2003) we are able to accede to a certain degree to the 'North Korean Personality'. One thing deserving comment at the beginning is the *a priori* proposition about the cultural homogeneity of Koreans, South and North, which serves unchanged as the most important essential fact for the Korean unification policy and Sunshine Policy. The experiences of Germans with East Germans after the Unification show that on the both sides of Germany two personalities completely diverged. West Germans, especially West German unification policy makers were ignorant of the growing heterogeneity of Germans evinced, above all, by East Germany-dissident novelists, poets, and lawyers such as Stephan Heym, Christa Wolf, Rudolf Bahro, and Rolf Heinrich. "Der Gefühlsstau" by Hans-Joachim Maaz first drew attention to the false assumption about the cultural homogeneity of Germans after the unification (Maaz 1989/90).

In Korea the concept of 'cultural homogeneity' has existed persistently for a long time forming the ground for the South Korean unification policy. Even a reflection upon this was tabooed. This notion will probably continue far into the future. However, the realities of cultural homogeneity are quite different from belief and emotions buttressing the official unification policy. I have tried to remind the audience of a necessary recourse to the realistic capturing of cultural homogeneity (Park et al 2005).

The above-mentioned reports by NGOs pointed *unisono* to the cultural and mental differences between North and South Koreans. Here is a list of some 'negative' and 'positive' traits of North Koreans.

negative traits:
-authoritarian personality
-concealing the real nature of human-beings
-lack of emotion and frankness
-passive and receptive attitude
-lack of creativity
-permissive, power-, order-orientation
-regarding North Korea as paradise
-food shortage for helping South Koreans in starvation

positive traits:
-diligence, eagerness to learn
-ascetical life to get Korea united
-humble
-cooperative
-community-oriented/family oriented

Western experts writing articles and trip reports about North Korea tend to generalize some mentioned attitudes and characteristics of North Koreans as 'confucian-oriented'. I have doubts about this hypothesis and think some of them to be 'authoritarian' in association with the socialistic socialization which was also the case in East Germany and Communist China. I am not supportive of this cultural interpretation. Only by taking critical distance from this culturalism can one find useful comparative nominators.

Harmony between Kim Jongil and Christian NGOs?

This title may evoke prejudice that Kim Jongil's politics eventually complies with the Christian spirit. However, this is definitely not the case, due to the fact that he is convinced that: *'Dieu, c'est moi!'*

In North Korea, missionary work is forbidden. Freedom of religion is non-existent. The Christian NGOs are not operating for the purpose of pursuing missionary work. Had any Christian NGO done missionary work even in an indirect sense, they would have been banned from North Korea.

However, Christian European NGOs pray and conduct service in presence of North Koreans. These behaviours are tolerated, because North Government agencies are convinced that these NGOs are doing nothing other than humanitarian assistance in the sense of solidaric rationality. This is not regarded as a missionary work. What they do is to contribute to solving food shortage which complies with the policy of North Korean government.

European NGOs are operating in the countryside at grass roots level far away from Pyongyang, based upon living with local people. However, they have conviction that 'a real development must come from the local people'. They emphasize common experiences with local people and do not ask for any kind of compensation. Sacrifice and devotion to development with local people is *ultimo ratio*. This makes it possible to set up reliable relations with local people. NGOs think with this engagement to be able to create a small room of freedom which is expected to get expanded in the long run. They are not interested in a mass media show, but satisfied with a 'calm existence'. Flake (2004) described Christian NGOs' activities as follows: "while generally smaller in scope, such organisations were frequently able to negotiate more effectively with the DPRK and respond more directly to needs as they arose, because they implemented their programmes apart from political considerations and did not draw attention to their efforts (Flake 2004, p.4)."

'The small-sized operation, direct response to arisen needs, separation between politics and aid, and indifference towards populism' are strategic characteristics of NGOs. NGOs formed in 1997 a consortium called Private Voluntary Organisation Consortium (PVOC), to which the following NGOs belong: ADRA, Amigos Internationales, CARE, Catholic Relief Service, Church World Service, Korean-American Sharing Movement, Latter Day Saints Charities, Mercy Corps, and World Vision.

The North Government agencies are not ignorant that there is a close relation between Christianity and the human rights issue, and especially take into account one of the important reasons for the collapse of East German Communist regime. It collapsed due to the resistance groups assembled and supported in churches of East Berlin and Leipzig. Therefore, it was no coincidence that those NGOs claiming human rights in North Korea such as MSF, MDM, Cap Anamur, etc. were forced to cease their operation.

In contrast, Christian NGOs have been trying to operate within the framework of humanitarian guidelines agreed-upon in 2001 by WFP and UNICEF jointly with the North Korean government (cf. as follows), by which it is greatly doubtful to which extent the 'signed clauses' are respected by the North Korean government. Considering the realities of the situation, some of the following clauses sound like a mockery!

"knowledge about the overall humanitarian situation in the country according to assessed needs; assurance that humanitarian assistance reaches sectors of the population in greatest need; access for assessment, monitoring, and evaluation; distribution of assistance only to areas where access is granted; protection of the humanitarian interests of the population; support to local capacity building; beneficiary participation in programme planning and implementation; adequate capacity in terms of international staff; meet the health and safety needs of the international humanitarian community (Smith 2002)"

ADRA's head, Herbert Bodenmann replied to the question how ADRA operat es, "he cannot understand why Campus fuer Christus and ADRA are so much fa vored in North Korea". Furthermore, he stressed that "the pure solidarity of Cam pus fuer Christus and ADRA is not concurring with the instrumental rationality of the North Korean government (http://www.livenet.ch/www/index.php/D/artic le/190/16150). In addition, the following statement by Hans Peter Nüsch of Diak onie (on his personal experiences in North Korea) seems to strongly support the thesis on the absence of conflict between instrumental rationality (of the North Korean government) and the solidaric rationality (of NGOs) as the most essentia l pillar for NGOs' activities in North Korea:

"We Christians enjoy special relations with government agencies in North Korea. They think we Christians are good people, even though we behave in a naive way, for we have nothing to conceal. We do not bow before Kim Ilsung's statue. We always pray before we take meal. We do not talk badly about North Koreans. Instead, we pray for them. They often say that they have good reliable relations with us. We always live together with village people in the countryside. We rarely live in Pyongyang, a district reserved for foreign diplomats. We often lead frank discussions about God and our belief with the North Korean cadre and government officials. We are convinced that only if we are honest and open can we reach our goals. The North Korean officials are not comfortable with us talking with the local people about politics and ideology. Nevertheless, we Christians can help them realize their goal in solidarity and idealism (Imhof 2005) (slightly modified translation by the author)."

Does Kim Jongil like God? No, definitely no, because he thinks: Dieu, c'est moi!

Conclusion

During the SNU-Hanns Seidel Foundation Joint Conference (June 1, 2007) I was asked by a commentator whether Christian European NGOs envision an expansion of their activities to a larger scale, possibly to such an extent that a Christianity-minded 'mass movement' can be eventually expected. This question came from an expert from USA. Is this a typical way thinking for an American cold war falcon? I am very sceptical about this probability, because first of all, NGOs have no intention to enlarge their activities beyond their current activity radius and, I am quite sure Christian European NGOs are sticking to their current policy of gradual local development with local people, and secondly, the North Korean government eliminates sufficient chances to exercise perfect control over details of NGOs' operations.

The intention and strategy of Christian European NGOs regardless of operation site have always respected the principle of "alteri vivas oportet, si vis tibi vivere". The solidaric rationality will and should remain with NGOs in North Korea.

References

Attali, Jacques (2004, September 10). Proceeding of Keynote Address closing the 57th Annual DPI/NGO Conference at the UN General Assembly Hall.

Campus für Christus (2002). Zwischenbericht 2002. Zukunft 200. url

Campus für Christus (2003). Zwischenbericht Nordkorea.

Damasio, Antonio R. (2005). Descartes' Irrtum, List Taschenbuch Berlin

Deutsche Welthungerhilfe (2003). Freedom from Hunger. Portrait of German Agro Action, Annual Report

Deutsche Welthungerhilfe (2005). Freedom from Hunger. Portrait of German Agro Action, Annual Report

Fehr, Ernst (2004). Die Natur des menschlichen Altruismus. Rede zur Cogito Preisverleihung

Flake, L. Gordon (2004, April, 24) Testimony before the Subcommittee on Asia and the Pacific. House Committee on International Relations

German Agro Action (2003). Annual Report 2003, url

German Agro Action (2004). Annual Report 2004, url

Imhof, Fritz (2005). Diakonie ohne Grenzen, livenet.ch. url

Joint CIDSE and Caritas Europa contribution (2005). European Commission consultation on the future of EU Development Policy.

Kant, Immanuel (1795). Zum ewigen Frieden in: Kant Werke Band 9

Maaz, Hans Joachim (1990). Der Gefühlsstau. Ein Psycho Programme der DDR, Berlin

McCarthy, Thomas (2000). CARE's Withdrawal from North Korea. Policy Forum online (http://www.nautilius.org/fora/security/0003A_McCarthy.html

Medico international (2004).Jahresbericht 2004

Noland, Marcus (2003). Famine and Reform in North Korea, Institute of International Economics, WP03-5, url

Otten, Nadine (2005). Kooperation zwischen öffentlichen und privatwirtschaftlichen Partnern. Eine Analyse am Beispiel des Programmems' Entwicklungspartnerschaften mit der Wirtschaft' des Bundesministeriums für wirtschaftliche Zusammenarbeit, Kölner Arbeitspapiere für internationalen Politik, nr.21

Park, Sung-Jo (2006). Hanbando bunge (The Collapse of the Korean Peninsula), Random House JoongAng (in korean)

Park, Sung-Jo et al (2005). Nambukhan Mungchi myun juknunda (South and North Korea, they come together, they fall), Random House JoongAng (in Korean), 4th edition (in korean)

Schloms, Michael (2000). Divide et Impera - Totalitärer Staat und Humanitäre Hilfe in Nordkorea, Wissenschaftszentrum Berlin POO-304

Schloms, Michael (2004). North Korea and the Timeless Dilemma of Aid. A Study of Humanitarian Action in Famines, LIT Berlin

Smith, Hazel (2002). Overcoming Humanitarian Dilemmas in the DPRK (North Korea), url

VENRO (2000). Abschlussbericht. Umfrage zur Zukunft der deutschen Entwicklungspolitik

Zellweger, Kaethi (2006). DPRK Trip Report by Caritas-Hong Kong, NK brief no.06-8-14-1

4

Human Rights Crisis in North Korea: Basic Understanding from the Perspective of International Law

Dae-Soon Kim

I. Prologue changing status of individuals and the protection of human rights in international law

The purpose of this article is to provide some insight into the international legal framework on human rights particularly in the context of ongoing suffering of the North Korean people. With this in mind, let us first go over how individuals had been perceived and treated through the lens of international law.

First, as far as the obligations are concerned, individuals under international law, as it existed before World War II, already had the obligation not to commit serious crimes ranging from piracy to war crimes, then further expanding to include crimes against humanity and so forth. The list of such crimes has been supplemented. The efforts of the international community since World War II to prosecute and punish an individual perpetrator who has committed egregious crimes culminated in the adoption of the Rome Statue of the International Criminal Court on July 17, 1998.[1]

However, as far as the "rights" go, individuals were not allowed to derive any rights directly from international law. When an individual was injured by a foreign state, his final remedy was to try to seek diplomatic protection from the state of which he was a national. International law did not endow obligations on the states to afford diplomatic protection; from an international law perspective, the exercise of diplomatic protection was the sole right of the states, and whether

[1]UN Doc. A/CONF. 183/9; 2187 UNTS(no. 38544) 90 ; Entered into force July 1, 2002.

or not to exercise such right fell entirely within the discretion of the states. In addition, whenever an individual had been injured by the state of his nationality, it was regarded as domestic affairs of that state, thereby taking place beyond the regulatory boundary of international law.[2] This classic opinion was reiterated by the Permanent Court of International Justice, which stated in the *Mavrommatis Palestine Concessions* case:[3]

"It is an elementary principle of international law that a State is entitled to protect its subjects, when injured by acts contrary to international law committed by another State, from whom they have been unable to obtain satisfaction through the ordinary channels. By taking up the case of one of its subjects, and by resorting to diplomatic action or international judicial proceedings on his behalf, a State is in reality asserting its own rights –its right to ensure, in the person of its subjects, respect for the rules of international law."

In short, individuals under traditional international law were subject to the complete control of the states of their nationality. Has such a viewpoint been fundamentally changed or modified by the modern international law? The answer is still 'No', though a glimpse of a change in thinking seems to make headway. The International Court of Justice states, for example, in *Barcelona Traction Co.* Case:[4]

"that, within the limits prescribed by international law, a State may exercise diplomatic protection by whatever means and to whatever extent it thinks fit, for it is its own right that the State is asserting. Should the natural or legal persons on whose behalf it is acting consider that their rights are not adequately protected, they have no remedy in international law. All they can do is resort to municipal law, if means are available, with a view to furthering their cause or obtaining redress.... The State must be viewed as the sole judge to decide whether its protection will be granted, to what extent it is granted, and when it will cease. It retains in this respect a discretionary power the exercise of which may be determined by considerations of a political or other nature, unrelated to the particular case. Since the claim of the State is not identical with that of the individual or corporate person whose cause is espoused, the State enjoys complete freedom of action."

---

[2] See L. Oppenheim, *International Law: A Treatise*, 8th ed. (edited by H. Lauterpacht) (London: Longman Group Limited, 1955), 19, fn. 12.

[3] 1) PCIJ (1924), Series A, no. 2, 11-12.

[4] ICJ Reports (1970), p. 3 at 44 (paras. 78-79)

So far, as the current regime persists that a state is represented only by its government and not by its nationals individually, it seems almost inevitable that the international community will remain decentralized. However, injuries occurring to individuals are more likely to be caused by the States which they belong to rather than by foreign States. The period following World War II saw a shift towards the protection of individuals as part of an effort by the international community, which subsequently assigned such task to the realm of the international human rights law. The modern principle on which respect for basic human rights is based proposes that individuals should be protected not in their capacity as members of a State or a certain group, but *qua* a single human being; as the respect for or the protection of basic human rights is no longer an entirely domestic affair of the states, individuals should no longer be subjects at a complete disposal of the state of which they are nationals. Furthermore, the principle of respect for human rights has now become *jus cogens* (peremptory norms of general international law), which will be mentioned later.

With the substantial progress made in the legal field of human rights, traditional notion of diplomatic protection is being reconsidered, which can be palpably felt from what the UN "International Law Commission" (hereinafter "ILC") stated in its Commentary, para. 3, to the "Draft articles on Diplomatic Protection" of 2006,[5] Article 1:

"Diplomatic protection has traditionally been seen as an exclusive State right in the sense that a State exercises diplomatic protection in its own right because an injury to a national is deemed to be an injury to the State itself. This approach has its roots, first in a statement by the Swiss jurist Emmerich de Vattel in 1758 that "whoever ill-treats a citizen indirectly injures the State, which must protect that citizen," and, secondly in a dictum of the Permanent Court of International Justice in 1924 in the Mavrommatis Palestine Concessions case that "by taking up the case of one of its subjects and by resorting to diplomatic action or international judicial proceedings on his behalf, a State is in reality asserting its own right, the right to ensure, in the person of its subjects, respect for the rules of international law". Obviously it is a fiction - and an exaggeration - to say that an injury to a national is an injury to the State itself. Many of the rules of diplomatic protection contradict the correctness of this fiction, notably the rule of continuous nationality which requires a State to prove that the injured national remained its national after the injury itself and up to the date of

[5] http://www.un.org/law/ilc/

the presentation of the claim. A State does not "in reality" - to quote Mavrommatis - assert its own right only. "In reality" it also asserts the right of its injured national."

On a similar line, the Arbitral Court of the case *Government of the State of Eritrea and Government of the Republic of Yemen* (*Phase Two: Maritime Delimitation*)[6] said that "the western legal fiction-which is in any event losing its importance-whereby all legal rights, even those in reality held by individuals, were deemed to be those of the State."

Moving onto the main part of this paper, "human rights," we sometimes find a few remaining totalitarian states telling the human rights-friendly states to "mind their own business." However, it ought to be borne in mind that the respect for the basic human rights is the ultimate and supreme value upon which the whole international community should be, and already is, built.

At the same time, there would be, by any means, no state on earth that does not report a single incidence of human rights violation by state authorities: the threshold at which this principle operates on the international plane is the 'massive', 'gross' or 'repeated and systematic' violation of human rights. If a certain violation falls short of this level, it cannot be blamed in the eyes of general international law. Blaming for a single violation arising out of treaty is entirely another matter.

With regard to which human rights are classified as "basic," numerous international instruments have been adopted, including the 1948 Universal Declaration of Human Rights and the two of 1966 Human Rights Covenants, i.e. the International Covenant on Civil and Political Rights[7] and the International Covenant on Economic, Social and Cultural Rights.[8]

It is also worthwhile to note that many human rights-related international instruments stress the close connection between the respect for human rights and the international peace and security. For example, Article 55(c) of the Charter of the United Nations states that "with a view to the creation of conditions ... necessary for peace and friendly relations among nations ... the United Nations shall promote ... universal respect for, and observance of, human rights and fundamental freedoms..."; and the two Human Rights Covenant of 1966 state in their preambles respectively that "recognition of the inherent dignity and of the equal

---

[6] Judgment of December 17, 1999, para. 101 (available at http://www.pca-cpa.org/).

[7] Adopted December 16, 1966, effective March 23, 1976; GA Res. 2200A(XXI), annex, UN Doc. A/6316; 999 UNTS (no. 14668) 171 ; http://www.ohchr.org/english/law/ccpr.htm.

[8] Adopted December 16, 1966, effective January 3, 1976; GA Res. 2200A(XXI), annex, UN Doc. A/6316; 993 UNTS (no. 14531) 3 ; http://www.ohchr.org/english/law/cescr.htm.

and inalienable rights of all members of the human family is the foundation of freedom, justice and peace in the world."

Along with a brief general overview to this point, this paper focuses on what international law authorizes us to do when we make an attempt to improve the situation of human rights in North Korea. That is, is there anything we can or must do if we truly want to liberate North Korean people who are being beaten, tortured and finally shot to death in a way beyond our ordinary imagination? Holding down my anger towards the brutal group, I will attempt to set out the reality and human rights issues in North Korea from the perspective of international law.

II. What is going on within and without North Korea?

Before discussing issues relating to international law, we need to first identify what is going on in North Korea. One of the issues that deserve our attention is international abduction. It is an indisputable fact, partly admitted by North Korea itself, that it had abducted a number of people overseas, mainly including, but not limited to, South Koreans and Japanese.

Since the cease-fire of the Korean War in 1953, four hundred and eighty six South Koreans, most of whom were fishermen, are strongly presumed to have been taken away to North Korea. There is an ongoing dispute between Japan and North Korea even after Junichiro Koizumi, then-Japanese Prime Minister, visited Pyongyang in September 2002 and made Kim Jong-Il admit that the abductions of Japanese nationals during the 1970s and 1980s were manoeuvred and carried out by North Korean special institutions (it is comic-opera that he said as if he himself had not involved in such crimes) ; five surviving Japanese abductees were thereafter temporarily allowed to visit Japan, but they did not return to North Korea; and it is the sparkling issue whether Ms. Megumi Yokota, who was abducted at the age of 13, has died as North Korea claims or is still alive as her parents together with Japanese government believe based on forensic analysis of the alleged cremated remains of Ms. Yokota. Why did North Korea headed by Kim Jung-Il perpetrate such so many wanton abductions? As one of possible answers thereto, I'd like to recall here what one of Modern Great Thinkers, Professor Hayek properly said: "The principle that the end justifies the means is in individualist ethics regarded as the denial of all morals. In collectivist ethics it becomes necessarily the supreme rule; there is literally nothing which the consistent collectivist must not be prepared to do if it serves "the good of the whole," because "the good of the whole" is to him the only criterion of what ought be done."[9]

Another issue of international concern in a similar context is state-sponsored terrorism. The fact that North Korea exports terrorism and grants asylum to foreign terrorists is not much astonishing if we read Article 80 of its Constitution, which provides that "The DPRK shall grant the right of asylum to foreign nationals persecuted for struggling or peace and democracy, national independence and socialism for the freedom of scientific and cultural pursuit." A paradox faced by North Korea is that it regards escapees from North Korea desperately seeking food or freedom as traitors and cracks down on them in a cruel manner.

Now, let us take a look at what North Korea's New Constitution of 1998 (the so-called Kim Il-Sung Constitution) says about basic rights of nationals. Its Chapter 5, consisting of 25 articles starting from Article 62, contains "Fundamental Rights and Duties of Citizens". Among others, by Article 67 "Citizens are guaranteed freedom of speech, of the press, of assembly, demonstration and association. The State shall guarantee conditions for the free activity of democratic political parties and social organisations." ; by Article 68 "Citizens have freedom of religious beliefs. This right is granted by approving the construction of religious buildings and the holding of religious ceremonies. No one may use religion as a pretext for drawing in foreign forces or for harming the State and social order." ; by Article 74 "Citizens are free to engage in scientific, literary and artistic pursuits. The State shall grant benefits to inventors and innovators. Copyright and patent rights shall be protected by law." ; by Article 75 "The citizens shall have freedom to reside in and travel to any place." ; and by Article 79 "Citizens are guaranteed inviolability of the person and the home and privacy of correspondence. No citizens can be placed under control or be arrested nor can their homes be searched without a legal warrant."

The text itself seems to be seemingly fine on its surface, but the truth lies in the opposite of what it says: in North Korea you cannot expect at all to enjoy "freedom of speech, of the press, of assembly, demonstration and association", "conditions for the free activity of democratic political parties and social organisations", "freedom of religious beliefs", creative activities without any interference including "scientific, literary and artistic pursuits". "freedom to reside in and travel to any place", and "inviolability of the person and the home and privacy of correspondence". In connection with this, you cannot miss Article 63 which provides that "In the DPRK the rights and duties of citizens are based on

[9] Friedrick A. Hayek, *The Road to Serfdom* (Chicago: University of Chicago Press, 1944), 146-147.

the collectivist principle, One for all and all for one." In North Korea, living a life dedicated to the "Dear Leader" (Kim Jung-Il) is an honor not only for yourself, but for your whole family. You will now understand why Kim Jung-Il and his regime do not feel the slightest bit of remorse for prohibiting people from moving freely even within what they claim is a country and doing business for their minimal survival. What is worse, they are not hesitant to starve and/or torture their own people, operate prison camps on an enormous scale and execute people publicly. Judging from facts like these, North Korea as it exists now is as such a huge concentration internment camp.[10]

International community as a whole has been expressing serious concern over the complete lack of notion of human rights within North Korea; one of the most recent responses from the international community is Resolution 62/167 adopted by the General Assembly on December 18, 2007 by a vote of 101 in favour, 22 against and 59 abstentions, wherein it "[e]xpresses its very serious concern at", *inter alia,* "[t]he persistence of continuing reports of systematic, widespread and grave violations of civil, political, economic, social and cultural rights in the Democratic People's Republic of Korea, including:

(i) Torture and other cruel, inhuman or degrading treatment or punishment, including inhuman conditions of detention, public executions, extrajudicial and arbitrary detention; the absence of due process and the rule of law, including fair trial guarantees and an independent judiciary; the imposition of the death penalty for political and religious reasons; and the existence of a large number of prison camps and the extensive use of forced labour;

(ii) The situation of refugees and asylum-seekers expelled or returned to the Democratic People's Republic of Korea and sanctions imposed on citizens of the Democratic People's Republic of Korea who have been repatriated from abroad leading to punishments of internment, torture, cruel, inhuman or degrading treatment or the death penalty, and in this regard urges all States to ensure respect for the fundamental principle of non-refoulement and to treat those who seek refuge humanely;

(iii) All-pervasive and severe restrictions on the freedoms of thought, conscience, religion, opinion and expression, peaceful assembly and association, and on equal access to information, by such means as the persecution of individuals exercising their freedom of opinion and expression, and their families;

---

[10] See http://en.wikipedia.org/wiki/Human_rights_in_North_Korea.

(iv) Limitations imposed on every person who wishes to move freely within the country and travel abroad, including the punishment of those who leave, or try to leave, the country without permission, or their families;

(v) The violations of economic, social and cultural rights, which have led to severe malnutrition, widespread health problems and other hardship for the population in the Democratic People's Republic of Korea, inter alia, women, children and the elderly;

(vi) Continuing violation of the human rights and fundamental freedoms of women, in particular the trafficking of women for the purpose of prostitution or forced marriage and the subjection of women to human smuggling, forced abortions, gender-based discrimination and violence;

(vii) Continuing reports of violations of the human rights and fundamental freedoms of persons with disabilities, especially on the use of collective camps and of coercive measures that target the rights of persons with disabilities to decide freely and responsibly on the number and spacing of their children;

(viii) Violations of workers' rights, including the right to freedom of association and collective bargaining, the right to strike as defined by the obligations of the Democratic People's Republic of Korea under the International Covenant on Economic, Social and Cultural Rights, and the prohibition of the economic exploitation of children and of any harmful or hazardous work of children as defined by the obligations of the Democratic People's Republic of Korea under the Convention on the Rights of the Child."

The Resolution also "[r]eiterates its very serious concern on unresolved questions of international concern relating to the abduction of foreigners in the form of enforced disappearance, which violates the human rights of the nationals of other sovereign countries, and in this regard strongly calls upon the Government of the Democratic People's Republic of Korea urgently to resolve these questions, including through existing channels, in a transparent manner, including ensuring the immediate return of abductees".

All in all, the Resolution depicts well, although in an epitomizing manner, what is happening within North Korea. Simply because we do not live there will not mean we cannot see what everyday life of North Korean people would be like.

III. What does international law demand from North Korea?

As the above Resolution implies that North Korea is being asked to comply with international rules and norms legally and validly imposed on them. It'll be required to identify rules and norms applicable to North Korea.

Among others, we can think of human rights-related treaties to which North Korea is a party. With North Korea being a member of the United Nations, the first instrument to be mentioned is the Charter of the United Nations. In contrast to the Covenant of the League of Nations of 1919 which merely stated in the Preamble that "The High Contracting Parties, in order to promote international co-operation and to achieve international peace and security ...Agree to this Covenant of the League of Nations," the Charter of the United Nations of 1945 cleared in its Chapter I (Articles 1 and 2) the purposes of the organisation and the basic principles in accordance with which the organisation and its Members shall act. The Charter states, *inter alia*, in Article 1, paragraph 3, that one of the Purposes of the United Nations is "to achieve international co-operation ... in promoting and encouraging respect for human rights and for fundamental freedoms for all without distinctions as to race, sex, language, or religion". Based on Charter authorisation provisions including this, the UN General Assembly, the primary organ responsible for the promotion of human rights, has adopted a number of international conventions (in other words "treaties") up to now. As the Resolution 62/167 noted in its preamble, second paragraph, North Korea is a party to such conventions as the International Covenant on Civil and Political Rights,[11] the International Covenant on Economic, Social and Cultural Rights,[12] the Convention on the Rights of the Child[13] and the Convention on the Elimination of All Forms of Discrimination against Women.[14] The Resolution indicates that North Korea is, on the whole, not fulfilling its obligation imposed by those conventions.

The quintessence of treaties of whatever kind is that they cannot bind non-parties. The 1969 Vienna Convention on the Law of Treaties confirms this point in its Article 34, which states: "a treaty does not create obligations or rights for a third State without its consent." Following this line, Articles 35 and 36 of the Convention respectively require the expressed acceptance in writing by the third, non-party state of the obligation the states parties of a treaty wish to impose on

[11] supra, note 7.
[12] supra, note 8.
[13] Adopted November 20, 1989, effective September 2, 1990; 1577 UNTS (no. 27531) 3.
[14] Adopted December 18, 1979, effective September 3, 1981; 1249 UNTS (no. 20378) 13.

the outsider and the presumed assent by the third party to the right the states parties of a treaty wish to give to the outsider. In other words, treaties including those governing human rights are generally thought to be a tool for establishing rights or duties only among states parties, therefore, creating *subjective* regimes. An interesting debate is going on about whether or not there could be *legislative* treaties or treaties creating *objective* regimes. The adjective 'legislative' or 'objective' suggests that such treaties create obligations and rights valid *erga omnes*. Do or can they really exist under the present decentralised international community based upon the principle of state sovereignty? The Vienna Convention does not touch upon this matter, probably considering its controversial potentiality.[15]

And, furthermore, global treaties concerning human rights, including those to which North Korea is a party, vest individuals with the standing to sue their own governments for the infringement of human rights before international institutions. Regrettably, the final decisions of such institutions still fall short of being binding upon the respondent states, except for some judicial protection systems on the regional plan such as that of the European Convention for the Protection of Human Rights and Fundamental Freedoms. The international personality of individuals is left to the will of states and therefore still remains unstable.

International rules originate from "custom." Although conventions and custom are two different law-making procedures, they have one thing in common, - to wit, that their binding force rests ultimately on the consent of states participating in their making. No legal rule, whether emanating from customs or treaties, cannot bind the outsiders: although a different approach based on the majoritarinianism is being attempted by some international lawyers, the system of majority is, in principle, not allowed when making inter-state rules or decisions. This is a corollary of the basic rule called 'the principle of sovereign equality of states' upon which the international community was and still is founded. In the *Lotus* case[16] the Permanent Court of International Justice pointed out that: "International law governs relations between independent States. The rules of law binding upon States therefore emanate from their own free will as expressed in conventions or by usages generally accepted as expressing principles of law and established in order to regulate the relations between these co-existing independent communities or with a view to the achievement of common aims. Restrictions upon the independence of States cannot therefore be presumed."

---

[15] Sir Ian Sinclair, *The Vienna Convention on the Law of Treaties*, 2nd ed. (Manchester: Manchester University Press, 1984),104; Mark W. Janis, *An introduction to Introduction Law*, 3rd ed. (New York: Aspen Law & Business, 1999), p. 33.

[16] PCIJ (1927), Series A, No. 10, p. 18.

However, there is a vast difference between convention and custom in terms of nature: Western international lawyers generally agree that once a "general" practice is subsequently accompanied with the psychological element commonly called "*opinio juris*", it binds in principle "all" states on earth. They argue that the custom is, in kind, not a tacit or implied agreement but a legal form separated from the treaty. According to this opinion, the customary rule would bind those states which kept silent, remained passive, or showed no interest during its formation period of time and newly emerging states would be bound by the existing rules of custom, -to which extent it might be said that custom consists of certain heteronymous elements.

One exception is allowed: the persistent objector, i.e. the state which argued unambiguously and persistently against the emergence of a new custom during its formation period lies beyond its binding sphere. The subsequent objector, i.e. the state which kept silent during the formative stage of a new custom and belatedly dissents from what already has been consolidated as a legal norm, is, by definition, not a persistent objector and cannot evade the binding force of the new custom in question, although there might be an exception if other interested countries acquiesce in such an evasive behaviour by the subsequent objectors.

As respect for human rights has now become one of the core principles established under the framework of international custom, numerous types of human rights abuses by North Korea will be able to be condemned in accordance with the relevant customary rules.

Here we cannot fail to mention two basic norms or duties of modern customary international law, -to wit, "peremptory norms of general international law" (simply called "*jus cogens*" in Latin) and "duties *erga omnes*". There seems to be no evidence that North Korea has argued against the emergence of those two concepts, which are crucial standards in deciding whether we will, or whoever can, blame North Korea for its unacceptable behaviour. These two concepts are very technical and a brief clarification of them will be given below to help laymen understand the human rights crisis of North Korea in an international legal aspect.

Some early international lawyers contended that natural law exists and that it binds states irrespective of their will. For instance, Vattel (1714-1767) stated:[17]

[17] Emerich de Vattel, Le Droit de Gents, ou Principes de la Loi Naturelle, applique's a la Conduite et aux Affaires des Nations et des Souverains (The Law of Nations or the Principles of Natural Law Applied to the Conduct and to the Affairs of Nations and of Sovereigns), Volume Three (Translation of the Edition of 1758 by Charles G. Fenwick) (Washington: Carnegie Institution, 1916), 4-5.

"We use the term necessary Law of Nations for that law which results from applying the natural law to Nations. ... Since this law is not subject to change and the obligations which it imposes are necessary and indispensable, Nations cannot alter it by agreement, nor individually or mutually release themselves from it. It is by the application of this principle that a distinction can be made between lawful and unlawful treaties or conventions and between customs which are innocent and reasonable and those which are unjust and deserving of condemnation."

This line of thought, however, was nearly overshadowed by the 19th century positivism, which placed the sovereignty or will of states before natural law. It seemed to have died out when the *Lotus* case[18] was decided in 1927, although the lip-service had been paid to it.

The contemporary debate centres upon how to look at the 'peremptory norm of general international law (*jus cogens*),' introduced by Article 53 of the 1969 Vienna Convention on the Law of Treaties which states:

"A treaty is void if, at the time of its conclusion, it conflicts with a peremptory norm of general international law. For the purposes of the present Convention, a peremptory norm of general international law is a norm accepted and recognized by the international community of States as a whole as a norm from which no derogation is permitted and which can be modified only by a subsequent norm of general international law having the same character."

At one end of the spectrum, some scholars contend that the peremptory norm of general international law is entirely a new source of international law. They argue, among other things, that the traditional sources of international law listed in Article 38, paragraph 1, of the Statute of the International Court of Justice are not suitable to represent 'the international community of States as a whole' and that such community can only be convened at the Assembly of the United Nations or a universal international conference. But one thing is not to be forgotten: the peremptory norm of the 1969 Vienna Convention still belongs to the category of 'general international law.'

Other scholars, standing at the other end of the spectrum, therefore, refuse to see this formula as the introduction of a new source. They think that the peremptory norm also can only come out from (general) treaty and (general) custom, not from other sources including natural law. However, they still have not

[18] PCIJ (1927), Series A, No. 10, p. 18.

reached an agreement on one point. Some argue that the peremptory norm still allows persistent objectors to slip out of the binding force of the peremptory norm because it is derived from the treaty or custom. In contrast, others insist that the peremptory norm, whether coming from treaty or custom, binds all states of the international community including a handful of possible dissenters: this argument, in fact, leads to introducing rule-making by majority into the international community. The controversy goes on, but it seems to be wise to remember Professor Sinclair's admonition: "*Jus cogens* is neither Dr. Jekyll nor Mr. Hyde; but it has the potentialities of both".[19] And, whichever opinion of the two turns out to be more convincing, the peremptory norm of general international law is not eternal, either: by definition, while the derogation therefrom is not permitted, it can be modified by, and only by, a subsequent norm of general international law having the same character.

It is generally agreed that the formula and idea of 'peremptory norm of general international law', initially intended by the 1969 Vienna Convention to be one of the grounds of invalidity of treaties, has been transferred into the realm of customary international law, extending its applicability to other areas beyond the law of treaties. Article 53 of the 1969 Vienna Convention does not enumerate the rules falling under the roof of the peremptory norm of general international law: it is left to the development of the international community and at the moment the prohibition of threat or use of force, the respect for the basic human rights, and especially the rule against genocide seem to be the most persuasive examples of *jus cogens*.

Meanwhile, in the judgment of 1970 concerning *Barcelona Traction Co.* Case[20], the ICJ confirmed the presence of duties/obligations *erga omnes* in the international community:

"When a State admits into its territory foreign investments or foreign nationals, whether natural or juristic persons, it is bound to extend to them the protection of the law and assumes obligations concerning the treatment to be afforded them. These obligations, however, are neither absolute nor unqualified. In particular, an essential distinction should be drawn between the obligations of a State towards the international community as a whole, and those arising vis-à-vis another State in the field of diplomatic protection. By their very nature the former are the concern of all States. In view of the importance of the rights involved, all States can be held to have a legal interest in their protection; they

[19] Sinclair, op. cit., p. 223.

[20] Belgium v. Spain, ICJ Reports (1970), p. 3 at 32 (paras. 33-34).

are obligations erga omnes. Such obligations derive, for example, in contemporary international law, from the outlawing of acts of aggression, and of genocide, as also from the principles and rules concerning basic rights of the human person including protection from slavery and racial discrimination. Some of the corresponding rights of protection have entered into the body of general international law (Reservations to the Convention on the Prevention and Punishment of the Crime of Genocide, Advisory Opinion, I.C.J. Reports 1951, p. 23) ; others are conferred by international instruments of a universal or quasi-universal character."

The Court mentioned the outlawing of aggression and genocide and the protection from slavery and racial discrimination as examples of duties *erga omnes*, and later added to the list the self-determination in *East Timor* case[21] and many rules of international humanitarian law in *Legal Consequences of the Construction of a Wall in the Occupied Palestinian Territory* case.[22] When a state breaches an international obligation, in normal situations, only the directly affected state is entitled to seek remedy from and against the wrong-doing state, whereas, if the breach arises out of the duties *erga omnes*, any other state including the affected state can invoke the responsibility of the wrongdoing state and ask for remedy.[23] Although duties *erga omnes*, an emerging concept in modern international law, cover very limited cases, they are in a sense revolutionary as in the case of *jus cogens;* the traditional international law scarcely knew of them because it thought that all the ultimate relations between states ended in bilateral ones irrespective of whether they rest on bilateral treaties, multilateral treaties or customary international law.[24] In short, duties *erga omnes* are kind of community-oriented ones. To be more precise, duties *erga omnes* are sometimes distin-

---

[21] Case concerning East Timor (Portugal v. Australia), ICJ Reports (1995), p. 90 at 102 (para. 29). See also Joost Pauwelyn, *Conflict of Norms in Public International Law: How WTO Law Relates to other Rules of International Law* (Cambridge: Cambridge University Press, 2003), 62.

[22] Advisory Opinion of 9 July 2004, para. 157 ; Christian J. Tams, Enforcing Obligations Erga Omnes in International Law (Cambridge: Cambridge University Press, 2005), 123.

[23] UN ILC, "Conclusions of the work of the Study Group on the Fragmentation of International Law: Difficulties arising from the Diversification and Expansion of International Law" (2006), para. (37), available at http://www.un.org/law/ilc.

[24] Tams, op. cit., p. 45, puts this as follows: "Although the legal rules apply between a plurality of States, the obligations arising under them are owed to one State in particular. In the case of a breach, that State therefore is specially affected and entitled to respond. A brief reference to obligations in the field of diplomatic or consular relations may illustrate the point. Despite their multilateral (customary or conventional) character, these obligations have to be performed between pairs of receiving and sending States. ...Since all of these rules are required to be performed between pairs of States, they are frequently referred to as 'bilateralisable' obligations, or 'bundles of bilateral relationships'." See also UN ILC Report 2001, 297-299.

guished by writers from duties *erga omnes partes* (or duties *erga omnes contractantes*) which indicate 'treaty'-based obligations in whose performance 'all contracting parties' are said to have a legal interest.[25]

As for the difference between *jus cogens* and duties *erga omnes*, Pauwelyn properly says: "in the notion of *jus cogens*, the focus is on the higher hierarchical status of certain norms; in the notion of *erga omnes* obligations, the focus is on who can invoke responsibility for breach."[26] And for the connection between the two concepts, the UN ILC said in its Report of 2006: "It is recognized that while all obligations established by *jus cogens* norms...also have the character of *erga omnes* obligations, the reverse is not necessarily true. Not all *erga omnes* obligations are established by peremptory norms of general international law. This is the case, for example, of certain obligations under the 'principles and rules concerning the basic rights of the human person', as well as of some obligations relating to the global commons."[27]

Applying to North Korea what has been discussed so far, it seems apparent that its government has been persistently breaching the rule of respect for human rights as well as some peremptory norms concerning human rights, automatically exposing itself to breach of duties *erga omnes*: North Korea is grossly and repeatedly persecuting its nationals and any state including South Korea is entitled, but not "duty-bound", to demand rectification from it, -to wit, "in view of the importance of the rights involved, all States can be held to have a legal interest in their protection".

Apparently international law looks plausible. Caveat. Just because "all States can be held to have a legal interest in their protection" does not mean any state can bring North Korea before one of the international rectification mechanisms including ICJ without its (express or implied) consent: these are two different matters. There exists no means which has been vested with compulsory jurisdiction by the general international law. No pacific means can exercise compulsory jurisdiction without referring to a particular treaty. This is where the international community presently stands today. For example, in the case of the ICJ, the Court said in *Armed Activities on the Territory of the Congo* case[28]:

---

25 Tams, op. cit., p. 120.

26 Pauwelyn, op. cit., p. 99.

27 UN ILC, "Conclusions of the work of the Study Group on the Fragmentation of International Law: Difficulties arising from the Diversification and Expansion of International Law," para. (38), available at http://www.un.org/law/ilc.

28 Democratic Republic of the Congo v. Rwanda, (Jurisdiction and Admissibility), Judgment of 2006, para. 64.

"The Court observes, however, as it has already had occasion to emphasize, that "the erga omnes character of a norm and the rule of consent to jurisdiction are two different things" (East Timor (Portugal v. Australia),Judgment, I.C.J. Reports 1995, p. 102, para. 29), and that the mere fact that rights and obligations erga omnes may be at issue in a dispute would not give the Court jurisdiction to entertain that dispute. The same applies to the relationship between peremptory norms of general international law (jus cogens) and the establishment of the Court's jurisdiction: the fact that a dispute relates to compliance with a norm having such a character, which is assuredly the case with regard to the prohibition of genocide, cannot of itself provide a basis for the jurisdiction of the Court to entertain that dispute, under the Court's Statute that jurisdiction is always based on the consent of the parties."

Alas. Then, what can we do? Is there no effective alternative but to merely watch people dying of hunger, suffering from assault, battery and torture, being executed publicly or being confined in political prisoner camps? How about taking unilateral actions outside courts to ease the pain of North Korean people, that is, will the so-called humanitarian (or physical) intervention be allowed under international law? Is such intervention discretionary or mandatory?

IV. Are Unilateral Actions Possible?: "Humanitarian Intervention" into "responsibility to protect"

While we roughly say, probably just out of a lucid explanation, that the concept of human rights was introduced into international law very lately, that is, with and since the World War II and that the concept of community-oriented duties or "duties *erga omnes*" became clear in the *Barcelona Traction Co.* case brought before the ICJ, the traditional international law as it stood before the two Great Wars did not turn its back on the on-going pain of humans altogether. First, it will be helpful to recall that Hugo Grotius (Huig De Groot)(1583-1645), a Dutch jurist known as "father of international law,"[29] had already suggested something similar to duties *erga omnes* as follows:

"The fact must also be recognized that kings, and those who possess rights equal to those kings, have the right of demanding punishments not only on account of injuries committed against themselves or their subjects, but also on ac-

---

[29] http://www.judicialmonitor.org/current/leadingfigures.html.

count of injuries which do not directly affect them but excessively violate the law of nature or of nations in regard to any persons whatsoever."[30]

Possibly influenced by this kind of humanism-oriented thinking, the concept of "humanitarian intervention"[31] was introduced into the traditional international law although not without a doubt about its validity even at that time. Humanitarian intervention, by its definition, suggests that the unilateral use of force should be admissible in the situation where the purpose is to save the lives and/or property of those who are, irrespective of nationality, helplessly in extreme pain and whose territorial state is not able and/or willing to alleviate their pain. According to Adams Roberts, humanitarian intervention in a classical sense means "coercive action by one or more states involving the use of armed force in another state without the consent of its authorities, and with the purpose of preventing widespread suffering or death among the inhabitants."[32]

---

[30] Hugo Grotius, De Jure Belli Ac Pacis-Libri Tres, Book II, p. 504. See also Georg Nolte, "From Dionisio Anzilotti to Roberto Ago: The Classical International Law of State Responsibility and the Traditional Primacy of a Bilateral Conception of Inter-state Relations," EJIL (2002), Vol. 13 No. 5, 1083 at 1084-1085. In this perspective, what Tams said, op. cit., at p. 96 is also noteworthy : "... assertions that (by necessity and without exceptions) States, prior to the Court's Barcelona Traction judgment, could only respond to violations of international law that had affected their individual positions, are not only simplistic, but incorrect. Even before that judgment, it was hard to ignore the trend towards the recognition of general legal interest in the observance of specific categories of obligations. Paraphrasing a famous dictum by Judge Weeramantry, it seems fair to say that even prior to 1970, something not dissimilar to the 'erga omnes concept...[had] been at the door of [the] Court for many years.'" The opinion of Judge Weeramantry mentioned here by Tams is what the Judge expressed through his dissenting opinion in Case concerning East Timor (Portugal v. Australia), ICJ Reports (1995), p. 216 : "The erga omnes concept has been at the door of this Court for many years. A disregard of erga omnes obligations makes a serious tear in the web of international obligations, and the current state of international law requires that violations of the concept be followed through to their logical and legal conclusion."

[31] On this subject, see generally W.D. Verwey, "Humanitarian Intervention under International Law." (1985) XXXII Netherlands International Law Review 357 at 374-375 ; Steven Wheatley, "The NATO Action against The Federal Republic of Yugoslavia: Humanitarian Intervention in the Post-Cold War Era." (1999) 50 Northern Ireland Legal Quarterly 478 at 479, fn. 4 ; U. Beyerlin, "Humanitarian Intervention." in: R. Bernhardt (ed.), Encyclopaedia of Public International Law, vol. 3 (Amsterdam: North-Holland Publishing, 1982), p. 211 ; F. Kofi Abiew, The Evolution of the Doctrine and Practice of Humanitarian Intervention (The Hague: Kluwer Law International, 1999), p. 18.

[32] Adams Roberts, "The So-called 'Right' of Humanitarian Intervention", (2000) 3 Yearbook of International Humanitarian Law 3 at 5. He added here that "Confusingly, in the 1990s the term has sometimes been used, especially by some relief agencies, with a much broader and less precise meaning: major humanitarian action in an emergency situation, not necessarily involving use of armed force, and not necessarily against the will of the government. Some writers have used it in both senses." In my opinion, this kind of confusion came out as a result of laymen not distinguishing between humanitarian intervention and humanitarian assistance. In Military and Paramilitary Activities in and against Nicaragua (Nicaragua v. United States) case, ICJ Reports (1986), paras. 242-243, ICJ said that the purpose of humanitarian assistance is "to prevent and alleviate human suffering" and "to protect life and health and to ensure respect for the human being" ; the Court also said that "an essential feature of truly humanitarian aid is that it is given "without discrimination" of any kind".

Under the traditional or classical rules of international law, the threat or use of force between states was not forbidden, which was interpreted to mean that the use of force or initiating a war was permissible. Therefore, under international law before the World War I, the humanitarian intervention as a unilateral action by an outsider state was generally thought by Western international lawyers to be a legal tool or an excuse for resorting to force "short of war." With the advent of the UN Charter which prohibited any kind of threat or use of force including war except in some cases including self-defence (Article 51 of the Charter), the admissibility, -under the Charter and/or customary international law,- of humanitarian intervention as an additional cause for resort to force became a burning issue, still leaving no definitely agreed answer.

Some NATO states relied on humanitarian intervention when they carried out aerial bombardment against Serbia to desist it from crack downing on Kosovo, one of its autonomies, which had made a move towards independence in March, 1999. Serbia and Montenegro filed suits before the ICJ against 10 NATO states respectively which joined this operation, but to no avail for lack of jurisdiction.[33] Rosenne is of the opinion that the NATO states' bombardment was *ex post facto* recognized by Resolution 1247 of the Security Council, dated June 18, 1999.[34]

But, under the UN Charter, humanitarian intervention seems to be inadmissible in light of Article 2(4) of the Charter which prohibits "threat or use of force against the territorial integrity...of any State; in *Military and Paramilitary Activities in and against Nicaragua*,[35] ICJ mentioned that "humanitarian intervention could not be the appropriate method to monitor or ensure such respect (i.e. respect for human rights)." Also, an additional issue remains: is humanitarian intervention still admissible under the guise of a customary rule, or -at least- is such a customary rule emerging in parallel with the UN Charter?[36]

Similarly, in the Resolution on Humanitarian Assistance adopted at Bruges Session of 2003, the Institut de Droit International defined humanitarian assistance as "all acts, activities and the human and material resources for the provision of goods and services of an exclusively humanitarian character, indispensable for the survival and the fulfilment of the essential needs of the victims of disasters."

[33] Cases concerning Legality of Use of Force (Preliminary Objections), Judgments of 15 December 2004 (Serbia and Montenegro v. Belgium ; Serbia and Montenegro v. Canada ; Serbia and Montenegro v. France ; Serbia and Montenegro v. Germany ; Serbia and Montenegro v. Italy ; Serbia and Montenegro v. Netherlands ; Serbia and Montenegro v. Portugal ; Serbia and Montenegro v. United Kingdom). Two other suits against United States and Spain which also joind this operation had been readily dismissed because the lack of jurisdiction was too obvious.

[34] Shabtai Rosenne, The Perplexities of Modern International Law (Leiden/Boston: Martinus Nijhoff Publishers, 2004), 142.

[35] Nicaragua v. United States, ICJ Reports (1986), 14 at 134 (para. 268)

[36] On this issue, see Antonio Cassese, "Ex iniuria ius oritur: Are We Moving towards International Legitimation of Forcible Humanitarian Countermeasures in the World Community?," (1999) 10 EJIL 23.

It will be yet another matter that states resort to force with the intention or purpose of humanitarian intervention under authorisation by the Security Council. When bloody strife took place between different clans within Somalia in 1992, the Security Council, acting unanimously, authorised Member States "to use all necessary means to establish as soon as possible a secure environment for humanitarian relief operations in Somalia" without consent of the local Government.[37]

The responsibility of the Security Council for this matter is now emphasized in the name of "responsibility to protect". This new concept, which was an outcome of the World Summit held in 2005 and subsequently adopted by the UN Assembly, attempts to change the right or admissibility of humanitarian intervention into its responsibility or duty. It states:

"Each individual State has the responsibility to protect its populations from genocide, war crimes, ethnic cleansing and crimes against humanity.... The international community, through the United Nations, also has the responsibility to use appropriate diplomatic, humanitarian and other peaceful means, in accordance with Chapters VI and VIII of the Charter, to help to protect populations from genocide, war crimes, ethnic cleansing and crimes against humanity. In this context, we are prepared to take collective action, in a timely and decisive manner, through the Security Council, in accordance with the Chapter, including Chapter VII, on a case-by-case basis and in cooperation with relevant regional organisations as appropriate, should peaceful means be inadequate and national authorities are manifestly failing to protect their populations from genocide, war crimes, ethnic cleansing and crimes against humanity...."[38]

In 1999 and 2000, then UN Secretary General Kofi Annan urged the international community to make out consensus on humanitarian intervention and raised the following issue straightforward : "...if humanitarian intervention is, indeed, an unacceptable assault on sovereignty, how should we respond to a Rwanda, to a Srebrenica - to gross and systematic violations of human rights that affect every precept of our common humanity?" Stimulated by his question, the Canadian Government instituted an "International Commission on Interven-

---

[37] UN Security Council Resolution 794 of December 3, 1992.

[38] UN A/Res/60/1 (16 September 2005), paras. 138 and 139. See http://www.un.org/Depts/dhl/resguide/r60.htm;http://www.un.org/summit2005; http://en.wikipedia.org/wiki/Responsibility_to_protect http://en.wikipedia.org/wiki/2005_World_Summit http://www.un.org/largerfreedom.

tion and State Sovereignty"[39] and asked it to present an answer for that. After a 12 month-long intensive research, the Commission adopted a report entitled "The Responsibility to Protect",[40] which served as the very basis of the conclusion, quoted above, the World Summit of 2005 reached on this matter.

In line with this understanding, the humanitarian intervention is no longer a right or discretion of states: it is a responsibility of the whole international community stood for by the Security Council as far as it concerns protection of populations from "genocide, war crimes, ethnic cleansing and crimes against humanity."

According to the logic of duties *erga omnes*, each state has duties towards the international community as a whole and each and every other state has corresponding "legal interest" to interfere. "Responsibility to protect" goes beyond this and imposes "responsibility" to act on the international community as a whole which will act through the Security Council of the United Nations when an individual state fails in the primary responsibility to protect its populations from genocide, war crimes, ethnic cleansing and crimes against humanity.

In response to this urgent demand, the Security Council adopted Resolution 1674 on April 28, 2006, at paragraph 4 of which it "reaffirms the provisions of paragraphs 138 and 139 of the 2005 World Summit Outcome Document regarding the responsibility to protect populations from genocide, war crimes, ethnic cleansing and crimes against humanity."

It is touching and timely that a US NGO, "U.S. Committee for Human Rights in North Korea", applies this logic of "responsibility to protect" to human rights crisis in North Korea and argues in a report of 2006 named "Failure to Protect: A Call for the UN Security Council to Act in North Korea" that "the North Korean government's violation of its responsibility to protect its own citizens from crimes against humanity creates a need for Security Council intervention. An equally compelling reason for intervention is that the situation in North Korea constitutes a non-traditional threat to the peace."[41] In this report, the Committee's final recommendations read as follows: "Initially, the UN Security Council should adopt a non-punitive resolution on the situation in North Korea in accor-

---

[39] The commission consisted of 12 persons including two joint presidents, Gareth Evans of Canada and Mohamed Sahnoun of Algeria.

[40] The Responsibility to Protect: Report of the International Commission on Intervention and State Sovereignty, Published by the International Development Research Centre (PO Box 8500, Ottawa, ON, Canada K1G 3H9), (http://www.idrc.ca ; http://www.iciss.ca/menu-en.asp.

[41] U.S. Committee for Human Rights in North Korea, *Failure to Protect: A Call for the UN Security Council to Act in North Korea,* October 30, 2006, 94, (http://www.hrnk.org/). See also (U.S.) CRS (Congressional Research Service) *Report for Congress, North Korean Refugees in China and Human Rights Issues: International Response and U.S. Policy Options*, September 26, 2007, 28-29.

dance with its authority under Chapter VI of the UN Charter and past Security Council precedents. ...Should North Korea fail to comply with a Chapter VI resolution, the Security Council should consider adopting a binding resolution under Chapter VII."

V. Epilogue: Towards the new doctrine, "responsibility to protect"

Frankly speaking, before writing this paper I wondered where to begin to tell the devastating story of human rights situation in North Korea.

We hear tragic and heartbreaking news about North Korea almost every day among other ordinary news: public executions are frequently conducted, people deserting North Korea out of hunger and/or political persecution are taking a risk to get shot, large-scale imprisonment camps similar to Gulag are being operated, and approximately three million people are estimated to have starved to death for some years in the 1990s.

An indisputable fact that North Korea is grossly and persistently violating duties validly imposed by the international law of human rights means that the international community has "legal interest" and, what's more, "responsibility" to protest or interfere against the tyrannical acts of the North Korean government. The new doctrine of international law, "responsibility to protect", suggests some points: first, to protect own nationals is more of a responsibility of each state than its right or competence; second, if the national state fails in its primary responsibility, the international community is duty-bound to respond to it ; and, last, the Security Council of the United Nations is in a position to act on behalf of the international community. If we agree that the promotion and protection of human rights is the supreme value that we must uphold, the "responsibility to protect" should remain at the heart of safeguarding the utmost value of the international community.

Before concluding this paper, I must add one thing. No doubt, the ultimate origin of this kind of man-made human rights disaster happening in North Korea lies in the very idiosyncrasy of its totalitarian regime: the unelected leader, standing above the law, dictates every corner of North Korea pursuant to its own Constitutional rule of "one for all, all for one," or more accurately, according to his whim. North Korea, by contrast, is a member of the United Nations, whose admittance is allowed only to "peace-loving" countries; its members are obliged to cooperate to respect and promote human rights. Such a contradictory situation surrounding North Korea both internally and externally is being made by its very own regime. Personally, I do not expect at all Kim Jung-Il regime to fulfil its primary responsibility of protecting its populations from genocide, war crimes, ethnic cleansing and crimes against humanity. If we simply express concerns over human rights disasters in Korea without praying for the eventual collapse of a brute of a Kim Jung-Il regime, it would be hypocritical.

PART II

Economic, Political and Ideological Relations between East/West Germany and North Korea, and their legacies

5

Reunification in a Constitutional State

Kolja Naumann

Introduction

Issues surrounding Korean reunification are mostly discussed through political, economic, military or sociological perspectives. Yet, if reunification takes place in a constitutional state, the constitution will have to be respected, providing a legal framework for the political decisions to be taken. The exact contents of this framework however are very vague and they are seldom at the centre of constitutionalists' debates. Given the very special circumstances of reunification and the fact that reunification is one the Korean constitution's main goals, it seems conceivable that the interpretation of the constitution can allow a certain flexibility to adapt to the special challenges of reunification.

To ascertain the constitutional parameters more precisely, it seems promising to compare Korean reunification to the German reunification process as the only reunification so far, which was set in the clear context of a constitutional state. Of course, it is today all but certain in which political circumstances Korean reunification will take place, and many scholars contend that these circumstances will greatly differ from German reunification. However as long as reunification to one constitutional and democratic state is the goal of the reunification process, it seems very possible that the legal premises of reunification show great similarity in Korea and Germany despite economic and sociological conditions being very far apart.

This paper will thus analyze constitutional problems of reunification on a comparative basis. A first part will outline constitutional problems of German reunification. In a second part this paper will try to develop a coherent approach for the constitutional parameters of Korean Reunification on the basis of the existing South Korean Constitution. Likely problems in constitutional law will be outlined and aspects of possible solutions presented.

1. The role of Constitution in Reunification in Germany

The German reunification process shall be outlined in the following chapter from a constitutional point of view. However, the object and scope of this study allows some restrictions. In most cases, details of legal questions in German law can be ignored, since the circumstances in Korean reunification would be different and the Constitutional texts and its interpretations will differ, too. Therefore this study will restrict itself to the main legal issues in reunification, the diverging interests on these issues and finally the decisions of Executive, Legislature and Constitutional Court. For further case studies on this topic, refer to the two volumes and over 2000 pages concerning legal questions in German Reunification in the "Handbuch des Staatsrechts" tomes VIII and IX and the numerous studies referenced within.[1]

1.1 The German reunification process and legal cases

When German Reunification occurred, it took most political leaders by surprise. As late as in summer of 1989 (four months before the Berlin wall fell) many political leaders in the West were convinced that the division of Germany would continue as it had for the preceding four decades. Consequently when the civil rights movement in the East gained momentum and the Soviet Union refused to support the Eastern government making a military abatement of the movement impossible, virtually no politician in the West was prepared for the changes that were to rapidly follow. A democratic East German government was elected for the first time in the March of 1990 making it apparent that fast and full-fledged Reunification was about to happen. In the negotiations about reunification the Kohl-government had to face and resolve a very complex set of situations in very short time. This enormous pressure led to many decisions which caused considerable problems later on. In addition Germany, as would be the case in Korea, was hampered by the concerns of other regional powers, notably the US, Russia, the UK and France, with the UK and France demonstrating considerable reluctance.

1.1.1 Why no "new" Constitution?

The first main legal question to be answered was whether a new constitution should be drafted or if the West German "Grundgesetz" should become the Con-

---

[1] See Josef Isensee/ Paul Kirchhof (editors): Handbuch des Staatsrechts, Band VIII: Die Einheit Deutschlands – Entwicklung und Grundlagen – and Band IX: Die Einheit Deutschlands – Festigung und Übergang. For a concise summary see Kempen, Wiedervereinigung, Evangelisches Staatslexikon, p. 2712 ff.

stitution for the reunified German State. The Grundgesetz itself provided for both solutions as in article 23 it included the possibility of accession of Eastern Germany to the Federal Republic and in article 146 GG it stipulated that after Reunification a new Constitution might be composed. Even though the question was fiercely debated in the West, where many were fervent supporters of a new Constitution, it was the Eastern position, which had the power to decide upon the question. If the East had demanded the negotiation of a new Constitution, the Federal Republic could not have insisted on the endurance of the Grundgesetz. However as the GDR pushed for its accession to the Grundgesetz, the FRG was unable to refuse, since article 23 GG included the binding constitutional offer to accede to the East; an offer the East just had to approve.[2] During peaceful revolution in the East, most voices had insisted on negotiations about a new Constitution or proposed further existence of the GDR to give socialism another try, but the leading opinion changed drastically after the first free elections in the East on March 16th 1990. In these "Volkskammerwahlen" the parties in favor to accede to the Federal Republic won a clear cut majority of the seats and the new government proposed that the procedure of accession provided for in article 23 GG would be applied.[3] Two reasons were particularly important for this decision. First, the Grundgesetz had strong support both in the West and the East. The population in the West knew the Grundgesetz and was close to it[4] and the population in the East saw the Grundgesetz as the basis for Western Germany's political and economic success after World War II. Thus on both sides, the Grundgesetz was seen as a well-functioning, appropriate constitutional basis for the reunified Germany. Second, and perhaps more important, in the rapidly developing international environment of 1990 most German politicians were aware that reunification could well be a matter of time and that any hesitation or time costly constitutional negotiations could destroy the hopes for reunification once and for all. To prevent such an outcome the majority of political forces in the East preferred to take the presumably faster and safer way of accession to the Federal Republic.

1.1.2 Inter-German Treaties and Constitutional Amendments

Accession of the East to the West was agreed on and theoretically this could have been it. The Eastern Länder could have become part of the Federal Repub-

[2] See for example Isensee, in: Guggenberger/Stein, Die Verfassungsdiskussion im Jahr der deutschen Einheit, 1991, p.214 (216 f.); Kempen, Wiedervereinigung, Evangelisches Staatslexikon, p. 2712.

[3] See Lerche, in: Isensee/Kirchhof, Handbuch des Staatsrechts VIII, § 194, para 13.

[4] The so called "Verfassungspatriotismus" of Habermas was the first reappearance of patriotism among left intellectuals in Germany after World War 2.

lic; the Western laws could have just been applied in the East. However, from the very beginning there were no doubts that the legal transition in the East from a socialist society to a democratic, capitalistic and pluralistic one would be very complicated and that many difficult questions had to be adjudicated upon before reunification could be realized. For these reasons, it was clear that extensive negotiations would take place and treaties between East and West Germany – the former actually preparing its own disappearance – had to be concluded.

In the first of such treaties – the so called "Staatsvertrag", which was signed on May 18th 1990 and came into force on July 1st – the question of economic transition was adressed. Market economy was introduced in the GDR, a unitary monetary system agreed on, custom inspections abolished, labour law and social security in the East were thoroughly reformed.

The second important treaty agreement, actually regarded as core piece of reunification, is the "Einigungsvertrag". This agreement prepared East Germany to become part of the Federal Republic by stipulating were the new German boarders in the East should be. To prevent large scale discussions about necessary constitutional amendments, it was agreed that only Unification related amendments to the Grundgesetz should be included in the "Einigungsvertrag".[5] This meant the abrogation of norms in the Constitution dealing with issues of reunification (preamble, article 23 GG) and the adjustment of the number of votes of the Länder in the "second chamber" in parliament the "Bundesrat".

Furthermore article 135a § 2 GG was introduced, which stipulated that the federal republic under certain circumstances did not have to assume all obligations of the GDR existent at the time of reunification. The article's intention was obviously to give the FDR a certain margin of appreciation in fulfilling such obligations and to avoid unbearable costs.[6] Moreover the new article 143 GG provided that Eastern laws, which were applied for some time after reunification, did not have to conform to the Constitution in all respects. Until December 31st 1992 they could derogate from almost all provisions of the fundamental law, until the same day in 1995 they were exempted from the constitutional rules of the federal state, for the execution of federal laws and some other constitutional provisions. Lastly, article 143 § 3, was introduced, which ruled out the possibility of claims for restitution of expropriated property in the east, while promising compensation to the expropriated. To calm the demands of those who advocated a new Constitution at the place of the Grundgesetz, article 146 GG, which pro-

---

[5] As we will see below, this procedure created serious problems with regard to the rights of the parliament to decide upon constitutional amendments.

[6] See Koch, in: Sachs, GG, Art. 135a, para. 5.

vided such a possibility for the case of reunification was not abrogated but only modified, in a way that allows the elaboration of a new Constitution without requiring any special situation. Article 5 of the Einigungsvertrag recommended discussion about amendments to the Grundgesetz take place in the future.

Beside these constitutional amendments, the Einigungsvertrag confronted the question of approximation of laws. It was stipulated that generally speaking all West German laws should be applied in the East from the moment of Reunification with the exception of specially mentioned West and East German norms. This solution included the advantage of high simplicity, however it quickly became apparent that nobody in the negotiating bodies had had any notion of how complicated the approximation of laws still would be and how many problems would later have to be resolved. Yet, today most scholars believe that this was the only feasible approach to reach unity of laws.[7] Any eastern norm, which should further be applied after reunification, had to conform to the Grundgesetz in the latest after 1995, if it was not, it would be declared void.[8] Contrary to the principle of non-continuation of laws, administrative acts and court judgments were largely to be upheld and only if they were in contradiction to principles of a constitutional state could be declared void upon request of the concerned citizens.

Beyond the streamlining of general law, the organisation of administration in the East had to be thoroughly reformed. Even before reunification was carried out, major restructuring took effect. In the aftermath of reunification the highly centralized administration in the East was abolished and the self-administration of local entities introduced.[9]

Moreover article 12 of the Einigungsvertrag provided further guidelines for the future of East Germany's international treaties. Because of the controversies surrounding this question, the article only provided that except for membership in international organisations, which should be terminated automatically, consultations were to be held with the treaty partners and a set of formal criteria enlisted, so as to determine whether a treaty ended or not. In practice this meant that concurrent to the principle of discontinuity of treaties after the disappearance of the state most international treaties of the GDR were cancelled, however the trustworthy expectations of the other parties to these treaties were duly respected.

---

[7] See Haverkate, in: Isensee/ Kirchhof, HbStR IX, § 209, Rn. 9.

[8] See Isensee, in: Isensee/Kirchhof, HbStR IX, § 202, Rn. 116, who ascertains that this is only true for the conformity with material rules of the constitution.

[9] See to the very complex problems Loschelder, in: Isensee/Kirchhof, HbStR IX, § 217, Rn. 44.

Finally, the two Germanys agreed on the "Wahlvertrag", in which the procedure of the first common elections was codified. There were some disputes at first over whether one common election based on equal rules in East and West should be held or if two separate elections following different rules should lead to the constitution of one new Parliament. However, when it became clear that Reunification would take place prior to the elections, all parties unanimously agreed that one common system should be applied.

These were the legal premises under which Reunification took place on October 3rd 1990.

1.1.3 Major Legal Disputes and Decisions of the BVerfG

These legal solutions now have to be scrutinized within the context of the constitutional problems and issues of legal policy they raise. For the purpose of this study a particular approach will be applied. Only such problems will be examined, which might arise during Korean reunification or which give interesting hints for comparable problems. Furthermore, this study does not necessitate a thorough discussion about the exact constitutional parameters of these problems in German Law. It will suffice to outline the diverging interests, the politically agreed solutions and the jurisprudence of the Federal Constitutional Court. The latter's judgments will be given special attention, since in these judgments the special nature of legal problems in the context of reunification are particularly apparent.

1.1.3.1 Constitutional amendments in international treaties

Highly problematic in German constitutional law, was the fact that Constitutional amendments were agreed upon in the Einigungsvertrag, which was considered as an international treaty. Yet, according to a widespread opinion in German constitutional doctrine such a modus operandi is unconstitutional.[10] Of course the conclusion of the Einigungsvertrag did not in itself effectuate these amendments of the Grundgesetz. Bundestag and Bundesrat still had to vote about the proposed amendments. Yet, since the amendments were included in the Einigungsvertrag as international treaty, the parliament could only approve or disapprove the treaty, but no amendments to the proposed constitutional amendments were possible. Furthermore, long time before the necessary votes in both chambers took place, it was clear that neither chamber could vote against the Einigungsvertrag without seriously endangering German Reunification and

[10] See Meyer, in: Badura/Dreier, FS-50 Jahre BVerfG, p. 83 (86).

thus could not even make adjustments about the wording of the Constitutional Amendments.

Some legal scholars contended that this procedure was a serious threat to the usually preponderant role of parliament in the German process of constitutional revisions. For this reason eight conservative members of parliament went to the federal constitutional Court in Karlsruhe to secure their rights. The Court however declared these demands as "evidently unfounded".[11] It argued that in the case of the "historic chance to achieve the unification of Germany", the government was competent to agree upon constitutional revisions in an international treaty, as long as these revisions were absolutely necessary to reach a consensus about reunification with the GDR and with the International Powers involved.[12] The main concern behind this ruling was apparent: the Court did not want to trouble the schedule of reunification and thus let pass, what never would have passed in other circumstances. Still the Court saw that the situation bore considerable difficulties and insisted that only amendments necessary for reunification, or otherwise demanded by the other negotiating parties could lead to constitutional revisions. These conditions however make it doubtful whether the agreement about a new voting system in the Bundesrat in article 51, which strengthened the role of the big Länder, was conforming to the constitution.[13]

When the judgment about the Einigungsvertrag first came up, it posed what would become a constant argument in the Courts jurisprudence: the "historic chance to achieve the unification of Germany" requiring and justifying special measures.[14] This jurisprudence would become a corner stone of all constitutional jurisprudence in unification-related cases and would be used to consider measures as conforming to the constitution, which in regular circumstances presumably would have been declared void by the Constitutional Court.[15]

1.1.3.2 Common elections

A second big issue to be adjudicated upon by the Constitutional Court during the reunification process was the procedure and electoral law of the first all

---

[11] "Offensichtliche Unbegründet". The German constitutional doctrine today is unanimous that the evidence was not given, but that the Constitutional Court overruled as evidently unfounded, because this was the fastest possible to reject the lawsuit and in this way it could be avoided to slow down and possibly endanger the reunification process.

[12] BVerfGE 84, p. 90 (118).

[13] Meyer, in: Badura/Dreier, FS-50 Jahre BVerfG, p. 83 (86) asserts that this was unconstitutional.

[14] See the analysis of this jurisprudence by Klein, in: Eckart/ Hacker/ Mampel, Wiedervereinigung Deutschlands, p. 417 (426).

[15] See BVerfG 85, 360 (377), 92, 277 (327), 82, 316 (321), 84, 90 (119), 94, 12 (34 f.), NJW 1997, S. 383 ff., NJW 1997, S. 1977.

German elections for a common Parliament. The traditional German election system is strongly proportional, even though it includes some majority voting elements. To ensure the possibility of establishing stable majorities the election law prescribes that only parties receiving 5% of the nationwide votes will be granted seats in the parliament.[16] In the political situation of 1990 it was clear that the successor of the communist party in the East, the PDS, would certainly not be able to reach 5% nationwide, since it would receive almost no votes in the West and thus would need 23,75% of Eastern votes to reach 5% and enter parliament[17], what again seemed impossible. Thus to apply the 5%-clause nationwide meant to keep the Socialist party out of parliament, the main reason behind why all the major Western parties insisted on the upholding of this clause.[18] However if the Constitutional Court had been very generous in its judgment on the Constitutional amendments, it became relentless in the case of the 5%-clause. It had been the Court's constant jurisprudence that the principle of equality of vote could not be examined in a purely formal way but that the concrete political situation in the moment of elections had to be taken into account by the legislature. However, this condition had obviously and intentionally been ignored by the legislative, since it was widely known that the East German parties and especially the Communist party had not been able to build a large base of supporters in the West during the few months between Reunification and the common elections. Thus contrarily to the Western parties they had almost no chances to enter parliament, if no Western German Party was willing to form a coalition with them. The Constitutional Court held this rule to be discriminatory in the context of Reunification and thus censored it.[19] Given the high importance of the principle of equality of votes, the Court ruled that it had to suffice in the 1990 elections to reach 5% of the votes in the East.

The contrast between the two first judgments of the Constitutional Court with regard to reunification is striking. Concerning the question of how to reach reunification the Court renounced almost completely to review the measures judged appropriate by the government. Yet, on the issue which held great influence on party politics and which had no potential to effectively hinder reunifica-

---

[16] For this reasons in the German Bundestag, there had been a maximum of four represented parties: CDU/CSU, SPD, FDP and since 1983 the Greens.

[17] This result is caused by the much larger Western population of above 64 million people compared to 16 million in the East in the moment of reunification.

[18] See for example the statement of the speaker of the social-democrats in the Bundestag Vogel in BT StenProt. 11/217 S. 17168 C/D.

[19] BVerfGE 82, p. 322 (340 ff.).

tion, the Court was a strict controller and overruled the attempt by the old West German parties to hinder the emergence of any new party.[20]

1.1.3.3 Rehabilitation

A further problem of German reunification, which shall be presented in this study, is the necessity of rehabilitation for the victims of the socialist regime. This included victims of the socialist state, who were imprisoned for political reasons, who were tortured by the Stasi, whose children were taken away as a result of their non-socialist political convictions. In all these cases restitution was naturally impossible and rehabilitation in money often could not give back what had been lost. Most constitutionalists did not see an obligation of the state to grant compensation in the fundamental rights, as the organs of the Federal Republic had not violated fundamental rights. On obligation to compensate only existed based on the principles of the social and democratic constitutional state.[21] Two major aspects of rehabilitation had to be carried out. First, the legislation for the recompense of socialist injustices tried to compensate for disadvantages in professional careers, suffered by GDR citizens because of their democratic beliefs, for example in cases of bans from profession, dismissals and other such disadvantages. However, compensation was only granted if this discrimination still continued to put a heavy burden on the victim of such acts. The second aspect was penal rehabilitation. Victims of political persecution in the GDR were granted compensation in form of nullification of judgments and financial compensation for unjustified imprisonment. Needless to say, such compensation was usually considered too low and unequal to what had been lost.[22]

As a result, one can assert that the Federal Republic was constitutionally obliged to grant compensation to victims of the socialist dictatorship. Yet in view of the very large number of victims and the difficult financial situation in the aftermath of reunification, there was a large constitutional margin of appreciation of how much money should be given to the victims. If it was almost impossible to deduct absolute numbers from the Constitution, the Grundgesetz obliged the legislator to grant compensation according to the principle of equality between the different groups of victims.

These principles also applied for the demands for restitution of owners of property expropriated by the Soviet Union and later the GDR. Some of these

---

[20] This has had considerable effects on German politics because the post-communist party has been represented in the Bundestag since 1990 with exception of the 2002-2005 period.

[21] See BVerfGE 84, 90 (126) and Dreier, in: Badura/Dreier, 50 Jahre-BVerfG, p. 159 (186).

[22] Dreier, in: Badura/Dreier, 50 Jahre-BVerfG, p. 159 (186) quotes an example of 12,000 DM (at the time about 6,000 US $) for 2 years of prison.

owners were granted restitution but most of them only received financial compensation, which in many cases was far below the market price.

1.1.3.4 Penal prosecution

Another tangled challenge of reunification litigation was the question of penal prosecution of acts by GDR-officials, which were considered crimes in the West, while legal in the East. The most famous example is of the so called "Mauerschützen"[23] but also judges and spies from the GDR were the targets of penal prosecution for acts committed in the name of socialism. In this regard, it was always unambiguous that prosecution was possible, if the deed was punishable under Socialist law in the socialist interpretation. However, if the letter of the law in the East seemed to allow punishment, but in socialist practice the deed was considered to be legal, most jurists and the German Courts agreed that no punishment was principally possible. However, the Courts accepted one exception: If the legal situation in the East was in sharp contrast to international obligations of the GDR or to "überpositive Rechtsnormen", which must be accepted by any law, Federal Germany's justice could condemn the involved criminals.[24] This solution was above all applied in the cases of shootings of refugees at the inner German border, as well to the political decision-makers. The solution drew very severe critiques since it seemed to be in clear contrast to the absolute non-retroactivity of penal laws prescribed for in article 103 § 2 GG[25], but the finding was finally accepted by the Constitutional Court.[26] The Constitutional Court considered that the principle of non-retroactivity was only absolute with regard to laws adopted by a democratic legislator and thus not to the law in ex-GDR.

In contrast, the Constitutional Court put strict limits to the penal prosecution of spies of the former GDR.[27] It stated that their punishment violated the principle of a state of law if these spies had acted in compliance with the socialist law without any risk of being punished, which included all spies acting only from Eastern territory, since the GDR – naturally – did not threaten to punish its own agents.[28] However, if the spies were acting on western soil, they could be pun-

[23] Wall shootings.

[24] The penal Courts took according decisions in BGHStE 39, p. 1; 40, p. 218; 41, p. 101.

[25] See for example Dreier, in: Badura/Dreier, 50 Jahre-BVerfG, p. 159 (205 ff.); Isensee, in: Isensee/Kirchhof, HbStR IX, § 202, p. 99 ff.

[26] See Dreier, in: Badura/Dreier, 50 Jahre-BVerfG, p. 159 (205 ff.).

[27] See BVerfGE 95, 86.

[28] See BVerfGE 92, p. 277 (351 f.), and Klein, in: Eckart/ Hacker/ Mampel, Wiedervereinigung Deutschlands, S. 417 (427).

ished after Reunification as had been the case before 1990.[29] The solution of the Constitutional Court came close to a general amnesty, and was thus criticized by the dissenting opinion and some scholars as usurpation of the powers of the legislature.[30]

The system of penal prosecution thus had to content with two strongly diverging interests: The trust of the citizens of the East in the system they were living in, and the demand for punishment of crimes against humanity. The solutions found in Germany were constantly swinging between these two extremes without being completely convincing. The call for a politically decided amnesty however was barely audible.[31]

1.1.3.5 Employees of the GDR

In the aftermath of reunification the public service system in the East was oversized and could not be assimilated as a whole by the Federal Republic after Reunification and many GDR employees had been fervent supporters of the socialist regime.[32] It was thus hardly conceivable to entrust them with the creation of a new administration. Therefore, legislation provided that employees seemingly unable to serve a democracy and employees who were not needed for administration could be dismissed. The BVerfG accepted these measures but insisted in its decision, that the sole fact to have been loyal to the socialist regime was not sufficient for the dismissal of employees and that even if dismissal was admissible in principle, it had to respect the social rights of the employees and especially the rights of mothers.[33]

1.2 Conclusion

The large number of decisions reached by the constitutional court proves that the process of Reunification was a legally challenging enterprise.[34] Throughout the BVerfG constantly found itself in a very difficult situation. It could neither take decisions which endangered reunification nor such which caused unbearable costs for the federal republic. Consequently many legal questions had to be

---

[29] Articles 94 and 99 of the West German Penalcode (StGB) penalized espionage of the GDR against the FRG even from the territory of the GDR.

[30] BVerfGE 92, p. 277 (351 f.).

[31] Such a demand did not come up in negotiations about reunification either, what was certainly due to the fact that the negotiating persons of the East were not the leading cadres of the Eastern state before the peaceful revolution took place.

[32] See for a comprehensive overview about public employees in the GDR, Trute, in: Isensee/Kirchhof, HbStR IX, § 215.

[33] BVerfGE 92, 140 (154)

[34] Until today there have been close to 100 judgments by the Constitutional Court regarding unification-related matters.

decided under enormous pressure what meant that the interpretation of legal norms could change considerably. Yet, the Constitutional Court and in many cases the legislature did their best to respect fundamental rights as much as possible. As to all others professions, the process of reunification caused specific difficulties for the constitutionalist that enforced solutions which might have been considered unconstitutional in any other context.

One further observation might prove instructive. Almost all of the Constitutional Court's decisions are related to special and distinctive problems in the transition process. That is to say that the Constitution did not prescribe the general political decisions during this transition process, like the question of whether or not to pass by a stage of confederation or what demands of the Soviet Union and the GDR had to be fulfilled. To answer such questions government and parliament were given a broad, potentially unlimited margin of appreciation. By contrast the Constitutional norms played an important role when the fundamental decisions had been taken and it came to precise decisions, directly affecting individual and collective rights. With regard to these questions, the constitutional review of such measures was still less strict than in "regular" times, but the Constitution did not lose its normative power. To avoid the potentially costly censoring of laws by the Constitutional Court, it is thus desirable for decision makers to be prepared for the moment of reunification and to carefully consider if restrictions on citizens' human rights are proportionate.

2. Constitutional law in Korean reunification

The following chapter will analyze constitutional problems in a prospective process of Korean reunification. Keeping in mind the legal solutions in Germany in 1990, possible advantages and disadvantages will be analyzed without however giving clear-cut solutions to the arising problems. Such solutions can only be found in the concrete economic and socio-political situation of reunification and by Korean scholars. This research project only tries to make the modest contribution, German constitutional doctrine can make to this important process. The following chapter will first consider general constitutional question, then examine some particular constitutional problems and finally propose necessary constitutional amendments.

2.1 Are there any constitutional limits in case of reunification?

Yet, the analysis of the constitutional limits of reunification would be vain, if one attacked and refuted the basic assumption of this work, which is that legal boundaries exist in the process of Korean reunification.

In German constitutional doctrine, some scholars have supported since a long time that in cases where the very survival of the state is at stake, the constitution cannot restrain the political power from acting as necessary.[35] This position finds its justification in the idea that the state has created the constitution, so the constitution cannot set limits which would make the state disappear, since there would be no constitution without a state.

This "Etatism", however collides with the very idea of a constitutional state, in which all legitimate and official power has to be executed in a way conforming to the Constitution. It is true that the Constitution's intention is to assure the survival of the state. Yet, it is already designed to provide all means necessary and legitimate for that. If in extreme situations unusual measures are necessary, article 76 ROKC provides rules for the state of emergency, which allow far going restrictions on human rights and an exceptionally fast decision-making by the President. To contend that in special situation the executive is given even further going powers, without anyone to control it, could endanger democracy much more than the scenarios usually put forward to justify the temporary Non-application of the Constitution.

Yet, if one believed in this "raison d'Etat"-approach, one could try to transfer it to the situation of reunification. It could be argued that when the constitution's final goal of reunification of the entire state is at stake, the question how to achieve this goal could not be prescribed by the constitution. For it is only reunification, which will allow the creation of the state the constitution actually wants to achieve and the process of reunification cannot be limited by the Constitution of the interim state. Furthermore one could argue that in this situation the executive power has to be given a large margin of manoeuvre instead of the unfitting restrictions of everyday constitutional law, so that the perhaps nonrecurring chance of reunification can be seized.

All this might seem convincing and still it is not. The question of whether or not the executive has to be given a large margin of appreciation in the context of reunification can be answered within the framework of the existing constitution.[36] The question rather is, if the normative power of the Constitution ends when the chance for reunification comes up. Such an approach could only be justified, if the Constitution regards the objective of reunification as more important than any other of its principles. The constitution includes the answer to

---

[35] This position has had its most influential supporter in Carl Schmitt whose "étatism" can still be found in Germany's constitutional doctrine, see for example Depenheuer, Selbstbehauptung des Rechtsstaats .For critiques of Schmitt see Kennedy, Constitutional Failure. Carl Schmitt in Weimar, Durham 2004, S. 70 ff.

[36] See below 2.2.4.

this question, when it prescribes that the Republic of Korea carries out a policy of peaceful unification based on the principles of freedom and democracy. This statement in the Constitution cannot be interpreted as a mere wish by the "pouvoir constituant". It certainly constitutes a legally binding norm stipulating the principles, which have to be respected in a Reunification process as long as the South Korean Constitution has not been abrogated. This means that the South Korean Constitution, even though it gives a clear mandate for reunification, does not want any kind of reunification, but only one which brings democracy and freedom to the entire Korean nation. As a consequence, there can be no doubt that the South Korean constitution premises its validity in the case of reunification and thus has to be respected in a reunification process.

2.2 The constitutional framework for reunification – General Considerations

As the German Grundgesetz did, the South Korean Constitution mentions reunification in some of its articles. Both fundamental laws had to cope with a similar situation. In law, the Federal Republic of Germany after 1949 and the Republic of Korea after 1948 see themselves as the only legitimate successor of the one state prior to division. The Korean Constitution allows no doubt about that, when it reads in article 3: "The territory of the Republic of Korea shall consist of the Korean peninsula and its adjacent islands." However this legal statement stands in contrast to the "de facto" existence of two states – until 1990 in Germany and to this day on the Korean Peninsula. And of course the Korean Constitution – as was the "Grundgesetz" – is aware of this fact when it stipulates in article 4: "The Republic of Korea seeks unification and formulates and carries out a policy of peaceful unification based on the principles of freedom and democracy." The apparent contradiction between these two norms has been much discussed in Korean Constitutional doctrine.[37] These articles show clearly that the relation to North Korea is as a matter of fact none of internal relations, but that from a South Korean constitutional point of view North Korea cannot be regarded as independent state.

Yet, the Constitution is unambiguous about the fact that the South Korean government is to pursue reunification actively and that in the case of reunification the existing South Korean Constitution should be the Constitution of a reunified Korea. Furthermore, as it has been contended before, the limits set by the Constitution have to be observed in the case of reunification.[38] Given the de-

[37] See Jang, Yeong Su, Introduction to Constitutional Law, p. 174.
[38] See above 2.1.

scription of the German reunification process above, it seems obvious that in the context of reunification special problems will arise, which can hardly be adequately solved with the conventional interpretation of the Constitution. However, the Korean Constitution today includes numerous rules, which insist on the goal of reunification but very few provisions, dealing with constitutional issues in a reunification process. Thus, one of the core questions of this work is, if there are adequate mechanisms to design reunification within the existing constitutional framework.

Regarding these questions, it has to be kept in mind that the answers can depend on the demands of other parties in discussions about reunification. For example the DPRK could insist on full immunity for its officials. Such demands possibly leading to constitutional amendments would change the Constitutional basis for answering these questions fundamentally. However, such demands will depend on the political powers negotiating reunification and it would thus be purely speculative to include such demands in the following considerations. When appearing very likely such demands will be mentioned, but in general the following chapter will take the Constitution, as it is today, as a basis.

2.2.1 No new Constitution

The first issue to be decided before reunification takes place and which will influence all further consideration is whether to uphold the existing ROK Constitution or if rather a new Constitution has to be drafted. There are a certain number of reasons favoring the perpetuation of the ROKC. First, it hardly seems conceivable that in the already very complex situation of reunification, the ambitious task of negotiations on a new constitution can be successfully carried out. There is a high probability that in necessary negotiations about a new constitution various political groups would try to constitutionalize parts of their political programme and it would therefore be extremely difficult to come to a satisfying consensus. Besides, such a process would probably take up much time; time, which might be very disadvantageous to lose. Second, the ROKC is a generally well functioning fundamental law. Of course, there might be wishes about amendments to the Constitution, like strengthening the role of parliament. However, the ROKC has brought two decennials of peaceful democracy to South Korea including a steadily improving human rights situation and the guarantee that, unlike in many other newly democratized countries, the decision of voters for democratic change is respected. There are no good reasons perceivable why this all in all well working fundamental law should be given up in the mere hope that something better might be negotiated. Third, the ROKC intends its own maintenance after reunification. Contrary to the German Grundgesetz's article 146, it does not provide a provision for its own termination, but is obviously designed to apply to the entire peninsula, argumentum ex article 3 ROKC. This does not mean that the ROKC effectively prevents the draft of a new Constitution; it just does not include any rules about it. However, if the Constitution itself does not contain a provision for change, this decreases chances that politicians will opt for such an option. For these three reasons chances appear high that the parties in a reunification process would take the current constitution as a normative basis of the reunified Korea and under certain circumstances agree on some amendments; thus such an outcome is the basic assumption to the following chapter. Yet, there is no way to know for sure, nor is there a constitutionally binding answer to this question.

2.2.2 *Procedure of constitutional amendments*

As it was pointed out before, one of the legally most challenging problems in the process of German reunification was the fact that constitutional amendments had been agreed on in an international treaty. In this situation the parliament could only accept the constitutional amendments and the treaty or reject both, but it could not insist on modifications to the amendments, what would have been within its discretion in a normal amendment procedure. The same would be true in Korean reunification. Constitutional amendments would probably be necessary to actualize the Constitution, i.e. to change or abrogate the norms related to reunification and perhaps to adapt relevant norms to some special problems.[39] If constitutional amendments were agreed upon in a treaty by the President of the ROK and the negotiators of the North Korean state, this treaty usually would have to be ratified by the national assembly. In ratifying an international treaty, the national assembly cannot insist on any changes of this treaty, but only approve or disapprove it.[40] If furthermore the treaty includes amendments to the Constitution, the procedure of article 130 ROKC will apply. Article 130 stipulates special requirements for the vote of the national assembly and requires the people consent to the proposed amendments in a referendum. In this situation a mélange of rules of approving international treaties and of constitutional amendments would apply as it has been the case in German. This is to say, Constitutional amendments will be adjudicated upon with the enormous pressure that, if they fail, this will effectively stop the reunification process. Thus the executive can negotiate constitutional amendments, which as a matter

[39] See below 2.4. and the amendments to the Grundgesetz in article 135a § 2 and 143.

[40] Parliament can only consent to international treaties not amend them, see article 60 ROKC.

of fact have to be accepted by parliament. Furthermore, when voting about an international treaty the National Assembly only has the right to consent to the treaty, but not to modify it. As it has been described above, such a procedure was considered highly problematic in German constitutional law. Yet, the Constitutional Court judged this procedure justified by the special circumstances of reunification as long as the constitutional amendments only comprised reunification-related amendments.

Similar considerations apply to the Korean case for the following reasons. The fact that the decisions of national assembly and referendum have to be taken under high pressure originates from the very nature of the process of reunification. If this process requires constitutional amendments, it is impossible to decide about these amendments without the pressure of impeding reunification by a negative vote. This situation is caused by reunification and has to be accepted. The further fact that parliament will not be able to change the wording of the constitutional amendments, as they are included in an international treaty, resides within the inner-logic of reunification based on negotiations with the North. The historically unique situation of reunifications requires fast and decisive actions and is thus foremost the time for the executive. That is why the Constitution in article 66 § 3 ROKC gives the competence to deal with Unification primarily to the President. This reasoning serves to justify the narrowing of competences of parliament in the process constitutional revisions. This only applies to amendments directly related to reunification or if they are a prerequisite of the other negotiating parties involved, without the fulfilment of which the negotiations would have failed. Further constitutional amendments have to be negotiated and decided after reunification.

2.2.3 Common elections

The democratic principle requires holding elections a short time after reunification to make sure that the entire Korean population is duly represented by the elected representatives of the state. This is a basic requirement of article 1 ROKC. However, the case of reunification entails major irregularities necessitating some adjustments of the usual election procedures. Other than in German Reunification, where only a new parliament had to be elected, in Korea two popular votes would be necessary: presidential and parliamentary elections. The election of a new president should take place in an appropriate time after reunification. What appropriate time means can only be judged with regard to the concrete situation of reunification, especially for how much time reunification had been prepared. An important question would be, if the President holding office in the moment of reunification could be re-elected. The wording of article 70 ROKC seems to give a negative answer to that question prohibiting the re-election of the president and article 128 § 2 ROKC even withstands a constitutional revision in the reunification process allowing re-election. However, this is an exclusive question of Korean Constitutional law, where no German experiences exist and which thus shall not be discussed in this study.

In the contrary, some comparative problems exist with regard to the necessary parliamentary elections. First, it is doubtful whether the entire parliament should be re-elected or if only the Northern Part of the Unified Korea should elect new representatives to send them to the parliament already constituted in the South. This question is one of political practicability rather than of constitutional law, since there is no rule in Korean Constitutional Law stipulating that all members of parliament have to be elected in the same time. However, it certainly has to be prevented that in the long term elections to the national parliament take place on different dates in the Northern and Southern part of Korea. Such an outcome would be especially disadvantageous in case of a clear cut majority after the elections in the South, which could not be changed by elections in the North, because of the numeric superiority of the Southern population. For this reason, it seems the most convincing, if legally not mandatory, solution to hold common elections for an all-Korean parliament shortly after reunification. The other possibility to elect in a certain way "interim" members of parliament in the North, until the next general elections are due, seems less convincing, since then the first northern members of parliament would in a certain, time related way be second-class members. Such an outcome is hardly desirable.[41]

Given the procedure of these elections, it goes without saying that they have to be conforming to the general ROKC-standards of elections, thus have to be universal, equal, direct and secret as prescribed in article 41 ROKC. In particular it would be necessary that an election campaign takes place, which besides presenting the parties to the voters would introduce the North Korean population to the rules of democratic election.

A possible lesson from German reunification is that a fair chance of Northern political parties to succeed in these elections has to be guaranteed. That is true for newly founded as for the already existing parties prior to reunification, as long as they accept the democratic principles. This results from the equality of vote demanded by article 41 § 1 ROKC. In view of the majority voting system for members of parliament this means that parties from the North have to be en-

[41] There is of course the possibility that the date of reunification coincides with the date of parliamentary elections in the South in which case the described problem would not come up.

abled to be present with a candidate in these local ballots like any other party and to receive the seat in case they obtain the majority of votes. The equality of vote becomes especially relevant and poses special requirements for the seats distributed on the basis of the proportional elements of electoral law demanded by article 41 § 3 ROKC. Conforming to this principle, one-third of Korean parliamentary seats is distributed due to the votes received nationwide, as long as the party has received more than 3% of them. These rules have to be adjusted to the special circumstances of reunification. Therefore it has to be carefully considered how to allow a ballot, which gives chances to the North Korean population to be represented with independently formed parties in the parliament. One could imagine that in the unified Republic of Korea, concurring to the judgment of the Constitutional Court in Germany, the nationwide 3%-clause for the proportional vote should only apply to the formerly divided parts of the country. If this solution was not applied, a party, only represented in the North of the Country, would need about 9% of the votes in the North to receive any seats.[42] Such an electoral law would pose serious problems with regard to the principle of equality of vote.

Furthermore, this principle indicates that newly formed parties in the North should receive some aid for their electoral campaign from the state to compensate for their funding deficiencies. Given the poor economic conditions in the North, a party without such help would not be able to raise the funds necessary assuring a nationwide electoral campaign. It thus would have a serious disadvantage compared to the long-established parties in the South. It seems constitutionally and politically very important to carry out the first all-Korean parliamentary elections in a way to give equal chances to South and North Koreans to be represented in parliament.

A possible further existence of the old Workers' party in the North or other small parties having supported the Juche-regime might raise some additional issues. In the first place these parties would have to fundamentally transform their organisation and objectives to conform to article 8 § 2 ROKC. In particular they would have to accept the fundamental democratic order of the ROKC to evade their dissolution through a judgment by the Constitutional Court as provided for in article 8 § 4 ROKC. In short, such parties would have to do what most formerly communist parties in Eastern Europe did after the breakdown of the states they ruled: Adapt to the new democratic order. In this case, the Workers' party as could other ex-communist parties could be on the ballots in the first general

[42] This is due to the fact that in North Korea only live around 23 Mio. People, while in the South is living a total of 49 Mio. people.

elections after reunification and experiences in other post-socialistic states suggest that it would probably be able to achieve a relevant score and would thus later be present on the Korean political scene.

A big problem regarding this party would be how to handle its property. In view of the Workers' party's close connections to the state, it is not surprising that its property is huge and very valuable. However, it will be difficult to judge, what can be considered to belong to the state and what constitutes property of the party. In this situation, it seems justified to consider that all property belongs to the state and thus after reunification to the unified Republic of Korea. The workers' party might be left with the party's main building and some operational funds, the spare of the party property will be used to cope with the extremely difficult economic and social situation in the North. From a constitutional point of view it is not conceivable why the ex-state party should be given the immense properties it acquired only as a result of its symbiosis with the state.[43] The right of property only guarantees property to individuals, but not to state agencies. And it seems evident that a state agency, "privatized" in the process of reunification, has no constitutional right to retain all the goods it acquired as a state agency. This "metamorphosis" enforces a fundamental change of the structure of the organisation of the workers' party, which is furthermore necessary to turn it into a normal party in Korea's pluralistic politics.[44] In the contrary, a decision to leave all the property with the communist party would raise reasonable doubts with regard to the principle of equality of parties founded in article 8 and 11 ROKC.

Thus the first common elections of parliament have to be free, universal, direct and secret and should take place simultaneously in all the country. Furthermore, they are to be carried out in a way to give parties in the North a fair chance to succeed in these elections. The workers' party can participate in these elections, if it has accepted the fundamental democratic order.

2.2.4 Reunification as exception and the restriction of fundamental rights

One of the main concerns in any reunification scenario will be the protection of the citizens' fundamental rights, while at the same time the effectiveness of measures to be taken by the government has to be secured. The Constitutional Court of the Republic of Korea has developed a very demanding and keen jurisprudence on fundamental rights over the last 20 years. In numerous cases the

---

[43] For a similar argument see BVerfGE 84, p. 290 (297 ff.); Meyer, in: Badura/Dreier, FS-50 Jahre BVerfG, p. 83 (86).

[44] See Kunig, in: Isensee/Kirchhof, HbStR IX, § 216, Rn. 44.

Court has declared laws or administrative acts void, because they violated human rights of individuals. However, in Korean constitutional law not any provision restricting human rights is unconstitutional, but it rather has to be analyzed, if the restriction is conforming to article 37 § 2 ROKC and to the principle of proportionality. The reasons enumerated in article 37 § 2, which can justify restrictions on human rights, are national security, the maintenance of law and order and a necessity of public welfare. There is no special mention of reasons related to national reunification. Given this wording of article 37 § 2 ROKC, one might think that in the situation of reunification the same level of human rights protection has to be guaranteed as in any other situation. Thus the special difficulties of reunification could not be taken into account and from the day of reunification the citizens in the North would enjoy the same freedoms and rights as the citizens in the South. Yet, such an interpretation would lead to a very high level of human rights protection, which might not be adequate in the difficult situation of reunification and in particular could cause an uncontrollable, since legally unstoppable, wave of immigration from the North to the South.[45] If such an outcome, which might put unbearable burdens on the state, is to be prevented, the constitution must be amended and the possibility of restriction of human rights broadened.

To propose such an interpretation, however, might fall short of the existing content of the Constitution. The Constitution stipulates the central goal of reunification in numerous of its norms, for example in paragraph three of the preamble, in articles 4, 66 § 3, 69, 72, 92. Given the fact that a constitution as other laws shall usually be interpreted in a systematic and interrelated way, it seems hardly convincing that these norms should not have any effects on the possibility of restriction of human rights in reunification. Instead these norms insinuate that the special situation of reunification has to be taken into account, when adjudicating upon the constitutionality of human rights restrictions as upon other constitutional cases. Such an approach can be found in the jurisdiction of the German Constitutional Court, which stated on several occasions that the unique circumstances of reunification allowed measures to be taken, which in regular times would have been considered contrary to the Constitution.[46] Thus article 37 § 2 ROKC, even though not especially mentioning the case of reunification, has to be read in the light of the numerous provisions of the Constitution making clear that reunification has to be considered as a main goal of the Republic of Korea. This could be interpreted as leading to a fourth reason - unwritten in arti-

[45] To such fears see below 2.3.2.

[46] See above 1.1.3.1.

cle 37 § 2 – which legitimizes restrictions on fundamental rights, i.e. the cause of national reunification. The creation of such unwritten norms is something familiar to most constitutional orders and there are many prominent judgments of Constitutional Courts "discovering" such unwritten norms.[47] Yet, such jurisprudence has always been object of fervent critiques, because judges, in developing unwritten principles, are not saying law anymore, but are creating it. Critiques then usually argue that creating law should be the task of the legislator and Courts, in doing so, usurp this power. Even if such a conception of Courts as mere "bouche de la loi" hardly seems convincing today, it should be examined, if no other possibilities of judicial construction exist to avoid such criticism.

The Constitutional Court could interpret the wording of article 37 § 2 ROKC in a broader way including the goal of reunification in the three written reasons. In some cases, measures in reunification already serve national security and the maintenance of law and order and thus could be justified by these goals. In cases, in which there is no direct link between National Reunification and national security or the maintenance of law and order, it should be contended that the goal of public welfare in article 37 § 2 ROKC can comprise the goal of reunification in a general way. The Constitution intends to be applied to the entire Korean peninsula, as it is clearly stated in article 3 ROKC. Thus, "public welfare" arguably should not be understood as comprising only public welfare in South Korea, but public welfare in Korea within the boundaries of article 3. And from a South Korea point of view there is no doubt that reunification in a peaceful and democratic way would provide increasing welfare for the population in the North. This is even more convincing as Public Welfare does not only include the satisfaction of everyday needs, but also the guarantee to the population to live in a pluralistic, democratic and liberal society.[48] If article 37 § 2 ROKC is thus read in the light of articles 3 and 4 and the preamble of the Constitution, it is contended here that the cause "public welfare" includes the mission of reunification which provides "public welfare" to the North. This is to say that not only measures taken during reunification, which directly concern questions of public welfare in the North can be considered to serve public welfare, but that the goal of reunification itself can be considered to provide public welfare.

---

[47] See for example the Volkszählungsurteil by the the BVerfGE 65, p. 1, which develops a unwritten fundamental right and the Capital movement case by the Korean Constitutional Court 2004Hun-Ma554, which states – acknowledging that there is no written provision – that Seoul constitutionally has to be the Capital of Korea.

[48] Even though the concept of "public welfare" is controversial in Korean constitutional doctrine, most scholars support that it has to be understood in a broad sense, see Kim Nam Sik, Treaties of fundamental rights, p. 84; Jang Yeong Su, Treaties of fundamental rights, p. 149.

Furthermore, given the repeatedly stated goal of reunification, it is conceivable to award it a special weight. This would allow more severe restrictions of fundamental rights in the context of Reunification than in regular times, what basically means that the powers of parliament and executive are widened in the situation of reunification. This seems crucial as in the very moment of reunification, important decisions may have to be taken in a very short time and the competent authorities will not have the time to wait for an constitutional analysis about the admissibility of a measure. In this way, the existing Constitution can adapt to the very complex situation of necessary restrictions to human rights in the context of reunification.

This argumentation can be extended to other constitutional problems. The ROKC insists on the goal of reunification in many of its articles. In the system of a constitution, where colliding norms often have to be restrained to reach "praktische Kohärenz", it seems clear that no provision of the Constitution should be read in a way, which obstructs one of the Constitution's main goals. That does not mean that any measure taken by the government can be justified by a mere reference to the problems caused by reunification. It is within the jurisdiction of the Constitutional Court to examine whether or not the problems of reunification plausibly necessitate such measures to be taken and if advantages and disadvantages of these measures are in a sound relation. Thus, reunification does not give a "carte blanche" to the government, but its margin of appreciation is widened and important decisions can be taken without overwhelming constraints. In reviewing the constitutionality of such measures, the Constitutional Court always has to be aware that the measure in question was taken to realize one of the Constitution's main goals.

2.2.5 Liability of a unified Korea for North Korean acts

A further general question to be analyzed is whether or not the unified Republic of Korea will be liable for acts committed by North Korea during its existence from a constitutional point of view. There are two possible legal bases for demands of individuals for reparation: Fundamental rights or the principles of a social and constitutional state and its concretizations.

Fundamental rights do not only give the individual the right to prevent violations of these rights, but in case of afflicted violations give a right to compensation of the individual against the state. At first glance one might think that since South Korea fusions with the North, has never accepted the latter's independent existence and the South Korean constitution always claimed to apply to the North, the citizens in the North de jure always enjoyed the freedoms granted in the Southern Constitution. As the Unified Korea in some ways will be the successor of the North Korean state, the citizens in the North could claim restitution or compensation for the uncountable violations of human rights committed by the North Korean state based on their fundamental rights from the unified Korea.

However such an argumentation falls short of the real Korean situation. It ignores the division of the country and misinterprets the Constitution in one decisive point: the Constitution and its fundamental rights only bind the organs and agencies of the Republic of Korea. For these reasons the violations of human rights by the North Korean government cannot be attributed to the South Korean state. Consequently the unified Republic of Korea is not obliged to confer compensation to all citizens based on the ROKC's fundamental rights because of violations of these rights by the North. It is not the obligation of a Constitutional state and the guarantee of human rights to secure retroactive historical justice, but to allow to its citizens to live in freedom and dignity today.[49] In the process of reunification this task is already very demanding and should not be further complicated by demands to compensate all injustices occurred during the last century. In a technical wording: In the case of a claim for state liability, the North Korean official, who committed the act, was not a public official in the sense of article 29 ROKC and the human rights guaranteed in the ROKC did not apply. Thus the unified ROK is not obliged to pay compensation. Similarly, political prisoners in the North are not entitled to damages against the ROK out of article 28 ROKC.

Still there is a strong moral, political and possibly legal need to grant some kind of compensation to the victims of a totalitarian regime. In German Reunification the constitutional norms, which contained guidelines for this problem, were the principles of a social and democratic constitutional state enshrined in article 20, 28 GG. In the Korean case one might take another normative basis. Article 30 ROKC prescribes that those, who have suffered bodily injury or death from the deeds of others, may receive aid from the state under the conditions prescribed by law. "Deeds of others" can be interpreted as including acts of North Korea and thus a law could be passed on the basis of article 30, which entitles the victims in North Korea to just compensation. It is doubtful whether or not there exists a constitutional obligation of the legislator to pass such a law.[50] Given the assumed cruelties in North Korean prisons or labour camps, it seems

[49] See Ossenbühl. In: Isensee/Kirchhof, HbStR IX, § 209, Rn. 54.

[50] Most Korean scholars believe that in general there exists no such obligation of the state, see Jang Yeong Su, Treaties of Fundamental Rights, p. 672.

like a moral obligation to give some a kind of compensation to the victims of those deeds. The existence of such an obligation seems even more evident as the North Korean victims have been kept away from any justice since 1945. Still, to constitutionally determine an obligation to give financial aid to the victims of totalitarian oppression or even its exact amount is just not feasible. It is the duty of the legislature to cope with the situation after reunification and parliament and executive have to determine to what extent help should be given to the victims. In these considerations the suffering of victims of the totalitarian regime in the North has to be duly weighted. But still many other burdens will have to be taken care of by the unified Korea and the financial costs of reunification will be very high anyway. If compensation for victims of the North Korean state seems very important, the same is true for measures aiming at making the North Korean economy recover and to ensure sufficient food supplies for the North. The Constitution cannot respond to the question, to which aspects priority should be given in these deliberations. For this reasons a constitutional obligation to provide financial recompense to the victims does not exist. The only constitutional prerequisite is that these sufferings have to be taken into account, thus the government cannot just ignore what happened and that if compensation is to be given, this compensation has to comply with the principle of equality.[51] That is to say, the necessary differentiations between the compensation for victims should be based on rational differences and corporal damages should give place to higher compensation than mere losses of property. Thus the question of compensation for the victims of the North Korean regime is one of politics rather than of constitutional law. This of course does not obstruct the government form granting compensation, but the Constitution does not oblige the government to spend more money for this purpose than what it deems necessary.

2.2.6 Conclusion

The Constitution gives a wide margin of appreciation to the competent authorities in handling uprising issues in case of Reunification. As long as the Constitution is not abrogated, it does not lose its normative power, but allows a flexible interpretation, which in general does not restrain the competent authorities from taking necessary steps. These general considerations shall be applied and discussed for some concrete problems in the following chapter.

[51] See below 2.3.4.

2.3 Human rights to be respected in transition

In German Reunification some of the issues, giving place to the most litigation and very heated discussions, were protection and compensation for violations of fundamental rights. Since the concept of fundamental rights is similar in Germany and Korea, but questions of constitutional law with regard to the organisation of the state are very different, this chapter will concentrate on issues of fundamental rights. As a starting point we take the results found above that the situation of reunification justifies more severe restrictions of human rights than in regular interpretations, but that these rights are only modified not abrogated.

2.3.1 *Right to property*

An issue of huge economic importance in any transition process is the issue of (re)-distribution of land property in North Korea. It is without the scope of this article to give an exhaustive analysis of the problems which might arise. Considering questions of restitution of properties expropriated by the DPRK it seems convincing to apply the same rules outlined for compensations of victims of the Communist regime in general. Thus some kind of compensation should be granted but the legislature has a broad margin of appreciation when adjudicating upon this issue. In the contrary, North Koreans possessing land in the moment of reunification could not be taken away these rights without granting them compensation.

2.3.2 Freedom of movement

A second constitutional human right requiring special attention in the case of reunification will be the freedom of movement. One of South Korea's main concerns in reunification is how to prevent a wave of immigration of desperate North Koreans to the South. The attention to the freedom of movement in this case will be in strong contrast to the generally low importance of this freedom in constitutional, market-economy states. This low importance is due to the fact that, in a liberal society based on market economy principles, only very few restrictions on the freedom of movement are necessary, citizens being usually allowed to travel freely and to move their residence at their discretion. Thus, even though the freedom of movement is a widely respected human rights, its importance in most democratic states is low and relatively few litigation exists on this freedom in Korea as in many western states.

Korean Constitutional doctrine generally accepts that the freedom of movement protects the movement of citizens inside Korea.[52] After reunification, it is unambiguous that the movement from the North to the South – or vice versa – falls within the scope of protection of article 14 ROKC. The validity of this freedom could prove very problematic as many observers believe that reunification and the opening of borders could trigger a wave of immigration from North, suffering from malnutrition and poor living conditions, to the "promised land" in the South.[53] If the government shared these fears, it might consider it necessary, to restrict the freedom of movement from the North to the South relying on the possibility of restrictions in article 37 ROKC. Such restrictions can be justified by two main reasons: First, the Southern Part of the country would be hopelessly overburdened by the task to take care of a supposedly very high number of refugees. Second and even more important, it would be disastrous to the Northern economy, if most of the citizens, who are able to move and who thus constitute the major part of the Northern work force, would flee to the South, letting behind a Northern population, which will depend on money from the South for incalculable time. Such an outcome of reunification should be prevented by all means and a restriction of the freedom of movement could be part of a prevention strategy. Such restrictions would easily fulfil the requirement of a necessity of "public welfare" in the sense of article 37 § 2 ROKC. However, restrictions of fundamental rights of the Korean Constitution are only admissible, if, additionally to the pursuit of a legitimate goal, they do respect the principle of proportionality and do not violate an essential aspect of this right.[54]

Proportionality means that the intensity of restriction of human right has to be in a sound relationship to the goal that shall be secured.[55] Such proportionality of measures to prevent an exodus from the North might be highly problematic, depending on how restrictive these rules would be. As it has just been stated the goals pursued by measures to prevent an exodus from the North to South are high-ranking goals and in general could easily justify restrictions of human rights. However, the restrictions could also be very intense. For example, a gen-

---

[52] See Kim Nam Sik, Treaties of fundamental rights, p. 232.

[53] There are some observers who contend that these fears are exaggerated, Bowring, International Herald Tribune, September 27, 2005, or that a high cross-border mobility is one of the keys to successful economic development, see Noland/Robinson/Liu, The costs and benefits of Korean Unification. These questions however lie within the competence to assess of legislator and government and will largely depend on the socio-economic situation on reunification.

[54] See Jang Yeong Su, Treaties of fundamental rights, p. 150; Kim Nam Sik, Treaties of fundamental rights, p. 89.

[55] To German influences on the Korean doctrine of proportionality see Chan Jin Kim, KJICL vol. 34 (2006), p. 29 (86 f.); Jang Yeong Su, Treaties of fundamental rights, p. 150.

eral prohibition of travelling from the North to the South over years would leave little or even no room for the freedom of movement for citizens in the North. It could be contended that such restrictions violate the essential aspect of this freedom and are thus prohibited by article 37 § 2 ROKC. Less intense measures, like the necessity of administrative approval of any travelling to the South would be less problematic, even though this depends on the conditions under which this permission is granted.

If highly intense measures like a general prohibition of travelling were considered indispensable by the government, it would be necessary to allow exceptions from these rules to secure the proportionality of the restrictions. There should be an exhaustive codification of exceptions to these rules, which should be adjudicated upon by the competent authorities and courts. Furthermore, far going restrictions would require a regular and critical examination in the following years, if they are still necessary, or if the situation in the North has improved to such an extent that no mass exodus has to be expected anymore. If restrictions are not necessary anymore, the government would have to adapt them to the improved situation. This means that although very restrictive measures could be admissible and proportional in the beginning of the reunification process, they would remain highly problematic throughout this process and in case of improvements in the economic situation in the North could become disproportional in very short time. To prevent judicial insecurity and to allow to the state to found its freedom of movement policy in the Reunification process on firm ground, the Constitution could be amended to explicitly allow further restrictions of this freedom during the transition process.[56]

2.3.3. "nulla poena sine lege", Article 13 ROKC

Korean reunification, as the overcoming of totalitarian states in general, raises several problems with regard to penal law. On the one hand, after reunification there is usually a strong demand by the victims of state acts, which were in contradiction to principles of humanity, for prosecution of the state officials or citizens, who committed these deeds.[57] Many of these deeds in the same time violated human rights recognized by international customary law or even "ius cogens". On the other hand in most cases, these deeds have been conforming to the legal situation in the totalitarian state or at least have not been persecuted by the competent state agencies. To analyze to what extent the persons responsible for

[56] For proposals for such amendments, see below 2.4.

[57] For a comprehensive overview of human Rights violations in North Korea, see White Paper on North Korean Human Rights statistics 2007.

these acts can be persecuted in a reunified Korea, it is necessary to analyze three distinct groups of "crimes": first, criminal acts, which were usually prosecuted as such in North Korea; second, acts, which were not considered illegal acts in the North, but which can be considered crimes against humanity and third, formally illegal acts, which however because they were silently accepted by the state were not prosecuted. Furthermore, the results contended below would change considerably, if in negotiations about reunification special rules were agreed upon for penal prosecution. For example, it seems possible that a general amnesty would be passed or a procedure comparable to the Truth and Reconciliation commission in South Africa would be introduced. The negotiating parties would be free to agree on such rules and could thus exclude penal prosecution. Even though such a solution might be considered problematic, because it prevents judicial justice and for some crimes against humanity there might exist obligations in international law to prosecute them, it is quite probable that if some of the old communist cadres would be the negotiators on the North Korean side, they would only accept reunification, if it was unambiguous that they do not have to fear penal prosecution. The probability of such agreements depends on the negotiators from the North. If they are old cadres of the Juche-regime they will certainly insist on a general amnesty, whereas if they are the ones, who have overcome the old regime, they might even demand penal prosecution. The following chapter does takes as a starting point that no such amnesty or other mechanisms of dealing with the past are agreed on and instead the general penal and constitutional rules apply.

2.3.3.1 Criminal offenses

Fewest constitutional problems exist with regard to crimes, which where labelled and handled as such by the North Korean regime. If they have not been judged by the courts back then for some reasons and if they are not prescribed in law, there exist no legal barriers to judge these deeds after reunification. In this case, the Northern Law has to be applied except in the case that the South Korean law provides less severe penalties. However there exists no obligation to prosecute such crimes, especially if punishment does not seem necessary anymore.

This solution applies also to deeds, which were illegal but due to the breakdown of the North Korean judiciary system were in all or almost all cases not judged. As long as in a possible trial the criminal would have been found guilty under North Korean law by North Korean Courts, he can still be judged after reunification. The trust in the non-functioning of the legal system is not protected by the "nulla poena sine lege"-principle in article 13 ROKC. However, given the desperate situation of the population in the North, it seems possible to pass an amnesty everyday criminal offenses, so that the tribunals and courts in the North will not be overburdened with judgments concerning the past and the population in the North could restart their new lives without having to fear penal prosecution for deeds committed in absolute misery. Anyway, for the clarity of law the reunification treaty should explicitly provide rules for this question.

2.3.3.2 Formally legal acts violating human rights

Very problematic is the penal prosecution of acts considered legal in North Korea, but in clear contrast to fundamental human rights, international human rights treaties or metaphysic norms. In this case two principles of law collide: judicial justice and judicial security!

Any constitutional analysis of this problem has to take as a starting point the constitutional norms. Article 13 is relevant in this context, as it provides that "No citizen may be prosecuted for an act which does not constitute a crime under the law in force at the time it was committed ...". This seems to be exactly the case discussed here, as in the time the act was committed, this act did not constitute a crime under the applicable North Korean law and thus article 13 ROKC seems to rule out any possibility of punishment. The problem could be solved if the possibility of restriction of fundamental rights would apply to article 13 ROKC as to other fundamental rights. However, it is generally accepted today that not all the human rights guaranteed in the Korean Constitution can be restricted because of article 37 ROKC. For example the interdiction of torture is mostly believed to be absolute in the sense that, even if the general goals enumerated in article 37 ROKC cannot be achieved in any other way than by using torture, torture remains illegal. The same is traditionally true for the procedural rights of citizens in criminal cases.[58] These rights cannot be legally restricted, since they protect the belief of citizens in judicial security. In other words any restriction of such a right constitutes a violation. If one follows this opinion in the context of reunification, North Koreans, who committed acts like murder, torture etc., justified under North Korean law, cannot be prosecuted after reunification.

As we have seen above the German Constitutional Court principally agreed with this solution, however it insisted that exceptions were admissible in cases of severe violations of human rights. The Constitutional Court contended that

[58] See to the problem of application of article 37, Jang Yeong Su, Treaties of fundamental rights, p. 151-153.

the absolute trustworthiness of the "nulla poena sine lege"-principle only applied for laws passed by a democratic legislator. Thus in the case of grave violations of human rights, restrictions of this principle were possible. These decisions were heavily criticized by the German doctrine, which convincingly contended that the "nulla poena"-principle dates back to times, when there was no democratic legislator but an authoritarian monarchy.[59] The principle thus draws its legitimacy not from the democratic act of lawmaking but from the trust of citizens not to be retroactively punished for acts, which were legal when they were committed. It is hardly convincing that only citizens, who are lucky enough to live in a democracy, shall enjoy this advantage, while those in a dictatorship have to fear prosecution after the dictatorship's collapse. If one follows this reasoning, northern officials cannot be judged for acts like torture or executions of political prisoners without trial, as long as their acts were conforming to North Korean law.[60] Such a position might be refuted with the argument that these acts violated international "ius cogens" and thus were already illegal, in the time they were committed. Regarding deeds which doubtlessly disrespect fundamental values of the international society, it is argued that there can be no trustworthy belief of individuals in the legality of their deeds.[61] However such an argumentation is not convincing for two reasons. First, "ius cogens" might prescribe that torture is always illegal. But this in itself is not a penal norm, but a norm which obliges the state to pass such a penal norm. Thus the international "ius cogens"-norm which prohibits certain acts, is not the penal code necessitated by "nulla poena"-principle. Second, already in democratic states it seems very difficult to judge which acts doubtlessly disrespect fundamental values.[62] To argue that such judgments could be made without any problems in a totalitarian state, completely shut off from the rest of the world, by individuals, indoctrinated during all their lives, seems utterly unrealistic.[63] Thus, it shall be contended that the "nulla poena"- principle withstands the prosecution of acts, which were not illegal in the DPRK.

---

[59] See Dreier, in: Badura/Dreier, FS-BVerfG, p. 159 (206 f.).

[60] Another example might be the legally authorized "in-flagranti"-executions of thieves of food during the great famines in North Korea, White Paper on Human Rights in North Korea, 2006, p. 24 ff. Of course, such executions violated human rights in multiple ways and left the relatives of the victim in great pain, but still the "nulla poena"-principle would withstand the punishment of the acting persons.

[61] See Klein, in: Eckart/ Hacker/ Mampel, Wiedervereinigung Deutschlands, p. 417 (425).

[62] A good example is the actual dispute whether or not the so called „waterbording" practiced by American officials in the "War against Terror" constitutes torture.

[63] For similar critiques in Germany see Dreier, in: Badura/Dreier, FS-BVerfG, p. 159 (206 f.).

Such an outcome might be very unsatisfying to the victims of crimes against humanity in the DPRK, but this is what article 13 ROKC suggests. Furthermore, studies on transitional justice put forward that it is all but certain that (severely) punishing officials of an overcome dictatorship is an effective way to achieve reconciliation.[64] However, without such reconciliation the future of a unified Korea is very uncertain. Nevertheless, if one wants to punish responsible person, it should be contended that a constitutional amendment must be passed in the course of reunification to allow exceptions from the "nulla poena"-principle.[65]

2.3.3.3 Criminal offenses accepted by the government

A third category of acts, which might be prosecuted after reunification, are those, which, when reading the law texts of North Korea in a sense conforming to fundamental principles of interpretation, were illegal and penalized, but in the North Korean state and judicial practice were favoured by the state or at least silently accepted. In these cases the question arises: What does it mean "law in force" in article 13 ROKC? Is law in force the legal text only or is it to a certain degree the living text, hence including interpretation by non-democratic jurisdictions. We think that in any case a clear distinction must be drawn: In cases where there was a certain interpretation of a norm by the North Korean Courts, which one might argue about, but which seems after all possible, the situation is not any different from the situation examined above.[66] The individual in the North could trust in this legal situation and thus should not be punished after reunification. South Korean Courts should not pretend that they understand the former North Korean law better than the North Korean Courts did.

However in case the wording is clear but for political reasons the deeds violating this wording were not considered as criminal acts, the situation is quite difficult. For example one might think of the often stated suspicion that North Korean officials are actively pursuing drug-traffic or counterfeiting of currencies as a mean to provide foreign currencies to the North Korean state.[67] If these suspicions could be proven, the question of whether or not to punish the North Korean officials would be raised. In these cases, there was no real trust that the act committed was no criminal offense, but only that these acts were not prosecuted. On the one hand, such acts constituted criminal offenses under North Korea law. On the other hand, such acts were in a certain way regarded as official acts,

[64] See for example Teitel, Transitional Justice, Oxford, 2002.
[65] See below 2.4.
[66] See above 2.3.3.2.
[67] See the analysis by Perl, Drug Trafficking and North Korea: Issues for U.S. Policy, CRS Report for Congress December 5, 2003.

which, in a country like North Korea, were sure to be exempted from any penal prosecution. These cases are on the brink between trustworthy belief in non-prosecution and obvious and thus punishable breach of penal law. For some reasons, the position taken by the German Constitutional Court about the spies of the ex-GDR seems convincing and transferable to the Korean situation.[68] If the principle of "nulla poena" finds its justification in the fact that the trust in non-prosecution should weigh more, than the demand for justice, this principle can be transferred to our case. Principally, it is not the fault of citizens to live in a state, which disrespects law. Therefore, the trust of these citizens in non-prosecution of certain acts should weigh as much the same belief of citizens in a democratic constitutional state. However, this reasoning brings with it a restriction of the trust in non-prosecution by the public officials. If they committed their acts abroad and thus risked to be punished by the competent authorities, if they were seized, there was no trust-worthy belief in non-prosecution.[69] In these cases they just hoped not to be caught and punished like ordinary criminals and it goes without saying that such belief is not protected by article 13 ROKC.

The Constitution puts high limits to the penal prosecution of acts, considered legal in the North prior to reunification, but constitute criminal offenses in the South. In this way the trust of the Northern citizens in the Northern penal system prevents retaliation for acts committed in the North.

2.3.4 Principle of Equality

Finally, the principle of equality would create certain problems in the case of reunification. In Korean Constitutional doctrine it is generally accepted that the idea of relative equality has to be respected.[70] This means that in similar situations citizens have to be treated equally by the state. The principle thus does not respond to the question of whether or not to grant an advantage to citizens or to restrict their freedoms, instead it requires that if such measures are taken, these measures have to treat citizens equally. Of course, this principle is not absolute. Unequal treatments of citizens can be justified, if there is a legitimate reason for this.

In the context of reunification, two main problems with regard to the principle of equality will probably occur. First, for a transition period it will be necessary to apply different laws in the North and the South. To give only two possible ex-

[68] See above 1.1.3.4.

[69] Thus members of North Korean special units, who committed sabotage acts in the South, can still be punished under South Korean law.

[70] See Kim Nam Sik, Theory of Fundamental rights, S. 151.

amples: public officials in the North and in the South will have to be paid differently for doing the same work and Southerners will be allowed to travel freely in the North and to move their residence there, while Northerners might be prohibited from travelling to the South for some time. However, such unequal treatment could be justified by differences between North and South. The big difference in economic productivity justifies very different salaries and these differences have also to be applied to public officials to prevent an enormous income gap between public and private employees in the North. The same is true for restrictions of the freedom of movement, since there is certainly no high probability that waves of Southerners will immediately move to the North in contrast to the other direction. As long as fundamental differences persist between the North and the South, many different treatments between citizens in the North and in the South will be tolerable.

A second possibility of unequal treatment raises much more constitutional concerns. As it has been asserted before, article 11 ROKC of the Constitution requires the legislator and the executive to distribute advantages equally. In the process of reunification many different victims of the North Korean regime will claim compensation for their losses and political pressure presumably will lead to the fulfilment of at least some of these demands. When such compensation is granted, the principle of equality has to be respected, thus differentiations between different victims are only permitted when legitimate reasons justify such unequal treatment. Of course, differentiations are allowed and necessary between different groups, which suffered from different hardships. Yet, there always has to be a reason, why one group is receiving a certain amount of compensation and another one receives none or lower compensation. For example it would probably be a non-justified unequal treatment to grant financial compensation to the ones, who were expropriated without compensation by the DPRK and to deny compensation to those, who were politically prosecuted and imprisoned in North Korean work camps. There remains a certain margin of appreciation of the competent authorities to judge, who needs compensation the most, but these decisions have to be non-arbitrary and just. If they are not, the disadvantaged might be able to claim compensation based on the principle of equality and additional costs would be caused. These constitutional requirements make it necessary to examine very cautiously, to whom compensation should be granted and why other groups can be neglected. When granting compensation to one group, one should ascertain before why this group needs compensation more than other groups. To reach convincing and in conclusive results, it seems desirable to adjudicate upon one general law of compensation for injustices committed in the North, in which all demands are to be settled. Such a procedure would have the big advantage to allow a good overview over the different victims and would thus reduce the risk of granting compensation unequally. Furthermore, the overall financial burdens caused by compensation could be foreseen and unbearable burdens prevented in such a procedure. To say it again, there exists no constitutional obligation to grant compensation. But if compensation is granted, the principle of equality has to be respected.

2.3.5 Conclusion

As an overall conclusion one might say that the existing constitution is able to cope with most problems in a transition process, which today can be foreseen. In some cases, necessary measures would have to be very carefully analyzed, to make sure they are constitutional but in many other situations the margin of appreciation will be broad and most measures can comply with the Constitution without too much uncertainty. As long as the Constitutional Court will follow the concept proposed by the German experience – that reunification broadens the margin of appreciation of the government – and the government respects human rights as much as possible, only few constitutional problems will arise. Still, some amendments to the Constitution are desirable to counter doubts about the constitutionality of certain measure.

2.4 Necessary Constitutional amendments

In this paper, several possible necessities of constitutional amendments have been mentioned and such amendments shall be outlined in this chapter.

A first option of constitutional amendments would be the abrogation of norms in the Constitution, which are directly related to unification. Paragraph 3 of the preamble, articles 4, 66 § 3, 69, 72, 92 all regard question of how and by whom to reach reunification and could thus be deleted, if the constitutional goal of reunification has been achieved. It is questionable, if they should be replaced by other norms. As it has been pointed out before, the interpretation of the Constitution could adapt to the special circumstances of reunification on the basis of today's wording of the Constitution. Thus from a juridical point of view, it is not necessary to introduce a norm into the constitution, which mentions the special possibilities of the government in the context of reunification. However, one may debate if a declaratory norm codifying the broad margin of appreciation of the competent authorities, would be beneficial to the clarity of constitutional law and should thus be included.

One could also think about replacing some of these norms by articles, which declare the intention to preserve national unity in the future. In Germany not only the goal of reunification was deleted from the preamble of the Grundgesetz, but also the affirmation of the will to strive for national unity. This decision led to heated discussions among constitutionalists, who discussed, if it was constitutional to delete the affirmation of this will.[71] Even though the question of the constitutionality of such a deletion would probably not arise in the Korean case, political discussions might come up about this issue. To prevent such discussions, it would be possible to change the preamble, deleting the goal of reunification in paragraph three, but retain the wording of paragraph four, which pronounces the goal of consolidation of national unity. Such a solution would have the further advantage, to show clearly that after more than half a century of division, the mere fact of formal reunification is not sufficient to achieve the long term goal of an overall sentiment of Koreans being one nation again.[72] Thus, after deleting and substituting the reunification-deleted articles of the Constitution the matter of unification would be present in one or two norms. Paragraph 4 of the preamble would pronounce the goal consolidation of national unity. If judged necessary, a new article 4 would ascertain that in the process of transition the special circumstances of reunification should be taken into account, when judging the constitutionality of measures decided on in the reunification process.

Beside these general constitutional amendments, caused by the changes in reunification, two other possible amendments have been proposed above. First, one might think about allowing prosecution of persons, who committed certain, enumerated and especially grave crimes in North Korea, but which are protected from prosecution by the "nulla poena"- principle. If the ones responsible for these acts should be prosecuted despite this principle, it has been contended above that a constitutional amendment would be necessary.[73] For example one could introduce a second sentence in article 13 § 1 ROKC, reading:

"These principles shall not apply to crimes against humanity committed on the North Korean territory prior to Reunification."

Of course, the exact wording of such exception is debatable. The acts, which could give place to prosecution, can be defined in an abstract way as proposed above, or with an exact enumeration of crimes, of which penal prosecution

[71] For unconstitutionality Murswiek, in: Dolzer/Vogel, Bonner Kommentar, Präambel, Rn. 184; for constitutionality Dreier, in: Dreier, GG I, Präambel, Rn. 77.

[72] This is another possible lesson from German Reunification: long years of division cannot be just forgotten in the euphoria of reunification. The great costs for the West and the still existent disadvantages in the East have led to a still visible division between the two former parts of the country.

[73] See above 2.3.3.2.

seems indispensable. This is a question of political will rather than constitutional points of view. Yet, given the exceptional character of this rule, one should refrain from retroactively punishing acts, which cannot be considered as grave crimes. Furthermore, one could narrow the scope of the exception by only allowing the prosecution of high-ranking officials. By doing so, one could probably still fulfil most wishes for retaliation, without however threatening potentially many people in the North with penal prosecution. Such an approach would limit the restriction of the "nulla-poena"-principle and would perhaps counter the reproach of victor's justice, most certainly used by the adversaries of this exception.

This article has proposed constitutional amendments for one other human right protected by the Constitution: The freedom of movement. If the government believes that in the process of transition an exodus from the North to the South is probable, which might have devastating humanitarian and economic consequences, very restrictive measures like a general prohibition for Northerners to move their residences to the South for a certain period of time could be considered necessary. Such measures could come close to violating essential aspects of this freedom and their constitutionality would thus be very dubious.[74] To respond to such doubts a constitutional amendment could be passed, ascertaining that during the transition process the freedom of movement can be restricted more severely than in normal times. Alternatively, it could be provided that this freedom cannot be immediately enjoyed by citizens in the North, but that during a certain period of time, they can only travel at the discretion of the legislator. It is within the discretion of the competent authorities for constitutional amendments, to what extent to restrict this freedom by a constitutional amendment. However, if a constitutional amendment seems necessary, one should pay attention to guarantee as much freedom as possible to the citizens in the North. Therefore, the special possibility of restrictions on the freedom of movement should be limited in time and quality. A limitation in time is relatively easy to codify, and could just be included in the constitutional amendment. The exact length is of course debatable, but it seems probable that such restrictions will be necessary for many years. Much more difficulties would arise in finding a convincing limitation of the quality of the restrictions on this freedom. In this respect the constitutional amendment could provide that the freedom of movement cannot be enjoyed by the citizens in the North as long as the risk of large scale immigration from the North to the South is susceptible to en-

[74] See above 2.3.2.

danger the successful handling of the transition process. However it seems impossible to give a crystal-clear solution to this question via constitutional amendment. It rather seems advantageous to include in the constitutional text of article 14 a new paragraph, which makes clear that this freedom can be restricted more severely during the transition process, but which leaves the decision on the exact limits of such restrictions to the Constitutional Court. In this way the two constitutional main concerns in reunification could be reconciled: On the one hand, it would be clear that measures required by the special circumstances of reunification, restricting the freedom of movement severely, would be admissible for a certain time. On the other hand, it would be ensured by the Constitutional Court that citizens in the North are able to enjoy this freedom as soon as possible.

To conclude it can be ascertained that in most cases, constitutional amendments are not a question of legal necessity but of political intentions. This would be true in the process of reunification and thus any discussions about constitutional amendments will foremost depend on political interests and representation of these interests in reunification.

3. Concluding observations

In a reunification process many constitutional problems will occur, posing important challenges to political decision makers. Some of these problems are described above; many others probably cannot even been foreseen today. Still, the contribution of constitutional doctrine to the reunification process is crucial. The respect of the norms of the Constitution guarantees that fair and non-arbitrary decision, not unnecessarily narrowing the liberties of the citizens, will be taken. This will certainly improve on the population's perception of reunification. In the same time, the Constitution does not withstand indispensable actions by the government required by the reunification process, even if they lead to strong restrictions of citizens' human rights.

When analyzing Korean reunification from a constitutional point of view the German experiences can be very valuable. Not because they provide a perfect procedure which just has to be copied, but because they showed the many problems of reunification and proposed answers, many of which worked out fine and some of which did not.

References

Bowring, Philip (2005, September 27). Modelling Korean Unification, *International Herald Tribune*

Chan Jin Kim (2006). Constitutional Review in Korea. *Korean Journal of International and Comparative Law*, 34, 29.

Depenheuer, Otto (2007), *Selbstbehauptung des Rechtsstaats.*

Dolzer, Rudolf et al. (Ed.). (2008, June). *Bonner Kommentar zum Grundgesetz.*

Dreier, Horst (Ed.). (2004). *Grundgesetz. Kommentar*, tome I, second edition.

Dreier, Horst, Verfassungsstaatliche Vergangenheitsbewältigung. In Horst Dreier/ Peter Badura, Festschrift. 50 Jahre Bundesverfassungsgericht, 159.

Gomà, Daniel. The Chinese-Korean Border Issue. An Analysis of a Contested frontier, *Asian Survey*, 46, 867.

Haverkate, Görg, § 209, Rechtseinheit als Aufgabe, in Josef Isensee and Paul Kirchhof (Ed.), *Handbuch des Staatsrechts*,9, 403.

Isensee, Josef (1991), Abstimmen ohne zu entscheiden? Ein Plebiszit über die Verfassung ist nicht vorgesehen und auch nicht wünschenswert, In Guggenberger, Stein, *Die Verfassungsdiskussion im Jahr der deutschen Einheit* (pp. 214).

Isensee, Josef, § 202, Rechtsstaat – Vorgabe und Aufgabe der Einheit Deutschlands, In Josef Isensee, Paul Kirchhof (Ed.), *Handbuch des Staatsrechts*, 9 (pp.9)

Jang Yeong Su (2002). *Introduction to Constitutional Law.*

Jang Yeong Su (2002). *Treaties of Fundamental Rights.*

Kempen, Bernhard, Wiedervereinigung Deutschlands. In Werner Heun et al. (Ed.), *Evangelisches Staatslexikon* (pp. 2712).

Kennedy, Ellen (2004). *Constitutional Failure.* Carl Schmitt in Weimar.

Kim Nam Sik (2000), *Treaties of Fundamental Rights.*

Klein, Eckart, Die verfassungsrechtliche Bewältigung der deutschen Wiedervereinigung, in: Karl Eckart et al. (Ed.), *Wiedervereinigung Deutschlands* (pp.417).

Kunig, Phillip, § 216: Die Parteien und ihr Vermögen, in: Josef Isensee & Paul Kirchhof (Ed.), *Handbuch des Staatsrechts,* 9, 705.

Lerche, Peter, § 194 Der Beitritt der DDR – Voraussetzungen, Realisierung, Wirkungen, in: Josef Isensee/ Paul Kirchhof (Ed.), *Handbuch des Staatsrechts,* 8, 403.

Loschelder, Wolfgang, § 217, Verwaltung, Armee, Gerichte, In Josef Isensee & Paul Kirchhof (Ed.), *Handbuch des Staatsrechts*,9,745.

Meyer, Hans, Die Wiedervereinigung und ihre Folgen vor dem Forum des Bundesverfassungsgerichts. In Dreier/Badura, Festschrift. *50 Jahre Bundesverfassungsgericht* (pp.83).

Noland, Marcus, Robinson, Sherman & Liu, Li Gang (1998). *The costs and benefits of Korean Unification.*

Ossenbühl, Fritz, § 212: Eigentumsfragen, in: Josef Isensee/ Paul Kirchhof (Ed.), *Handbuch des Staatsrechts*, 9, 521.

Perl, Raphael (2003, December 5). Drug Trafficking and North Korea: Issues for U.S. Policy. *CRS Report for Congress.*

Sachs, Michael (Ed.). (2003). *Grundgesetz Kommentar.*

Teitel, Ruti (2002), *Transitional Justice*. Oxford.

White Paper on North Korean Human Rights statistics (2007).Seoul.

6

Differences in Self-Confidence: East Germany, North Korea and Concepts of the Nation

Bernd Schaefer

After the foundation of their respective states in 1948 and 1949, the Democratic People's Republic of Korea (DPRK) and the German Democratic Republic (GDR) both adopted similar concepts of the German and the Korean nation. They stipulated the building of one united nation in the future despite the current provisional stage of two antagonistic states divided by foreign "imperialist" powers. In both cases, the socialist state was viewed as the healthy national core and nucleus to foster unification. The capitalist entity was denounced as a temporary aberration occupied by "American imperialists". A complete restoration of the nation was supposedly accomplished by unification of the divided parts under socialist auspices after the political defeat of the "imperialists". Yet over the course of time, the initially similar concepts GDR and DPRK conceived about their respective nations began to differ markedly. Now modified perceptions mirrored different levels of self-confidence, and of the awareness to grasp and interpret political and economic realities.

GDR Concepts

The 1949 constitution of the GDR adopted several provisions from the 1919 German "Weimar Republic" and thus also maintained the term of "German nation". During the 1950s, as well as before and immediately after the 1961 building of the Berlin Wall, the GDR claimed to strive for eventual German unification as a historically "progressive" nation. East German leaders could only envision a united German nation in its post-World War II borders to be a socialist system without explaining in detail how to achieve such. It castigated capitalist

West Germany for allegedly abandoning the idea of unification by firmly integrating its state into Western military and economic alliances. Talking about vague ideas of a confederation between both German states as a preliminary stage to their unification, the GDR aimed at portraying itself as the only truly German and authentic standard-bearer of the "unity of the nation".

Yet the West German state also claimed the mantle of the German nation and declared itself to be the sole legitimate representative of all German people East and West and to act on their behalf (*Alleinvertretungsanspruch*). East Germans moving to, or just visiting, the West German territory were entitled to instant redemption of West German citizenship and passports. This position was strongly denounced by the GDR which continued to challenge the "rotten Americanized" Federal Republic (FRG) in nationalist unification rhetoric.

In fact, however, this was rather a propaganda ploy to expose West Germany than a sincere effort by the GDR to achieve a united Germany.[1] In reality, East Germany was completely preoccupied with stabilizing and preserving its own precarious state and the leadership monopoly of the SED (*Sozialistische Einheitspartei*/Socialist Unity Party), the communist party, in the political system. In order to prevent the GDR from falling apart, like during the crises surrounding the uprising of 1953 or the period before and after the 1961 building of the Berlin Wall, communist rulers in East Germany internally did not view German unification as an imminent priority at all.

Despite the continuation of nationalist confederation rhetoric and subsequent propagandistic activities for some time after 1961, the GDR officially began to adapt its concept of the nation when proximity to influences from ever more prosperous West Germany affected the stability of the GDR and questioned its self-perception as the superior German state. Also, the SED had come to realize that no relevant political forces in West Germany could serve as a partner to ultimately turn the capitalist state there into a socialist one. In multiple stages from 1967, and in reaction to a new West German "Ostpolitik" of engaging the East, the GDR abandoned the idea of the existence of one German nation.[2] Confederation proposals were shelved and disappeared from the public and internal agenda. Instead strict delimitation from West Germany was propagated and implemented in several steps.

---

[1] Fritz Kopp, *Kurs auf ganz Deutschland? Die Deutschlandpolitik der SED* (Stuttgart: Seewald, 1965).

[2] Gerhard Naumann/Eckhard Trümpler, *Der Flop mit der DDR-Nation 1971: Zwischen Abstand von der Idee der Konföderation und Illusion von der Herausbildung einer sozialistischen deutschen Nation* (Berlin: Dietz Verlag, 1991); Karl-Heinz Schmidt, "Die Deutschlandpolitik der SED", in Deutscher Bundestag ed., *Materalien der Enquete-Kommission "Aufarbeitung von Geschichte und Folgen der SED-Diktatur in Deutschland",* Volume 5 (Baden-Baden: Nomos, 1995), p. 2114-2293.

The amended GDR constitution from 1968 defined East Germany as a "socialist state of German nation" and official propaganda called the GDR "our socialist fatherland". From 1970 the SED completely avoided the term of the "German nation" to distance and insure the GDR against FRG Chancellor Willy Brandt's "New Ostpolitik". In 1971 the East German leadership announced the "German reunification question" to be historically obsolete through the existence of two different German nations that had emerged after 1945. With one of them socialist and the other one capitalist-imperialist, unification was declared virtually impossible unless socialism might triumph one distant future day in the "imperialist nation" as well. The GDR constitution was amended again in 1974 and the last remaining traces of the "German nation" disappeared. The GDR now defined itself as a "socialist state of the workers and peasants" and said to be "irrevocably linked to the Soviet Union". National issues of the past were exclusively defined in class-based terms and selective so-called "progressive traditions of German history". Ethnic inter-relations and family ties between the two German states were dismissed as politically irrelevant and completely subservient to "the class question". These definitions remained basically intact as official GDR concepts until 1989, notwithstanding certain attempts during the 1980s to uncover and claim certain "progressive" national traditions in pre-1933 German history as antecedents of the established "socialist GDR nation".

DPRK concepts

In stark contrast to GDR political defensiveness and hidden feelings of economic inferiority that led to official delimitation from West Germany, for a long time the DPRK was convinced of its superiority and overconfident to win the system contest with South Korea. It never abandoned its self-perception of being the sole legitimate and superior representative of the Korean nation, and it never put into question the existence of one Korean nation. Until the early 1990s when both Korean states acceded to the United Nations, i.e. until the end of the Cold War in Europe and the dissolution of the Soviet Union, North Korea pursued unbending maximalist positions. Implementing socialist unification during the lifetime of Kim Il Sung was heralded as the central and dominant priority of its public policy and propaganda. The DPRK viewed itself as the only true embodiment of the Korean nation, while the South was seen as only temporarily separated from the nation by foreign imperialist military and economic intruders, namely the United States and Japan. The North did not recognize the Republic of Korea (ROK) in the South as a state or considered its governments as legitimate. It was viewed and treated as a provisional administrative entity and dependent colony established by foreign powers and their Korean collaborators.

Only socialist reunification was seen as the acceptable path to restoration and fulfilment of the Korean nation's destiny. North Korea's unification policy was based on the sincere but actually fictitious presumption that the vast majority of South Korean "masses" harboured the same "desire" as the entire population of the DPRK, namely to live in a united Korea under the leadership of North Korean ruler Kim Il Sung. Propaganda portrayed him as Korea's designated and only legitimate leader, as he allegedly liberated the peninsula from Japanese occupation but was subsequently hindered by the United States through the Korean War to take over the reins of the entire nation. Instead, the saying went, the "Southern entity" was ruled by "puppets" of the Americans or former collaborators of colonial Japan guaranteeing the latter vast and undue influence.

Therefore it remained North Korea's main goal between the 1950s and the early 1990s to apply various means, strategies, and tactics to sideline, trick or eliminate the various regimes in Seoul. The winding historical trajectory of North Korean unification policy and tactics cannot be outlined here in tail.[3]Suffice it to say, that from 1971 (with a brief interlude in the first half of 1975 when revolutionary unification triumphed in Indochina) the DPRK moved away from embracing military options in earnest. China's suddenly moderating influence[4] and the increasing military strength of South Korea, bolstered by the deployment of U.S. nuclear weapons on ROK territory, served as an effective deterrence. Until 1970 the DPRK had preferred "adventurist means" but now it proposed a negotiated confederation model with the ultimate goal of socialist reunification. This model remained more or less intact as the North Korean concept for the entire duration of the global Cold War.

The strategy of "unification through confederation" was first unsuccessfully explored and practiced during the first secret and then open North-South Korean unification talks and negotiations between 1971 and 1973.[5] The inter-Korean dialogues briefly culminated in the "Joint Declaration of South and North", issued simultaneously in DPRK and ROK on 4 July 1972. It called for the "unifi-

---

[3] Bernd Schaefer, "Die Koreanische Demokratische Volksrepublik: Wiedervereinigungs- und Sicherheitsstrategien 1966-1989" [DPRK Reunification and Security Strategy, 1966-1989], *Die Friedens-Warte – Journal of International Peace and Organisation 81* (2006), pp. 119-132.

[4] Bernd Schaefer, *North Korean 'Adventurism' and China's Long Shadow, 1966-1972*, Cold War International History Project (CWIHP) Working Paper # 44, Washington D.C. 2004. See: http://www.wilsoncentre.org/topics/pubs/swp44.pdf.

[5] Bernd Schaefer, *'Evil Deception': North Korean Unification Policy, 1971-1975*, CWIHP Working Paper, Washington D.C. 2009 (upcoming).

cation of the fatherland" and emphasized the following three main principles to achieve it:

- No foreign interference but through self-reliance of the Korean people
- Peaceful and non-violent implementation
- Building one unified nation regardless of ideological and social differences[6]

Those three principles had been drafted by Kim Il Sung himself and were accepted at the time by South Korean Intelligence Head Lee Hu-rak as the authorized representative of the government of President Park Chung-hee in Seoul. Back then in the 1970s, the DPRK still believed in an inter-Korean process of understanding independent from foreign interests. Pyongyang simply assumed such a process would lead to the expulsion of U.S. forces from the peninsula through a newly established pro-Northern regime in Seoul. Later the North slightly adapted somewhat more to reality and envisioned signing a peace treaty and/or a mutual non-aggression agreement with the U.S. and South Korea as a first step to start the inter-Korean process leading to American withdrawal and subsequent unification.

In any event, it was basic North Korean presumption to establish inter-Korean talks and negotiations on all levels of society as a first step. Those talks would, according to the Northern scenario, demonstrate DPRK superiority, subvert the regime in Seoul through involvement of pro-Northern mass movements in South Korea, and create in a second step a confederation with both domestic systems still formally intact but under a joint constitution, army and foreign policy. In a third step following open inter-Korean contacts, revolutionary upheaval and transformation would come about in the South and culminate in the full adoption of the superior Northern system of *juche* under Kim Il Sung's sole leadership and the expulsion of American forces. From Northern perspective, this way the "restoration of the Korean nation" was accomplished.

This scenario was based on two premises, both of which the DPRK refused to recognize in their rather wishful and fictitious character:

First, complete superiority of the North Korean system and society will become evident in open exchanges and competition between Pyongyang and Seoul

---

[6] See Kim Il Sung, *On the Three Principles of National Reunification. Conversations with the South Korean Delegates to the High-Level Political Talks between North and South Korea. May 3 and November 3, 1972* (Pyongyang: Foreign Languages Publishing House). http://www.kcckp.net/en/book/reading.php.

and lead to a surrender of the supposed anti-Northern minority holding power in the South.

Second, all Koreans will always value national unification higher than ideological, economic and social interests that developed during the peninsula's division, and therefore will opt for the authentic Northern embodiment of the Korean nation.

It is anything but surprising that this kind of North Korean self-confidence, maybe better called over-confidence, ran completely counter to the experiences and defensive strategies of the GDR in its attempts to delimit itself from a German nation.

Clash of concepts and mutual pretension

As an interesting curiosity, North Korean concepts of the "nation" rather resembled ideas harboured in capitalist West Germany than in communist East Germany. This was publicly noted when international attention was paid in 1972 to the inter-Korean unification talks. The July 4 Korean North-South Declaration on "Unification of the Fatherland" was seized upon by West German media in an attempt to play off the unsympathetic East German versus the positive North Korean position regarding the question of the "existence of one nation".

Such developments annoyed the GDR to certain extent, as it had not been consulted by the DPRK on inter-Korean unification talks and strategies in advance. East Berlin was afraid this might create problems for GDR-FRG relations and the upcoming GDR accession to the United Nations. East Germany issued an official public statement to dismiss similarities and to emphasize the differences to the Korean case. According to East Berlin, in Korea unification of one nation has to be achieved against "external imperialist forces" on ROK territory. In Germany, however, after 1945 one former nation had been divided into two independent sovereign states with antagonistic systems. Eventually they emerged as two different German nations, one being bourgeois-imperialist, the other socialist.[7] In general, the GDR officially supported the DPRK in its efforts for Korean unification, but professed ignorance of the third point of the 4th of July Declaration with regard to its claim for the existence of two different systems within one nation – a provision that ran completely counter to GDR positions and interests.

---

[7] GDR Foreign Ministry, Statement, 12 July 1972. Politisches Archiv des Auswärtigen Amtes (PolA AA) [Political Archive of the Foreign Ministry], Ministerium für Auswärtige Angelegenheiten der DDR (MfAA) [Ministry for Foreign Affairs of the GDR], C 951/76.

Overall, from 1972 both GDR and DPRK merely referenced each other's policies and strategies without becoming too specific in details. Mutual acknowledgement existed that situations were completely different, and both sides agreed to reject any efforts to enable West Germany to drive a wedge between DPRK and GDR. North Korea flatteringly told the GDR "we have basically the same goal of socialist reunification of our nations". In fact, however, both sides agreed not to take the ideas of the other side as a model, mutually respect their different concepts on nation and unification, and refrain from drawing comparisons in public. Form and methods of DPRK and GDR starkly differed mainly for historical reasons: In the German case, it was the capitalist state that maintained the existence of one nation against the two-nation-position of the socialist state – and in Korea it was almost the other way around.

Ideological and historical differences aside, however, in the end it was also boiling down to notions of confidence and a sense for realities - or the lack thereof. As far as the DPRK is concerned, it neither attempted to proselytize East Germany nor did it recommend applying the Korean model to the German situation. Also Pyongyang did not criticize East Berlin for its intra-German policies. The GDR, however, did repeatedly dismiss North Korean policy. East German diplomats in Pyongyang, as well as their Soviet counterparts, thought of North Korea to pursue an ideologically false and dangerous course that, if followed through, would lead to the end of socialism on the Korean peninsula and the swallowing of the North by the economically superior South. Fortunately from the GDR perspective, North Korean unification efforts were said to lead nowhere due to their flawed premises. With the unification question for the Korean peninsula hitting a dead end, North Korea's incorrect ideas would never be tested in reality, the GDR thought.[8]

Conclusion: East German dead end, North Korean Continuity

In the late 1980s the GDR basked in the notion of a firmly established socialist nation in the Eastern part of Germany and was content with its achievements. North Korea, however, was dismissively regarded as having completely failed to reach its propagated maximalist goal of restoring and reunifying the Korean nation. Yet in 1990 it was the GDR that disappeared and was swallowed up by economically superior West Germany. North Korea had toned down its over-

---

[8] GDR Embassy Pyongyang, On Future Developments of the Korea Problem, 13 January 1988. Die Bundesbeauftragte für die Unterlagen des Staatssicherheitsdienstes (BStU) [Federal Commissioner for Stasi Records], Zentralarchiv (ZA) [Central Archive], ZAIG 14077, Bl. 39-54.

confident unification rhetoric but it survived as a nominally socialist state. Actually, the DPRK felt great vindication that its own revolutionary vigilance and societal formation had made it invulnerable to a "counter-revolution" unlike the Soviet Union and its Eastern European allies.

Unlike all the European socialist states that tended to lecture North Korea, the latter had developed a pragmatic strategy mix of public rhetoric and internal realism. Kim Il Sung exploited to utmost extent his claim to embody the Korean nation in the North and hoped for sympathy in the South, as long as the prosperity gap between both Korean states had not yet skyrocketed. By the 1980s at the latest, however, it had become clear that the DPRK was losing the economic competition with the South and better focus on maintaining and preserving itself. Internally abandoned were any notions of winning a competition with the ROK under conditions of open contacts and borders. Yet the propagandistic value of Kim Il Sung's claims to restore the Korean nation and his constant outlining of unification scenarios, however far from reality, remained always high in order to enforce sympathy and subservience among the Northern population.

Concerning the question of national unification North Korea pretended to be overconfident but internally distinguished between hard reality and useful propaganda without becoming a victim of the latter. Despite its almost sentimental rhetoric of the nation, North Korea always behaved hard-nosed, shunned any real exchange with the South, and kept its borders close and tight. The GDR leadership on the other hand was eager to come across as realistic on questions of national unification. It confidently believed in survival as a distinctive German nation of its own with only semi-closed borders and partially controlled open exchange and competition. However, the GDR leadership failed to convince its people with its propaganda and committed the fatal mistake in believing its own rhetoric. Eventually, in 1989 it was the GDR and not North Korea that had become too over-confident – with all too well-known historical results.

7

Aspects of North Korean Defectors' integration in South Korea: Reflection and Application of the German Unification Experience on North Korean Defectors with Cultural Homogeneity

Soon-Hyung Yi

Contents

1. The similarity of acculturation conditions between North Korean defectors and East Germans after the unification
2. Data
3. Culture shock and cognitive dissonance of North Korean defectors and East Germans after the unification
4. Insecurity of life due to unemployment
5. Settlement and stability of family life
6. Self-identity and cultural integration
7. Conclusion: Meanings and perspectives of the integration of North Korean defectors in South Korea

1. The similarity of acculturation conditions between North Korean defectors and East Germans after the unification

When an individual enters into a new society one experiences cultural differences between their previous society and the new society. Especially when one has to face a different ideology, religion, history, or customs than that of the previous society, adaptation to the newly exposed is inevitable. Berry (1997) proposed a theoretical acculturation model that introduces four acculturation strategies an individual chooses to take when adopting to a new culture integration, assimilation, separation, and marginalization. The two acculturation strategies that reveal a main acculturation model are assimilation and integration. Immigrants tend to assimilate to the new society during the early stages of immigration, but gradually integrate with the new culture over time. Assimilation is when one identifies with a newly adopted culture while rejecting his or her culture of origin whereas an integrative person values traditions from a new culture while retaining traditions from his or her culture of origin. Assimilation can be viewed as passive when compared with integration, which is a more aggressive strategy in acculturation.

North Korean defectors are put in a situation where they must choose to adopt either the mainstream culture or their own culture, accept or reject both cultures. North Korean defectors could be classified into three out of the four strategies mentioned in Berry's acculturation theory: Separation, assimilation, and integration. The North Korean defectors may choose to maintain the value orientation and customs of North Korea, they may choose to adopt those of South Korea, or they may take in both cultures. The tasks that North Korean defectors had to face due to acculturation to South Korean society resemble that of East Germans after the unification with West Germany. Both North Korean defectors and East Germans share the similar experience of moving from a socialist to capitalistic economy system.

1) Similarity of political experience

After World War II, Korea was divided into two separate countries and has remained divided for the last 60 years. South Korea pursued economic exchanges with outside countries openly, whereas North Korea retained the Juche (주체) ideology limiting foreign exchanges. With the competitive heavy industry, North Korea was better off economically than South Korea until the early 1920s, yet its closed economic policy led North Korea to suffer from economic hardships later on. North Korea's economic situation worsened and food rationing was discontinued in 1995. By the year 1998, the serious food crisis caused large numbers of people to suffer from starvation. The serious food crisis acted as a push factor for migration of many North Koreans to other countries. North Koreans crossed the Chinese border seeking food or headed to Thailand, Vietnam or Mongolia to avoid arrest from the Agency. The estimated number of defectors from North Korea can only be assumed to be hundreds of thousands. Most North Korean defectors passed through a third country to migrate to South

Korea, whose people share the same ethnicity and language. As of 1992, there were only about 600 North Korean defectors; yet by 2008 the number has grown to about 13,000 people forming a culturally heterogeneous group within the South Korean society.

North Korean defectors experience feelings of alienation and psychological conflict, socially and culturally, in a new society as is expected of foreigners. Both North and South Koreans share the same language; nevertheless 60 years of closed policy had isolated North Korea, creating big differences from South Korea in terms of language, daily life, consumption pattern, and workplace culture; this caused North Korean defectors to struggle in adjusting to South Korean society and culture (Yi, Cho, Kim & Chin, 2007).

2) Similarity of economic crisis experience

The North Korean defectors' daily life experience prior to the food crisis appears to resemble that of East Germans. In East Germany, when children were born, nursery care, education, and jobs were to be provided by the government until they were grown up. Despite the seemingly ideal system, not everyone who wishes to pursue an academic career was allowed for college entrance. Even though one's choice of career was not solely made by the individual, unemployment was never the case in East Germany.

As for East Germans, like North Koreans, their lives centred around their jobs. Their lives including their social lives and hobbies, all depended on their jobs. Thus unemployment was beyond losing a job for East Germans; rather it was as if their foci of life had been taken away. The people of a capitalist society such as West Germans and South Koreans may not be able to perceive the meaning as well.

Unemployment after the unification sent East Germans into great chaos. As soon as the unification took place in 1992, 16.1% of the East Germans were laid off with a male unemployment rate of 10.5% and female unemployment rate of 19.6%. When compared to the West Germans' average unemployment rate of 6.6% with the male unemployment rate at 6.2% and the female unemployment rate at 7.2%, East Germans showed a higher rate of unemployment. In 1992, the unemployment rate of East Germans had continued to be higher than that of West Germans for the past 10 years.[1]

[1]Das Statistische Bundasamt, Memorandam, 1999.

As the merging of East German banks and financial restructuring took place, banks went through a reconstruction, thus causing the laying off of even more employees. In one bank branch, of the 22 employees, only eight would maintain employment after the restructuring (Rita, 28). In the course of the financial restructuring process, the price of housing, rent prices and the commodities market prices rose fast. The rent for housing in East German had been provided and controlled by the government allowing for affordable housing.

After the unification, the German nation treaty returned the ownership of properties to the previous owners before the East German establishment. The returned estates climbed up to their realized market values, eventually raising housing prices.

The gap in economic power between East and West Germany was followed by a big difference in labour costs as well. The industrial labour cost of East Germany in the early '90s was only 7.5% of that of West German labour. After the monetary integration on July 1st in 1990, East Germans' labour cost was about 36.8% of that of West German labour, and the labour cost rose to be about 50% of that of West Germans in 1991. In fact, the hourly labour cost of East Germans surpassed that of the United States in 1992. By 2002, East German industrial workers were receiving only 77.5% of the pay that West German workers were. In fact, since the cost of living including housing rent, is higher in West Germany, the government estimates the labour cost of East Germany reaching 80% of the West German wage is considered to be fairly balanced.

Given the consumption levels of East and West Germany, recent labour costs in East Germany have reached a somewhat similar level to that of West Germany; yet its labour productivity is still falling behind the goal. Why is labour productivity in East Germany lower than that of West Germany? Lower productivity of East Germany can be attributed to outdated production facilities impeding the production of competitive products compared to West German production goods. A lower rate of operation compared to its West German competitors is also an important factor that hinders East German labour productivity. The manufacturing production index of East Germany rose from 72.6% in 1993 to 81.9% in 1998, but failed to reach the level of West Germany which was 90%. The low production index in East Germany is due to its economic structure providing surplus job openings to everyone with 0% unemployment rate in their pre-unification period. The lack of experience in the international arena along with the lack of management philosophy and experience worked as big obstacle in obtaining economic success as well. In addition, East Germans' negative attitude towards the capitalist system resulted in reduced motivation in the service industries, leading to the deterioration phenomena of productivity with lack of experience. (Lee G, 2008, p. 85) The low production rate and a shrinking job market are similar circumstances that both North Korean defectors and East Germans after unification have faced. East Germans and North Korean defectors with lack of knowledge or expertise in capitalist society had higher chances of becoming subject to unemployment.

As mentioned above, sharing many factors in common in regards to the economic conditions and employment conditions, North Korean defectors and East Germans after the unification are very likely to exhibit similar pattern of culture shock and acculturation tendency in their everyday lives. Therefore, reflecting the process of acculturation of the East Germans to that of North Korean defectors would reveal meaningful similarities and differences between the two groups.

2. Data

This study's analyzed data was collected by interviewing 19 North Korean defectors and 13 East Germans. The interview data for North Korean defectors was obtained from a book (Yi, Cho, Kim & Chin, 2007)[2].

As for the interview data for East Germans, 5 professors who had majored in German literature visited Dresden, East Germany on January 2004 and held 3 group interview sessions. The interview data was published into a book[3] in Korean in 2006.

---

[2] Yi, Kim & Chin. The Disorganisation & Reorganisation of a North Korean Defector Family, 2009.

[3] 15 years after the German unification of Eastern German people (Seoul: Hanul academy, 2006)

Table 6.1 Demographic information of North Korean defectors

Case	Gender	Birth Year	Family Status	Year Out NK	Year In SK	Residential Area in NK	Occupation
1	female	1967	Single	1999	2007	HwanghaeDo	Factory Worker
2	female	1979	Single	2002	2007	Kangwon Do	Unemployed
3	female	.1970	Single	2004	2006	Pyongyang	Restaurant Business
4	female	1974	Single	1998	2006	HamgyungDo	Unemployed
5	female	1972	Daughter	2005	2006	HamgyungDo	Accounting clerk
6	female	1975	Daughter, Boyfriend	2005	2006	HamgyungDo	Unemployed
7	female	1975	Husband, Son	2005	2005	HamgyungDo	Unemployed
8	female	1979	Husband, Son	2004	2004	HamgyungDo	Unemployed
9	female	1974	Daughter	2000	2005	HamgyungDo	Unemployed
10	male	1968	Single	2006	2007	-	Welder
11	male	1968	Single	2003	2003	HamgyungDo	Transportation worker
12	male	1971	Brother	2007	2007	HamgyungDo	Unemployed
13	male	1961	Girlfriend, Girlfriend's daughter	1998	2004	HamgyungDo	Unemployed
14	female	1951	Daughter, Son	1999	2007	HamgyungDo	Restaurant business
15	female	1964	Husband, Son, Daughter	1998	2004	HamgyungDo	Unemployed
16	female	1965	Daughter, Son	1998	2007	HamgyungDo	Clergyman
17	female	1965	Daughter, Son	2006	2007	HamgyungDo	Unemployed
18	male	1977	Wife, Daughter, Son	1999	2007	HamgyungDo	PC room manager
19	female	1969	Daughter	1997	2005	HamgyungDo	Student

Table 6.2 Demographic Information of East Germans

Group	Case	Gender	Name	Year of Birth	Age	Family Status	Occupation before Unification	Occupation after Unification	
middle age	1	female	Rita	1949	49	divorced, 1 child	white-collar labour	Clerk	unemployed
	2	female	Gudrun	1949	49	married, 2 children	engineer	Secretary	unemployed
	3	female	Inge	1952	52	divorced, 2 children	clothing alteration	Labourer	unemployed
	4	female	Irmgart	1952	52	married, 3 children	library clerk	Clerk	employed
	5	male	Michael		35				
	6	male	Torsten		37				
	7	female	Anna		40				
	8	female	Pranka		41				
	9	female	Michaela		42				
adolescence	10	female	Denis		16		college student		
	11	female	Romi		17		college student		
	12	male	Ronne		18		college student		
	13	male	Raas		19		college student		
	14	female	Carola		17		college student		
	15	male	Heinrich						

3. Culture shock and cognitive dissonance of North Korean defectors and East Germans

1) Culture Shock

Before unification, East Germans were able to access information about West Germany via mass media such as TV. After the unification, the East Germans had to go through sudden changes in the social system. The evaluation on social change after the unification has a view that institutional unification has been relatively successful (Diewald & Mayer, 1996), whereas some point out that socio-cultural unification is rather hard to achieve (Diewald & Mayer, 1996).

Rapid social change may put a psychological burden on the individual yet at the same time, may also be a chance for new challenges and opportunities in the new world. In fact, socially well-adapted groups positioned themselves with vested rights after the unification whereas groups who did not successfully adapt suffered from psychological and economical difficulties along with homesickness for their past lives.

Along with the change of regime, East Germans experienced changes in their economic and social lives some of which were positive and some of which were negative. These ambivalent feelings about the regime change may lead to cognitive dissonance. Since the unification, individual and political freedom has increased yet people had to pay for the freedom they gained as a consequence. Although Germany prior to the unification did not promise wealth, it did guarantee economic stability; yet the affluence of the capitalist society rather caused economic anxiety to the East Germans (Diewald & Mayer, 1996). In particular, people who have experienced the pain of unemployment since the reunification show more dissatisfaction along with homesickness for their past lives (Witruk, 1998, 1999; Witruk, Marquardt, and Quast, 1999). The risk of unemployment was higher for women, especially if they were not professionals and if they were of older age (Betram, 1998). The aspects of the culture shock that East Germans experienced are reflected on that of North Korean defectors.

Ever since they have arrived in South Korea, North Korean defectors have been experiencing culture shock due to big differences between the socio-cultural environments of North and South Korea. To move from a social system where the government allocates the recourses with restricted freedom to a society where individuals have to make decisions for themselves puts a great psychological burden on their shoulders (case 1, 9).

The rapid change in the economic system environment might be a crisis or challenging opportunity for an individual. Those able to cope with the change successfully could occupy high positions, yet those who failed in coping with the change experienced economical and psychological difficulties in South Korea. They had to cope with living problems and experience social adjustment difficulties at the same time creating ambivalent emotions (Yi et al, 2007), which may cause cognitive dissonance (case 11).

North Korean defectors had more individual and political freedom in South Korea and yet they were not aware about responsibilities that would follow as the cost of the freedom. They may have experienced hunger in North Korea, but jealousy from economic inequality was something they did not have to worry about. Their exposure to rich materials and economic affluence of the South has caused them to feel relatively poor drawing them back to China or another third country (Yi, Kim & Chin, 2009). Especially, when they could not find a job after coming to South Korea and suffered as a result, they tended to think fondly upon the sense of security they had felt in North Korea although they had not possessed freedom in choosing their jobs (case 2). Actually female defectors are employed in low income jobs as salespersons and service employees easily, and male defectors are also easily employed as manual labourers in low income/ unstable jobs. The risk of unemployment among women is higher if she has not received specialized vocational training of is older in age (case 7). Entering South Korea means that North Korean adults have to accept the uncertainty of unemployment and the future, as well as experience negative emotions towards the new values and customs that conflict with their familiar values and customs. Negative perceptions towards their existing values and customs in the society may lead to cognitive dissonance. Cognitive dissonance is a feeling of uncomfortable tension which comes from the detachment of a person's existing knowledge from his contradictory current knowledge. North Korean defectors' beliefs in North Korea's leader, ideology and social system is broken apart once they enter into South Korean society. Feeling psychological imbalance from the cognitive conflict, North Korean defectors may try to seek psychological stability by acknowledging their existing knowledge to be intact. The belief that North Korea is more plentiful, and is a stable and happier society reflects their desperate effort to seek psychological stability from the cognitive dissonance. Cognitive dissonance eventually leads people to manipulate their faith to gain back their psychological stability and adjustment.

2) Cognitive dissonance

After the German unification, East Germans were forced to accept the uncertainty of employment and at the same time experience emotional issues, i.e. negative emotions, due to conflicts in their existing lifestyle with the new values and ways of capitalist society. The negative emotion might cause dissonance. Cognitive dissonance was defined as cognitive disequilibrium caused by two cognitive elements which are not agreeable. Extensive cognitive dissonance[4] causes psychological tension, thus forcing people to overcome the condition of cognitive dissonance even if they might have a false belief. East Germans believe that East Germany before the unification was Utopia. It exhibits their

[4] The concept of cognitive dissonance was introduced by Lean Festinger, American social psychologist, in book, Theory of Cognitive Dissonance, published in 1957

struggle to maintain their emotional stability caused from the dissonance of cognition by reinforcing the existing beliefs.

First, cognitive dissonance appears in the daily life culture. East Germans and West Germans feel alienated in their life culture. An East German female who had lived in the suburbs of Munich for four months stated that she felt West Germans were foreigners and she was treated as a foreigner by the West Germans as well (Kim N. et al, 2006, p.41[5]). The discrepancy between their life cultures are evident in many aspects such as their child rearing values and methods. An East German female witnessed a West German mother who was stopping a 4-year-old child with a pacifier in her mouth from getting off a stroller and walking by herself (Kim N. et al, 2006, p.42). According to her, West German females seem to be more self-centred in raising their children whereas East German females tend to be more devoted to their children.

In East Germany, though considered a restricted society, sexual freedom was allowed. There were nudist camps located in East Germany (Kim N. et al, 2006, p.49) and remarried families and couples living together were prevalent. Despite the presumption that a socialist country would restrict sexual freedom and would try to maintain a similar family structure, in fact they are more open when it comes to sexual freedom and showed more acceptance of diverse forms of marriage or families (Km N. et al, 1996, p.50).

In case of North Korean defectors as well, North Korean society forced restricted freedom in regards to political or ideological issues but allowed freedom pertaining to sex, marriage or divorce. Rather, as a way to escape from the anxiety and extreme oppression, intemperate sexual aspects may appear (Yi et al, 2007). To alleviate the pressure from political and ideological restrictions, except for political opposition and murder, North Korean law enforcement is somewhat lenient on other issues such as civil rights, fairness and justice. For example, the sexual harassment of a female by a male boss in the workplace or rape in North Korea might pass by unrecognized which reflects the lenience of the law enforcement in such issues.

Secondly, cognitive dissonance arises with wealth and consumption. East Germans were fascinated with the huge influx of goods from West Germany. Coming from a communist society background, where they had limited experience in the production of goods, they were delighted to see overflowing goods in department stores and boutiques. The fact that those goods were from overseas enchanted them even more. An East German female stated that the desire to buy

[5] Page of the book, Kim N. et al

goods was so serious that it almost became an addiction (Kim N. et al, 2006, p.142). According to another East German female, she feels caught up in the payment of unmanaged spending and housing loans. As a result, she is unable to afford any trips (Km N. et al, 1996, p.137). North Korean defectors, too, were delighted with the affluent supply of goods. The problem arose when they made purchased of goods without considering the limited size of their house goods such as a big refrigerator, piano and the latest advanced mobile phones from a department store. It may have looked strange to the North Korean defectors when South Koreans did not readily purchase all the goods available to buy.

Is the ownership of material goods a way of proving existence? North Korean defectors realize that the ownership of material goods may function to raise their status in the eyes of others, which was never the case in North Korean society. How can consumption indicate the meaning of one's existence? Dose owning luxury goods then show a superior state of being? These are some of the confusions and questions that North Koreans may face when entering a different culture in South Korea that holds in esteem wealth and the consumption of goods.

Thirdly, cognitive dissonance arises from one's capability and competition. One of the major differences between socialist society and capitalist society is the existence of performance oriented competition. In a socialist society, though wage may be low, everyone is employed without fail, thus maintaining a uniform wage structure. Unlike socialist society, employment depends upon capability and performance affects the wage differences in a capitalist society, which creates keen competition in the labour market. The emphasis on capability and competition in the capitalist society was the most difficult part of adjusting after the unification for East Germans. With a lack of expertise and skills, it must have been very challenging for East Germans to compete with West Germans. Short-term retraining of people in East Germany was provided to catch up with the knowledge and skills of West Germans and yet it did not help reduce the gap between them. After experiencing the restructuring of the job market for three years since the unification, East Germans finally started to grasp the concept of competition. As they have adjusted better to the competitive market, the workplace atmosphere has changed. The facial expression of the people and the atmosphere of the workplace have become hostile (Kim N. et al, 2006, p.44). The competitive market structure made if often necessary for one to broaden their job search, eventually leaving less time and chance for families to get together and communicate. An East German female stated that their family has hardly had the chance to meet with each other since her son has left to work in Switzerland or the Netherlands. She also stated that her chef daughter has to work 12 hours per day (Kim N. et al, 2006, p.45). Another East German female stated that she could not see her daughter until late at night because of her daughter's frequent overtime work hours (Kim N. et al, 2006, p.45). Regardless of age, in order to lead an independent life with a job, competition in life is inevitable (Kim N. et al, 2006, p.45) and yet they did not wish to go back to the East German system before the unification (Kim N. et al, 2006, p.55). It is just the excessive competition that makes people miss the old East German times (Kim N. et al, 2006, p.54). According to her, in the old days of East Germany, lack of competition allowed colleagues to have more consideration toward each other and yet with the unification they feel that it is gradually disappearing. Once the principle of competition was introduced in the management of a business and organisation, workers started to feel the psychological pressure.

Fourth, North Korean defectors feel cognitive dissonance in their relationships. The fact that two societies that are rooted in the same ethnicity sharing a common history and language background have difficulties understanding and communicating with each other is surprising, as is in the case of West and East Germans and South Korean and North Korean defectors. Close relationships with relatives experiencing a shortage of goods before the unification rather deteriorated with a surplus supply of goods (Kim N. et al, 2006, p.243). The workplace atmosphere used to be very friendly and yet it became more self-centred without the close relationships with colleagues that used to exist in the old days of East Germany (Kim N. et al, 2006, p.44). Colleagues or workers recall their past experience to be more ideal, feeling that the warm consideration for each other has disappeared at the workplace after the unification. That is, relationships became complex and people became more self-centred after the unification because the relationships that were formed were based on materialistic purposes. As friendships turned into competition, relationships once thought as true friendships are believed to have deteriorated (Kim N. et al, 2006, p.125).

It is surprising to find out that North Korean defectors and South Koreans have difficulties understanding and communicating with each other as well. South Koreans find it rather easier to communicate and understand foreigners such as Japanese or Americans than with North Korean defectors. North Korean defectors feel the anxiety from unexpected communication difficulties when they enter into South Korean society. With all the unfamiliar hardships, North Korean defectors miss the old days in North Korea where they were able to feel content even from sharing little things together. Their disappointments in the relationships they have formed in South Korea are often expressed by speaking of their wishes to go back to North Korea (case 15).

As mentioned above, both East Germans and North Korean defectors undergo similar experiences upon exposure to a new society in that they both experience differences in language, differences in the concepts of public and private spaces, and differences in the concepts dealing with relationships. Therefore, their instability of life and experiences are expected to be similar as well.

4. Insecurity of life due to unemployment

The employment structure East Germans were familiar with changed after the unification. With the existing system of East Germany allocating jobs to everyone, people had no interest in competition at the workplace. The time and type of work was given to workers and all they had to do was to follow the given manual instructions. Since everyone had to be assigned with some work, a small amount of workload was distributed evenly to everyone. Competition nor efficiency was not a concern among the workers at the workplace.

The restructuring of the employment structure after the unification was one of the biggest changes that East Germans had to face. Most professional jobs were taken over by the West Germans with expertise and skills, and machinery replaced many labourers. The utilization of labour was emphasized in East German workplaces as well and job re-training that provides skills and information helped East Germans to find jobs. Despite the effort, some East German workers were employed and some were not. Especially many East German females were laid off and were unemployed. According to an East German female who had lost job and had sent in 25 resumes during a period of 5 months from August 2003 until January 2004, she has not yet heard from any one of the hiring companies (Kim N. et al, 2006, p.29). She stated that sometimes there are at least 300 applicants for a single job opening (Kim N. et al, p.29). The older the age, the less chance of getting employed and females found it harder to be employed than men; thus elderly females stood very little chances of getting a job.

With the unemployment rate of East Germans being 20%, the unemployment issue for women was more serious than that of men. Most women in East Germany had jobs and rarely stayed at home (Kim N. et al, 2006, p.33). Most of the women gave birth while working and came back to work after maternity leave, then sending their children to a public nursery.

Even though the wage of East German women was only 450 marks after working for 4 to 8 hours per day, since the prices of commodities were relatively cheap, there were no serious difficulties in everyday life. However, after the unification high-quality goods were made more available, yet the prices went up very high. With the unification the wages went up and yet the price commodities went up as well. On top of that, the unemployment rate increased. An East German confessed that her wage was 450 euros during the East German regime prior to unification, and although she received 500 euros for unemployment benefits, the increased prices for commodities forced her to always be on a tight budget (Kim N. et al, 2006, p.32-33).

The employment structure changed after the unification. Few jobs that required advanced technology and knowledge offered high salaries, but other jobs were replaced with machines or cheap foreign labourers. East German women who were used to receiving a low salary without any competition had to compete for a job, and people who were not qualified for high salary jobs were discouraged. Moreover, it was proven that fewer workers were required to fulfil the job that required more workers. In the eyes of East Germans, West Germans were viewed as workaholics and competing with them seemed very tiring. People were discouraged as they compared their situation to that of people of higher socioeconomic status and with higher salaries.[6] The unemployment rate in East Germany was twice as high as that of West Germany. This condition continued in early 2000. After the unification, as the female unemployment rate and the number of housewives rose, East German women felt they had reverted to doing work in the home. As women's unemployment rate increased after the unification, the number of housewives increased (Kim N. et al, 2006, p.35).

Such a case can be applied to North Korean defectors' employment. A defector who graduated from a famous engineering school in North Korea got a job at Hynix in South Korea. The job was offered as a favour from the government but he was very disappointed to know that his skill was not useful to his company in South Korea (case 11). Getting laid off from a company never crossed his mind and he could not understand his colleagues' worry and fear. His colleagues were nice and yet it was a burden to him because he felt he was being pitied. When he felt his skills or knowledge were useless, he quit the job and complained to the government for not giving him another job. In the eyes of South Koreans, he was given a big favour but he did not understand the employment structure of a capitalistic society because he was used to getting jobs given by the government. The fundamental problem is that an individual has to get out of the mindset of the government providing jobs. Although the workload is heavier and in return the compensation is higher, many North Korean defectors who have doubts about living such a life ask the question; "why do people do nothing but only

[6] Das Statistische Bundasamt, Memorandam, 1999.

work? Are South Koreans workaholics?" Competition in a workplace is one of difficulties they face. Although North Korean defectors receive re-education of job skills, they have difficulty in learning since the gap between the technology of South and North Korea is very wide.

East Germans miss the old East German times. Nostalgia about the times of former East Germany is caused by their psychological oppression from the workplace. Psychological burdens due to work rarely existed in times of East Germany. However, after the unification, individuals faced difficulties of getting laid off from work when work efficiency was not guaranteed.

5. Settlement and stability of family life

There was a difference in East and West German women's family settlement and stability. Women living in West Germany were more eager to have a career and achieve self realization through their work rather than devote their lives to reproduction and child rearing. But women living in East Germany were used to both having jobs and child rearing. They were encouraged to have more children for better productivity thus resulting in a high rate of childbirth. They felt the women in West Germany chose either to work or raise children, whereas East German women were used to doing both at the same time. As an East German female has stated, women in West Germany seemed to have stronger self-awareness making choices by themselves between working fairly with men and caring for their children (Kim N. et al, 2006, 41). On the other hand, women in East Germany viewed themselves as naive and modest people who perform the dual tasks of working and child rearing. They think their characteristics are frugal, simple, naive, and passive. According to her, it was easy to distinguish between East and West German women even from their way of walking. East German women seem hesitating and timid (Kim N. et al, 2006, p.40) whereas West German women seem arrogant and selfish (Kim N. et al, 2006, p.42). For example, a person returned to East Germany from West Germany after living in a house whose landlord was very picky with many restrictions and limitations (Kim N. et al, 2006, p.40). East German women feel alienated from West German women who dress up and are enthusiastic about their child's education.

There were many differences in life culture between East and West Germany. East Germany, before the unification, allowed sexual freedom. Even a nudist camp existed there. And yet, the government had a policy to encourage marriage by supporting housing only to married couples and not to unmarried couples living together. In addition, housing was no longer provided when married couples got a divorce. This policy caused divorced couples to live in the same house with a curtain for privacy. Bank loans were also allowed only to married people. These government policies in regards to housing and financial support encouraged and supported legitimate family formation.

An East German female states that people who rented a house in West Germany were scandalized by arrogant West Germans and landlords placed a lot of restrictions on them (Kim N. et al, 2006, 42). Moreover, East Germans got frustrated by the fact that as the West German's welfare system was introduced, the process became very complex and there were many documents that gad to be prepared (Kim N. et al, 2006, 46). A procedure to claim unemployment benefits became complicated as well (Kim N. et al, 2006, 46). People who used to live in East Germany were not familiar with such complicated bureaucratic procedures.

6. Self-identity and cultural integration

It takes a long time to change from a communist society to a capitalist society. For East Germans, beliefs and thoughts were given to them and they were managed to be maintained by the government. Their value for equality was bigger than anything else and especially their jobs, labour, and wages were fixed. East Germans remembered East Germany before the unification to be a humane society that promoted equality. In the past, they knew how to live. Things that were once considered clear were not definite anymore after the unification. Uncertainty was reflected on self-identity as well. They felt that their job-identity became vague and they did not feel they were part of the German nation. Despite the fact that East Germans moved to West Germany to look for jobs, they believed that they were treated as foreigners. They did not form an identity as citizens of a united Germany, but rather they still viewed themselves as Germans instead of East Germans, and yet they felt West Germans were still West Germans but not Germans.

Studies on the identity of Germany can be divided into three stages (Mutterlose, 2004). First is a period of propaganda, a period where the approach of study moved from an ideological and normative to a socio-scientific approach. Right after the unification, West Germans judged East Germans as undemocratic, authoritative, and conservative people. Financial, cultural and communication difficulties that were faced by East Germans are referred to as unification stress (Schmitz, 1995). It was explained that people brought up in a collectivist culture that demands alignment have difficulty adjusting to socio-economical changes are based on individuality and autonomy.

When people who did not have an opportunity to learn flexibility, responsibility, and social ability faced difficulties, they returned to their past behavioural style or escape, and in turn this resulted in other types of failure such as alcoholism. This phenomenon does not apply only to individual cases but also it spreads to the social atmosphere so that people experience defeat and trauma. In terms of politics, they fell into either the ultra right or ultra left parties.

Second is a period of functional analysis on two independent cultures, which understands both an approach focusing on the financial side from the first period and normative functions of the socialization theory approach. The movement of socio-scientific, and cultural and political integration formed mainly by West Germans in the late 1990s was reflected. They interpreted that they became more enriched both politically and culturally from differences between East and West Germany after the unification. The concept of 'internal unification' was accepted negatively in this perspective. A claim that insists East Germans were authoritative or potential fascist with repressive attitudes was proven to be wrong through an experience research study (Wagner, 1999).

At the same time, psychoanalysis of West German was carried out. They had aversion to nationalism due to the Nazi experience and they tried a paradigm shift from a nationalistic country to a constitutional country and capitalistic country. Thus, they preferred the functional concept of constitutionalism rather than the unification of the German nation. They thought East Germans could not act by the constitution because of learned enervation. That is, they believed that East Germans were just devoted to a German Mark from their repressed psychological structure and trauma.

Understanding the origin of the West German identity issue, East Germans were able to redirect their biased perception of West Germans being initiative over East Germany. It was then the West Germans could finally free themselves from their biased identity of being exclusive toward the East Germans. At this point, interaction and communication between East and West Germany became possible. A claim that says recognizing 'strangeness' in themselves plays a great role in forming identity was raised.

After the unification, the concept of group identity or social identity had normative and ideological functions. This can be interpreted that group identity is owned by many people but its existence is still in question. Does the group identity, 'weness', really exist? There were attempts to explore the group identity after the 1980s, but the attempt to find it after the unification had failed. (Mutterlose, 2004).

East German residents' identity change was somewhat similar to that of the Third World's modernization in terms that the change started from the top. Since I became useless to define I. It was me, as a member of a certain group, from which I has o be driven. Then, I became the person who is expected by outside world. East Germans experienced weak self-awareness and psychological trauma. On the other hand, nostalgia for East Germany came from the bottom. This is alienation between the socio-psychological state of East Germans and social expectation or social support. It can be interpreted that they are experiencing psychological retreat (Mutterlose, 2004).

Third is an period of emphasizing an inter-cultural identity that focuses on a separated and localized society without content or formality. There was a task of integrating the multiple identities that were broken into pieces by expectations of the multiple roles and needs from the organisation. Such a perspective shift recognizes the differences between East and West Germany without overvaluing one culture over the other. This can be understood as a shift from nationalism to regionalism. Rather than focusing on what kinds of problems East Germany has or what is lacking in East Germany, their different socio-political attitudes and potential to change were examined (Mutterlose, 2004). Cultural identity was focused on understanding the other.

Different schemata in recognizing and interpreting social interaction by individual exist in different cultures. The difference comes from values, cultural regulations, and meaning construction. The Meta communication approach is needed to analyze culture shock (Mutterlose, 2004). That is, not only accepting intercultural differences but also openness to accepting others' principles are needed. What's the real difference between East and West Germany's culture? Wagner describes East Germany's cultural characteristic as a 'moralism' that is based on the characteristics of Prussian and Protestantism. Such a characteristic had been melted in communistic human form. Agony and labour were understood in this context as well. On top of it, typical German characteristics such as order, perseverance, and diligence were added. East Germans perceived that their social rise was blocked. This resulted in them to be pro-PDS (Party of Democratic Socialism, a succeeding party to the Socialist Unity Party), ultraright, and followers of a fundamentalism that emphasized the moral.

From now on, cultural changes must occur. Cultural change refers to a change in perception style and communication style. Cultural change and cultural integration have a gap. Cultural integration means moving from being one-culture-oriented to becoming an inter-cultural state. There has been a debate on group and individual identity within West Germany's globalization, and yet the loss of identity from the division of a country could not be recovered. As a result, German shifted the direction from an integrated identity through assimilation to a separated identity that accepts differences (Mutterlose, 2004).

Communication on cultural identity started in South Korea. North Korean defectors should accept their own cultural identity and communicate with South Korean culture. North Korean communistic human form is based on Goguryeo's strong and masculine culture (case 11). This has to be differentiated from capitalistic human form with a strong self-awareness which is based on Silla's delicate culture. North Korean defectors with cultural identity can differentiate and maintain their identity by accepting the differences between the two cultures. Doing so, they can find the meaning of existence and enhance their self-identity.

7. Conclusion: Meanings and Perspectives of Integration of North Korean Defectors in South Korea

Social conflicts between West and East Germany after reunification can be explained in two ways. One is non-democracy and Deformations these in East Germany's regime. 40 years of Stalinism and Fascism in East Germany had demolished democracy and thus creative potentiality and crushed the free spirit of democracy from the system. Today, the majority in East Germany have difficulty in adapting to the discipline of parliamentary democracy due to the typical non-democratic character of East Germany where no virtues and ideas had any place to be rooted (Pollack, 1997). Hans-Joachim Maaz (1990), an East German psychotherapist who has criticized the disability of East Germany, has commented that East Germany was a big mental hospital. He had also added his criticism that East Germany was in a state of such disability and derangement that had been planted into not only politics but also scholarship, education, everyday life and the psychological structure of individuals. In a state of a parental and supervisory role, the state has covered up the immaturity of their people and thus created a system-dependency human nature, he commented. Consequently, the dependency of people has become a praised role model that is believed to lead to social stabilisation. Due to this particular system-dependency human nature, East Germans had demanded strong social security benefits because they were so used to depending on the system, Maaz added. In fact, the claim has been discovered in actual interviews. According to Maaz (2008), the East Germans' tendency to feel victimized, as a developmental retarded, has caused the conflict between East and West Germans. The government of West Germany has even provided privilege to East Germans by selling East German territories only to them. The excessive social welfare policy of East Germany was the very factor that caused the nation's economic crisis after all. Contrary to the general notion, East Germans' underestimation of and bias toward West German was another (Kim N. et al, 2006, pp.257). How would it be considered discrimination to give preferential treatment to Western Germans for their outstanding intelligence and ability. (Kim N. et al, 2006, p.261)

Maaz (1990) had suggested that Transformations these, which pointed out of the problems that occurred during he conversion process of East Germany, is the cause of the conflict between the East and the West Germans. A complicated and questioning bureaucracy in the post-unification era, serious crime and unemployment rates, weakly-structured social security policy, negative perspectives on reality for new living standards(experience these), desire to be compensated for being a victim of West Germans' underestimation were suggested as legitimate examples. East Germans had felt that their experiences and life in East Germany had been devalued and neglected as their qualifications, training, exercises and job practices were all ignored. Likewise, they had begun to think that they were alienated and that they were then following the norms built by outsiders; consequently, they had felt that overwhelmingly inadequate in their homeland (Pollack, 1998). Making a bad evaluation of West Germany's political order is because East Germans want to compensate their unrespected past (Pollack, 1997). Thus, they are re-evaluating East Germany positively not because they want to go back to old times but because they want to compensate for their hurt past.[7] After the unification, they learned the freedom and responsibility that comes along and difficulties of decision making. Because systems like welfare, benefits, and insurance are distributed selectively, they realized it is hard to make a decision on a free will. When they were in East Germany, they lived and acted as they were told by the government. That is, they have come to realize that it is a hard task to become a political and autonomous person.

North Korean defectors face difficulties in adapting to a new culture and they experience conflicts with South Koreans but they do not want to go back to North Korea (Yi et. al, 2009). People who have experienced freedom cannot go back to a state of repression. After realizing what they can achieve and do for

[7] The Colonythese explains the conflicts between East and West Germans. That is, East Germans believed that the political dictatorship of socialist East Germany moved to economical dictatorship of West Germany, a capitalist society after the unification (32). This means that in the process of East German property asset redistribution after the unification, they claimed that more than 90% of East German property went to West Germ‘s ownership. On top of that, the expectation for East Germans to internalize West Germany's life style and labour pattern has to do with colonist ruler's perspective (31). This perspective does not apply to the North Korean defectors due to their different conditions and circumstances from East Germany.

themselves, they cannot go back to North Korea. Even if they face relative deprivation, it is hard to leave a bountiful society. Sometimes there are a few men and women who wanted to go back to North Korea after saving some money but they gave up the hope in fear of getting punished by the North Korean government (case 15).

Nowadays, North Korean defectors came out of being passive in adapting to South Korean culture and they try to act on their own by informing their identities through grouping.[8] Such a circumstance was shown in East Germans as well. After the unification, East Germans went through stages where they rejoiced first, then tried to assimilate into West Germany, and finally to making self-reflections. [9]

They tried to fulfil individual adaption and think critically about the new society while looking at the unified Germany with a new perspective. A new phenomenon of devoting to daily life and culture arose. In addition, a dominant model that encouraged East Germans to be like West Germans faded (Reißig, 2000). Especially from the mid 1990s, East Germans raised their self-esteem by remembering they were not losers but winners who had achieved their accomplishments on their own. At that time, their partial culture based on a sense of community and group identity was formed. They remembered East German players winning sports games and supported the social welfare system of East Germany (Kim N. et al, 2006, p.103). The 'we-consciousness' of East Germans is expressed as a strong sense of unity and it became the source of a strong sense of belonging and identity. East Germans' self-consciousness is not reflecting upon them as inferior citizens to West Germans but accepting their differences with West Germans. This concept helped them to form a partial culture that belonged to their unique partial nation.

Their awareness of a partial culture depends on the regional history. East Germany had a history of the Eastern Roman Empire and also a long history of Prussia, the birthplace of an ancient culture. Historically East Germans had a structurally unique culture, and their lifestyle such as dietary habits, awareness

---

[8] There are over a hundred gatherings of North Korean defectors with their total number being about 13,000 people.

[9] East German's attitude towards the unification has changed over 3 stages (Reißig, 2000). The first stage of 'joy' is from collapse of the Berlin Wall on November 1989 until their official declaration of the unification of Germany on Nov. 3rd, 1990. They felt pride and pleasure about their peaceful revolution. The second stage starts from the early 1991 to 1994 characterized as the 'shock' stage. The conversion of system and unification has caused them a lot of frustration and challenges in their life and cultural identity. There was a fundamental overthrow took place in their previous social values, orientation, norms and symbols after the unification. They felt great pressure to assimilate to the West Germans. The 3rd stage, the reflection stage, began from 1995 and continued until present.

of money and methods of dealing with money, self-expression, a preference of a political party were very much different from that of West Germany. This is the heart of East Germany's 'labour court culture' (arbeiterliche kultur) and although it essentially differs from the 'civic culture' of West Germany, it only shows cultural difference and not the superiority of one culture over the other (Engler, 2002). Engler argued that as East Germans face West Germans who believe in competition, in the name of solidarity, they would adapt better to changes in the future. These experiences by East Germans give many implications to North Korean defectors. Even though it was the financial reasons that made them leave North Korea, they realize that it was their own decision to come to South Korea rather than viewing themselves as losers.

They had strong pride for their own and experienced group identity in Communism. This pride and group identity can sometimes be an obstacle to a flexible adjustment. However, on the other hand, it also can be an efficient way for them to achieve what they want and hope to possess. Despite the differences between North Korea's labour culture and South Korea's civic culture in their nature, North Korean defectors are coping with the crisis by forming a supportive group by themselves as they try to compete with the mainstream culture sometimes and strive to adjust in South Korean society (Yi, S., Cho, S. Kim, C. & Chin, M., 2009). With their efforts and governmental support, the North Korean defectors will be able to form an integrative identity and accommodate with South Korean society in the future.

References

Akzeptanz von Demokratie und Markwirtschaft in Ostdeutshland. *Aus Politik und Zeitgeschichte* Bd. 13, S. 4.

Berry, J. W. (1997). Immigration, acculturation, and adaptation. *Applied*

Betram (1998). Character theory of finite group. Berlin: de Gruyter.
Budrich.

Diewald, M. & Mayer, K. U. (1996). *Zwischenbilanz der Wiedervereinigung :*

Engler, W. (2002). *Die Ostdeutschen als Avantgarde*. Berlin : Aufbau-Verlag.

Find good things of North Korea. *Hankeyore Sinmun*, retrieved April, 27, 2007 from http://h21.hani.co.kr/arti/society/society_general/19652.html

Jin Mikyeong, Lee Soonyoung and Kim Changdae, *Social network and social capital of North Korean defectors.* Seoul: Hakjisa.

Kim Nuri (2006). Political and economic integration and socialand cultural division. In Kim Nuri (Ed.), *The wall in mind* (pp. 20-61). Seoul:Hanul.

Kim Nuri et al (2006). *15 years after the German unification of Eastern German people*. Seoul: Hanul academy.

Lee Gishik. *Small white paper on 15 years after the German unification.* Seoul: Korea university press.

Maaz, H. (1990). *Der Gefühlsstau- Ein Psychogramm der DDR*. Berlin:

Mutterlose, F. (2004). *Aus- und Einschliessung om Ost-West-Verhältnis*. Verhaltenstherapie & Psychosoziale Praxis, 36(2), 233-272.

Pollack, D. (1997) Das Bedrürfnis nach sozialer Anerkennung- Der Wandelder

Pollack, D. (1998). Ostdeutsche Identität - ein multidimensionales Phänomen. In: Meulemann, Heiner (Ed.) : *Werte und nationale Identität im vereinten Deutschland.* Opladen: 301-318.
Psychology: An International Review, 46, 5-68.

Reißig, R.(2000). *Die gespaltene Vereinigungsgesellschaft. Bilanz und Perspektiven der Transformation Ostdeutschlands und der deutschen Vereinigung*, Berlin.

Schmitz, M. (1995). *Wendestress: die psychosozialen Kosten der deutschen Einheit*. Berlin, Rowohlt.
Strukturwandel und Mobilität im Transformationsprozess. Opladen: Leske

Wagner, W. (1999). *Vergleich von ringförmiger und sektoraler Stadtstruktur bei Nachbarschaftsexternalitäten im monozentrischen Syste* http://www.uni-potsdam.de/fakultaeten/wiso.html

Witruk, E. (1998). *Transformationsprozesse in Ostdeutschland*, Research Institute for women's problem in Mokpo University

Witruk, E. (1999). Arbeitsgedächtnisleistungen bei Legasthenie –nicht nur ein Defizit. In: 13. Fachkongress des Bundesverbandes Legasthenie e.V. Würzburg.

Witruk, E., Marquardt, F. and Quast, U. (Hrsg.) (1999). *Psychische Dimensionen sozialer Wandlungen in Sachsn.* Leipziger Universitaetsvertag GmbH.

Yi, S., Cho, S. Kim, C. & Chin, M. (2007). *The social and psychological acculturation of North Korean defector families*. Seoul: Seoul National University Press.

Yi, S., Kim, C. & Chin, M. (2009). *The Disorganisation & Reorganisation of a North Korean Defector Family*. Seoul: Seoul National University.

PART III

Capacity-Building and Development

8

Capacity Building for Economic Change in North Korea: The Experience of Hanns Seidel Foundation

Bernhard Seliger[1]

Abstract

Capacity building has been on agenda in North Korea since the beginning of foreign aid in the mid-1990s. While for political reasons cooperation was mainly (and, for some organisations, depending on the donor state, entirely) restricted to humanitarian aid, in practice such a distinction became soon fiction. This paper discusses the experience of Hanns Seidel Foundation (HSS), a German NGO and think tank involved in development projects around the globe. Since 2003 and 2004, HSS took various approaches to capacity building in North Korea, through seminars, scholarships, frequent discussions with officials, provision of educational materials, etc. While North Koreans due to the breakdown of the official economy, especially the Public Distribution System, all to a smaller or larger extent have to rely on market activities, the understanding of the market remains poor, since the North Korean market is fragmented, corrupted and in varying degrees market activities are illegal. This leads to a first gap between the understanding of the breakdown of the former economic system and its ideological dismantlement and the understanding of a working alternative. There is a second gap between the will of participants in capacity building activities to embrace learning and reform and the strong limitation of learning and implementing lessons learned by supervising state agencies. Therefore, though capacity

---

[1] Representative for Korea, Hanns Seidel Foundation. The author is also senior lecturer (*Privatdozent)* at the Faculty of Economics, University Witten/ Herdecke (Germany). All views are solely those of the author, not necessarily those of Hanns Seidel Foundation.

building can contribute in a meaningful way to prepare North Korea for inevitable changes, its impact under the current political circumstances is limited. Political support from the outside is an important precondition for success of capacity building by NGOs in North Korea.

1. Introduction

Capacity building has been on agenda in the Democratic People's Republic of Korea (henceforth North Korea) since the beginning of foreign aid in the mid-1990s. While for political reasons cooperation was mainly (and, for some organisations, depending on the donor state, entirely) restricted to humanitarian aid, in practice such a distinction became soon fiction. All projects other than the most basic forms of food aid, which merely had to be distributed, involved some form of capacity building. The first reason for this was the gap in technologies between North Korea, which had been virtually closed for sixty years from most (academic, scientific, economic) exchange with the rest of the world. For example, if medical supplies were delivered, it could not work without basic training of doctors and nurses. Local staff of NGOs had to be trained. Without capacity building most humanitarian projects were not effective. For example, the provision of clean water and the establishment of a waste water system in rural communities by German Agro Action, financed by ECHO, the European aid organisation, needed additional training on the use of lavatories and basic hygienic knowledge. The second reason is that NGOs tried to overcome the problems of dependency of the local population on goods brought from the outside and instead focused on rehabilitation of the environment and local economy, often in the field of agriculture. This became gradually more important, when the general economic situation of North Korea did not improve, at least not fast enough to eradicate hunger and poverty, and when the outside relations of North Korea did not allow increased exchanges with foreign countries. Nevertheless, for political reasons capacity building, which smacks of official development aid, was and is largely a topic which remains with a dubious status: everybody tried to do it in North Korea, but nobody really acknowledges it.

Given the ambiguity of North Korea's policy itself this is not necessarily a bad situation since it means NGOs are trying what is possible, being limited by a country not willing to embrace comprehensive reform and scared by the possibility of the loss of control once reforms are implemented. But given these limiting factors, is capacity building possible?

This paper discusses the experience of Hanns Seidel Foundation (HSS), a German NGO and think tank involved in development projects around the globe. Since 2003 and 2004, HSS took various approaches to capacity building in North Korea, through seminars, scholarships, frequent discussions with officials, provision of educational materials etc. The second part reviews the framework of EU-North Korea relations, in which these activities take place. Then, the need for capacity building and the possibilities for its implementation are discussed in the third part. Section four reviews the projects of HSS in the field of economic policy capacity building, followed by a conclusion looking at the experiences of HSS, using among other indicators the monitoring of seminar participants in North Korea.

2. From Humanitarian Assistance to Development Aid – A European Perspective[2]

"[T]he EU strongly supports the Six Party Talks. Though not a participant, the EU follows this process closely, and a solution to the nuclear issue would open the door to closer relations between North Korea and Europe."

Benita Ferrero-Waldner, EU Commissioner for External Relations and European Neighborhood Policy, New York, September 19th 2005

"The nuclear test which North Korea claims to have conducted at Gilju in Hamgyong province on the morning of 9 October is an extremely serious matter, which I unreservedly condemn. Not only does it threaten regional stability in northeast Asia: it also constitutes the latest in a series of challenges by Pyongyang to the international nuclear non-proliferation regime. ... The international community will have to take appropriate actions towards the North Korean regime. Someone will have to talk to this regime to bring it out of its paranoiac and aggressive posture. ... Let me say finally that I think that it is absolutely necessary to continue with our humanitarian aid for the suffering and most needed North Korean population who should not be punished for these acts of their government."

[2] This section of the paper is based on Seliger (2006a; 2007).

Benita Ferrero-Waldner, EU Commissioner for External Relations and European Neighbourhood Policy, European Parliament Plenary, Brussels, October 11, 2006

The two statements above give – in a nutshell – quite a good view on the political position and also perceived role of the EU towards North Korea. The first statement above was issued during a meeting of EU Commissioner Ferrero-Waldner with the North Korean Minister for Foreign Affairs, Choe Tae Bok, on the margins of the UN summit in New York in September 2005. First of all, the EU is no regional power with its own regional agenda. Consequently, there is no direct interest into the solution of the numerous conflicts and problems of North Korea and the Northeast Asian regions, foremost the nuclear issue, but also other important questions like human rights concerns. The EU is no member to the six party talks on none of the participating countries has an interest in inviting the EU to become a member of this body. While there has been speculation of a role of an "honest broker" for the EU, in the Bismarckian tradition of the Berlin Congress of 1878, brokering an agreement on the future of the Balkan states, such a role has few adherents, and none among the parties directly affected.

Rather, the relations of the EU and North Korea are mainly focusing on a second track of diplomacy. Being not specifically interested in the region, but being generally interested in a peaceful development of the world, without the burden of a colonial history, the EU has the chance to support peace initiatives on the second track, namely not by direct diplomacy, but by "soft power" (Nye, 1990; 2004). Humanitarian assistance, membership in the now defunct KEDO, and capacity building measures are among the policy instruments the EU uses vis-à-vis North Korea. Though the nuclear issue overshadows all other relations, there are by now a multitude of bilateral and multilateral initiatives from the EU to North Korea. Nevertheless, without a solution of the nuclear issue, flourishing relations between the EU, its member states and North Korea are not likely. Official Development Aid (ODA) has been frozen after the admission of a nuclear weapons programme by North Korea.

While the EU was willing to continue relations informally through the work of its aid organisations, the re-organisation of humanitarian assistance and the end of much of it at a very short notice in December 2005 dealt another blow to the good intentions of many European organisations involved in North Korean affairs. There are indeed some good reasons to discontinue purely humanitarian projects and the EU-based donors for a long time had adjusted their programmes to the need of capacity building. The aim of North Korea, however, was not to re-adjust aid, but its foremost aim was the eviction of aid workers based in North Korea. Though some of them had a long history of relations with the reclusive state, dating back to 1995, when North Korea first opened its gates to international aid, and sometimes even longer, they were still regarded as potential trouble makers and spies. This shows that the inflow of information, which cannot be completely controlled by the state in the case of resident aid workers and their daily exchanges with North Korean counterparts in particular, is still a threat to regime survival, more than the alleged hostility of the US.

It is important to see that even the complete solution of the nuclear issue and a potential solution of pressing human rights issues are nothing more than a necessary, but not a sufficient condition for the flourishing of relations, in particular economic relations. Still, after the introduction of fully-fledged ODA North Korea would need long periods of training in all areas of the economy, before a successful recovery of its economy can be expected. Due to the relatively small size of the economy and the important impact bilateral Chinese and South Korean aid can have on the country, this is sometimes forgotten. But North Korea still has to build up its economy from the scratch. Can the EU help in this endeavour?

The missile test of July 2006 and the nuclear test of October 2006 seemed to have tipped the balance further in a direction, where the use of soft power becomes useless. The second excerpt, from a speech of Commissioner Ferrero-Waldner before the European Parliament just two days after the nuclear test in October, shows the helplessness vis-à-vis North Korea, a regime "to whom somebody has to talk…" But who? The new agreement of February 13, 2007, gives hope that North Korea is more willing to listen to talk of the EU. As the following short overview shows, the EU has been outreaching a lot to make such a dialogue possible.

The EU established diplomatic ties with North Korea in 2001. By now, it has become a major partner for the DPRK in humanitarian aid, with frequent visits from the EU or EU countries' representatives in the last years. The deterioration of North Korea's relations with other powers meant that the relative weight of European relations, European business and European visits to North Korea increased. However, the outlook for political cooperation is not so bright. The EU had hoped, as a "distant power" with no strategic interests and colonial legacy on the Korean Peninsula to play a role as a mediator between North Korea and the United States. However, this "turned out to be a case of wishful thinking, although a recent European Parliament initiative to set up a seven-nation meeting in Brussels to discuss nuclear issues with Pyongyang suggests that the EU hasn't caved in just yet. The well-meant initiative, however, still needs the EC's go-ahead and follow-up, and Pyongyang's strategy of snubbing the EU on security issues does suggest that food and cash are all that North Korea wants from Brussels." (Berkofsky, 2003) This harsh statement on the reality of the EU's limited role in the North Korean issue is still true, since relations have not fundamentally changed in the last two years. As mentioned above, the nuclear test of October 2006 even tipped the balance more in the direction of a military confrontation, where the EU's potential role becomes increasingly unrealistic.

Preconditions of establishing diplomatic ties in 2001 were the agreement for a political and a human rights dialogue. That there is not much else left to talk about would indeed be a very sobering conclusion after five years of political dialogue between the EU and the DPRK (Democratic People's Republic of Korea). Five rounds of political dialogue have been held since 1998, although the EU has usually revealed very few details on the outcome of the talks beyond calling them "useful" and "constructive". Less useful and everything but constructive when human rights were on the agenda, though. The EU and the DPRK started discussing human rights two years ago, only to see the talks break down after only one session. Despite this setback, the EU still insists that human rights remain a "natural topic" for discussion, admitting, however, that talks with North Korea "do not yet match," in quality and substance, the EU's human-rights dialogue with China. Given the poor quality of the EU-China dialogue, however, this assessment seems even less encouraging.

When the EU established relations with North Korea, it set out its strategies on relations in a country strategy paper (European Commission, 2001). Technical assistance was an important part of this strategy and a total of 35 million euros has been set aside for EU technical assistance projects until 2006, making the EU a substantial donor of technical assistance to the DPRK. The EC-DPRK Country Strategy Paper (CSP) and the EU's National Indicative Programme (NIP) for the DPRK set out the framework and objectives for technical assistance projects in North Korea. The CSP and NIP, if ever implemented, provide for training in market economic principles and projects designed to support and promote sustainable management and the efficient use of natural resources and energy in the DPRK, the development of a reliable and sustainable transport sector, rural development as well as institutional support and capacity-building. However, the admission of a nuclear weapons programme by North Korea stopped ODA and the EU froze the money earmarked for technical assistance.

Instead, humanitarian projects alone were allowed, executed by a multitude of bilateral and multilateral donors and implementing organisations, and coordinated on the European side by ECHO, the office for humanitarian aid of the EU. When in 1995 flooding as a result of environmental degradation brought upon the country by its dysfunctional economic system as well as famine brought North Korea to the brink of collapse, it opened its doors to international aid. The EU, via the Food Aid and Food Security Programmes, provided significant aid since 1997. While originally food aid to the needy has been the focus of the programme, soon it shifted to structural food assistance, in particular, the provision of inputs and technical assistance. ECHO assistance already started in 1995, targeting the improvement of access to safe water and sanitation, providing drugs and medicines to health institutions (European Commission, 2005).

The focus of the two programmes shows that the aid of the EU was not designed simply to bring food to North Korea, with the negative side effect of possibly making people dependent on the food. This happened only in the first years of the crisis, when there was an immediate need for feeding millions of undernourished people left alone by their regime. Rather, the EU saw the necessity for structural assistance, i.e. capacity building and training to broaden the domestic North Korean food supply. While it has been frequently pointed out that North Korea is not an agricultural country and that North Korea should rather focus on the rehabilitation of industrial production, earning by exports the money necessary to import food, the rehabilitation of agriculture nevertheless offers abundant potential for improvement and possibly could lead to self-sufficiency in food production, once a household responsibility system (i.e. privatization) of the agriculture begins. Under the current circumstances of collective farming, such improvements are not likely. Nevertheless, the eviction of most foreign aid workers in December 2005, which in particular affected the European NGOs, shows that not the pretext of a shift to development assistance, but rather the fact that aid workers were in the country at all has been bothering North Korea. Also, substitution effects had set in: the unconditional aid of South Korea was much more attractive from the point of view of North Korea, since no stringent monitoring requirements were attached and since the flow of information in dealing with South Koreans, who were accepted every controlling step by the North, could be much more effectively controlled.

An additional, yet also ultimately unsuccessful chapter of EU-DPRK relations was the membership of the EU in the Korean Peninsula Energy Development Organisation (KEDO). A total sum of 118 million euro has been provided by the EU, plus additional bilateral funding, to KEDO. However, with the breach of the international proliferation commitments of North Korea, KEDO was frozen and ultimately disbanded. The second summit of the North and South Korean leaders in sixty years in October 2007, though conspicuously close to the South Korean presidential election and therefore regarded as an attempt to help the ruling party in South Korea was nevertheless widely seen as another real sign of détente. By now, the European NGOs as well as the EU Commission had found a *modus vivendi* with the new rules for NGO activities in North Korea. Inside the country, the focus is still largely on food security, i.e. the increased efficiency of the agricultural sector. But, additionally North Korea has been integrated with pilot projects into the general activities of EU-Asian relations on the NGO level. This allows also projects like the EU-DPRK trade capacity project of Hanns Seidel Foundation.

The relations of the EU and North Korea go far beyond the few aspects sketched above. By now, numerous experts of EU countries participate in low-key activities in industrial re-organisation, among them joint ventures, training activities from language training to business related training activities and in cultural activities. Germany, the largest economy of the EU, is particularly active; among others, there is now more frequent culture exchange and a library (study room) with German media has been provided to Pyongyang. Nevertheless, the activities have reached a form of plateau, from which it is difficult to conceive progress without a resolution of the nuclear issue and a willingness to tackle other problems, among them the pressing human rights questions.

And another important caveat has to be made about the future relations: Often it is alleged (in particular, by North Korea itself, but also by many foreign observers) that the sanctions of the US and the hostility of the international community are reasons for the bad state of the North Korean economy. This is clearly wrong, since the reasons can be found exclusively in the mismanagement and dysfunctionalities of the North Korean economic system (Seliger, 2004). Also, the reforms of July 2002 only marginally altered this fact, since no basic decision for economic transformation has been taken (Seliger, 2005). However, the often heard conclusion is wrong that a lifting of sanctions or a peaceful resolution of the nuclear issue will bring prosperity to North Korea. While it might bring a massive inflow of aid (in particular, there are prospects of Japanese reparation payments, though they are by no means legally binding and politically secured), it does not alter the state of the North Korean economy and the lack of human capital development. It can, therefore, only be the beginning of serious efforts to change North Korea.

This requires much more than the possibility of free exchanges and trade: it requires the competitiveness of North Korean products, it requires a legally and financially safe environment for trade and it requires that North Korea tackles its problem of old debt, which it defaulted on long time ago. All these issues are often forgotten in the debate about the impact of the external relation on North Korea's economy. Capacity-building measures like the EU-DPRK trade capacity project can help to raise awareness of these issues and, eventually, lead to the required change.

All in all, relations between the EU and North Korea are on the crossroads: to overcome donor fatigue and also political wariness of an extremely unreliable partner, important efforts by North Korea have to be made. It is currently, despite the February 13th agreement, a great question, if North Korea is willing to do so. Still, North Korea has to declare its nuclear arsenal and agree on its complete destruction. Donor fatigue also set in South Korea, as the presidential elections there showed. On December 19, 2007, the presidential election in South Korea brought the candidate of the opposition centre-right Grand National Party, Lee Myung-Bak, to power. The new president was elected on an economic agenda and a domestic agenda. Many South Koreans were disappointed with the rapprochement process with North Korea, on which South Korea poured huge amounts of generous aid without any strings attached and few tangible results. This is important for the prospects of EU-DPRK relations, since South Korea is the largest donor of aid to the North. The change of its policies might have a considerable impact on the stance of North Korea to embrace change.

In terms of EU policies towards North Korea and EU coordination with its partners in South Korea, the US, and to a lesser extent, China and Russia, the EU policies can give some additional push into the direction of a peaceful resolution for the nuclear standoff, i.e. providing additional incentives for fulfilling its promises of February 2007. However, overall EU influence on the issue remains small. Among the possible benefits, given close policy coordination with South Korea and the US (which is not always the reality until now) would be the establishment of an additional informal channel of conveying information about intentions of the international community to North Korea. Such an understanding of using European policies towards North Korea could be particularly helpful in the current situation, given the amount of time and money invested by Europe into building trust with North Korea and its role as an observer directly not involved in the crisis and the negotiations. But currently, this role seems to be not considered as important by either of the relevant parties, leaving the EU for now clearly on the sideline of the endgame on North Korean development.

Can the EU have a role besides "funding the bill?" Certainly, major powers are not interested in an institutionalized involvement of the EU in the emerging Northeast Asian security system, be it the six-party-talks or other approaches.

But, the EU has one important asset, namely experience in setting up a multilateral security system, under the adverse conditions of systemic conflict. This system, CSCE (and later OSCE) did not work particularly well, but it did work, and it encouraged, among other developments, the wave of democratisation in Eastern Europe. The EU should use its experience to participate in the establishment of a similar system in Northeast Asia through capacity building, through close political and economic cooperation and through becoming indeed the disinterested, "honest" broker.

3. Assessment of Needs: What Do North Koreans Know, What Do North Koreans Need to Know and What Are North Koreans Allowed to know about the Market Economic?

Capacity building, i.e. the upgrading of societal and governmental abilities in technical matters, organisational and managerial skills broadly understood, has emerged as the main focus of worldwide development efforts in the 1990s and 2000s. It overcame the dissatisfaction with failed development efforts centred on technological solutions like large industrial or infrastructure construction projects. In the case of North Korea, capacity building is necessary in all conceivable fields. The country has virtually been closed to the knowledge transfer and exchange for almost sixty years, with some exceptions in narrowly defined technical fields, especially weapons technology. At the same time, preconditions for efficient capacity building are barely given due to the strict political control of information flows. This is true in terms of general limits to teachings, which usually have to refrain from being directly aimed at North Korea, but rather have to be framed as "experiences of other countries" without calling directly for change (or, worse, reform) in North Korea, and this is also true in practical terms, since there is no access to North Korea other than through official channels pre-selecting knowledge and tightly controlling its flow. For example, participants to capacity building activities are not only selected by the state, but also it is impossible to ensure that they are receiving related information, e.g. study materials, prior to and after measures. Also, the permanent control situation makes open question sessions, which are an important tool for the success of capacity building, not easily possible. There is always the danger of censoring ex post for participants. The ex ante censoring, in the mind of the participants, cannot be measured, but might be much more severe.

As said before, capacity building is important in North Korea in all conceivable areas. In the economy it can mean more technical capacity building, upgrading bureaucratic knowledge, e.g. in the field of national accounting or legal trade practices and terms. It also has to include a general understanding of market mechanisms, e.g. of chances to participate in the world economy through trade and investment. In this relation it might be interesting to ask the question what North Koreans already know about the market economy. After all, the North Korean economy from the point of view of its main participants, the consumers, since a long time is a market economy. As a recent study by the Bank of Korea among refugees from North Korea revealed, the state provided for less than 10 percent of the needs of population in terms of food, i.e. market relations are overwhelmingly important (Bank of Korea, 2007).[3]

It would be a wrong conclusion that the market principle is already firmly embedded in the mind of the people and there is already a basic understanding of the market. The market as experienced by North Korean consumers is fragmented, is characterized by varying degrees of illegality and corruption, is unfair, and works not smoothly, but in a disrupted way. Market relations in North Korea are to large degree power relations. (see Seliger, 2006b) So, also the view of the market economy is one of a fragmented, corrupted, and unfair system with dubious legality. While there is a clear understanding that the state failed in providing goods and services for more than a decade by now and while there is increasingly low credibility in the assurances of the North Korean state that foreign pressure is the reason for this, there is no clear idea of how markets works. But such an understanding is the preconditions for the acceptance of the need for capacity building and also for the possibility of the implementation of lessons learned by capacity building. This is not only true at a grand, national scale, the basic decision for a market economy, for example, but also on the lower, individual (e.g. company-level) scale, for example in the implementation of new management methods.

In terms of policy-making, it is possible to draw lessons from transition economies to establish the way of reform. In particular, experiences of former centrally-planned economies in Central and Eastern Europe give a fairly accurate blueprint of what should happen in North Korea. Consider the field of monetary policy, for example. Monetary policy is of utmost importance for North Korea, since inflation has been threat to the functioning of markets and

[3] Given the free, though meagre supply of housing, water, basic medical services and educational services, as well as the varying amount of food supplied by the public distribution system (PDS), it is not possible to calculate the amount of market relations in total provision of goods and services to consumers. But the failure of the PDS means that every North Korean citizen has to cope with market relations for the largest part of his daily necessities, with the general relation that the higher the rank, the more of the needs are cared for by the state and vice versa.

the regime's stability (Seliger, 2007b). Certainly, first of all a basic decision for introducing market mechanisms has to be made and this decision, contrary to the more optimistic view of some observers, has not yet been made. It might be argued that the coming into existence of a new, private sector in North Korea (additionally to the special economic zones of Gaesong), Geumgangsan, and maybe Rajin-Sonbong and Shinuiju or the new projects of inter-Korean cooperation discussed for Haeju and other places) heralds the adoption of a Chinese-style transition process. This, however, is not likely. First, the strong, though now defunct industrialization of North Korea does not allow North Korea to rally its support for transition, and thereby guarantee the stability of political leadership, by sharp increases in agricultural productivity, as was the case in China and Vietnam in the early transition stage. Second, the large inflows of foreign currency as a side effect of heavy foreign investment, which upheld exchange rate stability, allowed for a growing degree (though not full) of convertibility of the Chinese Yüan and even now puts heavy pressure towards revaluation cannot be expected in North Korea.[4]

Assuming a general decision for a market economy, the first task in North Korea would be the introduction of a sufficient degree of transparency, in particular the publication of statistics on monetary growth, inflation, the government budget, subsidies etc. This is the precondition for the assessment of the degree of the monetization of deficits of the state and the degree of subsidization of state firms (and the decision, which firms are bankrupt and which are, eventually, viable). To make such a publication possible, not only have the relevant laws to be revised – today, all these figures are state secrets, but also economists and accountants with modern training are needed. This is the only point, where already some attempts for capacity building can be seen: beginning with visits to the Chinese Central Bank in 2001, there have been various training measures for accounting, central banking and commercial banking for North Korean officials. For example, Hanns Seidel Foundation of Germany in 2004 and 2005 carried out training measures for medium-level officials from the Central Bank, the Ministry of Finance, specialized banks, other authorities like the Price Committee, and academics in Pyongyang. Also, an increasing number of students of management and economics have been sent abroad, especially to China and

[4] This does not mean that North Korea cannot learn from China. Indeed, its most valuable lessons may come from China, since they are the most politically accepted lessons. Lee (2006) sketches a possible North Korean monetary and financial reform based on Chinese experience. The argument above just refers to the possibility to expect similar results than in the Chinese transition process. Also, the existence of the successful other, namely South Korea, gives North Korea far less leeway in economic reform without the danger of regime destabilisation.

European countries, which gives some hope for future change in economic policy. However, to make this come true, a much bolder approach is necessary.

Once the relevant experts are educated, it is necessary to strengthen the institutional framework, by giving the Central Bank a sufficient degree of independence and establishing clear norms for central banking as well as government finance and separating both functions. The introduction of a two-tier banking system would be the last step towards the introduction of a market-based monetary and financial framework. A two-tier banking system also would require the establishment of a supervisory authority, either inside the central bank or in form of a Financial Supervisory Commission. The introduction of this framework does not mean that the task of transition is successfully concluded. Gaining experience with a market-based system, and gaining reputation for defending it, for example in inflation fighting and against political meddling, are tasks which will require not only experts, but also time. Nevertheless, as the old Korean saying goes, a long way cannot be gone until one begins with the first step.

This example shows what North Korea needs in terms of capacity building: experts able to understand, and ultimately to implement, market-based reforms. Such experts cannot be created overnight. Their education takes time, money and political will. Occasional training sessions by non-resident NGOs like HSS are certainly not enough to provide such training. They are rather teasers, showing the need for more thoroughgoing capacity building activities. Some attempts to achieve this have been made, e.g. the so-called MBA programme organized by the Swiss Aid office, the only European country providing ODA to North Korea, and the attempts to establish the Pyongyang University of Science and Technology, which might open as soon as 2008.

But is it possible to carry out capacity building in a more organized way? Certainly, it is not yet possible on a large scale. Even for the existing capacity building projects, reminders on the limitations on topics and political sensitivity are the rule. If participants or trainers are talking about topics somehow deemed dangerous by the officials in place, immediate warnings are issued. Given the control mania in North Korea, these warnings are not necessarily reflecting the ideological predilections of the officials, but rather attempts to cover their position from possible bureaucratic backlashes. So, an answer to the question posed in the heading of this section could be this: First, North Koreans need to know almost everything, since their knowledge is limited. They do know one thing however, and that is that the current politico-economic situation brought poverty, backwardness and isolation to North Korea. This is a knowledge shared by the population and the bureaucracy, though – other than through interviewing refugees, who openly can voice dissent – it can only be concluded implicitly. Second, North Koreans are allowed to know something, namely technical, technological and also managerial knowledge considered as beneficial by the state. In this sense, the substitution (or supplementation) of *juche* ideology by *songun* ideology brought positive changes in that sense that learning from foreign countries is not condemned per se, as it was before. However, learning still is strictly limited to issues which are in conformity with the existing economic system, however poor it works. Learning leading to changes, not only revolutionary changes, but also reforms, is not accepted.

Nevertheless, the chance to conduct capacity building activities in North Korea by the use of successful examples from other countries allows participants to evaluate necessary policies themselves. When talking about the success of open trade policies of a small country like Estonia, or talking about the inflation fighting experiences of transition economies like Russia and the Czech Republic, the analogy to North Korea is not too difficult.

4. The Capacity Building Projects of Hanns Seidel Foundation in North Korea

Hanns Seidel Foundation (HSS), based in Munich in Bavaria and sharing a political basis with the Christian Social Union, a centre-right governing party in Bavaria, is a German NGO and think tank, active in civic education in Germany and in political and economic development projects worldwide, with more than 30 offices and projects in more than 60 countries. Since 1987 HSS has an office in Seoul, South Korea. Projects were first aiming at promoting rural development, local autonomy and decentralisation. Over time, the topic of unification and comparative lessons from German unification for Korea became more and more the focus of the work of HSS. In the 1990s and early 2000s there had been several contacts between HSS and North Korea, however to no avail. This changed in 2003 during a delegation trip of the German Bundestag German foundations were explicitly invited by Kim Yong-Nam, nominal head of the state, to start capacity building projects in North Korea. At that time, a number of new organisations, so-called NGOs, had been set up in North Korea with the aim to engage with foreign organisations. These NGO, like the Korean European Technology and Economic Services (KETES), a now defunct organisation, had some leeway to cooperate with foreign institutions. HSS could start with two capacity building projects in the field of international finance, one dealing with international financial institutions and one dealing with inflation and exchange rates, in 2004 and 2005. Though this does not seem particularly impressive in the context of other countries, the fact that more or less unhampered free market theories could be presented to a large number of ministerial officials, academic researchers, professors, and managers, was encouraging. However, this situation of relative freedom was short-phased. All the time, since the opening for foreign aid in 1995, North Korea had been displeased by the influence of foreign actors, like monitoring, bringing them into contact with the population. The fear to loose control plus the hope to become less dependent on international aid (mainly due to the fact that South Korea by the mid-decade became the largest donor and virtually did not attach strings to its aid) led to a policy change.

When in the autumn of 2005 North Korea threatened the aid organisations to expel them from the country or to reorganize their work along the lines of development assistance, this was not only a typical example of North Korean brinkmanship, raising the bar for NGOs who had their own agenda in staying in North Korea, since it meant jobs for their people and money from the EU. It also disguised the fact that a reorientation towards capacity building had begun a long time before; the alleged wrong focus on food aid was a fiction. This orientation can be seen not only in the reorientation of ECHO and food programmes towards structural assistance. It also was clear from the fact that from early 2005 onwards North Korea was included in most "calls for applications" the European Union sends around for its numerous exchange and development assistance programmes to NGOs. The focus on NGO-level cooperation allows the EU to stay true to its mantra that ODA can only be given after a peaceful solution of the nuclear crisis; at the same time NGOs could explore the willingness of North Korea to embark on serious training and economic transformation programmes as well as the possibilities and areas of successful cooperation. Among the calls were those in the field of "open NGO cooperation", environmental programmes and, also, the ASIA Invest II programme, which will be discussed here.

Many of the newly established organisations like KETES were either closed down or were forced to give up contacts with foreign actors. Instead, new agencies for the contact with the outside world as direct subsidiaries of the Ministry of Foreign Affairs were established. For European NGOs, the contact point was called "Korean-European Cooperation Coordinating Agency" (KECCA), an agency not only monitoring or facilitating NGO-contacts, but taking them in fact over from the NGOs. In terms of the preferences for programmes the focus is clearly on technical issues. Technical issues are those most urgent in the mind of North Korean officials since they are first, according to the North Korean official understanding, responsible for North Korea's relative backwardness and decline and second of all they are politically least dangerous. The one positive change after the breakdown of the political and economic system of North Korea during the 1990s is that at least in the field of technology, learning from abroad was encouraged, as long as it is about technology, not about political and economic ideas. So, North Korean proposals for cooperation projects and for educational programmes (like sending North Korean students abroad) always include energy issues (in the case of dealing with European organisations, often "renewable energy" is proposed as a topic, due to the idea that this is more appealing to European organisations), issues of agricultural and fisheries technologies etc. Economic training is also accepted on a limited basis. It is known to North Korea that for example the German foundations active in North Korea are by purpose involved only in non-technical projects (though fields like energy often are inside the field of activities) and some allowance to this fact has to be made. North Korea hopes not only to benefit directly from the activities of foundations and other actors (like, for example, the German cultural institute, Goethe Institut), but also to use the activities with the foundations as precedence for later ODA. Second, economic training is seen as useful as long as it helps in technical terms (like, facilitating exports of North Korea) and does not challenge the leading ideology.

The EU-financed programme Asia-Invest was launched in 1998 and aims to promote the internationalisation of European and Asian small and medium-sized enterprises (SMEs). It supports the exchange of experience, networking and matchmaking among European and Asian business organisations to promote the greater integration of European and Asian companies and the transfer of know-how and technology between the two regions. This is achieved by supporting multilateral partnership projects between intermediary business organisations in the European Union and South Asia, South East Asia and East Asia. The EU-DPRK trade capacity project aims at meeting the 3rd priority of the ASIA-invest II – programme, i.e. achieving an institutional reinforcement consisting of capacity building of North Korean intermediary business organisations and enhanced networking with European counterparts. Over and above this the project meets also the top priority of the EU foreign policy strategy on North Korea, viz. to provide the necessary impulse for reaching long-term benefits in the DPRK through institutional change.

The EU-DPRK Trade Capacity project is a joint project by Hanns Seidel Foundation from Germany with the Pyongyang International Information Centre for new Technology and Economy (PIINTEC) and the EU-Korea Industrial Cooperation Agency (EUKICA) from Brussels. The broad objective includes the following aspects: Capacity building in North Korea first of all contributes to the general purpose of promoting peace and reconciliation on the Korean peninsula. Dialogue and cooperation between EU and North Korea partners fosters mutual understanding and trust as well as improves general relations. This should thus allow the EU to gain a greater presence as a trusted economic and political actor in the region. Moreover, reducing institutional shortcomings and investing in human development of business intermediary and trade promotion organisations gives an impetus for economic innovation. In this respect, the project also envisages better living conditions for the North Korean population. Implementation of measures proposed by seminars produces opportunities for viable economic development. This contributes to the long-term goal of economic growth and combating poverty in one of the poorest states of the region.

As far as a more narrow definition of the project objectives is concerned, the emphasis lies on institutional capacity building to increase the potential of North Korean trade and business promotion organisations. Imparting business related knowledge and improving their services, serves the purpose of strengthening local expertise and competence in these organisations. As an important prerequisite for economic development the project supports the country to help itself in building up trade and business relations, export capabilities and foreign investment prospects. A more beneficial business environment should allow European businesses to lead the way on foreign trade with North Korea.

The main activities include seminars and workshops held by invited economic specialists in North Korea as well as study visits of DPRK experts to European organisations, such as Chambers of Commerce, which have an interest in exchange. DPRK experts taking part in the activities will be mainly drawn from business intermediary and trade institutions in North Korea.

As of 2007, four seminars on international business, international trade, business intermediaries (chambers of commerce) and export strategies have been carried out. Given the difficult political circumstances, this is a result which is better than expected, though many improvements are still necessary. Also, the participants approved of the programmes, as the regular monitoring of seminars shows. In the next section, the review of the capacity building experience of HSS in North Korea will be partly based on answers from the monitoring.

5. Does Capacity Building in North Korea Work? A Tentative Conclusion

In the last four years, HSS could gain some experience with the specific circumstances of capacity building in North Korea. The following five "lessons" are condensed from this experience.

(1) Relations to the bureaucracy are central and at the same time the most challenging variable in conducting capacity building in North Korea. Personal connections are helpful to overcome certain obstacles, beginning with the possibility of direct e-mail communication, and to get more leeway for activities. Understanding the bureaucratic position is important, since it does not only reflect official ideology, but also the fear of sanctions by higher echelons of the bureaucracy. These fears are not imaginary, but real, and frequently sanctions are issued.

(2) The overwhelming desire of participants in all our capacity building seminars was "more practice" and more "practical lessons for Korea" instead of theories. This might be partly related to the fact that there is no sound theoretical basis in many participants (e.g. to discuss problems related to the economy), but mainly it reflects the honest will to learn from capacity building activities. In monitoring questionnaires of our capacity building activities, filled in on the spot (i.e. without direct interference by possible minders) and evaluated anonymously, this was the single most important item. At the same time, such practical lessons are explicitly unwanted by the bureaucracy fearing for negative sanctions when allowing direct calls for changes in the economic system. Occasionally, during the capacity building measures, such calls came occasionally from the participants, but were later censored by the North Korean officials responsible.

(3) Though many participants obviously have no prior knowledge of the seminar topics and occasionally even feel deceived by titles, there must be a certain supply of educational materials available in research institutes, universities and bureaucracies. Participants had access to macroeconomic teaching materials in a seminar on trade strategies, for example. Even, it was written that "recently books related to that topic (exports and export strategies) have been published lately in our country." So, to some extent participants and not only personally knowledgeable about the market they encounter on a daily basis, but also have a prior preconceived idea of how the market economy works – yet another sign that the ideological basis for the current economic system is long gone and that

political reasons, i.e. fear of regime change, are responsible for the maintenance of the ideological system.

(4) Capacity building would require step by step approaches to participants, building upon each other and allowing them to accumulate learning. This is not yet possible in North Korea. Participants are selected completely by the North Korean side and information on study materials for participants are irregular, to say the least. The lack of direct supervision of the preparation of seminar tasks is specifically severe for non-resident NGOs. Therefore, capacity building is quite limited. The existing measures can only show North Koreans the importance to conduct much grander, large-scale capacity building activities.

(5) Political support for capacity building projects is a main factor of success. This is true for support inside the country, though this is a variable out of control for most actors. It is also true for support from the outside, for example support by European politicians for EU-funded projects in North Korea. This gives some leverage to demand the acceptance of contents, even if it might not be a priority for the North Korean bureaucracy. Especially, political support is necessary to move away from technical or technological projects to projects related to the institutional system. Such a support also helps the Korean bureaucrats to justify programmes vis-à-vis their superiors.

Capacity building in North Korea has still a long way to go. However, it is important that there are projects, that there is a diversity of actors from abroad, among them NGOs, and that topics do not only include technical projects. As one participant of our activities put it: "*It is better to train our specialist related to management and planning by help of your organisation or the EU. I feel that that the lack of experienced managers is an urgent issue.*" In this sense, HSS tries to understand its activities as a programme to assist North Korea in its need for economic modernization and at the same time showing possible routes of reform towards prosperity.

References

Bank of Korea (2007), Survey of refugees from North Korea, Seoul: BOK.

Berkofsky, Axel (2003), EU's North Korea policy a non-starter, Asia Times, July 10th, 2003, in the Internet: http://www.atimes.com/atimes/Korea/EG10Dg01.html (file retrieved May 23rd, 2006).

European Commission (2002), The EC – Democratic People's Republic of Korea (DPRK) Country Strategy Paper 2001-2004, in the Internet: http://ec.europa.eu/comm/external_relations/north_korea/csp/01_04_en.pdf, (file retrieved May 23rd, 2006).

European Commission (2005), The EU's relations with the Democratic People's Republic of Korea – DPRK (North Korea), in the Internet: http://ec.europa.eu/comm/external_relations/north_korea/intro/index.htm, (file retrieved October 22nd, 2006).

Ferrero-Waldner, Benita (2006), North Korea, European Parliament Plenary, Brussels, 11 October 2006, Reference SPEECH/06/587, in the Internet: http://europa.eu.int/rapid/pressReleasesAction.do?reference=SPEECH/06/587&format=HTML&aged=0&language=EN&guiLanguage=en (file retrieved October 22nd, 2006).

Lee, Dong-Wook (2006), Banking Reforms in North Korea and China (in Korean), Seoul: Samsung Economic Research Institute.

Nye, Joseph S. (1990), *Bound to lead. The changing nature of American power*, New York: Basic Books.

Nye, Joseph S. (2004), *Soft power. The means to success in world politics and understand international conflict*, New York: Public Affairs.

Seliger, Bernhard (2004), "The North Korean Economy: Nuclear crisis and decline, or peace and reform in the last Asian dynastic regime?," *Korea's Economy 2004*, Korea Economic Institute, 77-86.

Seliger, Bernhard (2005), The July 2002 reforms in North Korea – Liberman style reforms or road to transformation?, *North Korea Review*, 1, 22-37.

Seliger, Bernhard (2006a, November), *The European Union's policy toward North Korea after the twin missile and nuclear tests*, presentation at the conference "North Korean Nuclear Test: It`s Impact on North East Asian Political Order", Seoul ASEM Institute for International Relations, Seoul.

Seliger, Bernhard (2006b), "Income, Wealth and Political Power in an uneven Transformation Process – the Case of North Korea," *North Korea Review*, Vol. 2 (2) autumn.

Seliger, Bernhard (2007), Monetary and Exchange Rate Policy in Declining Centrally Planned Economies and in Early Transition Economies: Some Observations in North Korea, in: Korea Economic Institute Joint U.S.-Korea Academic Studies, 17, 111-137.

Seliger, Bernhard (2007, May 21), *The European Union and North Korea – more than "funding the bill"?*, paper for a conference of the Research Institute for International Affairs, Seoul.

9

Specific Structural Features and Future Development Perspectives of the South Korean Province of Gangwon

Peter Jurczek

When we take a closer look at the research area, the province of Gangwon is one of the less populated parts of the country. Regarding its population in 2007 (1.5 million), it belongs to the smallest administrative districts of South Korea. Within the province, there are also significant differences (fig. 1): In 2007, the most populated cities were the cities of Wonju (301,101), Chuncheon (260,439), Gangneung (222,100), Donghae (97,199), Sokcho (86,104), Samcheok (71,256) and Taebaek (51,697); followed by the districts of Hongcheon (70,929), Cheorwon (47,719), Pyeongchang (44,303), Jeongseon (42,084), Hoengseong (43,799), Yeongwol (40,505), Inje (32,317), Goseong (30,794), Yangyang (28,699), Hwacheon (23,107) and Yanggu (21,594).

Within two years the population decreased by 17,585 people (- 1.1%). However, there are significant differences inside the province (cf. table 1). The two biggest cities record an increasing population: Wonju by 19,076 people (+ 6.8%) and Chuncheon by 6,073 people (+ 2.4%). In contrast, most of the districts have a decreasing population, where those regions neighboring North Korea are particularly affected: Goseong (- 6.3%), Hwacheon (- 6.2%), Cheorwon (- 5.4%) und Yanggu (- 2.5%).

Table 8.1 Level and development of population in the cities and the districts in the South Korean Gangwon province (2005 – 2007)

city/district	inhabitants 2005	inhabitants 31.12.2007	Population development	
			absolute	%
Chuncheon	254,366	260,439	+6,073	+2.4
Gangneung	230,080	222,100	-7,980	-3.5
Sokcho	89,458	86,104	-3,354	-3.7
Donghae	102,032	97,199	-4,833	-4.7
Samcheok	75,941	71,256	-4,685	-6.2
Taebaek	54,043	51,697	2,346	-4.3
Wonju	282,025	301,101	+19,076	+6.8
Hoengseong	44,599	43,799	-800	-1.8
Cheorwon	50,450	47,719	-2,731	-5.4
Hwacheon	24,631	23,107	-1,524	-6.2
Yanggu	22,146	21,594	-552	-2.5
Goseong	32,868	30,794	-2,074	-6.3
Inje	32,188	32,317	+129	+0.4
Yangyang	29,744	28,699	-1,045	-3.5
Hongcheon	71,733	70,929	-804	-1.1
Pyeongchang	46,531	44,303	-2,228	-4.8
Jeongseon	46,362	42,084	-4,278	-9.2
Yeongwol	44,134	40,505	-3,629	-8.2
Total	**1,533,331**	**1,515,746**	**-17,585**	**-1.1**

Sources: Korea National Statistical Office (2005); Gangwon Development Research Institute (2007)

When looking more into detail at the administrative district Goseong in the far North of the province Gangwon, it becomes evident that it is one of the entities with the lowest number of inhabitants and with the highest loss of inhabitants.

Between 2005 and 2007 Goseong has lost 2,074 inhabitants, what marks an above-average decrease in population within the province. The district of Goseong consists of five populated municipalities. The largest is Geojin, which benefits from its coastal location (harbor function). It is followed by Toseong (tourism function) and Ganseong (district town). On a large scale, the district Goseong is situated peripherally and hence difficult to reach (there is no motorway). Additionally, it is mainly agricultural so that possibilities of further development – especially near the North Korean border – are exceedingly limited.

1. The Province of Gangwon and the Demilitarized Zone (DMZ)

The province Gangwon belongs to those regional entities that 'share' the longest border section with North Korea. Hence, this results in unfavorable factors for a positive development; particularly for those cities and districts close to the border. In equal measure, this means that the Demilitarized Zone (DMZ) has a very high significance, what will be considered in more detail in the following. The DMZ is about 250 kilometers long and about four kilometers wide. It hermetically seals off the "Republic of Korea" (South Korea) and the "Democratic People's Republic of Korea (DPRK)" (North Korea). However, recently, some relaxations concerning the border crossings of South Korean visitors can be observed. Here, either short-term tourists, who would like to visit the Geumgangsan, or day-trippers to the special economic zone Kaesong) are concerned. Despite these few tolerated by the DPR border crossings, which are primarily due to financial reasons, there is no concrete evidence for an eminent stronger rapprochement between South and North Korea. Nevertheless, there are numerous speculations on how a closer collaboration in the future may look like and on how a possible unification may take place.

Therefore, various factors on the informational (politics, economy, society, culture, etc) and the regional level have to be taken into consideration. The Demilitarized Zone (DMZ), which was developed in 1953, is especially significant. Since not long ago, anticipatory considerations are made concerning the probable or necessary development of the DMZ in the case of a liberalization of the border formalities or a possible reunification of Korea. A consensus consists in the fact that besides the political and the economic (including infrastructural) aspects, numerous basic functions of human life should play an important role. In this context, concepts like "peace" and "environment" are often attributed to the DMZ. This means that in the future corresponding utilizations within the inner Korean border strip might have a chance to be considered as development impulses. In addition to that, various activities of "formation" appear to be important to guarantee a broad acceptance within the population. Eventually, sections such as "regeneration" or "gusto" might play a role in providing offers of relaxation and wellness to modern citizens in the "free" DMZ.

1.1 The DMZ – an area of peace

Regarding the advancement of the DMZ, first several elementary considerations concerning its future functions have to be taken. In the case of the reunification of Korea or a liberalization of the border formalities, the DMZ should be regarded and communicated as a symbol of peace. This applies to the national level as well as to the international context. This means that the DMZ could be developed to be a nationwide centre of attraction in the country. National and international visitors should, at a given moment, be motivated to travel to the DMZ and its surroundings. This again means that the destination of symbolic importance, the DMZ, has to be interesting for diverse age groups, nationalities, etc. The last point regards a user friendly design both of the DMZ and the neighbouring regions.

It is basically important that spatial planning specialists determine carefully the land use within the DMZ and make sure that it endures. It is assumed that differently used parts will be outsourced from the actual border corridor. As far as it is known, the Korean Research Institute for Human Settlements (KRIHS) has done valuable preparatory work, which needs to be realized on a small scale (in cooperation with regional planning institutions). By all means, the DMZ should be designed as an area of contemplation and relaxation in order to avoid vociferous usage. Prohibiting intensive cultivation in general would be the most consequent way. A high significance gains the optimal organisation of large-scale travel connections and of a small-scale path and road network. The latter should, to a large extend, – besides some few mainlines – renounce transit traffic.

Instead, it is necessary to offer plenty of 'gentle' activities that honours the idea of peace and the accompanying cultural, religious, military, political and other references. This includes, for instance, cultural events like poet readings, representations in theatres, and concerts with a serious background. When the weather is nice, they could take place open air and might be a convenient reason for the construction of simple venues. Further, it can be taken into consideration whether larger leisure resorts might be installed in the surroundings of the DMZ – for example in the North of Seoul – in order to centre big cultural events at locations with good traffic connections.

Religiously motivated events may also contribute to render the DMZ more valuable. In this case again open air events are convenient, which could be offered by all confessions in appropriately declared areas. Such actions would, on the one hand, symbolize the commitment concerning a free development of the life in this country realized by the temples and the monks as well as by the Christians and other churches. On the other hand, this would be a valuable contribution to a peaceful co-existence of the citizens of all Korean parts. Eventually, it is also about the religiously motivated consciousness and the active practice of religion at this traditional place.

For the military forces, the DMZ may become a kind of "Mecca" to claim constant peace. Actions of various groups of interest who demonstrate a worldwide disarmament might be added. This regards firstly the accounting of the recent inner Korean past, which aims at an intensive exchange of ideas concerning military issues. Therefore, existing military installations respectively barracks in the near of the DMZ could be used but need to be rebuilt and modernized. In this way the participants of such events would see the DMZ as direct visualization for a long lasting territorial separation and for different stages of development. Furthermore, military forces of other nations could be animated to visit the inner Korean corridor and to inform themselves on security problems and on defence issues. Finally, world-widely discussed topics with military, defence or political focuses might be debated so that Korea might eventually play an important role concerning this issue. There may perhaps be the chance for Korea to gain a new image of being a nation of disarmament and peace.

The visits, speeches and meetings of politicians also play a significant role. This means that it is more about those at a national or an international level than about local or regional decision makers. Regional decision makers could use the DMZ as a location for enunciating their political contents. Last but not least, the DMZ provides a kind of obligatory destination for foreign politicians on Korean state visits.

Hence, for such visitors it seems to be necessary to provide high quality accommodations, which should be settled at a scenically attractive location at the margin of the DMZ. Alike, for other visitors, who desire to stay for some days in the environment of the DMZ, bed and breakfast places or holiday apartments need to be available. That means that, in the future, there will possibly be an increasing demand for hotels, guesthouses, and private rooms that needs to be satisfied shortly. However, it is necessary, in general, to establish the biggest part of the tourist infrastructure (e.g. accommodations, large leisure resorts) outside the DMZ. That means that "gentle" forms of tourism should generally be preferred ("eco-tourism").

1.2 The DMZ - an area of natural environment

The demand for peace leads to another core function of the DMZ, namely the broad conservation and the permanent care of its natural environment. This is the reason why the DMZ should be made accessible in a "gentle" way (via an environmentally sustainable road and path network) but it should not be covered with buildings; least of all with high-rise buildings or large connected estates. That means that a certain infrastructural development would be necessary but it needs to be based upon a restrictive plan of land use and it needs to protect the most parts. The aim of such measures is to offer a nice stay in the frame of short-term visits to the visitors probably arriving in great quantities. Further, infrastructural facilities (e.g. accommodations, leisure resorts) may be established in the surroundings of the DMZ but they should nevertheless respect the symbolism (peace, calm, contemplation, etc) by their architecture.

In the core area of the DMZ, the rare plants should be preserved carefully and protected permanently for future generations. To realize this, the establishment of several botanic gardens is desirable. Similarly, the endangered animals living there are to be protected and looked after by specialized rangers in the wild. Additionally, parks with endemic animals could be installed at some locations to make them accessible for visitors. In that way especially families and pensioners would find attractive destinations for their visits.

In view of the occurring and possibly endangered flora and fauna in the DMZ, the installation of a research institution specialized in the protection of species may be considered. If necessary, even numerous research institutions should be established at various locations in order to concentrate on different research focuses (flora, fauna, etc). This regards also the settlement of one (or more) climate research station(s) in the surroundings of the DMZ to realize weather forecasts and scientific investigations concerning the climate change. Thus, the installation of numerous research institutions would produce a higher degree of efficiency: options of specialization, task specific location choices, spreading the regional advantages across the whole environment of the DMZ.

Moreover, significant natural monuments are to be identified and central viewpoints – partly with rest areas – offering visitors the opportunity to have an overview on the natural monuments should be installed. This offers visitors, on the one hand, the opportunity to experience nature. On the other hand, they can be led to places where it seems to be reasonable from an environmental point of view. Furthermore, rest areas that are free from noise and which are inviting people to relax and to feel comfortable should be systematically created. In addition to that an elaborated road and path network – as already claimed as being a basic principle – reducing the visitor traffic in the core area of the DMZ to a minimum needs to be worked out. Hence, preferably promenades for pedestrians – with eco-friendly materials – should be built, but they must neither affect the landscape conservation areas nor the nature reserves. Beyond that it cannot be excluded that some asphalted roads for supply purposes will be constructed. These could possibly be used as bikeways. Any kind of traffic within the DMZ should be designed environmentally-friendly (e.g. through application of electric driven buses or narrow-gauge railways) so that the disturbance caused by noise or emissions is as low as possible.

Both functions, "peace" and "natural environment", are the most important ones in this state of consideration. However, other development factors are also playing a strong role in achieving a reasonable shaping of the DMZ and its surroundings. This, for instance, includes the following functions: "formation", "regeneration and gusto", "strategic infrastructural connection and sustainable business locations" (cf. Jurczek , 2008).

1.3 Concluding evaluation of the prospective development of the entire DMZ

On a long-term basis, the DMZ will probably keep its political, historical and social symbolism. That is why the particularities of its territory should, on the one hand, be preserved and designed creatively as far as possible. On the other hand, it is essential to integrate this zone in an optimal way into the whole development process of the eventually reunited country. According to its national and international importance, the DMZ should preferably be used in an extensive way. In doing so, 'soft' but vitally important location factors (on the basis of peace, environment, formation, regeneration and gusto) would obtain priority for the inner Korean border strip.

By implication, this means that the DMZ should remain free from 'hard' kinds of traffic or economic use so that its sustainability can be guaranteed. In the surroundings of the inner Korean corridor, the settlement of various institutions would be imaginable or alternatively necessary. They would have to accomplish different functions (e.g. habitation, traffic, economy, leisure). Concerning the regional economic use patterns, the following ideal order for economically used areas can be considered (starting from the DMZ): agriculture, quaternary institutions (e.g. research), tertiary institutions (e.g. tourism) and manufacturing plants (e.g. SME).

However, numerous expert opinions are duly needed in order to receive concrete evidence for a reasonable spatial order and a desirable spatial planning within the DMZ as well as objective-orientated suggestions concerning a sustainable cultivation of its surroundings. The required conceptions need to contain, among other things, the following functional sections:

- Population structure and development
- Settlement
- Economy (primary, secondary, tertiary sector as well as job market)
- Technical and social infrastructure
- Ecology/ environmental protection

Thereby, the following ideal proceeding can be considered: inventory, rating analysis, needs for action, development principles and objectives, planning measures, and development projects. Moreover, the activity-oriented insights should be described on different levels of scales. This means that the elaborated expert opinions would be required on a large scale as well as on a small scale.

Besides, a planned preparation of the future land use and the resulting cultivation/ building, the conception and realization of so-called immaterial measures would play an important role. This refers, for instance, to the realization of information evenings, to worked-out teaching materials as well as to the training and the assignment of specialized "DMZ pedagogues". Due to the prominently social significance of the aspired reunion of the country and with it the future abolition of the inner Korean border, a broad further education initiative would be very important.

The development of the DMZ and its surroundings would only be possible through coordinated commitments of numerous decision makers. This means responsible politicians, scientists, and entrepreneurs. Further representatives of other social groups (e.g. trade unionists, priests) need to be activated. Finally, it seems to be indispensable to assure serious interest and disproportionately high commitment of the citizens for this unique national event.

Last but not least, in the case of necessary short-term development measures it needs to be ascertained that they might be financed ad hoc. That is why it is suggested to raise a kind of a reunion fund – amongst others with special focus on the DMZ (including donations) – in order to be prepared on time for necessary higher-than-average government purchases. Equally, it duly should be thought about which administrative level (nation state, provinces or municipality) takes on which tasks and which disbursements in the case of a reunited Korea. The most efficient way would be the division of the labour between representatives that would, according to the respective issue as regards content or space, require the application of national, regional and communal financial means.

2. Potential for Tourism in the Province Gangwon with Simultaneous consideration of the District Goseong

The district of Gangwon, situated in the northeast of the province of Goseong, is characterized by a multifaceted tourism structure. The spatial closeness of mountains and the East Sea coast is unique. Concerning the range of accommodation facilities, the so-called Condominiums, which can be characterized by distinctive hotels in the style of a multi-storey building, dominate. They are mostly located in an attractive landscape and, as a rule, have more than 100 guest rooms.

Furthermore, several trips are recommended and information about the regional gastronomy is given. In contrast, information concerning direct marketing (e.g. of fish or wine) is missing. Additionally, it seems necessary to further differentiate the leisure activities, as well as extend these offers (e.g. Golfing, sailing in the summer, skating in the winter [amongst others on flooded paddy fields]). There are already considerations on extended tourism offers among those responsible for the district. These new offers could be realized with the help of external investors.

The introduction of the Thalasso therapy is a new way to support spa tourism. It is a branch of medicine that deals with the therapeutic climate effects of sea air and of bathes in sea water as well as the therapeutic use of sea salt. In November 2006, a respective class, which is attended by almost 100 people, was launched at Kyungdong University. Sincethere is a course of studies called "Tourism" at this university, the cooperation with tourism practitioners should be continued at a high level and intensified for mutual benefit.

2.1 *Proposals for the intensification and further qualification of tourism in the district of Goseong*

In general, the district of Goseong has a remarkable potential for tourism. The existence of mountains and a coastline next to each other appears to be especially attractive. Therefore, the natural spatial resources of this region are qualified for a further development of alpine tourism as well as for an extension of bathing tourism. In the long term, a combination of both main focuses would be the best choice. The tourism of the cultural commemoration plays another noteworthy role. Organized tours to North Korea, visits of historically interesting memorial places (e. g. Unification Observatory, History security museum) etc.

belong to this type of tourism. At present, the regional economic importance of tourism in the district of Goseong is above the national average. However, there is the question of how the demand for tourism will develop in the future. In this regard, the following points should be taken into consideration:

On the basis of stable political and economic circumstances, the number of Koreans that spend their main holiday abroad could rise continuously. This, in all probability, will be accompanied by a constantly rising number of domestic multi-holidaymakers – while the average length of stay is waning. This leads to the conclusion that the district of Goseong on the one hand may lose Koreans on their primary holidays but, on the other hand, may gain domestic multi-holidaymakers. The tourism of cultural commemoration will initially keep its relatively high level. In the long term, however, the comparatively large number of people involved will rather stagnate - probably for the benefit of business travellers from and to North Korea (see corresponding experiences in Germany or Finland).

In the following, some important strengths of tourism that significantly increased the number of foreign travellers in the district of Goseong are listed:

- There is the impression that Korean managers are good organizers which has a positive effect on the problem-free transport of travellers. This equally concerns the air traffic, train and bus service or other means of transport (underground, taxi etc.).
- The air fares seem to be affordable and may be even more reasonable for package holiday providers; e.g. a good value flight for individual travellers from Europe to Incheon and return costs scarcely more than 600 Euro. The connecting flight to Yangyang in the district of Goseong costs about 50 Euro.
- This means that a one-week holiday package in the district of Goseong - including flight, accommodation (in a double room), transfer to and from the hotel - for a European costs scarcely more than about 1,000 Euro.
- In the district of Goseong, there are efforts to offer a differentiated and interesting programme for stays (see chapter 3).
- Number and variety of the local tourist offers are impressing.
- This also includes some highlights (e.g. hiking in Seoraksan, diving in the East Sea, Sushi or wine production).
- Not least, there are several well-equipped accommodation facilities (Condominions) and most of them satisfy international standards.
- Finally, the decision makers in the district of Goseong endeavor to further develop tourism and increase the resulting economic power (see Goseong-gun).

In contrast to this, there are still existing weaknesses that hinder the further development of tourism that cannot be overlooked. The following deficits are examples for them:

- The transport connection is in need of improvement including an extension of the airport Yangyang (definitive internationalization)
- Low differentiated range of accommodation facilities (dominance of Condominiums) and therefore, lack of small and medium-sized tourist accommodations
- Little commitment by international and regional tourism providers
- Partially insufficient quality or care of public and private tourism infrastructure
- No complete professional tourism marketing (e. g. insufficient knowledge of the English language) which, for example, do not meet with the specific culture of foreign travellers from different continents
- Limited range of gastronomy and retail trade, above all concerning foreign guests (e.g. European or American breakfast, foreign meals)
- Little tourism events that are also suitable for foreign guests
- Deterring security fences and military facilities along the coast which obstruct an unlimited bathing and spa tourism

In this case as well, it depends on a concrete planned tourism project to specifically plan and implement suitable measures. Nevertheless, it seems to be indispensable that the identified weaknesses concerning the tourism in the district of Goseong are soon to be eliminated completely. Only then, one can assume that the tourism in the research area - here examined with regard to the stay of foreigners - will obtain considerable significance. In the process, the preservation of natural and cultural resources should be persistently pursued since only their soundness will guarantee a successful future development of the region's tourism in the long term.

2.2 Establishment of a tourist "Romantic Road"

In order to give tourism further stimulus in the district of Goseong, additional marketing activities seem to be necessary to optimally bring the regional offers to the market. In several German tourist regions, this is achieved by the establishment of tourist routes. One of the best-known is the "Romantic Route" that runs from Würzburg (in the North) to Füssen (in the South). Along this tourist route there are several tourist places (e.g. Rothenburg ob der Tauber, Dinkelsbühl, Schwangau, Füssen) mostly with medieval characteristics and often with important sights (e.g. Castle Neuschwanstein). Taking into account the number of guests, these tourist places are not situated in one of the largest German tourist regions, but nevertheless, they are well known, especially abroad. In the past, most of visitors came from the USA. In the last years, Japanese tourists form the largest group of visitors that come to the region as part of their generally short stay in Europe.

Concerning the organisation of joint tourism activities, 26 municipalities coop erate in the "Tourist working group Romantic Route" (see: www.romanticroad.d e). They operate their own office in Dinkelsbühl and contribute to the tourism m arketing of their member-municipalities, to the local tourist businesses and the a ssociated tourist associations. Their work includes the publishing of several broc hures (partly in Korean), the attendance at special fairs etc. In spite of their own tasks, this working group primarily is a complementary institution that supports t he tourist measures of their member-municipalities through joint actions and that bundles activities - especially at a supra-regional level.

Additionally, there is a tourist association "Romantic Franconia" that includes the central part of the "Romantic Route" (www.romantisches-franken.de): several small towns with medieval character, the periphery of the "Franconian Lake District", the city of Ansbach (Head office of the administrative district Central Franconia) and its surroundings as well as the western neighboring municipalities of the city of Nuremberg. This tourist region in western Bavaria is largely rurally structured and is less known on the supra-regional level. It is managed by its own tourist association which is based in the market town of Colmberg (Jurczek, 1989). Regional tourist associations in Germany are financed by contributions of their members (municipalities, accommodation businesses, individuals etc.). They are oriented towards the objectives of the respective higher-ranking tourist association. In the case of "Romantic Franconia" the higher-ranking tourist association is the "Tourist Association Franconia e. V." settled in Nuremberg (www.frankentourismus.de). In this context, it has to be mentioned that in the federally organized Germany, the respective Federal State is responsible for the development and implementation of the political guidelines concerning tourism development. That means that tourism development in "Franconia" or "Romantic Franconia" is integrated in the superordinate tourism goals of the Federal State of Bavaria.

With regard to the district of Goseong, the following considerations evolve: Due to positive experiences in Germany and other states, a "Romantic Route" along the coast of the East Sea – with turn-off roads into the mountains – might be established in order to further develop tourism. The route should initially run from the Unification Observatory to the city of Yangyang or the city of Gangneung. In case of success, it should be continued towards Busan (in the South) and - across the present border - towards Wonsan (in the North). The underlying "romanticism" features several facets that are incomparable to the German situation. It concerns above all naturally and culturally spatial sights along the coast, in the mountains, at lakes as well as at historical, religious and other locations.

In order to meet the objectives that are connected with the establishment of a "Romantic Route", the following measures have to be implemented:

- Establishment of a working group "Romantic Route" at the East Sea (under the leadership of the district of Goseong and the participation of its municipalities, the city of Sokcho, the districts of Yangyang and its municipalities and, if applicable, the city of Gangneung, larger accommodation and gastronomic businesses and other tourism facilities)
- Acquisition of governmental funds for start-up financing
- Establishment of a tourist office "Romantic Route" in Ganseong, personnel and material equipment
- Defining the route of the holiday route while considering important tourism destinations (e.g. towards Seoraksan National Park)
- Multilingual signposts along the tourist route (Korean, Chinese, Japanese, English)
- Establishment of viewpoints, memorials, resting places etc. (in cooperation with the administrations of the districts/municipalities and local tourist offices)
- Creation of advertisement leaflets (in cooperation with the local tourist offices)
- Acquisition of further association members (e.g. public transport services) and acceptance inside the tourist region
- Realization of specific advertisement measures at national and international tourism fairs

It seems to be important that the working group "Romantic Route" at the East Sea supports bundles and contributes to the local tourism. Above all, the professional competence of the Kyungdong University (Department of Tourism) should be included in the process. This concerns the conduction of surveys by their tourism researchers as well as the employment of student apprentices and alumni of the course of studies "Tourism". To professionally and practically accompany the realization of the Korean project "Romantic Route", the "Gangwon Development Research Institute" would be a competent partner.

2.3 Perspective of the tourism in the future

The future significance of tourism in the district of Goseong largely depends on the future political and economic development, both at the national and the international level. Considering the future evaluation of this, three different courses of development can be formulated with the help of the so-called scenario method:

One speaks of a *linear process scenario* if no considerable chances occur. That means that the political situation will generally remain stable. Consequently, this would not include the unification of Korea. But a more liberal politics towards the neighbour could guarantee or further develop the ability of South Korean travelling groups to visit North Korea. The tourism in the district of Goseong would profit again because it has one of the most important national border check-points on its territory. Additionally, one could canvass travellers to North Korea to lengthen their stay in the South Korean border region (e.g. at the sea, in the mountains).

The economic situation in this scenario has to be stable as well. This means that the economic trend in the Republic of Korea would slightly rise or at least remain unchanged so that the wealth of its population will tend to increase. Thereby, again, favourable pre-conditions for travelling would exist, whereas the district of Goseong as a renowned national tourist destination might have advantages: during the main holidays, at weekends and holidays as well as for day trips and sightseeing tours.

In contrast to this, the *negative scenario* is based on an unfavourable political and/or economic development, while the respective degree of development is important. Concerning the political situation, this would include an intensification of conflicts in the East Asian region or the deterioration of the relationship with North Korea. The latter could have a negative impact on the tourism in the district of Goseong since cross-border travelling would then be limited or even restricted. Furthermore, the precautionary military measures in such a case would probably reach a dimension that could heavily obstruct holiday tourism and day trips in this region.

An unfavourable economic development might also negatively affect tourism. This could have global as well as national causes. One expected result of this would be a lower living standard. This might minimize - at least temporarily - the amount, length, etc. of national and international travels. The district of Goseong would be affected by the decreasing number of short-stay and long-stay tourists as well as by that of day-trippers. In this context, the tourism economy (e.g. accommodation businesses, gastronomy, public transport) and some complementary sectors (e.g. regional spare-time facilities, local retail trade) will presumably suffer from losses.

The *positive scenario* is based on a harmonic political and prosperous economic development. In the political context, an advancing liberalization of the neighbour relations is desirable for the Republic of Korea. The unification of the country would represent an absolute climax of the national development although it might cause new challenges (e.g. above average amount of investments to develop the infrastructure, especially in the northern part of a unified Korea). As regards tourism in the district of Goseong, a temporary boom could be expected. This would result from increasing tourist activities in the border region to North Korea that would involve North Koreans, South Koreans and foreigners. Similar to the German situation after the unification, the disproportionate rise of the number of guests would settle down after a few years.

If the positive scenario would be primarily based on a prosperous economic development, tourism could also gain more importance – not least due to the increasing yearly and weekly spare time of the Koreans. In this context, the (South-) Korean travel intensity abroad would grow initially. The national tourism, however, may equally profit since the number of multi-travellers and day-trippers will presumably rise. The district of Goseong, again, will definitely profit from this because it is, above all, suitable as a destination for short-stay travellers - a long-term trend in tourism. Additionally, further target groups (e.g. participants of conferences, businessmen, sportsmen, bathing tourists, recreation seeking guests, groups of tourists, foreigners) should be taken into consideration in order to guarantee a sustainable diversification of new offers for tourism.

3. Conclusion

As seen in the essay above, the province Gangwon is characterized by numerous problems. These are primarily due to the hermetically sealed border to North Korea. Because of this, there are more unfavourable preconditions for a positive future development in comparison to other provinces of Korea. In the future, tourism would play a more and more significant role for the research area. As the natural potential (sea and mountains) and the leisure infrastructure are advantageous, tourism could become an important economic and ecologic factor. Not least, the diversity of tourism might provide a valuable contribution for the intensification of these utilizations. However, tourism should not be overestimated in its effects on the regional economy. Nevertheless, recent activities in the fields of leisure and tourism restore hopes for the province Gangwon to develop into a renowned region for such uses in the years to come.

In this context, it will be the task of the province government and administration to reduce the disadvantages caused by the border proximity as well as to strongly promote those activities with promising success. In addition to that, the cities and the municipalities are asked to show commitment on the local level. Moreover, other institutions appear to have great importance to systematically support the national and local efforts. This includes for instance enterprises and economic associations as well as cultural, nature conservation associations etc. that might assist to shape positively the living conditions of the locals by a maximum of cooperation.

Last but not least, there are the educational institutions in the broadest sense that have to give new and innovative impulses. The more and more is spoken of a tendency to a knowledge-based society and this implies an optimal education and training in all parts of the country. This means that even a rather rural region such as the province Gangwon should further upgrade its offers for education. After all, there are already numerous universities that induce the aspired endogenous potential of knowledge, creativity and flexibility. These educational institutions should foster close contacts with foreign partners (e.g. from Japan, China, the USA or Germany), in order to get to know more of the international standards, which may be helpful for solving domestic problems.

References

Jurczek, Peter (2007). Economic and ecological aspects of the touristic development in the border region of Korea; In B. Seliger (ed.), *Sustainable economic and environmental development in the inner-Korean border area*, (pp. 118-135). Chuncheon.

Jurczek, Peter (2008). Meaning of DMZ as a Peace and Ecological Zone. In Gangwon Development Research Institute (Ed.), Peace and Stability in Northeast Asia and DMZ = Korea DMZ Peace Forum 2008 (Proceedings) (pp. 135-151 (in English) and p. 152-163 (in Korean), Chuncheon.

Jurczek, Peter. Challenges of land-use planning and development strategies of tourism in the Northeast of the Republic of Korea. In Quaestiones Geographicae, Poznan (in printing).

10

Building Up North Korean Foreign Trade Institutions from the Scratch: Lessons from New EU States and the Role of Capacity Building

Ralph M. Wrobel

1. Introduction

North Korea seems to be characterized as a closed society with only a minimum of political and economic relations to foreign countries. In the centre of the ideological underpinnings of the regime are the Juche ideology and system. Early on Juche ideology has been shifted to the economic sphere, meaning the development of a self-reliant economy. In this way the country is among the most isolated and poor countries in the world with limited global trade. But since the beginning of foreign aid in the mid-1990s capacity building as well as a careful opening process are on agenda in North Korea. (on the reform process see e.g. Wrobel, 2007a) While the level of North Korea's merchandise trade is still low, the volume increases. Especially the trade volume with China grew obviously in the last years.

But while the North Korean merchandize trade increases foreign trade institutions are in the early stages of development. For instance, North Korea is no member of the World Trade Organisation. The country is not associated to ASEAN or ASEAN plus 3. In contrast foreign trade is limited at most to imports and exports to respective from the Special Economic Zones like Kaesong Industrial Complex and to a partly illegal trade with China. Because the country has been closed to the knowledge transfer for almost sixty years only limited information about the functioning of a market economy as well as international trade exist. When the author himself participated in the DPRK Capacity Building Project of the German Hanns Seidel Foundation he taught basics of the theory and praxis of international trade. It has been necessary to inform the public – managers of state owned firms as well as scientists from Kim Il-Sung University in Pyongyang –about basic theorems of economic foreign trade theory as well as about advantages and the process of economic integration. Additionally, there exists an obvious gap between the will of participants of capacity building seminars to learn and the limitation of learning by supervising state agencies. For instance, while it was possible to talk about European integration and China's WTO membership in Pyongyang it was not allowed to adapt this knowledge to North Korea. Of course, in this way the understanding of market rules remains poor in North Korea and capacity building will be a long and difficult procedure. (See also Wrobel, 2007b)

In this paper the current status of foreign trade institutions in North Korea will be compared with the situation in Central and Eastern European states (CEES) in the first beginning of their transformation processes. Experiences of the former centrally-planned economies in this region can be imagined as a fairly accurate blueprint of what should happen in North Korea, too. Therefore this paper starts with an analysis of the current status of North Korean ideological underpinning of foreign economic relations, the countries foreign trade structure as well as the countries foreign trade institutions, especially according to the Special Economic Zones. Then recommendations for North Korea to build up foreign trade institutions supporting the reform process will be made by using the experiences from Central and Eastern Europe. As one can imagine North Korea is far away from a transformation process to a market economy but first steps are done and the country's development is worth to be supported.

2. North Korea and its International Trade

2.1 The Ideological Underpinning of the North Korean Self-Reliance

Basically the North Korean society and especially economy is organized along lines similar to all other socialist states. Additionally, in the centre of the ideological underpinnings of the regime are the Juche ideology and system. Literally "Juche" means "subject," meaning the subject thinking and acting to master the world. (Seliger, 2004a, p. 78) Together with its twin notion of "chajusong"(self-determination) Juche does mean a collective movement under the firm guidance of the Worker's Party and a strong leader ("suryong"), Kim Il-sung respective his son, Kim Jong-Il. (Pan, 1992, p. 73)

The concept of Juche first emerged in the mid of the 1950th and was used to justify extremely high levels of central command and autarky in the economic system. As the historical experience of the Soviet Union–especially in the Stalin era–has shown in this way the use of central determined economic targets and the ideological mobilisation of the labour force are possible. A high level of collectivisation of agriculture was an additional result of the Juche approach. Later Juche allowed Kim Il-sung to move away from the Soviet model in some important respects, for instance defending his essentially Stalinist methods of command in the economy at a time when Khrushchev was moving in new directions within the Soviet Union itself. (McKay, 2005, p. 88) Later, in the 1960s, Juche has been interpreted as the guiding through for military self-defence and as the principle of political independence. In 1970, Juche was introduced as the Worker's Party's guiding principle together with Marxism-Leninism, and two years later it became the leading guideline in the new communist constitution of the DPRK. (Seliger, 2004a, p. 78-79) In this way the first problem of building up a trade infrastructure in North Korea is to make changes in the Juche ideology. But this may be dangerous for the regime in Pyongyang because to avert fast from its own ideology may abolish the base of the regimes power. Only permanent capacity building activities to embrace learning in North Korea will help to change this.

2.2 The Structure of North Korean Trade

North Korea is among the most isolated and poor countries in the world with limited global trade. But although North Korea remains one of the world's autarkic countries in terms of merchandise trade, the country's exposure to the outside world is considerably higher when foreign aid or unconventional transactions are considered. From a balance of payments standpoint in recent years North Korea derived approximately one third of its revenues from foreign aid, one third from conventional exports, and one third from unconventional sources. (Noland, 2006, p. 36) First of all, foreign aid to North Korea comes from the South. The South Korean government's support to North Korea began with 150,000 tons of rice in 1995. It continued with the provision of fertilizers in 1999 as well as the launch of rice aid in 2000. Support was provided on a regular basis including direct support at the government level and support directed through international organisations such as the World Food Programme and World Health Organisation. From 1995 to 2006 total aid from South Korea to the North accounts for USD 15.52 billion. (Ministry of Unification, 2006a) But also the United States supported North Korea from 1995 to 2002 with foodstuff accounting for more than 1 billion USD. (Frank, 2005, p. 245)

The development of the North Korean merchandise trade is also interesting to observe. While the level is still low, the volume of North Korea's merchandise trade increases. For instance in 2005, North Korea's foreign trade volume is estimated to surpass 3 billion USD, compared to 2.860 billion USD in 2004. (Ministry of Unification, 2006a) Especially the trade volume with China increased. In 2005, the bilateral trade with China accounted for 39% of the total North Korean international trade. (Aden, 2006, p. 2) According to the energy sector North Korea dependents mainly on China which reportedly supplies about 70% of North Korea's fuel. (Chanlett-Avery/Squassoni, 2006, p. 5) Also inter-Korean trade has recorded an average annual 20% growth rate, increasing from USD 425.15 million in 2000 to more than USD 1 billion in 2005. The export from South Korea to the North increased by an annual rate of 21.3 % on the average while the import to the South grew by an average annual rate of 17.4 %. The increases in trade are largely attributable to the development of the Kaesong Industrial Complex, because the ratio of trade related to this complex to the entire inter-Korean trade grew from zero in 2000 to 16.7 % in 2005. (Ministry of Unification, 2006b) In 2005 inter-Korean trade surpassed $ 1 Billion and accounts for one fifth of North Korea's overall trade volume. (Lee, 2005, p. 175 Choe 2006, p. 28) In contrast, already since 2001 North Korean trade with Japan has been significantly curtailed due to worsening bilateral relations. (Choi/Lee, 2006, p. 27) Only remittances mostly come from a community of ethnic Koreans living in Japan and increasingly from refugees in China, who may account for 100,000. (Noland, 2006, p. 36)

The main unconventional source of foreign revenues comes from the military-party complex which dominates the entire system in North Korea. It is usual in communist states for the workers party to be the central focus, with the military also playing a key role. But in North Korea the armed forces are even more influential than in any other socialist state in recent history. In recent years the central role of the military has been articulated even more clearly as the "military-first" policy, in Korean called "Songun." Songun has now emerged as the dominant feature of the regime. (McKay, 2005, pp. 87-88) It must be emphasized that the military complex in North Korea includes a parallel military economy outside the central plan. The military maintains a completely integrated economic system, including farms and mines up to facilities to manufacture uniforms and weapons, with separate administrative structures, including foreign trade firms. This military complex has privileged access to technology and imports. So 95 % of weaponry is produced domestically, and much of what is produced is exported. (Noland, 1997, p. 34) Some analysts have estimated that North Korea earned USD 50 billion to 100 billion a year in the last years from the export of missiles to countries including Pakistan, Libya or Iran. (Jeffries, 2006, p. 413)

2.3 North Korean Trade Institutions and Special Economic Zones

The official North Korean foreign trade is concentrated in the Special Economic Zones. In these zones the rules of Juche and self –reliance are out of work. But it is questionable if these zones can be estimated as success at all. North Korea's first steps to implement Special Economic Zones in the country go back to 1984 when North Korea introduced a Joint Venture law apparently modelled on China's to attract Western capital. (Noland, 1997, p. 47) Most partners of estimated fifty joint ventures in the 1980s have been pro-North Korean businessmen from Japan (all members of the Chongryun organisation representing Korean residents in Japan). (Jeffries, 2006, p. 426) However, remarkable increases in inward foreign direct investment as well as in foreign trade did not realize. Until 1990, there were less than 135 cases in which foreign capital has been invested in North Korea. (Nam, 2005, p. 199) In the early 1990s, when the breakdown of the socialist bloc led to economic difficulties in North Korea, attempts to attract FDIs were strengthened. Already in 1990 a first "Special Economic Zone" (SEZ) has been established, three more in the beginning of the new century. They are to some extent, modelled after the Chinese system. Kim Jong-Il himself visited China various times and reportedly was impressed by the economic development observed. (Seliger, 2003, p. 263)

In 1990, North Korea established a first SEZ in the Rajin-Sonbong area in the so called Golden Triangle between Korea, China and Russia. The proximity to China and Japan, the rich endowment with seafood and the ice-free harbour are main natural advantages of this area. (Nam, 2005, p. 200) Favourable economic conditions like tax incentives, a guaranty for profit repatriation and the custom-free import and export of raw materials, intermediate products as well as products related to the industrial production of the SEZ were also among the features of Rajin-Sonbong. (Seliger, 2006a, p. 98) On paper, these conditions have been better than those in the Chinese or Vietnamese SEZs. (Noland, 1997, p. 47) Since then joint ventures as well as wholly-owned foreign enterprises from different countries in the sectors of telecommunications, transportation, tourism and fisheries have been established. Until 1999 about 150 companies–mostly from China–shall have opened offices or factories in Rajin-Sonbong. (Jeffries,

2006, p. 431) However, no lasting development took place. (Seliger, 2006a, p. 98)

Although there have been some improvements in the physical infrastructure, its serious bottleneck, the lack of an interregional and international transport network, has been reduced rather slowly. Additionally the original plan did not adequately consider the competition with the neighbouring SEZs like Hunchun in China or Vladivostok in Russia as potential location for foreign firms. (Nam, 2005, pp. 203-205) Nowadays Rajin-Sonbong (now called "Rason") is a directly governed city which future seems to be limited because a lack of infrastructure, the peripheral position and a lack of both transparency as well as economic freedom hinders the development of investment. (Jeffries, 2006, p. 429)

In summer 2002, North Korea announced the opening of an additional SEZ at the Yalu River in Sinuiju opposite the Chinese town of Dandong. Both cities are linked through bridges and a railway line. Main industries in Sinuiju, a town with 400.000 inhabitants, are chemicals, metal, and food processing industries. Like in Hong Kong, the plan was for a fifty year special basic law, which among other things allowed private property of means of production, a separate monetary and customs system, an autonomous budget and unrestricted capital movements (Seliger, 2004b, p. 74). By these regulations especially the inflow of hard currency from China to North Korea was intended. Unfortunately China was not previously informed about the North Korean plans of establishing a SEZ in Sinuiju, which would compete intensively with the Chinese SEZ in Dandong. Thus China took revenge and Pyongyang's chosen governor of the Sinuiju SEZ, the Chinese-Dutch entrepreneur Yang Bin, has been jailed in because of tax fraud in November 2002. (Hale, 2005, p. 839) Obviously, China has been striking back successfully. After Yang Bins imprisonment there has been no more progress in the establishment of the Sinuiju SEZ. (Seliger, 2006a, p. 100)

Nowadays the attention shifted to two new projects in the South of North Korea, the Geumgangsan Mountains and the SEZ in Kaesong, a city closed to Seoul, only a few kilometres from the inner-Korean border. Both projects have to be distinguished from the two earlier SEZs. While the Rajin–Sonbong SEZ is a trade-oriented centre that includes China, Russia, and Japan and Sinuiju SEZ has focused on the trade-oriented function in order to cooperate with countries in the Yellow Sea rim area, including China, Kaesong is envisaged as a production-centred SEZ, to attract small and medium-sized South Korean enterprises, as well as the Mt. Geumgang project focuses on tourism. (Kim, 2007, p. 7)

Already in the preparatory stage of the 2000 North–South–Korean Summit of Kim Dae-Jung and Kim Jong-Il a long-term cooperation of North Korea with the South-Korean Hyundai Conglomerate began. The showcase of this cooperation was the opening of the Geumgang Mountains and the shipping line to these mountains dear to Koreans on both sides of the border. In 2002 a "Special Tourism Zone" has been established in this area. Hyundai were given exclusive rights in this zone for the next thirty years. (Jeffries, 2006, p. 432) After initial hype wore off, the interest in the Geumgang Mountains tourism slowed down in the South, due to a combination of high prices, the complicated transportation logistics by ship from a remote South Korean harbour, the near-military rules for tourists, who could only travel in large groups along with a route surrounded by barbed wire. The opening of a land-based route in 2003 and bus trips considerably have lowered the costs. (Seliger, 2006a, pp. 99-101) Therefore the number of visitors to Geumgang Mountains exceeded 300,000 in 2005. (Cho, 2006, p. 28)

In contrast, the Kaesong Industrial Complex is the first major economic project undertaken jointly by the two Korean governments. During a three years preparation period, the North and South Korean governments worked on ensuring free passage across the demilitarized zone, and on establishing tax, accounting, banking, and labour laws to be applied to the Kaesong Industrial Complex (KIC). Although Kaesong is geographically located in North Korea, general North Korean laws do not apply. Instead, the KIC is governed by a special set of laws, since it was officially inaugurated in June 2003. As one can imagine, the KIC is the centrepiece of North–South economic cooperation. At present, roughly several dozen South Korean enterprises operate in the Kaesong Industrial Complex, with a total of 6,000 North Korean workers. It is planned to carry out the complex in three stages over 10 years, starting in 2003 and ending in 2012. The first stage shall be currently well under way and is expected to be completed by 2007. (Kim, 2007, p. 9) Relative to the income tax of 14 percent in case of general business and 10 percent in case of the sphere of encouragement (e.g. light industry or ultramodern science) as well as relative to the closed position to the South Korean border the Kaesong Industrial Complex offers a favourable investment environment for South Korean enterprises. (Korea Today, 2006, p. 38) Power and telephone service are supplied by South Korea. In 2005 already nearly 2,000 North Koreans and several hundred South Koreans are employed in the KIC. (Jeffries, 2006, p. 445) Hopes for Kaesong are high in South Korea. This SEZ seems to be the most direct parallel to the Chinese model of economic development as it began in Shenzen or other SEZs. But the parallel to China could be misleading, because the scale of production in Kaesong is minuscule, and if it grows at the current pace, no real change in North Korea's industrial output can be expected from it. (Seliger, 2006b, p. 66)

Other steps to open North Korea and establish foreign trade institutions, taken since 2004, include the revision of different laws and regulations, including those regarding joint ventures, foreign business concerns as well as foreign exchange management. Additionally, North Korea concluded an agreement on the encouragement and protection of investment with China in March 2005. (Bae, 2007, p. 47) In this way North Korea develops its formal foreign trade and foreign investment institutions. But North Korea is still far away from integration into world trade. How North Korea could learn from the experiences in Central and Eastern Europe will be analysed in the next chapters of this essay.

3. Recommendations for North Korea Building up Foreign Trade Institutions

North Korea is far away from becoming a market economy at all. But it can make steps forward to integrate into world trade. As the Central and Eastern European example has shown an absolute change of the political regime is a necessary precondition for the initialization of a real transformation process. The former communist regimes in Central and Eastern Europe became democracies in the beginning 1990s and replaced the leading political class. In contrast, the main restriction for the process of opening and capacity building in North Korea remains the fear of the regime of the inflow of information, which cannot be controlled by the state. Daily exchanges of North Korean merchants with foreigners are still seen as a threat to regime survival. However, a gradual reform of the trade regime may be initialized by the communist regime in Pyongyang, too, bringing the country step by step nearer to a market economy.

Anyway, from an institutional and political-economy point of view the building up of foreign trade institutions needs to be undertaken step by step in order to take advantage of an international and particularly an inter-Korean division of labour. A gradual integration process into world trade will avoid excessive demands on the political capabilities, the economic capacity, and the ideological receptivity of the North Korean political-economic system. Additionally, a gradual integration process will not avoid the financial capacity of South Korea which is needed to support and manage the integration process in the North. (Ahrens, 2003, p. 55) This gradual process may be divided into four or five steps:

A first step in the right direction is the current North–South economic cooperation on the Korean peninsula. This cooperation can be compared with the cooperation of the European Union with the transformation states in Central and Eastern Europe in the first beginning. The accession of the eight Central and Eastern European countries to the European Union in 2004 brought some important benefits to these countries. The new members gain from reduced barriers to trade and investment. Financial aid has been paid and will be paid in the future from the structural funds. In this way the process of Eastern Enlargement of the EU can be seen as a very successful example for the integration of less developed, former socialist economies into a trade block as well as into world trade. But the new member states from Central and Eastern Europe had a long way to travel. They lacked the established political, economic and legal structures that would allow them rapidly to join the Union. It was therefore clear that the accession process would take time, although EU leaders began sending positive political signals encouraging their membership shortly after the Berlin Wall fell in 1989. But helping the candidates move to a market economy and a stable pluralist democracy were the first priorities. (Tupy, 2003, p. 1) Additionally as early as June 1993, a summit of EU leaders set a list of criteria for the newcomers to meet. By the time they join, new members had to have stable institutions guaranteeing democracy, the rule of law, human rights and the protection of minorities, a functioning market economy that can cope with competitive pressures and market forces within the Union and the ability to take on the obligations of membership, including support to the aims of the Union. The new members had to have a public administration capable of applying and managing EU laws in practice. These criteria have been called the Copenhagen criteria. (Wrobel, 2000, p. 225 - 228)

However, also the North–South Korean cooperation can be seen as an accession process like in Europe. Equally this cooperation on the Korean peninsula will not only improve the knowledge of the functioning of a market economy in the North at all but it will also help to build up trade institutions from the scratch in North Korea. The existence of the special economic zones of Kaesong Industrial Complex, Geumgang Mountains and the new inter-Korean projects discussed for Haeju and other places will help to improve formal as well as informal (foreign) trade institutions in North Korea. They will implement a process of learning in the country. And in this way a permanent process of capacity building will take place. Maybe during this process also the North Korean underpinning of the current economic system, the Juche approach, can change step by step. (Wrobel, 2007, p. 490) But there exists a clear institutional lack in the cooperation process on the Korean peninsula. While the European Union demanded the fulfilling of clear defined criteria, South Korea supplies its support to the North without counter performance. It would be useful for both sides to make clear that economic as well as political support from South Korea to the North is dependent from the compliance of criteria and rules.

A second step for the implementation of foreign trade infrastructure may be a shift from project-style cooperation between North and South Korea to establishing a free trade area or ever deeper forms of trade integration on the Korean peninsula, including free investment in the whole country. Likewise the accession to the EU of a number of Central and Eastern European states began in the beginning of the 1990s by a Trade and Economic Cooperation Agreement. They have been replaced by Free Trade Agreements, which came in force mainly in 1995. By additional Europe Agreements an association between the EU and the Central and Eastern European countries has been established since 1998. In the following time between the EU and the CEES negotiations on the actual terms of accession began. The negotiations had been made possible by the willingness of the CEES to adhere to the principles respected in the EU and to accept the *acquis communautaire* and implement it from the moment of accession. (Wrobel, 2000, pp. 225–228) Then, on May 1, 2004, the Accession Treaty for the accession of the 10 candidate countries to the European Union came into force.

Such a rapid movement toward free trade and investment like in Europe will not be politically as well as economically feasible in the short term on the Korean peninsula. Nowadays competition from abroad and hence the introduction of world market prices could accelerate the he potential collapse of the domestic economy. Therefore North Korea's external opening has to be accompanied by internal reforms and safeguarded by international financial assistance (Ahrens 2003, p. 58). Additionally, it must be recognized that each type of economic integration on the Korean peninsula reduces South Korea's possibilities to integrate itself into an East Asian trade community like ASEAN plus 3 or to sign free trade agreements with other countries. (Kim 2007)

A third step may be a WTO observer status as well as preparations for a full WTO membership. Nowadays the most nations worldwide are members of the World Trade Organisation. Because WTO membership has been a precondition for accession to the European Union, all associated respective new member states of the European Union became members of the WTO parallel. Nowadays in Eastern Europe only Russia, Belorussia, the Ukraine and a few former Yugoslawian states are not members of WTO, but all of them are observers, ongoing accession. Any state or customs territory having full autonomy in the conduct of its trade policies may become a member ("accede to") the WTO, but all WTO members must agree on the terms. This is done through the establishment of a working party of WTO members and through a process of negotiations. (WTO, 2007, p. 105)

A government applying for membership in the WTO has to describe all aspects of its trade and economic policies that have a bearing on WTO agreements. (WTO, 2007, pp. 105) In this way transparency, in particular the publication of economical data like inflation, government subsidies etc., is necessary. Institutions like areal central bank have to be established. Also in this field capacity building is necessary in North Korea. Additionally, internal reforms into the direction of a market economy are on the top of agenda. It is impossible for North Korea to integrate into international trade structures on this level but to remain as a centrally planned economy.

At the end of this process–as fourth and fifth step on the way - a full membership in the WTO as well as in ASEAN plus 3 is possible. Especially an accession to the WTO will be both politically and economically a highly important step. The WTO membership ensures equal trade conditions between member countries, as this is the principle of the organisation. This means that all preferential terms and privileges that a country grants to another in trade relations are automatically extended to all member countries. As a member of the WTO, North Korea could take measures to balance unfair trade in accordance with the WTO agreement procedures. And the country could participate in the formation of world trade rules. This has been rather a symbolic benefit, because all WTO agreements are based on consensus reached in multilateral negotiations. Last but not least a WTO membership is a certain guarantee that internationally accepted trade principles apply in North Korea. This will give a more reliable image to North Korea and has a positive effect on North Korea's reputation. However, as one can imagine North Korea is only in the very first beginning of its reform and transformation process and this goal cannot be reached in the foreseeable future.

4. Conclusion

North Korea is only in the very first beginning of its reform and transformation process. The country's international trade is characterized by foreign aid (food and fuel), a low level of merchant trade and illegal trade transactions, e.g. in the military sector. Main trade partners are China and South Korea. There are two basic problems in North Korean policy being guilty for the disability to change institutions relative to foreign trade and foreign investments: first the ideological underpinnings of the North Korean self-reliance, the Juche ideology and system; and second the regimes fear of the inflow of information, which cannot be controlled by the state. In contrast the Special Economic Zones are a first step into the direction of openness. In these zones the rules of Juche and self –reliance are out of work. In this way especially the centrepiece of North–South Korean cooperation, the Kaesong Industrial Complex, can be seen as implementation of a process of learning in North Korea. And in this way a permanent process of capacity building will take place. Maybe during this process also the North Korean underpinning of the current economic system, the Juche approach, can change step by step.

Today, informal as well as formal institutions are lacking in respect to foreign trade institutions. But the situation is partly comparable with Central and Eastern Europe after the fall of the Berlin wall. As the experience of these countries has shown the building up of foreign trade institutions from the scratch is possible. In the Korean case the Kaesong Industrial Complex is a first step in the right direction. A second step should be a shift from project-style cooperation between North and South Korea to establishing a free trade area or ever deeper forms of trade integration on the Korean peninsula. Such a free trade area may be comparable to the free trade agreements between the European Union and the Central and Eastern European transformation states in the 1990s. Then a WTO observer status may be the third step to integrate North Korea into world trade. A full membership in the WTO as well as in ASEAN plus 3 may be the final goals. But to accomplish these goals a substantial transformation process in the country is necessary, too. In this way it will be a long way to go for North Korea to build up functioning foreign trade institutions from the scratch. Today especially capacity building will help the country to go this way ahead.

References

Aden, Nathaniel (2006). *North Korean Trade with China as Reported in Chinese Customs Statistics: Recent Energy Trends and Implications*, online: http://www.nautilus.org/ ora/security/ 0679Aden.pdf (accessed in February 2008).

Ahrens, Joachim (2003). Prospects and problems for Korean economic integration, In Choi E. Kwan, Kim E. Han & Yesook Merril (Ed.), *North Korea in the World Economy* (pp. 53–73). London.

Bae Chong-ryel (2007). Changes *in North Korea's external economic sector since the July 202 reform measures: evaluation and prospects*, In Vantage Point, August (pp. 44–55).

Chanlett-Avery, Emma & Squassoni, Sharon (2006, October 24). North Korea's Nuclear Test: Motivations, Implications, and U.S. Options, Congressional Research Service; The Library of Congress (Ed.), *CRS Report for Congress RL 33709*, 24.

Cho Young-suk (2006, December). The Inter-Korean Economic Cooperation: Achivements and Outlook, in: *Korea Policy Review* (pp. 27–29).

Frank, Rüdiger (2005). Nordkoreas Wirtschaft, In Kern, Thomas & Köllner, Patrik (Ed.), *Südkorea und Nordkorea: Einführung in Geschichte, Politik, Wirtschaft und Gesellschaft* (pp. 235-257).Frankfurt.

Jeffries, Ian (2006). *North Korea: a guide to economic and political developments*, London: Routledge.

Kim, Suh (2007, January 25) A Proposed Korea-U.S. Free trade Agreement and Kaesong Industrial Complex. In *Policy Forum Online* 07-007A, online: http://www.nautilus.org/fora/security/07007Suh.pdf (accessed in April 2007).

Korea Today (2006). Daily Face-Lifted Kaesong Industrial Zone, In *Korea Today*, 7 (601), 38.

Lee, Young-hoon (2005). An analysis of the effect of North Korea's international and inter-Koreantrade on its economic growth. In *Economic papers*, Seoul, 8(1), 175-211.

McKay, John (2005). How significant and effective are North Korea's "market reforms"?. In *Global economic review*, 34 (1), 83-97.

Ministry of Unification (2006a). *Humanitarian Support for North Korea - Support Status*, http://www.unikorea.go.kr/english/EUP/EUP0207R.jsp (accessed in November 2007).

Ministry of Unification (2006b). *North Korea: Facts & Figures*, In http://www.unikorea.go. kr/english/ENK/ENK0301L.jsp(accessed in November 2007.

Nam, Chang-woon (2005). Free economic and trade areas (FETA) as an instrument of economic transformation: the North Korean experience of Najin-Sonbong. In Friedrich, Peter (Ed.), *Regional competition under transformation conditions*. Neubiberg

Noland, Marcus (1997). Prospects for the North Korean Economy, In Suh, Dae-Sook & Lee, Chae-Jin (Ed.) North Korea after Kim Il Sung (pp. 33-58). London.

Noland, Marcus (2006, July). The Economic Implications of a North Korean Nuclear Test. In Asia Policy,2, 25-39.

Pan, Christoph (1992). *Nordkorea: Die ideologische und soziologische Basis*, Wien.

Seliger, Bernhard (2003). Die nordkoreanischen Sonderwirtschaftszonen: eine Wiederholung des chinesischen Erfolgsmodells?, In *Korea: Politik, Wirtschaft, Gesellschaft* (pp. 262-285).

Seliger, Bernhard (2004a). The North Korean Economy: Nuclear crisis and decline, or peace and reform in the last Asian dynastic regime? In the Korea Economic Institute (Ed.), *Korea's economy* (pp. 77-86).

Seliger, Bernhard (2004b). Nordkorea: Reformen im Sozialismus oder Reform des Sozialismus?, In *Orientierungen zur Wirtschafts- und Gesellschaftspolitik*, 99, 71-76.

Seliger, Bernhard (2006a). Towards a North Korea boom? Special Economic Zones in North Korea and their Effects on the North and South Korean Economies, In Oh, Yean-Cheon et al. (Ed.), *The Unification Research and Strategy in Korea and Germany: Affinity and Specifity* (pp. 93-122)

Seliger, Bernhard (2006b). North Korea's Economy at a Crossroads, In the Korea Economic Institute (ed.), *Korea's Economy* (pp. 62-71)

Tupy, Marian (2003, September 18). EU Enlargement: Costs, Benefits, and Strategies for Central and Eastern European Countries, *Policy Analysis.* 489.

World Trade Organisation [WTO] (2007) Understanding the WTO, Geneva.

Wrobel, Ralph (2000) *Estland und Europa: Die Bedeutung des Systemwettbewerbs für die Evolution und Transformation von Wirtschaftssystemen*, Tartu.

Wrobel, Ralph (2007a) North Korea after the Nuclear Crisis: The Future of the Economic Reforms, *Post Communist Economies*, 12(4), 483–504.

Wrobel, Ralph (2007b) Nordkorea - Impressionen aus Pjöngjang: Die letzte stalinistische Diktatur zwischen Stagnation und Wandel, *International– Zeitschrift für Internationale Politik*, 2, 6–11.

11

Creating a Good Bank for North Korea (and a bad bank within) – Creative Capacity-Building as a Domain for Asian-European Cooperation

Bernhard Seliger

Abstract

In the Northeast Asian region, a common perception of problems and challenges like energy security, economic integration and climate change is growing. In this respect, a regional finance opportunity for Northeast Asia like a Northeast Asian Development Bank (NADB) has been discussed in the last decade. While until now the NADB has not been realized, recent challenges from North Korea are favouring a reconsideration of NADB. Financial sanctions against North Korea aim to suppress illicit activities like money laundering and financing of illegal activities like smuggling and arms deals. However, they also prevent legal transactions for and with North Korea, with the side effect that these activities become relatively less attractive for North Korea. At the same time, the financial sector and experts in the financial sector of North Korea cannot develop. A Northeast Asian Development Bank (NADB) with a commercial arm could at the same time act as a legitimate and accepted intermediary between North Korea and the rest of the world in financial matters, and at the same time be the training facility for training of financial experts from North Korea. This paper discusses the features of such a regional development bank with special respect to North Korea upon the background of the experience of existing regional development banks.

JEL-Classification: N20, P2

Keywords: Northeast Asian Development Bank, Northeast Asia, North Korea, sanctions

1. Introduction

Among the most important approaches to the current financial crisis is the creation of "bad banks," which take up problematic, "poisonous" assets and try to turn them around and sell them off. South Korea after the crisis of 1997-98 gained experience with the quite successful Korea Asset Management Corporation.[1] For North Korea, however, the situation might reverse: a good bank is needed, a bank which can fulfil the classic banking functions without political interference, in the most transparent manner to refute any doubt about the legitimacy of financial transactions at that bank. The sanctions of the U.N. Security Council, which answered the missile and nuclear tests of North Korea in 2006, did not achieve their goal of preventing North Korea from embarking on its way to nuclearisation, and the sanctions of 2009 will probably not achieve their intended goal to cut off North Korea from financing its illicit activities. Though it might well be that North Korea is hurt by sanctions to some extent and that this requires a tactical return to the Six Party talks, a fundamental changes seems not to be achieved by the sanctions so far. If history and comparative experience of other states is a good guide, they will also not be able to achieve their goal.[2] Too difficult is the task to dry out the ways of uncontrolled finance. This is particularly true in terms of proliferation of arms, but also in other terms like drug trafficking, counterfeiting and smuggling.[3] The related departments of state, party and army are many and it is questionable how far they depend on a sound financial system for their success in business.

Where is the problem? We can presume that sanctions, or rather the warnings the U.S. Department of Treasury issued, are justified. Time and again North Korea has ignored the rules of international trade and financial transfers have

---

[1] See He (2004).

[2] For an extensive review of the issue of sanctions towards North Korea see Kim and Chang (2007). For a timeline until 2006 see Peterson Institute for International Economics (without year). Hufbauer et al. analyze 204 cases of international economic, trade and financial sanctions and come to the conclusion that their success rate is generally low, but highest in the case of "modest policy changes" and low in the case of regime change and military impairment, to which the sanctions towards North Korea tend; see Hufbauer et al. (2007), p. 159.

[3] The involvement of DPRK in such activities is well-documented though since the turn of the century it has considerably decreased; see Chestnut (2007) and Wyler/ Nanto (2008). The reasons for the seemingly declining illegal activities are discussed by Lim (2008), pp. 40-44.

played a major role in various illicit activities. The potential misuses of the international financial system are manifold ranging from money laundering and circulating counterfeited money to insurance scams. North Korea has been accused of all of them.[4] However, there is a problem. Together with dubious transactions, legal transactions will also be hurt.[5] One could even assume that legal transactions are hurt much more than illegal transactions. By their nature legal activities cannot easily turn to alternative ways of financing, such as cash transactions, which are feasible, though not comfortable, for illegal trade.

Cutting off both legal and illegal trade might be justifiable under two conditions: First, the goal of sanctions should be to strangle North Korea; Second, the sanctions should be able to achieve this goal. However, both conditions are not met. As officials not only from China and Russia, but also from South Korea and the United States have repeatedly said, sanctions are not intended to coerce North Korea by weakening its economy, they are simply meant to contain North Korea's illicit activities. Even if a hidden agenda of coercion is assumed, it will not work. As long as China, and to some extent Russia, do not start to isolate North Korea in terms of border trade, the United States and the rest of the world are simply not able to influence North Korea in this way. Recent research by Marcus Noland (2009) shows that after the sanctions imposed in October 2006, trade with China grew steadily. And North Korea does not really need other trading partners, as long as a minimum of imports is guaranteed consisting of goods distributed to the elite, in particular luxury goods, necessary military and technology inputs and some residual food needed to sustain the population at the meagre rates it has become used to during the last two decades. So, while legitimate as well as illicit trade might be forced to go underground and resort to cash transactions, life for the population might worsen, if that is possible, but the goal of sanctions will not be achieved.

Since North Korea opened up during the great famine of mid-1990s, the European Union, its member states and European NGOs have taken various initiatives to increase legitimate trade and business in North Korea as an alternative to illicit trade. Capacity-building for the trade and financial sector played an important role in this endeavour. Swedish institutions like the Royal Institute of Technology and the Stockholm School of Economics were involved in training programmes for the financial sector and German Hanns Seidel Foundation carried out the EU-DPRK trade capacity project, which tried to find ways to de-

[4] For the case of counterfeited money see the overview in Nanto (2009). For the case of insurance fraud, see Harden (2009).

[5] See Cowie (2006).

velop North Korean exports. These goals are certainly far from being achieved, not least due to North Korean political behaviour and the lack of commitment to economic reform in its leadership. However, at the working level, participants in training units are enthusiastic to embrace new knowledge. Certainly, training also generates demand for applying the new knowledge and by this it can be hoped to contribute to the goal to integrate North Korea peacefully into the world economy.[6]

Nevertheless, this is at best a long-term option and maybe, more can be done. But it has to be radically different from the current approach. Capacity-building for national North Korean banks and trade institutions, as long as it can be carried out, is good, and the fact that one North Korean joint venture bank, Daedong Credit Bank, has a foreign manager helps to create a technocracy more knowledgeable about the role of banks and finance in the modern economy.[7] But still, even these institutions cannot escape overarching political goals and the fact that other institutions have no more access to the international financial system due to the warnings issued by the U.S. Department of Treasury might even make the remaining institutions more the target of political, undesirable demands from the North Korean leadership. It is difficult to imagine that such institutions will ever gain the transparency trust necessary for integration in the international banking system.

The alternative is an international solution: Create a good bank for North Korea. This bank would have to be an international bank and, ultimately, part of the set of institutions called "International Financial Institutions (IFI)." At the same time, it would be governed by different rules than the current IFIs, but also be more than a mere "watered-down" IFI in terms of eligibility for membership. It would foster Northeast Asian integration and could be the nucleus of a closer Northeast Asian community. For North Korea, it would offer a more realistic membership perspective than the current IFI and at the same time, resolve the long-standing defaulted debt problem. In short, it would not only offer perspectives for North Korea, but also for its neighbours and the world community, to escape from the current "loose-loose" situation.

The remainder of the paper is organized as follows. The second section focuses on the experience of international development banks to date. Section three discusses features of the proposed Northeast Asian Development Bank

---

[6] For an extensive review of the experience of Hanns Seidel Foundation in North Korea see Seliger (2009).

[7] More information about the Daedong Credit Bank can be found at the website of its foreign investor, http://www.pcvltd.com/.

(NADB). The creation of "bad bank within" for the long-defaulted debt of North Korea as a precondition for reviving North Korea's international trade is reviewed in section 4, followed by a conclusion pondering the feasibility of such an approach.

2. The experience of regional development banks in Asia, Eastern Europe and the former Soviet Union – lending, politics, and regional integration

All regional development banks to a large extent follow the example of the World Bank or International Bank for Reconstruction and Development (IBRD), an organisation of the United Nations (UN), the aim of which is to spur economic growth and curb poverty in the Developing World by providing loans, policy advice, and technical assistance.[8] The World Bank (International Bank for Reconstruction and Development, IBRD) came into existence in 1945; its charter was drafted at the 1944 Bretton Woods Conference. As of 2009, 186 countries were World Bank members. Membership in the IRBD requires prior membership in the International Monetary Fund (IMF). This again means that transparency about macroeconomic data is a precondition for membership, an important point to have in mind when pondering the possibility of North Korea to participate in such institutions.

With a lending volume of 12 to 15 bn. US-$ per year, the World Bank is not only the largest lender, but also the oldest, with a history dating back to the end of World War II.[9] In July 1944, the United Nations convened a conference in Bretton Woods, New Hampshire to discuss economic cooperation after the war. Concerns over monetary stability were most pressing and so the IMF was established there. Post-war reconstruction and economic development issues were also addressed, which gave birth to the IRBD. In December 1945, the first IRBD members signed its charter, and in 1946 the organisation began its lending operations with a loan of $250 million for French post-war reconstruction. After the initial post-war reconstruction period in Europe, the second task of the World Bank, economic development, became most prominent. The World Bank used its status as a first-class debtor to pass on low-interest loan rates on funds

---

[8] There is sometimes confusion between IBRD and the World Bank Group. The latter also includes for more institutions, namely the International Development Association (focusing on the poorest countries), the International Finance Corporation (focusing on private sector investment) the Multilateral Investment Guarantee Agency (focusing on FDI to developing countries) and the International Centre for Settlement of Investment Disputes (focusing on investment dispute settlement).

[9] For the history of World Bank see Kapur et al. (1997), Salda (1997).

raised on international capital markets to project countries. Among these nations were newly-independent states in Africa and Asia.

Interestingly, among the first IRBD signatories were Poland and Czechoslovakia. In 1950, however, the Soviets forced them to withdraw, as they considered the World Bank as an instrument of U.S. "economic imperialism." Since then, IRBD members have consisted largely of nations with market-oriented economies. Japan and the Federal Republic of Germany (FRG) became members in 1952 and later were among the biggest donors of soft loans. The IBRD) charter specifically prohibits the body from interfering in the political affairs of states receiving World Bank aid and holds that only economic considerations will be used to determine need. Nevertheless, because the seat of Bretton Woods' institutions (IRBD, IMF) was in Washington, D.C., and the IRBD maintained close relations with American-based banking institutions, politics did come into play over the years. The United States has remained the most influential IRBD member, and the president of the World Bank has always been an American.

Because the establishment of credibility in capital markets was based on IRBD recipient nations' ability to repay loans, in the first fifteen years of its existence the body focused on lending not to the poorest countries, which posed too high risk of default, but rather to middle or upper middle income countries, like those in Latin America, for example. This policy, however, did little to alleviate poverty. It also became problematic in terms of Cold War geopolitics. Poverty presented itself as a powerful precondition for successful communist or nationalist movements throughout the Developing World. In recognition of this, in 1960 the International Development Association (IDA) was created as part of the World Bank, whose aim was to make concessional loans to the world's poorest nations, funded by contributions of member states. The two largest contributors were the United States and Japan. During 1962-1968, under the leadership of President George Woods, the IRBD broadened it conception of economic development, which had been formerly restricted to large, high-tech projects like highways or power plants. Because earnings from these initial projects allowed increased funding, the IRBD's new lending policy included longer repayment periods, involved technical and direct assistance, and provided loans for agricultural purposes, which became a major focus of World Bank priorities.

During 1968-1981, Robert McNamara, former CEO of Ford Motor Company and secretary of defence under Presidents John F. Kennedy and Lyndon B. Johnson, served as the World Banks' president. He profoundly changed the IRBD. Under his tenure, the World Bank became foremost involved in poverty mitigation programmes and increased its lending operations from $1 billion in 1968, to more than $12 billion in 1981. McNamara also had to cope with the 1971 breakdown of the international monetary system designed at Bretton Woods, the oil price shocks of 1973-1974 and 1979-1980, and the Developing World debt crisis. The first oil price shock led to the emergence of the so-called "petro-dollar market" of organisation of Petroleum Exporting Companies (OPEC) countries. Some of these funds were borrowed by the World Bank to finance development projects, especially rural development projects in Africa. Unfortunately, the expansion of lending did not always contribute to the reduction of poverty, but on the contrary locked many states into a vicious cycle of higher and higher debt, with no ability to serve the debt or accruing interest.

Because the IRBD raises its funds from international capital markets, it is largely independent upon interventions of member governments. During the 1960s and early 1970s particularly, the World Bank witnessed active intervention from the United States to prevent lending to North Vietnam and its other adversaries. This obviously politicized the IRBD. The 1980s saw, based upon successful IRBD-sponsored development projects in East Asia and Latin America, the emergence of a consensus view of economic development based upon free markets. World perceptions of the "East Asian Miracle" in nations like South Korea, Taiwan, and Singapore was largely based on a seminal book published by the World Bank in 1993. The end of the Cold War precipitated a dearth of nations clamouring to join the IRBD, many of them in former Communist Bloc areas. Today, the World Bank focuses on creating sustainable economic growth by combating corruption in recipient nations and by ameliorating the situation of the poorest, most heavily-indebted countries with poor growth records.

When the World Bank started to aggressively expand its lending in the 1960s, the set-up of regional development banks for the large world regions began as well. Already in 1959, the Inter-American Development Bank (IADB) was founded, under the auspices of the organisation of American States (OAS). In 1964, the African Development Bank (AfDB) was founded, which is currently with a volume of 2-3 bn. US-$ annually the most important lender in the region. Already one year before, in 1963, a resolution passed at the first Ministerial Conference on Asian Economic Cooperation held by the United Nations Economic Commission for Asia and the Far East on the establishment of a regional development bank for Asia. This vision became reality with the foundation of the Asian Development Bank (ADB) in 1966. Today, the ADB has 67 members (of which 48 are located in the region and 19 in other parts of the globe). Mostly lending to the public sector and governments, ADB also lends to private enterprises of developing countries and cooperates with NGOs, development agencies, community-based organisation and foundations. Its projects range from offshore oil and gas development in Taiwan to poverty reduction in the Philippines and, increasingly important, support for regional and sub regional integration. In particular, ADB has been involved in the Greater Mekong Sub-regional Programme in Southeast Asia. Its instruments and business rationale are similar to those of the World Bank: ADB hands out loans and grants, is involved in technical assistance and knowledge transfer and its triple-A credit rating allows to lend at favourable rates to developing countries. Currently, the so-called Strategy 2020, as a long-term framework adopted in 2008, sets inclusive and sustainable growth as well as regional integration as the foremost goals of ADB.

Membership in ADB is based upon membership or associate membership in the United Nations Economic and Social Commission for Asia and the Pacific, plus other countries and non-regional developed countries which are members of the United Nations or of any of its specialized agencies. As such, North Korea is clearly eligible for membership on both accounts. However, membership is decided by consensus among the existing membership. Given the strong position of the United States in the bank, with a voting power of currently 12,756 percent (though this might change in the future); membership is implicitly preconditioned by understanding with the US.

The fall of the Berlin Wall in 1989 and the disintegration of the Soviet bloc saw the emergence of a new regional development bank, the European Bank of Reconstruction and Development (EBRD). The idea for an EBRD was conceived by Jacques Attali, advisor to French President Francois Mitterand, who put forward the idea at the European Parliament in Strasbourg on 25 October 1989. In May 1990 EBRD was founded and in 1991 it started its work from its headquarters in London. The mission of EBRD was explicitly political, in that it supported the former communist countries in the process of establishing a market economy, with a focus on privatization and the creation of a new private sector, but also restructuring of state-owned or formerly state-owned companies and improvement of municipal services. For the large share of investment in the private sector, commercial partners play an important role in leveraging the EBRD's share of investment. The EBRD's mandate stipulates that it must only work in countries that are committed to democratic principles, which is quite contrary to the stipulations of "non-interference" in other banks like the World Bank. However, as the World Bank has been under political pressure (and so, to some extent, deviated from "non-interference"), EBRD frequently had to compromise on its stipulation of investment in democratic states, in particular when its focus shifted from the first, graduating group of transition countries in Central Europe to Southeast Europe and Central Asia. EBRD carried out projects in 30 countries. In 2008, 302 new projects were signed with commitments of 5.1 bn. Euro. The integration of Central and Eastern European states into the European economy and European institutions has been an important goal of EBRD.

One of the youngest attempts to create a regional development bank is the Eurasian Development Bank (EDB). It was founded by agreement between the Russian Federation and the Republic of Kazakhstan in January 2006. Armenia and Tajikistan joined in early 2009; the Republic of Belarus has applied for membership in 2008 and currently undergoes the necessary preparatory phase, after the EDB council approved its membership in December 2008. Also the Kyrgyz Republic is currently negotiating membership in EDB. The mission of EDB is to facilitate development and growth of market economies and to promote trade and economic integration in its member states. The investment portfolio of EDB, though considerably lower than that of the regional development banks discussed before, exceeds 1.2 bn. US-$, consisting of syndicated loans and eurobonds. Until 2010, the EDB aims to create an investment portfolio of not less than 4.5 bn. US-$. The effects of the global financial crisis of 2008 and 2009, however, will have a strong effect on the EDB, since Kazakhstan with a strongly exposed banking sector was in particular hit hard by the crisis. Key areas for investment of EDB are electric power, water and energy, transportation infrastructure and high-tech and innovative industries. Membership at EDB requires a decision by the Bank's Council as well as payment in the required share capital.

Table 10.1 A comparison of four regional development banks

	World Bank (IBRD)	Asian Development Bank	European Bank for Reconstruction and Development	Eurasian Development Bank
Founding year	1944	1966	1991	2006
Capital (as of 2008; EDB as of 2009)	189,9 bn. US-$ (11,5 bn. US-$ paid in, 178,4 bn. US-$ callable)	54,89 bn. US-$ (3,86 bn. US-$ paid in, 51,0 bn. US-$ callable)	20 bn. Euro (5 bn. EUR paid in, 15 bn. EUR callable)	1.500.600,00 US-$ (paid in)
Membership criteria	Membership in IMF	Membership in UN Organisations plus agreement among current member states		Agreement by current member states
Political criteria	non-interference	non-interference	Support for market economy and democracy	No clear statement
Involvement in regional integration projects	Yes (worldwide support for regionalization)	Yes (in particular Mekong river delta)	Yes (preparation for integration with West European institutions)	Yes (founding agreement, charter of EDB)

Source: own presentation after data of the respective institutions

Looking back at more than 60 years of history of international development banks, some features are quite common: lending has been consistently the most important activity, based on credit ratings, though this is less true for the last bank, the Eurasian Development Bank, which still has to work on its reputation. At the same time, politics played an important role at the banks, which were all founded by intergovernmental agreement, directly, as in the case of stated policy goals in EBRD, or indirectly, not least through the appointment of political figures as executives. At the same time, all development banks were involved in more than nationwide projects, namely in region-building or regional integration, in fact, they can be called regionalizing actors (Bull/ Boea, 2003). Regional development banks (if the IBRD is included) also from the start have been doubling existing efforts or complementing them, with a clear overlap, in the case of Central Asia between the IBRD, the EBRD and the EDB. The next section will discuss, if there is a rationale, based on this experience, for a Northeast Asian Development Bank (NADB).

3. The case for a Northeast Asian Development Bank (how it should look like and what it should focus on)

First of all, regional development banking depends on some form of region-building or regional identity. Only if there is a unifying theme among nations in the region, the work of an additional development bank makes sense. And exactly this has been traditionally very weak in the region. The strong Cold War cleavages, which for a long time – and on the Korean Peninsula until today – remained unchanged even after the end of the Cold War in Europe, prevented nations from seeking joint solutions to its problems.[10] In the late 1980s a conference on the development perspectives of the Sea of Japan in Niigata in 1988 brought experts from a number of regional players together. After the end of the Cold War, in 1991 the Northeast Asia Economic Forum was created, a network with a strong academic background with a secretariat in the East-West Centre in Hawaii, bringing together 40 institutions from China, Japan, South and North Korea, Mongolia and Russia.[11] First, common interests centred on the aforementioned question of the development of the Sea of Japan (Korean: East Sea) and the possibility of the development of the Tumen River delta, involving Russia, China and North Korea, which for some time in the early 1990s found strong interest and also involvement from international organisations like UNDP, but later was largely aborted. Today, the NEAEF in its annual conferences and other activities focuses on a broad range of topics like cross-border regional cooperation or energy cooperation. In this network, also the idea of a regional development bank was floating.

In 2002 in Japan, the Institute for Northeast Asian Study (INAS) called for the creation of such a bank, a call taken up by Takao Sato, lawmaker of the Democratic Party. Also, a former prime minister of the Republic of Korea, Duck-Woo

---

[10] Lambert (2002) lists ten impediments for cooperation in Northeast Asia.

[11] In the case of North Korea, cooperation functioned through the Committee for the Promotion of External Economic Cooperation (CPEEC). This was, however, largely limited to the initial idea of a Tumen River Development Project.

Nam, proposed the establishment of such a bank. Additional weight got the proposal through its promotion by S. Stanley Katz, former Vice President of the ADB (see Katz, 2004). The idea was to set up a bank to finance regional development projects and to cover that part of finance not covered by World Bank and ADB. Katz proposed a bank capitalized initially with 20 bn. US-$, with a share of 60 percent of members from the region and 40 percent from non-regional members.[12] However, governments in the region were reluctant to follow-up on the idea, maybe partly through the disappointing results of the Tumen River Development Project and the almost defunct Rajin-Sonbong Free Trade Area in North Korea.[13] Though the idea still is alive (see Pascha, 2007 and the Busan Declaration of the Northeast Asia Economic Forum of August 2009, which reiterated the call for a Northeast Asian Development Bank), it is certainly not on the forefront of regional policy-making.[14]

Nevertheless, in particular the recent experience with the inconsistent and bottom-up process of marketization in North Korea might provide a good reason to reconsider the case for the Northeast Asian Development Bank.[15] The NADB would be able to solve the impasse regarding the international financial system North Korea faces without compromising the system and rules set up with good reason by IFIs. The problem is that currently, while the membership conditions of these institutions are crucial to guarantee a maximum compatibility with the international financial system, they cannot be met by any institution in North Korea. Rather, the alternative is a bank of non-North Korean origin that is open to all legitimate transactions by North Korean entities – a "good bank" for North Korea. The creation of such a bank would fit into a scenario where positive offers accompany sanctions still in place. This does not mean the offers are new carrots for North Korea -- which did not work in the past -- but in the form of offering policy innovations to the country while bearing in mind the limited room for such initiatives that North Korea's political system allows. The good bank for North Korea would fit these preconditions.

Unlike the ADB, a strong offer should be made to North Korea to participate from the beginning. Funding could be regional, most probably from South Korea and China, but also Japan and non-Asian states and entities like the EU. Capacity-building should be, besides regional project funding, a main task of such a bank. It would be important that such a development bank was not seen as a

---

[12] For an outline of the NADB proposal see Cho/ Katz (2001).

[13] See on the Tumen River Development Project Hughes (2000) and on Rajin-Sonbong Kim (2001).

[14] The Busan Declaration can be downloaded at http://www.neaef.org/Busan%20Declaration%20FINAL.pdf.

[15] See for marketization as an unintended result of reform in North Korea Seliger (2005), Nam (2007).

"watered-down" international financial institution. Political credit guarantees for economically nonviable projects (which however are also not completely alien to existing financial institutions) would only make the institution prone to political attacks and would not be helpful for North Korea in the long run. This has been the weakness for many of the proposals on international policy cooperation related to the proposal of an Asian Monetary Fund in the wake of the East Asian economic and financial crisis of 1997 and 1998. In this respect, investment projects should be submitted to an "IFI-test," asking if other international financial institutions (IFI) would also carry out the project under their standards. The difference, however, would be that the political burden of the existing international financial institution would not exist. Though U.S. membership of the NADB might be desirable, no veto on political grounds for this institution should exist. North Korea should be barred from state membership -- the offers to the North should be limited to provision of services.

What would be the role of the NADB? As the name says, the first task of the bank would be regional development projects. A sectoral focus on cross-border energy, the environment and transportation issues could be beneficial immediately in the region, regardless of North Korea's involvement. Developing an energy pipeline network for the future, jointly fighting challenges like desertification in China that hurt other Northeast Asian countries, and developing transport links in the region are tasks where regional cooperation today seems compelling and is widely recognized also by the state actors.[16] Recently, also large-scale projects in clean energy became an important topic.[17] Perhaps interregional networks like the "iron silk road" could be considered as another important issue. Financial sector development and integration must be the second main function of the NADB. Capacity-building in all areas, but in particular the financial sector, would help achieve the goals of the bank.

Finally, the NADB could offer a commercial banking arm. The Northeast Asian Commercial Bank (NACB) could offer commercial banking particularly -- but not solely -- to North Korea. Operating under strict transparency rules, it would be open to all kinds of legitimate transactions under commercial standards, but with the political backing of the funding governments. Commercial banking would be the policy-innovation, which is unique to the case of Northeast Asia and would be markedly different from other regional development

[16] Thus, integration in Northeast Asia through the NADB would be functional, based on commonly perceived problems and common interests. This point has been stressed by Noriatsu/ Uyar (2006).

[17] For example, provision of solar energy through large-scale, desert-based electric power stations. See Seliger/ Kim (2009).

banks. While in other world regions sound banking might be scarce, it is not unavailable and it is according to market principles that state actors should refrain from meddling with activities best carried out by private actors. In the case of North Korea, this, however, is not a business problem or economic problem, but rather a question of political trust. While banking services are available in theory (a point strongly made by the foreign-invested Daesung Credit Bank), they are not trusted by the international community, due to the lack of transparency not inside particular institutions, but surrounding North Korea as a state. Accepting this situation means prolonging the exclusion of legitimate business of North Korea from sound finance and prolonging the practice of cash-based transactions with all the possible abuses – a point made, for example, with regard to the UNDP programme in North Korea, which had to close down temporarily due to allegations of misconduct.

Why would any state, but in particular North Korea, be interested in such a commercial bank arm of a regional development bank? For North Korea, there would be no credible excuse to refuse the activities of such a bank and no more credible complaints of allegations of "strangling" by financial sanctions. In this sense, it would not only be an olive branch extended to the North, but a branch having a cleaning function at the same time, different from the unrealistic and unwanted unrestricted access of dubious North Korean institutions to the international financial system. For the US and the regional players being founding members of the NADB, this would allow a two-tier strategy of maintaining a firewall against possible abuses of the international financial system and allowing access for desirable financial transactions. Among those, the transactions of international institutions working in North Korea would figure prominently, foremost the World Food Programme, UNDP and other UN organisations, but also for example the activities of the European Union. Together, these institutions had also some leverage to open up North Korea for such an initiative. The establishment of a Pyongyang branch of the commercial part of the NADB would then become a cornerstone of new financial relations between North Korea and the rest of the world. The opening of such a branch would have to be politically negotiated with strong guarantees from regional powers, in particular China, about the internal autonomy and transparency of the branch, including personnel sovereignty, a feature currently missing in foreign investment in North Korea.

Even for financial sanctions, effects could be beneficial. Though it might be argued that the additional pressure put on North Korea by restricting legitimate as well as unwanted financial transactions is necessary to make North Korea move, experience with sanctions worldwide shows that targeted and limited sanctions often offer a better chance of achieving their goal. In the case of North Korea, a policy shift might be achieved if it is clear that a maximum position – removal of all financial sanctions as part of a political bargaining – cannot be achieved for considerable time due to the fact that the counterparts, like the US, could deny it on the grounds that for legitimate business already opportunities exist. In this sense, it might put additional pressure on North Korea to offer more radical policy shifts to achieve a removal of sanctions – and this would mean, sanctions would have fulfilled its purpose.[18]

The commercial branch of the NADB would also be the natural starting point for capacity-building for North Korean bankers and officials. Grants as part of the banks regional development activities should offer generous possibilities for North Korean personnel to study modern banking and, in particular, modern project finance necessary for the restructuring of the North Korean defunct industrial economy. North Korean co-ownership – though based certainly on a small share of capital in the bank – would be another avenue, through which North Korea would have the possibility to gain knowledge about international cooperation direly needed. One important topic, where such cooperation is needed, is the case of defaulted old debt, which will be discussed in the next section.

4. Creating a bad bank within – Solving the Problem of North Korea's Defaulted Debt

The NADB would also be helpful in addressing an additional problem, which often is forgotten but will resurface once more immediate political and economic concerns are resolved. North Korea, like some other socialist and developing countries, defaulted on its external debt in the 1980s. This problem has to be resolved as a precondition for the re-integration of North Korea in the world economy, in particular for counterparts of North Korea being eligible for export credit guarantees.

North Korea's debt with Western countries dates back to the short, but aggressive phase of entering into commercial ventures with Western companies and receiving Western economic aid in the early 1970s. According to CIA estimates, between 1970 and 1975, North Korea signed contracts worth almost 600 mill.

[18] The nature of such a policy shift cannot be discussed here. It would, however, not be enough, like in the past, that North Korea claims to adhere to all international standards of anti-money laundering, when it assembled hastily a law against money-laundering.

US-$ with Japanese and West European companies.[19] This amount exceeded trade with the socialist bloc besides China and the Soviet Union, the most important trading partners of North Korea. With this borrowed money, North Korea built bridges and roads, bought heavy equipment and also grain.[20] Large German companies like Siemens and Mannesmann were active in rehabilitating industrial sites. But investment was not economically viable. Soon negotiations for larger investment, in particular with France, faltered. By the latter half of 1974, North Korea defaulted on its debt, being the first communist country to do so.[21] While being in arrears, North Korea began to negotiate with its private creditors in the framework of the London club and by 1979, it had renegotiated much of its international debt, standing at around 700 mill. US-$. However, it could not repay the debt and in 1984 also began to stop interest payments. Finally, in 1987, negotiations with the creditors in London, two syndicates representing 140 banks, finally broke down, when North Korea demanded 200 mill. US-$ in fresh loans instead of offering repayment (Kristof, 1987).

North Korea was not the only country defaulting on its debt. In the early 1980s, beginning with Mexico in August 1982, a worldwide debt crisis broke out. Aggressive borrowing for non-viable projects and a worsening economic climate brought many countries to the brink of bankruptcy. To deal with the situation, for decades the two "clubs" of private creditors (London Club) and state creditors (Paris club) existed. The Paris club dates back to debt negotiations with Argentine in 1956, when multilateral negotiations could prevent a major economic breakdown and at the same time solve coordination problems. Currently, in the Paris club, 19 creditor countries are coordinating and rescheduling public debt by meeting regularly at the French Treasury. Since the 1990s, debt reductions based on certain conditions for the poorest countries (the heavily indebted poor countries) became part of their strategy. Since the 1970s, procedures of the Paris Club have been codified, offering a "civilized alternative to gunboat diplomacy" (Cosio-Pascal, 2008, p. 2).

Analogous to the Paris Club, private lenders began to meet in the London Club, though on an ad-hoc instead of regular bases, to discuss outstanding private debt. A typical example of debt rescheduling of the two clubs is the outstanding debt of the Former Soviet Union. In 1991 the Russian Federation estimated all foreign liabilities (and most foreign assets) of the Soviet Union. After

[19] Cited after Armstrong (2009), p. 5. Armstrong provides a comprehensive overview over North Korea's outreaching strategy during the 1970s and its failure.

[20] Given external finance, it is no wonder that this phase is remembered in North Korea as a "golden phase" with the relatively least shortage of consumption

[21] Armstrong (2009), p. 5.

several rounds of difficult restructuring negotiations in the turbulent phase of transition during the 1990s, the face value of former outstanding debt was around 100 bn. US-$ in 1998, 55 percent of the total debt of Russia at the time. The Russian financial crisis (in the aftermath of the East Asian financial crisis) led to a renewed default and restructuring. Debt in the London Club was securitized, i.e. tradable, with principal notes at face value (PRINs) and interest arrear notes (IAN). After two years of negotiations, in February 2000, PRINs were devalued to 37,5 percent of face value, IANs to 33 percent of face value, with the remainder of the debt rescheduled into a 30 year eurobond with a seven year grace period.[22] Afterwards, Russia's debt with the London Club was reduced from around 31,8 bn. US-$ to 21.2 bn. US-$.

For North Korea, the experience of Russia and other reschedulers is highly relevant. Though the exact amount of the debt owed to foreign countries is not clear, it is considerable. Noland (2001) estimated the absolute debt in 1994 at 7.6 bn. US-$, but this is contradicting figures from the Paris Club, which estimates public debt at 9.5 bn. US-$ (see table 10.2). The South Korean Unification Ministry, in recent estimate, speaks of 18 bn. US-$ in 2008 and 30 creditor countries (Yonhap News, 2008).

Table 10.2 North Korea's Outstanding Debt with the Paris Club of official lenders

Debtor Country	Outstanding Debt (Official Development Aid)	Outstanding Debt (Non-ODA)	Total
Democratic People's Republic of Korea	142	9403	9544

(in mill. US-$, as of September 1st, 2008)
Source: Paris Club (2008).

Given the refusal to pay, North Korea seems not to be really burdened with its debt, but this debt has two long-standing problematic consequences. Defaulted debt means that North Korea cannot access international capital markets anymore and additionally it means that trade finance (trade credit insurance) is not available for North Korea. This last point is particularly problematic, since it also prevents North Korea from embarking on a strategy of trade-based growth

[22] See Buch et al. (2000), pp. 6-8.

and transition, as China and Vietnam successfully did. So, North Korea should urgently tackle with outstanding debt. This does not mean North Korea has to pay back all of that debt -- principal plus interest -- which is not possible in the foreseeable future. But it has to make an effort to relink itself with the creditor clubs. By this, it can gain more than painful negotiations: Looking at the experience of debt rescheduling of Soviet and Russian debt with the London Club (of private lenders) and Paris Club (of state lenders), it can be said that the process was helpful beyond solving the original problem. A new generation of debt and trade finance specialists emerged, more understanding of international trade followed and economic reform was forwarded by negotiations. Creating macroeconomic specialist, debt and trade finance specialists would be as well as a precondition and an outcome of negotiations. In both, the NADB could play a pivotal role. It could be the training centre for North Korean financial specialists. Having a branch in the country, even the problem of foreign travel – which is restricted to most North Koreans, particularly if they are young – would disappear.

In a second step, the NADB could also estimate the debt (where the possibility of repayment is currently zero anyway) after large write-offs, and for concessions in terms of reform in North Korea. A strong linkage of capacity-building, aid and trade would result.

5. Conclusion – Can North Korea be lured in international cooperation?

Overall, the NADB would have four functions as sketched in this paper: financing regional development projects, capacity-building, commercial banking for North Korea and the creation of a bad bank within for old North Korean debt. The last two functions go beyond that of the traditional regional development banks. One main question still remains unanswered: Can North Korea really be lured into international cooperation? Isn't the same approach which failed many times in the past? Certainly, it would be illusionary to think that North Korea would immediately come on board. But the proposal itself is not unrealistic and would have immediate positive effects: More regional cooperation, in particular in view of the North Korean situation, would be good for the region and would enhance an understanding of the newly emerging five-party grouping. Resolving current problems goes hand in hand with developing solutions for North Korea. Extending an olive branch to North Korea, particularly in the form of a regional initiative that includes China, would put pressure on North Korea to react positively. It would also show the population of North Korea, which by now has at least limited access to information from abroad, that the international community is not hostile vis-a-vis North Korea, but offering help.

This would open various possibilities: The most benign, but currently least probable, would be that North Korea itself becomes interested in capacity-building and economic integration. A more probable outcome, would be that growing Chinese frustration with its ally would lead to stronger Chinese efforts to convince North Korea to open up. There is no guarantee that the NADB will succeed with regard to North Korea. However, a lot of money has been spent on much more dubious inter-Korean cooperation projects to no avail. This approach might well be worth trying out.

References

Armstrong, Charles K. (2009). Juche and North Korea's Global Aspirations, *North Korea International Documentation Project Working Paper no. 1*, Washington, D.C.: Woodrow Wilson International Centre for Scholars.

Buch, Claudia M. - Ralph P. Heinrich – Lusine Lusinyan – Mechthild Schroten (2000). Russia's Debt Crisis and the Unofficial Economy, *DIW discussion paper no. 208*, Berlin: Deutsches Institut fuer Wirtschaftsforschung.

Bull, Benedicte – Morten Bøa (2003). Multilateral Development Banks as Regionalising Actors: The Asian Development Bank and the Inter-American Development Bank, *New Political Economy*, 8 (2), 245-261.

Chestnut, Sheena (2007). Illicit Activity and Proliferation: North Korean Smuggling Networks, *International Security*, 32 (1), 80-111.

Cho, Lee-Jay – S. Stanley Katz (2001). A Northeast Asian Development Bank?, *NIRA Review* 8 (1) Winter 2001. 41-47.

Cosio-Pascal, Enrique (2008). The emerging of a multilateral forum for debt restructuing: the Paris Club, UNCTAD discussion papers no. 192, Geneva: United Nations Conference on Trade and Development.

Cowie, Nigel (2006). Shutdown: US Financial Allegations Toward North Korea, The Asia-Pacific Journal: Japan Focus, http://www.japanfocus.org/-Nigel-Cowie/1783 (accessed October 1st, 2009).

Harden, Blaine (2009, June 18). Global Insurance Fraud By North Korea Outlined, *The Washington Post*.

He, Dong (2004). The Role of KAMCO in Resolving Nonperforming Loans in the Republic of Korea, IMF Working Paper 04/172, Washington, D.C.: International Monetary Fund.

Hufbauer, Gary - Jeffrey Schott - Kimberly Elliott and Barbara Oegg (2007). Economic Sanctions Reconsidered, 3rd edition, Washington, D.C.P: Peterson Institute for International Economics.

Hughes, Christopher W. (2000). Tumen River Area Development Programme: Frustrated Micro-Regionalism as a Microcosm of Political Rivalries, CSGR Working Paper No. 57/00, Warwick: University of Warwick - Centre for the Study of Globalisation and Regionalisation.

Kapur, Devesh, John P. Lewis and Richard Webb (Ed.) (1997). The World Bank: Its First Half Century. Washington, DC: Brookings Institution.

Katz, S. Stanley (2004). "An option for Northeast Asia: establishment of the Northeast Asia Development Bank," in: Joon-Kyung Kim (Ed.), Enhancing investment cooperation in Northeast Asia, Seoul: KIEP, 295-312.

Kim, Icksoo (2001). "The Rajin-Sonbong Economic and Trade Zone (RSETZ) : the sources of difficulties and lessons for the future," in: Lawrence J. Lau - Chang-Ho Yun (Ed.), North Korea in transition, Cheltenham: Edward Elgar, 301-333.

Kim, Suk – Seemon Chaung (Ed.) (2007). Economic Sanctions against a nuclear North Korea, Jefferson (NC): McFarland&Company.

Kristof, Nicholas D. (1987). "North Korea is Told of Loan Default," New York Times, August 23, 1987, Internet File: http://www.nytimes.com/1987/08/23/world/north-korea-is-told-of-loan-default.html, (accessed October 1st, 2009).

Lambert, Bruce Henry (2002). Northeast Asian dynamism: ten top impediments and countermeasures, Working Paper no. 145, European Institute of Japanese Studies, Stockholm School of Economics, Internet file: http://www.olemiss.edu/courses/pol337/lamber02.pdf (accessed October 1st, 2009).

Lim, Tai-Wei (2008). "North Korea's Shady Transnational Business Activities and Their Future Prospects," *North Korean Review*, 4 (2), 31-48.

Nam, Sung-Wook (2007). "Evaluation of the North Korean July 2002 Economic Reform," *North Korean Review*, 3(1), 32-44.

Nanto, Dick K. (2009). North Korean Counterfeiting of U.S. currency, CRS Report for Congress, Washington, D.C.: Congressional Report Service.

Noland, Marcus (2001). North Korea's External Economic Relations, Peterson Institute for International Economics, Internet File:

http://www.iie.com/publications/papers/paper.cfm?ResearchID=398, (accessed October 1st, 2009).

Noland, Marcus (2009). "The (Non) Impact of UN Sanctions on North Korea," *Asia Policy*, No. 7, 61–88

Noriatsu, Matsui - Aysun Uyar (2007). Loose functional integration in Northeast Asia: the Northeast Asian Development Bank, Working Paper 06-02, Yamaguchi: Yamaguchi University Graduate School of East Asian Studies.

Paris Club (2008). *Amounts due to Paris Club Creditor Countries by Foreign Sovering and other public debtors as of 1st September 2008*, Internet file: http://www.clubdeparis.org/sections/donnees-chiffrees/publication-creances-du/downloadFile/file/Publication_of_Paris_Club_claims_on_1st_September_2008.pdf (accessed October 1st, 2009).

Pascha, Werner (2007). "New options for Northeast Asian cooperation in development finance," The Journal of East Asian Affairs, 21(1), 139-161.

Peterson Institute for International Economics (without year). *Case Studies in Sanctions and Terrorism, Case US and UN v. North Korea (1950 -: Korean War)*, http://www.petersoninstitute.org/research/topics/sanctions/nk.cfm (accessed October 1st, 2009).

Salda, Anne C. M. (1997). *Historical Dictionary of the World Bank*. Lanham, MD: The Scarecrow Press.

Seliger, Bernhard – Gi-Eun Kim (2009). "Promoting an Asian Version of 'Desertec'," *Korea Herald*, September 24, 2009, p. C9.

Seliger, Bernhard (2005). "The July 2002 Reforms in North Korea: Liberman-Style Reforms or Road to Transformation?" *North Korean Review*,1 (1), pp. 22-37.

Seliger, Bernhard (2009). "Engagement on the margins – capacity building in North Korea," *Korea's Economy*, 25, 67-75.

Wyler, Liana Sun – Dick K. Nanto (2008). North Korean Crime-for-Profit Activities, CRS Report for Congress, Washington, D.C.: Congressional Report Service.

Yonhap News (2008). N. Korea's foreign debt estimated at US$18 billion," Internet File: http://english.yonhapnews.co.kr/northkorea/2008/10/07/2/0401000000AEN20081007005400315F.HTML, (accessed October 1st, 2009).

PART IV

Investment, Business and Business Schools

12

The Nampo-Pyongyang Corridor: a Strategic Area for European Investment in DPRK

Stanislas Roussin and César Ducruet

Abstract

This paper provides an overview of main problems affecting the development of North Korean regions. It recognizes the importance of transport and logistics as key factors in regional economic growth. A critical overview of main economic areas in terms of market size, industrial specializations, accessibility, and infrastructure provision, concludes that Nampo is the most efficient location for European companies that are willing to use North Korea as a base for producing and exporting their goods. Conclusions are based on recent figures about maritime traffics and hinterland characteristics.

Keywords: *DPRK, Europe, Logistics, North Korea, Regional Development*

Introduction

Several studies have addressed the different characteristics of North Korea's main economic areas. However, their results have remained mostly speculative and somewhat contradicting, due to data shortage. Therefore, most research depends on broad qualitative appreciations and external estimations of North Korea's regional economic performance. Very few works have provided a quantitative regional geography of the country. As for example, Jo and Adler (2002) show the difficulty providing accurate population figures by city and province, but they success in demonstrating key processes of a socialist developing country. They particularly highlight the precedence taken by economic factors over ideological factors, resulting in the formation of Pyongyang primate city, and the deficiency of intra and inter regional balance. One main explanation is that centralized socialist planning finds difficult to sustain its legitimacy and efficiency in a globalized environment where economic factors become dominant. Another set of studies based on international trading vessel movements demonstrated the gradual concentration of the North Korean port system favouring Nampo, the gateway to Pyongyang (Jo and Ducruet, 2006; Ducruet and Jo, 2007). Thus, both urban and port systems illustrate major spatial changes within the country, such as the "shift to the West" of populations and activities during the last two decades, as a result of geopolitical change, uneven accessibility, and overall industrial collapse (Roussin and Ducruet, 2006; Ducruet and Roussin, 2007a).

In order to address whether North Korean economic areas are differently attractive to foreign firms such as European firms, an overview of their main characteristics is provided in the first section. It is believed that European firms have a comparative advantage over other firms stemming from the absence of political issues between North Korea and Europe (Bridges, 2003). Besides, they can be seen as any potential investor for which location factors are the same than for other companies, in terms of market opportunities and logistics efficiency. Thus, this first section reviews the different economic areas according to their compatibility with global standards of supply chain management. In a second section and from this economic and logistics approach, the most relevant area, Nampo-Pyongyang, is selected and analyzed in terms of land-sea capacity, recent European investments and potential growth.

1. Regional panorama of North Korean logistics

1.1 Performance indicators of main economic areas

One major constraint to addressing the actual state of industrial activities in different parts of North Korea is the fact that only 20% of existing industries are still in operation or in semi-operation. The Soviet model based on heavy industry, the dramatic shortages of energy since the early 1990s, and the increase of defence-related expenditures at a time of diplomatic tensions and trade isolation all have provoked severe wounds to the whole economic system. As a consequence, any estimation of economic performance should not ignore that except Pyongyang and Nampo, most other cities have seen their economic base vanish over time. Cheongjin, a main economic centre of 800,000 inhabitants located in the northeast, has been described by a former UN representative as a 'forest of scrap metal' where the port is rather dormant (Pons, 2006).

Table 11.1 illustrates the actual and potential inventory of industries in DPRK by main areas. It shows that North Korea offers to investors an interesting mix of various natural resources highly demanded on the world market as uranium, copper or nickel, and an industrial tradition, the north part of Korean peninsula being industrialized since the 1920's. On the manufacturing heritage some new sectors have been introducing during this last decade like tourism or glass. By extension and based on the project announcements and various visits of foreign firms in DPRK since the warming between both Korea in 2000, we can extrapolate which possible industries could be located in the main North Korean industrial areas; Nampo-Pyongyang and Wonsan-Hamheung seemed to have the best and largest potential.

Table 11.1 Overview of economic activities in main economic areas of North Korea

	Traditional industries	Recent industries	Potential industries	Natural resources
Pyongyang – Nampo	Machinery, steel, electric, electronic, shipbuilding, cement, fertilizer, textile, clothing	Glass, chemicals, construction materials, automotive	Precision chemical, food and beverage, plastic and rubber, automotive spare parts and assembly	Coal, gold, iron ore, silver, zinc
Wonsan – Hamheung	Chemical, machinery, non-steel metal, cement, shipbuilding	-	Automobile, steel, non-ferrous metal, petrochemical, plastic and rubber, precision chemicals, chemical fertilizer, food and beverage, clothing, glass	Tungsten, zinc
Sinuiju	Machinery, metal, chemical, textile, paper, pulp	Sinuiju SAR (2002)	Precision chemicals, plastic and rubber, clothing, food and beverage, wood, glass	-
Rajin – Seonbong	Non-steel metal, petrochemical, coal	Construction, logistics, real estate, retailing, tourism, transport [Rajin-Seonbong Free-Trade Zone, 1991]	Wood, paper, pulp	Uranium, coal
Gaeseong – Haeju	Cement, fertilizer, textile, agriculture, marine products	Manufacturing [Gaeseong Industrial Park, 2004]	Electric, electronics, clothing, food and beverage	Graphite, molybdenum
Cheongjin – Gimchaek	Steel, metal, machinery, automobile, shipbuilding, equipollent, rubber	-	Non-ferrous metal, electric products	Coal, cobalt, copper, graphite, iron ore, lead, magnesite, nickel

Sources: compiled from Lee (2001) and various sources

Therefore, any interpretation of Table 11.1 should be cautious, as most traditional industries collapse and few new industries have been developed in the recent years. Economic specialisations of the different areas may not be regarded as crucial for new developments. In fact, foreign firms shall invest in North Korea whatever the mere traces of past local knowledge and skills. Those are not consistent enough to be considered as valid economic rents (Kaplinski, 2004). Moreover, the two examples of Gaeseong Industrial Park (GIC) and Rajin-Sonbong show that new developments have been taking place without any linkages with formerly existing industries. On the one hand, the South Korean government-based GIC continues to prosper since its start in 2004, even during peak diplomatic tension periods, such as summer 2006 nuclear tests. At the end of 2007, nineteen thousand North Korean workers were operating in eighteen South Korean factories and plans to expand the site are currently examined. On the other hand, Rajin-Sonbong has not prospered due to mismanagement (Ducruet, 2008a). Developers of the zone have selected high-tech industries, casino, and retail instead of using the port as both a catalyst for economies of scale in manufacturing and a remedy to geographical remoteness. Traffic data show that Rajin port has been used intensively for carrying construction materials to build the zone at early developmental stage rather than for trade activities (Jo and Ducruet, 2007). This is being partly recovered as China is willing to improve the connection between Rajin and Jilin province through highway development and the installation of a logistics-free zone at Namyang (Hankyoreh, 2006). China's ambition using Rajin as a gateway to the Pacific is somehow counterbalanced by Russia's strategy to provide the zone with energy in exchange of connecting Rajin to Siberia's oil and gas fields through pipeline and railways (American Shipper, 2008), what confirms the ambivalent position of North Korea towards China and Russia. Since several months, it seems that the Russian plans are more appreciate that Chinese proposal by North Korean authorities.

Despite its more favourable location at the border with China, where approximately 50 to 80 percent of North Korean exports pass, Sinuiju Special Administrative Region (SAR) has not much developed since the appointed manager Yang Bin has been arrested by Chinese authorities after the project has just been launched in 2002. Another reason in the failure of this zone and exposed by DPRK authorities, was the absence of free trade agreement for SAR with China, which completely minimized the competitively of Sinuiju. Although a Special Zone at Nampo area is mentioned by the South Korean Ministry of Unification (2005), there is not yet evidence of its realization. However, the example of Nampo shows that a special economic zone is not mandatory for economic development, as 120 Chinese firms have invested in the province in the recent years (Pons, 2004). Nampo and Wonsan are strategic locations and for this reason they have not been opened officially to free trade. Recent announcements about the free zone project on Bidan and Wihwa islands at the Chinese border near Sinuiju confirm the preference to peripheral locations remote from

Pyongyang (Yonhap News, 2007), and more specifically the wish of the authorities to keep Chinese firms, as much as possible, far from the country's heart and less visible for the local population.

Previous attempts to estimate the performance of main economic areas are synthesized in Table 2. Based on the hypothesis of further foreign investment, coastal locations are pointed by Kim (2000) as the most promising areas to matching the Chinese model of Open Cities. The author identifies five desirable factors for motivating investment for South Korean firms:

- coastal city area: economic advantages of water transport
- pre-existing industrial base: experienced workforce despite damaged facilities
- safe investment: areas far from sensitive sites such as military bases
- economic linkages with neighbouring countries: proximity to borders
- personnel attractiveness: educational facilities, skilled labour

According to this framework, factor such as remoteness from military sites does not apply to Gaeseong, a fruitful project near the Demilitarized Zone (DMZ). Also, the proximity to borders or ports, under the control of the Army, has proved wrong for Sinuiju SAR and Rajin-Sonbong FTZ. Of course, it is partly due to the elaboration of this framework prior to the reforms and special zones that take place from 2002. However, it implies that any rigidly objective analysis of North Korean economic areas is not sufficient to understand the current situation. There is more a complex mingling of different factors with a large share of unexpectedness. As indicated above, usual arguments explaining the demise of Rajin-Sonbong FTZ through geographical remoteness and lack of economic base have largely ignored the importance of ports and the fact that high-tech industries are not likely to grow without a previous developmental stage in the manufacturing / exporting industries sector. Even Silicon Valley in the US has not grown up from nothing but has benefited from already existing military sites where research activities became attractive for regional innovation (Howells, 2005). Thus, any attempt to rationalize investment factors in North Korea based on objective benchmarking remains very limited. There are no inherent qualities of places that turn them into economic centres 'naturally', but a set of ongoing processes and strategies varying through space and time.

In order to benchmark the different economic areas, a synthesis of Kim (2000) and Lee (2001) is proposed in Table 11.2 based on the given scores. As a result, the skilled, abundant, and cheap labour is one of the most important factors to attract investments, and constitutes a very strong advantage of North Korea over other developing Asian countries and notably China (Chabaud-Latour, 2006). Among the different zones, Pyongyang-Nampo is seen as the most promising investment area, as it is well represented in all factors, except raw material provision but this factor stands among the less important elsewhere.

Table 11.2 Benchmarking main economic areas of North Korea

	Pyongyang - Nampo	Wonsan - Hamheung	Sinuiju	Rajin – Seonbong	Gaeseong - Haeju	Total
Openness	3	2	3	3	1	12
Development potential	3	2	3	2	1	11
Labour quality / quantity	3	2	2	1	2	10
Social Overhead Capital	3	2	2	1	2	10
Market	3	2	2	1	2	10
Landward linkages	2	2	3	2	1	10
Industrial base	3	3	2	1	1	9
Land	2	2	1	1	2	8
Agglomeration effect	3	2	1	1	1	8
Raw material	1	2	1	2	1	7
Total	26	21	20	15	14	

Sources: adapted from Kim (2000) and Lee (2001)

Based on such estimations of economic performance, what could be the prime location for European firms willing to invest in North Korea? It seems that besides considerations on existing industries, markets, and development potentials, one main factor that is usually neglected by scholars is the ability of a place to provide efficient logistics. Therefore, a complementary analysis is necessary is order to further estimate how the different economic areas may be attractive for European firms in their global strategy of being inserted in supply chains and realize an export-based activity.

1.2 The diversity of logistics' efficiency

The overall characteristics of the North Korean transport system are very influenced by the Soviet model, with a major importance given to land transport (Table 11.3). This is explained by specialization in heavy industries, agriculture, and mining, of which the products take the largest share (80%) compared to manufactured goods (Tsuji, 2005). The predominant heavy loads have tended to damage the roads to such extent that without regular management, and in addition to very contrasted natural conditions, about 7% only of the entire road network is paved (Bang, 2004). Without sufficient coal due to the impossibility to restart flooded-mines due to lack of oil, some steam trains dating back to Japanese occupation even use old truck or car tires to fuel the locomotive. Also, short distance goods carriage is ensured by agricultural vehicles, of which animal-led, and also by hands. On the maritime side, no modern container-handling facilities are said to exist in North Korea, but at least containers are regularly handled in Nampo and Rajin ports (Ducruet and Roussin, 2007b), given the announcements in the press about new terminal facilities financed by (or leased to) China (Lloyd's Register, 2006). However, not only North Korean ports have not been much modernized since several decades, but also the army – which controls the ports – collects very high entrance fees, resulting in excessive shipping costs and prolonged shipping time (Ahn, 2002). For example, one TEU[1] carried between Incheon, South Korea, and Nampo costs US$1,000, i.e. as much as a journey to Europe, and takes 24 hours for a round trip of only 100 kilometres (Ahn, 2001). However, since the signature of the inter-Korean agreement (2004), the two ports have launched joint regular shuttle services (Lloyd's Register, 2005), and the cost as dropped to US$250, allowing more traffics (Choe et al., 2005).

---

[1]Twenty-Foot Equivalent Unit, standard measure of container traffics

Table 11.3 Estimated modal split in 1989 and 2005

	Railways	Roads	Sea	Air
1989	73.8	18.3	7.9	0.0
2005	70.0	17.0	10.0	3.0

Sources: Tsuji, 2000; Roussin and Ducruet (2006)

Another important aspect of the transport system is its very heterogeneous geographical coverage (Figure 11.1). Centred upon Pyongyang, the highway network is mostly reflecting militarist and political needs to circulate efficiently along main East-West and North-South axis. In turn, the core region remains protected from borders as it does not connect directly to other neighbours' highways. Moreover, the conditions of the highways are very unequal. If the highways connecting Pyongyang to Nampo, Gaeseong and North of South Pyongan Province are in quite good state, the highway to join Wonsan is in poor condition due to long, dark and dangerous tunnels along its way, where accidents are frequent between the trucks and other vehicles and pedestrians.

Figure 11.1 The North Korean transport system and truck accessibility of main cities

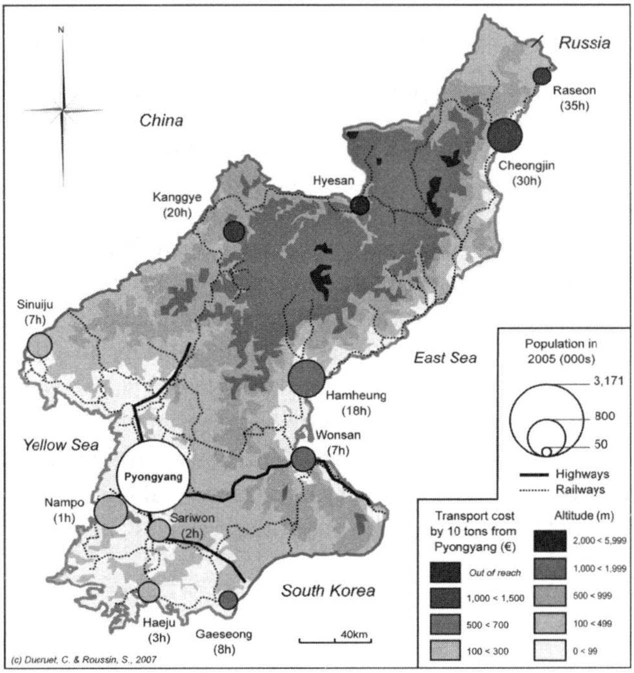

Sources: SERIC COREE(2005); Korea Research Institute for Human Settlements

Although it appears very well developed, the railway network is in fact poorly efficient, given the fact that it is approximately 70% electrified (CIA, 2005), and that the country runs out of energy. It has been observed that more generally, electricity spreads from Pyongyang to other provinces through a weekly rotation and in small quantities to minimize shortcuts. This gives a much contrasted regional distribution of domestic transport activities, with 30% around Nampo-Pyongyang, 10% around Sinuiju, 24% between Cheongjin and Rajin-Seonbong, and 17% around Hamheung-Heungnam (Tsuji, 2005). In terms of domestic circulation, there is an increasing separation between East, where several truck accidents are reported due to travel time, delays, lack of gas stations, repair facilities, and dangerous conditions notably along the coast and in the mountains; and West, where most of the operating factories are located. For foreign players, implications are enormous, as companies in North Korea have to spend 40% of their manufacturing costs on logistics (Foster-Carter, 2001).

As a result, foreign companies who want to invest in DPRK must be very careful regarding the location of their investments in order to not loss competitive advantage of the low-cost manpower in logistic cost. Thus, it appears at the term of this section that Nampo-Pyongyang area in the actual condition offer the best logistic solution for European firms, which will mainly use their facilities in North Korea for exportations to other most-advanced Asian countries or Europe. In the next section, we propose to analyze more specifically this area, the Nampo-Pyongyang Corridor (NPC).

2. The case of the Nampo-Pyongyang corridor

2.1 Recent developments around the corridor area

The Nampo-Pyongyang Corridor (NPC) is a plain with some smooth ills delimited by the administrative limits of Pyongyang's province and the agglomeration of Nampo (South Pyongan Province), both cities being only separated of 50 km or 1 hour of driving. With a population of 4.35 millions residents (around 1,500 residents per km^2, respectively 3,900,000 residents for Pyongyang area and 450,000 for Nampo), 18.5 % of national population, the NPC is the largest human concentration in DPRK and offers to foreign investors an abundant and cheap manpower. The monthly wage of a worker employed in a foreign company on Pyongyang is around 50 EUR (taxes included) and a specialist or a manager could be hired for 100 EUR per month, the NPC's area being the best place in DPRK to find skilled employees due to the location of the key national universities (Kim Chaek University of Technology, Kim Il-Sung University, the University of the Foreign Studies or the Pyongyang University of Science and Technology).

Beside this human factor, the NPC is also quite well connected with the other provinces (highways in good state to join Gaeseong and the north of South Pyongan Province, highway in more critical condition to go to Wonsan, railroads to reach the entire country) and most important for an European firm, NPC is connect to overseas through the port of Nampo for the goods, which is linked by regular service to Dalian port, and the airport of Pyongyang (Sunan International Airport) for the sensitive goods and the expatriates, with regular passengers and cargos flies to Beijing.

If the air road service does not show any specific problem except the age of the vessels, port service in Nampo faces two main difficulties. First, the access to Nampo port is limited by the West Sea barrage which allows only ships under

50,000 DWT[2] to enter, one time a day. Second difficulty, due to the trend of the containers to disappear in DPRK where they are easily recycling to other uses (storages, offices…), shipping companies ask now that the containers are loaded on board within the 24 hours after the arrival of the vessel. As a result, in order to minimize the transportation cost and to avoid buying its own containers, the port location is more advantageous. However, we can estimate that Nampo port in general is improving its services, but the city remains in very bad conditions, far from Pyongyang's environment. A new container terminal has been recently built there (Lloyd's Register, 2006), probably in order to sustain the trend of growth in container traffics (Figure 11.2).

Also, total traffic has been relatively stable along the last 20 years, except following the USSR's collapse (1991-1996). Between 1997 and 2001, the growth is mostly based on aid imports, while the growth from 2002 is more based on trade. This last trend is both explained by recent investments in the NPC and the betterment of inter-Korean relationships since 2000, reflected in their maritime agreement of 2005 (Ducruet and Roussin, 2007c). Notably, the cost of carrying one container on the Incheon-Nampo route has reduced fourfold after the agreement, as it is a main artery carrying 90% of inter-Korean sea trade

Figure 11.2 Evolution of traffic at Nampo port, 1985-2005

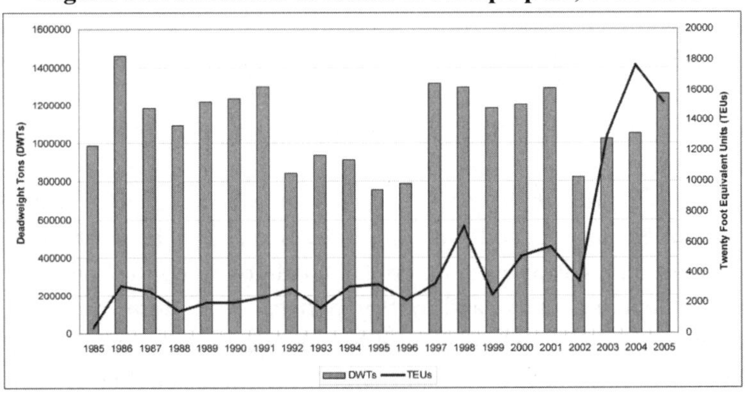

Sources: Lloyd's Marine Intelligence Unit

As we can see on figure 11.3, the NPC has been relatively well developed by the authorities during these last decades. A 6 lines road of 46 km follows the river Daedong and a large 10 lines highway of 44 km has been constructed later

[2] Deadweight Tonnage (DWT) represents the volume of the ship used for the carriage of goods

in 2000 lining more quickly Pyongyang and its port. Railways network is also widely extended with a main line between the both cities and several branches joining key industrials complexes; this area being one's of the main industrial district of DPRK with 2 mines, and 5 complexes specialized in mechanic and heavy industries, mostly still in operations.

Another important element in this area is the comparatively less lack of energy hitting it. Indeed, due to its political and economical key position, the NPC is privileged compare to other provinces and does not suffer of one-day-a-week shortcut. Factories located there can expect a better energy supply than in the entire country. In the same way and because of the same factors, diesel oil and gasoline are easier to find into NPC's area. As a matter of fact, Pyongyang and its nearby areas represented 50 % of the gasoline national consumption and 70 % of diesel consumption (Internal Report).

Figure 11.3 Overview of the Nampo-Pyongyang corridor

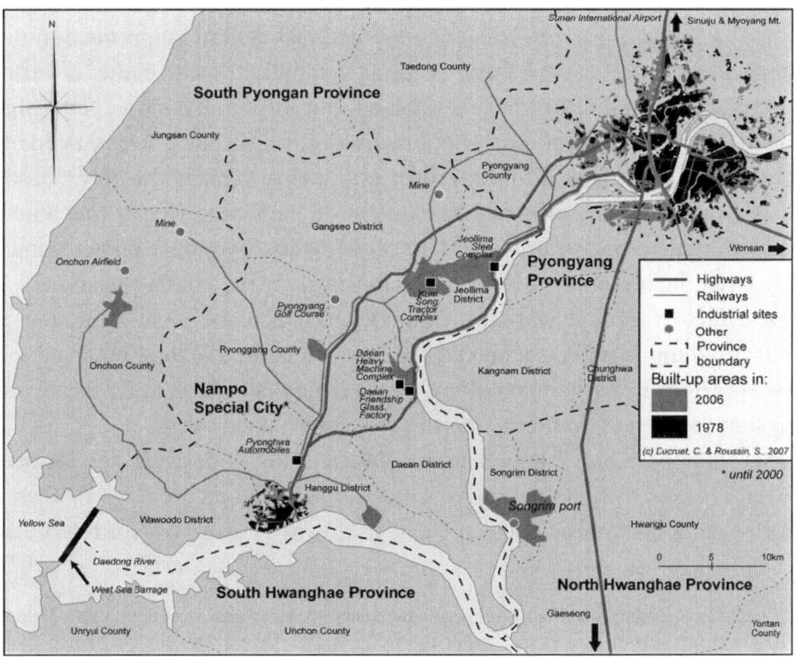

Sources: authors

As a result, most recent and main investments in DPRK (outside of mining sector) have been located on the NPC. Among them we can quote the Daean Friendship Glass Factory opened in 2006 in cooperation with the Chinese authorities. Equipments have been supplied by China, DPRK's army has built the facilities before to transfer it to the Cabinet (in DPRK, main factorises are under the control of the cabinet and smaller ones under the control of municipalities). To pay back this investment of US$24 million, DPRK has to buy raw material and energy from China. Following the same model, two other news factories have been inaugurated recently: a ceramics plant (with Italian origin equipments) and a synthetic painting industrial unit on Kiyang, near the Kumsong Tractor Complex. Also, the recent strategy of the Egyptian firm Orascom Cement (bought end of 2007 with the French company Lafarge) expecting to use Nampo as an export gateway reflects the importance of this region for North Korea's internationalization[3].

At last, we can quote the case of the Daean-Meccamidi (TM) joint-venture Company, an example of French-North Korean cooperation located on Daean and specialized in production of hydraulic power plant generator. TM has been created in 2004 in order to re-launch the national electricity production through a large programme of small and medium hydraulic power plants covering the entire country. Authorities have estimated that this solution was better than the construction of new large power plan using oil for instance which needs to import oil, to update the aged local power grill and to damage the air environment. TM is now employing around 100 workers on the Daean Heavy Machine Complex's site and plans to produce 1 to 50 M Watts hydraulic power generators. They have the ambition to open a R&D centre in the coming years, the North Korean factory should start the exportations when the local hydraulic power plants programme will be achieved. To proceed to the JV, the French partner has been agreed to bring its technology, management skill and cash, the North Korean side employees, building, mining concession and cash.

This example shows that because DPRK's key-industries are located into NPC, it is easier to find there more solid and potential partners for JV than in the other North Korean provinces, and that at this early stage of North Korean eco-

[3] Orascom Construction Industries, the Egyptian cement producer and construction group, announced an $115m investment in a cement plant in North Korea. The deal with state-owned Pyongyang Myongdang Trading Corporation will see OCI take a 50 percent stake in Sangwon Cement, which owns and operates the closest cement plant to Pyongyang. The increased capital will be used to modernise, rehabilitate and upgrade the plant's capacity to 3m tonnes a year. OCI's investment will also be used to invest in ready-mix concrete, distribution, related mining operations and a dedicated hydroelectric power station near the plant. See Griggs and Fidler (2007).

nomic opening it is more efficient to be geographically close to the authorities, situated in Pyongyang.

2.2 Potentials for further European investments

According to the North Korean regulation on foreign investments, foreigners have several options to open business. The most used is a joint venture company between an overseas partner and a local partner. Because of the local hard currency shortage, the North Korean part usually brings into the joint company, lands, buildings, vehicles and manpower. The foreign partner carries cash, machines, and technology or raw materials. In the case of strategic JV companies, authorities can provide special guarantees or advantages like mining concession, tax reduction or favourable legislation.

However and since the reform programme launched in 2002, foreign investors are now able to be owner at 100 % of their investment, except for the land which remains the exclusive property of the State. Nevertheless, due to the complexity of the local administration and in order to get a better access to skilled manpower, commodities supply or more efficient distribution channel, it is still more efficient to choose the JV business model's option.

As this stage, an alternative business model could be selected by European investors worried by the cultural gap between them and their local partner. This other solution is a tripartite joint company associating a European firm, with South Korean and North Korean partners.

- European side provides cash, technologies, strategic management skills; commercial debouches in Europe, and its flag. DPRK is willing to have cordial relationship with Europe in order to counterbalance the Tokyo-Washington axis and the too much influent China. As a result, European firms benefit of a quite welcome environment by Pyongyang and a better protection of their interest.
- The South Korean side, associated with the European partner in a joint company under the UE flag, brings cash, technologies, its dynamism, commercial opportunities on South Korean market, and pragmatic management come from its cultural knowledge and its geographical proximity.
- At last and like in regular JV business model, the North Korean side brings natural and human resources.

If this formula is not without confer some concerns regarding political issue or communication between 3 parties, we can object that a European presence in this deal can moderate the inter-Korean passion being keep advantages of the

Korean partners. After to have exanimate where to invest and how to invest, a last question is in which sector is it possible to invest in NPC?

First of all, an industrial implantation into NPC must be focus on exportation to European market or South Korean market (Chinese and Japanese markets in mid-term). Due to its low cost country characteristics and its easy access to various natural resources, steel and metallurgic activities, mechanic industries, automotive spares parts production (and in mid-term assembly), garments and shoes industries could be established there. Local manpower is ever qualified in these sectors and logistic system can support these activities. This is also facilitated by the proximity of Nampo to major load centres such as Dalian, Incheon, Busan, Singapore, Hong Kong, Osaka-Kobe, Yokohama, which connect to the world's busiest maritime lanes. Figure 4 represents 93% of Nampo's direct maritime connections, together with the recent weight of those pivotal ports in terms of direct calls for container lines. It shows the already existing linkages and the high potential for Nampo to get connected to international markets via neighbouring ports (Ducruet and Roussin, 2007d; Ducruet et al., 2008; Ducruet, 2008b).

Secondly and as we previously explained, demand has started to grow up into NPC's area, with around 20 % of the households earning more than 100 EUR per month. This population is composed of high ranking people in the administration or army, specialists (engineers in IT, mining or construction industries, translators…), companies managers and of various traders and businessmen who launched their own business (restaurants, transportation) or who are importing goods from overseas (mainly China). Largely represented on Pyongyang and also on Nampo, this population is demanding better services (taxi, banking, gas stations), improved public services (transport, waste treatment, water treatment and supply) understanding the idea that should be paid, and start to have a positive impact on construction and logistic industries. On all these sectors, European expertise is strong, world well-know and will not suffer of the local American or Japanese competitions like the Chinese firms are now using DPRK to be even more competitive.

Figure 11.4 Direct maritime linkages of Nampo port

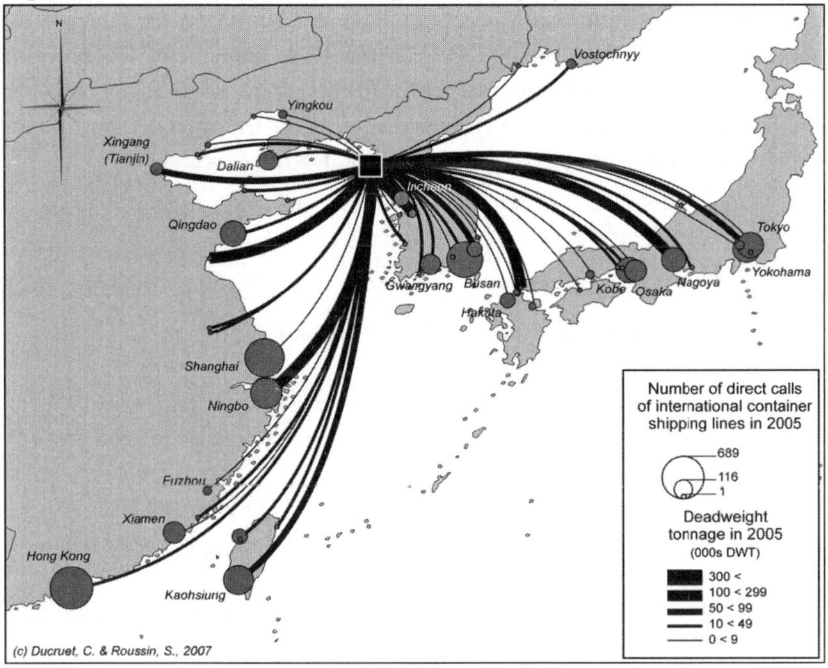

Sources: Lloyd's Marine Intelligence Unit ; Containerisation International

Conclusion

To invest in DPRK is a bet, a risky adventure seen from Europe, but from a Northeast Asian perspective it is a new frontier of business development, illustrated by the intense movement of Chinese companies in North Korea (around 130 companies have activities there), and the proactive involvement South Korean companies and authorities in the development of Gaeseong industrial complex and Geumgang Mountain tour. As a result, European firms should have a more rational vision of North Korea and see all the advantages that they can take from this country ready to open economic cooperation with Europe: low-cost and relatively well educated manpower, large panel of natural resources, and strategic location between South Korea, Japan, Eastern Russia and China. The purpose of this paper has been to show that nowadays and for European interests, the Nampo-Pyongyang Corridor offers the best alternative between risk and safety, compare to other areas in North Korea. However, we cannot forget that European Commission has opened FTA negotiations with South Korea and if we refer to the Korean-USA FTA case, the question of nationality of goods produced in Gaeseong Industrial Complex (GIC) will be put on the table. If European Union is agreed to include GIC in the FTA agreement, Gaeseong area could also become an interesting target for European investors focus on exportations, but with Damocles sword of any cooling in the inter-Korean dialogue process and the obligation to cooperate with both Koreas.

References

Ahn, M.B. (2002). Restoration of the Seoul-Sinuiju line: review and outlook, *East Asian Review*, 14(1), 107-119.

Ahn, M.Y. (2001). Slow boat to North Korea, *Cargo News Asia*, May 7th.

American Shipper, 2008, Russia, North Korea discuss port-connected cross-border rail link, January 28, http://www.americanshipper.com/SNW_story.asp?news=82882

Bang, H.K.(2004) Research notes: towards an integrated logistics system in Northeast Asia, *East Asian Review*, 16(2), 111-121.

Bridges, B. (2003) Western Europe and North Korea: new openings and old problems, *East Asia*, 20(3), 86-107.

Chabaud-Latour, P. (2006). Doing business in DPRK, *North Korea Forum*, Korea Research Institute for Human Settlements, Anyang, Korea, April 21st.

Choe, S.T., Cho, H.J.& Kwon, S.J.(2005). Is North Korea a viable economic partner?, *North Korean Review*, 1, 52-62.

Ducruet, C. and Roussin, S., (2007b). North Korea: towards the opening of seaports. *Journal de la Marine Marchande*, 4566, 6-9 (in French).

Ducruet, C. and Roussin, S., (2007c). Inter-Korean maritime linkages: economic integration vs. hub dependence. *15th European Conference on Theoretical and Quantitative Geography*, Conference Proceedings, Montreux, Switzerland, September 7-11, pp. 133-139 [ISBN 978-2-940368-05-1].

Ducruet, C. and Roussin, S., (2007d). The changing relations between hinterland and foreland at North Korean ports (1985-2006). *New Vision for Enhancing Asia-Europe Economic Cooperation*, Proceedings of the 6th Inha & Le Havre International Conference, Inha University, Incheon, Republic of Korea, October 10-11, 349-362.

Ducruet, C., (2008a). Free-trade zones in the Koreas. In: Bost, F. (Ed.) *World Atlas of Free-Trade Zones* (in French, forthcoming).

Ducruet, C., (2008b). Hub dependence in constrained economies: the case of North Korea, *Maritime Policy and Management* (forthcoming).

Ducruet, C., and Jo, J.C. (2007). Coastal cities, port activities and logistic constraints in a socialist developing country: the case of North Korea, *Transport Reviews*, 28(1), 1-25.

Ducruet, C., and Roussin, S., (2007a). The North Korean archipelago: economic transition and territorial blockages, *Mappemonde*, 87(3) (in French), Available at http://mappemonde.mgm.fr/num15/articles/art07302.html

Ducruet, C., Gelezeau, V., and Roussin, S. (2008). North Korea's maritime connections: territorial change on the peninsula and regional dynamics in Northeast Asia, *L'Espace Géographique* (in French, forthcoming).

Ducruet, C., Jo, J.C., Lee, S.W., and Roussin, S (2008). Geopolitics of shipping networks: the case of North Korea's maritime connections, *Sustainability in International Shipping, Port and Logistics Industries and the China Factor*, International Association of Maritime Economists (IAME), Dalian, China, April 2-4.

Griggs, T., and Fidler, S. (2007). Orascom takes stake in N Korea's Sangwon, *Financial Times*, July 15th, http://www.ft.com/cms/s/1/4c0d690c-32ee-11dc-a9e8-0000779fd2ac.html

Hankyoreh, (2006) China, N.K. agree to trade zone along border, *Hankyoreh*, http://english.hani.co.kr/arti/english_edition/e_international/150123.html

Howells, J. (2005) Innovation and regional economic development: a matter of perspective?, *Research Policy*, 34, 1220-1234.

Jo, J.C., and Adler, S., (2002). North Korean planning: urban changes and regional balance, *Cities*, 19(3), 205-215.

Jo, J.C., and Ducruet, C. (2007). Rajin-Seonbong, new gateway of Northeast Asia, *Annals of Regional Science*, 41(4), 927-950.

Jo, J.C., and Ducruet, C., (2006). Maritime trade and port evolution in a socialist developing country: Nampo, gateway of North Korea, *The Korea Spatial Planning Review*, 51, 3-24.

Kaplinsky, R., (2004). Sustaining income growth in a globalising world: the search for the Nth rent, Institute of Development Studies, Brighton.

Kim, C.K. (2000). Strategies for investing in North Korea, In *VIP Millenium Report*, (pp. 10-13). Hyundai Research Institute, Seoul.

Lee, D.H., (2001), Industrial location planning in North Korea, pp. 269-300 in: Yoon, C.H. and Lau, L.J. (Eds.), *North Korea in Transition*, Edward Elgar, Cheltenham and Northampton.

Lloyd's Register (2005), South Korean investors eye North's Nampo, September 22nd. http://www.portguide.com

Lloyd's Register (2006), North Korea completes container berth, May 12th. http://www.portguide.com

Ministry of Unification (2005). Recent changes in North Korea, March 14th. http://www.unikorea.go.kr

Pons, P., 2004, Fragile dégel en Corée du Nord, *Le Monde*, 16 Décembre.

Pons, P., 2006, Incursion en Corée du Nord, *Le Monde*, 4 Décembre.

Roussin, S., and Ducruet, C. (2006). Logistic perspectives in DPRK, *Proceedings of the Annual Fall Meeting of the Korean Society of Coastal and Ocean Engineers*, September 15-16, Seoul, Korea, 101-112.

Roussin, S., and Ducruet, C. (2007). Doing business in DPRK for the European companies: the logistic issue, Communication at Seogang University, Seoul, Republic of Korea, May 26.

Yonhap News, (2007). North Korea considering building special economic zone on two islands, March 23rd.

13

The North Korean IT Sector: "a hidden diamond" Some Observations from a Dutch Consultant

Paul Tjia

Introduction

Dutch companies are increasingly conducting IT and IT-related projects in low-cost countries. Also known as offshore sourcing, or off shoring, this way of working means that labour-intensive activities, such as the programming of computer software, are being done abroad. There are two major reasons for global sourcing: the possibility to reduce costs and the availability of specialized IT-skills. It must be noted that quality is always crucial: it makes no sense to use programmers from a cheaper location, when the software produced is of a lesser quality than in Holland.

So far, hundreds of Dutch organisations have executed offshore software projects, including small and medium-sized firms. Major Dutch enterprises, such as ABN Amro Bank, ING, Philips and KLM are active offshore users. Though as a country, The Netherlands is not particularly large, the deals that the Dutch companies have made have often been major. India is the most popular offshore destination for large Dutch enterprises, but smaller and medium-sized firms are working with a range of other countries, both nearshore (in Eastern-Europe) and farshore (especially in Asia). There are now dozens of offshore destinations, including the DPRK (Democratic People's Republic of Korea, or North Korea). It is a very interesting country, but not a well-known destination yet, and some outsourcing experts describe it as "a hidden diamond".

As a Dutch offshore consultant, I regularly advise clients about issues of country selection. A couple of years ago, when I noticed that Chinese companies were outsourcing IT-work to neighbouring North-Korea, I became interested in this country as well. After research, and after several visits, North Korea has been added to my personal list of most promising offshore destinations. It offers interesting business opportunities, and several European clients are already successfully outsourcing work to North-Korean service providers.

North-Korea: Information Technology Services

North-Korean companies offer two types of services; first of all activities in the field of Information Technology. These are software development services, such as programming various kinds of software (e.g. using programming languages such as Microsoft C++ or Java), testing of new software or building websites. Not all the work is being done by the North-Korean staff; in most cases the functional (and sometimes also the technical) specifications of the software are designed by the European client, who is also responsible for the final testing.

The North-Korean companies have experiences with a wide range of development platforms. They work with Assembler, Cobol, C, Visual Studio.Net, Visual C/C++, Visual Basic, Java, JBuilder, Powerbuilder, Delphi, Flash, XML, Ajax, ASP, PHP, Perl, Oracle, DB2, Sybase, SQL Server, MySQL, etc. They are also eager to learn new tools.

Software development can involve building new systems from scratch, but also maintenance work. Important are administrative applications, ranging from hotel management software to manufacturing and air traffic control systems. North-Koreans have also been working on ERP systems (Enterprise Resource Planning), e-Business, websites, Internet search engines, BPM systems (Business Process Management), BI (Business Intelligence) and vehicle tracking systems using GPS. Surprisingly, a North-Korean software company is involved in building a bank management system (Islamic banking) for a client in the Middle-East.

Compared with other countries, North-Korea is very advanced in the field of security systems. There is a lot of research and expertise in preventing systems from attacks from hackers, and services in the fields of firewall systems, encryption systems and specialized skills are being offered to foreign IT security firms.

Some of the locally made software is incorporated in hardware products (e.g. fingerprint identification products for access control of buildings and for time attendance) and are already exported. There are also software packages available in the areas of car number plate identification and face recognition.

Besides administrative software, North-Korea is producing technical software. It develops its own videoconferencing software, infrastructure management systems, specific software for radio communication and mobile communication, medical diagnostic software, embedded software and PLCs (programmable Logic Controllers).

North-Korea: IT-related Services

North-Korean providers are also offering various kinds of IT-related activities, also known as BPO (Business Process Outsourcing) or ITES (IT Enabled Services). There are various areas in this field:

Animation (e.g. production of cartoons) is very labour- intensive to produce, and is therefore ideal for offshoring to low-cost nations. North Korea is already famous as a production location for high quality cartoons and animation. International experts describe the country as one of the most talented centres of animation in the world. The most famous example is SEK in Pyongyang, one of the largest animation studios in the world with an artistic staff of more than 1600. SEK was established in 1957, and started cooperation with foreign organisations in 1985. Over the past dozen of years, it has made hundreds of animation, puppet and paper-cut movies pertaining to education and instruction of children. It is capable of producing more than 7.000 minutes of work every year. It has several foreign marketing offices and important European animation producing countries such as France, Spain and Italy are outsourcing to SEK on a large scale.

North Korea is also advanced in making computer games. I have seen a wide range of titles, including table tennis, chess, golf, or beach volley. The design of many of their applications is modern and according to the western taste. Games are made for export as well, and a Dutch company is outsourcing its game development to North Korea. There are now Korean games for PC's, Nintendo Wii and Playstation available. Some games to be used on mobile phones are quite popular in Japan. The Samilpho IT centre (part of the Korea Computer Centre) develops the award-winning Go computer game. Its office has a display showing all the trophies which were won during international competitions.

Data processing. In circumstances when data, stored on paper, needs to be converted into digital form and scanning is not an option, manual data entry is a solution. These services are offered by Dakor Company, established in cooperation with a Swiss firm. This joint venture works for European research companies, and it receives from them electronically scanned survey forms on a daily basis. It processes these papers and returns the results within 48 hours to their clients. The company is also conducting data-entry work for international organisations such as the United Nations and the International Red Cross. Dakor is offering additional services, such as producing 2D and 3D designs for architectural firms. A new area of expertise is energy reduction, and it has developed an innovative method to enlarge the capacity of batteries of UPS systems (Uninterruptible Power Supply) and to increase their lifecycle. It is now searching for European investors to market and to produce this innovation.

Document imaging also allows North Korea to perform finance and accounting services. Some companies in Pyongyang are involved in these back-office activities. Because of the available knowledge of the Japanese language, the North Koreans are also offering back-office services to western companies engaged in doing business with Japan.

A growing IT sector

In European countries, including The Netherlands, a shortage of software engineers is expected. This situation is different in many offshore countries, where a career in IT is popular among the youth. This is also the case in North Korea, and large numbers of students are interested to pursue a career in IT. Once, I visited in Pyongyang the large Kim Chaek University of Technology during the summer holiday, and there were still students around at the faculty of Informatics. In order to gain experience, some were conducting projects for foreign companies. I spoke with students who were Programming computer games or were developing software for PDA's (Personal Digital Assistants).

A large pool of technically qualified workforce is already available in North Korea. Companies employ scientists and engineers, having various degrees (e.g. PhD, MS and BS). Some of the staff is taking advanced courses abroad (in Asian countries such as India or China, and also in Europe). Foreign trainers are regularly invited to teach classes in Pyongyang. A European exchange project to train North Korean managers in the areas of project management, quality management and marketing is currently being prepared; European IT companies will arrange for the teachers.

The North Korean IT sector is dynamic, where new firms are being established, and where business units of larger organisations are being spun-off into new ventures. An example is the Gwang Myong IT Centre, which is a spin-off from KCC (Korea Computer Centre). It is specialized in network software and security, and it produces anti-virus, data encryption, data recovery, and fingerprint identification software. This firm is internationally active as well; it has an office in China and among its clients are financial institutions in Japan.

KCC (Korea Computer Centre) is the nation's single largest software corporation. Established in 1990, it has more than one thousand employees. For several years, KCC is active as an offshore services provider and it works for clients in Europe, China, South Korea and Japan. It has branch offices in several foreign countries, including China. It is divided in centres, such as the Milyong IT Centre (producing medical diagnostic equipment, including heart examination systems and vascular disease diagnostic systems). Its Chongbong IT Centre is involved in artificial intelligence (e.g. natural language processing, sound processing and image processing). KCC develops various software products, of which some are especially designed for the local market. Examples are a Korean version of Linux and translation software between Korean, Japanese, Chinese and English. They also produce software for Korean character and handwriting recognition and voice recognition. Another package is able to recognize music by humming a few sounds. In less than a second, a melody is being recognized from a database of more than 500 songs.

There are several other large North Korean IT companies, each employing hundreds of staff, such as PIC (Pyongyang Informatics Centre) and HTD (Hi-Tech Development Company). Other firms are part of huge general enterprises, such as Unha Corporation or Korea Roksan General Trading Company. Roksan has an IT Development Centre but is also involved in a wide range of other activities, including shipping, food production and electronics.

New companies are being founded as well, including foreign joint-ventures such as Nosotek, with a company from Germany. I also visited Tin Ming Alan CG Studio. This firm was set up in early 2006, and is located in a new office building in the outskirts of Pyongyang. Its main focus is in Computer Graphics and in 2D and 3D animation and it uses the latest hardware and software, including Maja. Some of the staff of Tin Ming Alan speak Chinese and the company has a marketing office in China. They are hired by Chinese advertisement companies to make the animation for TV-commercials. It also works on animation to be included in computer games. Several employees of this young company come from other animation studios and have more than ten years of experience in this field.

Business opportunities

In the current financial and economic situation, European companies face many challenges. They must cut costs, develop new products and find new markets. North-Korea is an interesting option because of its specific advantages. The local tariffs are lower than in India or China, thus giving European firms the option of considerable cost reductions. The commitment of North Korean IT firms is high, and the country is especially interesting for smaller or medium sized western software companies. Outsourcing work to North Korea could also be used to foster innovation (e.g. developing better products or new applications). The country can be used for various types of research (from Linux to parallel processing). Based from my interaction with Korean managers and software engineers, I do not believe that the cultural differences are larger than with China or India. My communication with them, both formal and informal, has been pleasant. Communicating with North Koreans is clearly less difficult than with Japanese. In addition, all local companies are eager to work for European clients.

Over the recent years, North Korea is opening up for foreign business. The introduction of modern technology (e-mail, Internet, FTP, Skype, etc.) makes communication much easier than it was in the past. North Korean IT companies are working toward quality improvement through the use of ISO9001, CMMI and Six Sigma. Nevertheless, it must be noted that offshoring always requires sound preparation. After all, we have to deal effectively with the differences in distance, in time zone, in language, in culture and even in political system. Communication is crucial when conducting offshore projects successfully. Various ways of electronic communication with North Korea are possible, but at the start of a project, personal contacts should take place and a visit by the client to the North Korean provider is advisable. I would also suggest to invite some of the North Korean staff to Europe, for a short period of familiarisation and additional training. In case a project is innovative, complicated or when it requires a lot of communication or knowledge transfer, it might be recommended to execute the first projects in Europe, by bringing North Korean staff to the facility of the client. In general, executing a small pilot project is always the best way to investigate the opportunities in more detail.

So far, the North Koreans were mainly focussed on trading with Asia; Europe has been a relatively new market for them. It is expected that this will change, since the Korean companies are putting more efforts on finding clients in Europe. The lack of visibility (country branding) is one of the main challenges, and North Korea is not a well-known IT destination yet. For this reason, the feasibility of an export promotion project is currently being investigated. External support in the field of export marketing can indeed be useful. Not all companies are using yet modern marketing material (e.g. company brochures, DVD's) and many do not even have a presence on the Internet (they might have a website, but often in the Korean language, and only visible on the local Intranet, which can only be browsed inside North Korea).

Conclusion

North Korea has a large number of skilled IT professionals, and has a high level of IT expertise in various areas. In addition, it offers various services in the field of Business Process Outsourcing. The country is evolving into an offshore destination for a growing number of clients from various countries. North Korean companies are now targeting the European market, and their low tariffs and the available skills are major advantages. Especially smaller and medium sized companies can consider North Korea as a potential offshore destination, and should research the opportunities for collaboration in more detail. Taking part in a study tour, as I have done several times, is an excellent way to get more insight in the actual business opportunities. For me, North Korea is currently one of the most interesting offshore destinations. It is also relatively unknown and I can fully agree with those experts who refer to this country as "a hidden diamond".

14

Software and Animation in North Korea: EU Firms' Activities, Korea Computer Centre Europe and Nosotek JV Company and EU's 'Route to DPRK'

Sung-Jo Park

"North Korea is well known for its nuclear ambitions. But it is relatively little-known fact that the country is a hidden outsourcing Mecca for the international animation industry..." (Sunny Lee, Asia Times Korea, March 14, 2007)

The following paper briefly describes the influence of East Germany on the development of IT in North Korea in the first part. The second part scrutinizes how North Korea has been trying to enter into the global business with softwares and animations films. In doing so, the cases of Korea Computer Centre Europe in Berlin and Nosotek JV in Pyongyang are analysed in detail. The final part touches upon the recent efforts by the EU to bring European and North Korean firms together under the name entitled 'Route to DPRK'.

1. Technical Assistance from East Germany to North Korea

Before the German unification in 1990 East Germany had relatively intensive economic relations with North Korea in terms of economic assistance and mutual trade, even though the volume of mutual exchange has been relatively small. It was essentially important that North Korea had a possibility to accede to the electronic and electric industry in East Germany, because this means that North Korea had a possibility to indirectly get in touch with West German electronic and electric expertises, since East Germany must have learned to a large extent from West Germany through technical cooperation projects between both countries. A series of cooperation agreements between North Korea and East Germany (before the German unification) contained West German and Western expertise and know how related to electronic and electric industry. (Extensively Park ,2007 p. 400 ff)

Shortly after the German Unification in 1990 the author had a chance to talk with former East German experts such as Professors G. Meyer, J. Ester and W. Thess who provided consultancy for North Korea in electronic industry. These professors were of opinion that the electronic technology of East Germany made a considerable contribution to development of IT in North Korea. Especially Professor W. Thess who is said to be responsible for developing one mega bit chip in East Germany told the author that "North Koreans who studied at Karl Marx University (now Chemnitz University) and joined his lectures in Pyongyang during his frequent visits in North Korea were extremely bright, smart and diligent, excellent in mathematics." "One of those students was writing a PhD dissertation but disappeared with other North Korean students when the Berlin Wall fell down." Further, he continued to tell his experiences in North Korea that "computers and other electronic equipments he saw in North Korea were very new, imported from Japan as donations by pro-north Korean residents in Japan."

An interesting question in this respect is to which extent North Korean students who played an essential role as the first generation of IT development in North Korea received a sufficient training in East Germany to develop their own electronic development capability.

Thomas Kudrass (2009, url) pointed out in his article on the study programme of informatics in East Germany, the fact that North Koreans' majoring in electronics in East Germany was possible at its full length at the Technical Institute of Dresden as the only education institution specialized to train students from various underdeveloped countries such as North Korea, Mongolia, Lybia and Algeria. Kudrass further stressed the significance of the informatics training in its inseparable coupling with internship-like practical exercise at plants, in particular, at Robotron.

At the Technical Institute of Dresden, there were North Korean students majoring in informatics until 1989. However, they disappeared at the time of Berlin Wall's fall. Kudrass' conjecture is that intensive internships by North Korean students at Robotron must have been very instrumental for development of electronic industry in North Korea.

How was the standard of ICT in East Germany? (See Boehme, Werner et al, 2007: VEB Robotron- Messelektronik "Otto Schoen" Dresden) The computer and automation technology in East Germany was thought to contribute primarily to the increase in labour productivity. (cf. the following table) Erich Honecker saw a possibility to catch up the labour productivity of West Germany by promoting computer and automation technology in East Germany.

Table 13.1 Labour Productivity Gap between West and East Germany

	West Germany	East Germany
1950	100	48%
1970	100	61%
1980	100	73%
1989	100	79%

Source: Marxismus-Forum (2006)

The development in microelectronics in East Germany began relatively late. In 1976 the first microprocessor 4-bit-processor was produced in series, soon followed by 8-bit processor U880 and UB880D. At the beginning of 80s the 18-bit processor came out which was followed by 32-bit processor at the end of 80s, with 1-Mbit memory chip being in development research at that time. In September of 1988 the first mega-bit memory chip produced in East Germany was brought to Erich Honecker personally who was said to be greatly satisfied with this ostensive success. Shortly before the unification the series of computer KCB85/4 in about 50000 pieces were produced. East Germany being allegedly lagged in development of computer technology was able to develop 1 mega bit memory chips and even small computers of its own accord. (Merkel, 2007)

The following table is a list of East Germany-produced computer programmes which we can be sure that North Koreans possibly came into contact during their study in East Germany and through East German experts' lectures such as Prof. Thess' ones in North Korea .

Table 13.2 Computer programmes developed by East Germans

Name of Programme	Programme producer
Autent	Dresden Institute of Construction Research
Comos	Humboldt University
Cosar	Magdeburg Institute of Technology
Surface CAD/CAM	Institute of Cybernetics
PSU	Dresden Institute of Applied Research
Petrinetz-Analysator	Leipzig Institute of Technology
Roscha	Dresden Institute of Technology
SEKOS	Humboldt University
System softwares (DOS, VMS, UNIX compatible)	Robotron Dresden
Wega (UNIX III compatible)	Koebnick Factory of Electric Tools

Source: Park (2007)

As regards characteristics of software development in East Germany, East German experts in their interview with the author argued unisono that the software development in East Germany was not tailored towards its practicability, but the competition with West Germany. Thus, these East German softwares were 'orders from above' which was to aim at enhancing political legitimacy and vanity of East German political leaders. (Park, 1991)

The close cooperation between East Germany and North Korea ceased at the moment of German unification in 1990. Years after, the cooperation between the unified Germany and North Korea has resumed in the recent time. North Korea has repeatedly shown a great interest to delegate researchers to German research institutes like Max Planck Institute, German Cancer Research Institute, other university institutes, etc, through the programmes financially supported by the German Academic Exchange Service, Gottlieb und Daimler-Karl Benz-Stiftung. The focus by North Koreans is supposed to be directed at basic research in biology, physics, mathematics, informatics, etc.

A very interesting story about the working conditions at research institutes in North Korea was given in the Report by Heidelberg University which held a joint seminar in North Korea in 2005 stated that: "The working conditions in North Korea are very different, especially as regards technical facilities. At those institutes we visited, no supercomputer was available. It was quite common that small-sized computers there are out of date, those models which we could buy in Singapore for about 500 US dollars. Also labs with books are very poorly equipped. In all, North Korean research is lagging behind the international standard. However, efforts by scientists to catch up to the international standard are in extreme contrast with their technical facilities." (http://www.uni.-heidelberg.de/presse/news04/240korea.html retrieved Dec.22, 2005)

North Korea has not been an important economic partner for both former East Germany and the United Germany. Despite this negligible importance of the North Korean economy, the so-called Asia-Pacific Economic Cooperation concept by former chancellor Helmut Kohl did not ignore it. He encouraged the German business world to deal intensively and systematically with markets in East and Southeast Asia. This concept implied inclusion of the socialist economies such as China, Vietnam, North Korea, Mongolia, etc., currently pursuing economic transformation which may trigger substantial aid, investments, technology transfer, etc.

Along with this initiative, Germany is, among all other European countries, the very country that has been extremely active in North Korea by pursuing trade activities, organizing industry and trade fairs with institutional and financial aids from the Federation of German Industries and the German Asia-Pacific Business Association (OAV, in German Ostasiatischer Verein).

Also, individual federal states took initiatives: Bavaria has been most active in initiating cooperation with North Korea - supported by the German-Korean Friendship Society - for the purpose of encouraging Bavarian firms to engage in North Korea by means of investment, technology cooperation and training of North Korean manpower in Germany. At the moment of signing the agreement, the North Korean side admitted serious problems with infrastructure, energy and metallurgical processing. The Bavarian state minister of economics Wiesheu called for creation of investment-promoting conditions, such as property rights, investment protection, payment guarantee, etc. and both sides established a joint working committee dealing with legal aspects of those investment-related conditions. (http://www.stmwivt.bayern.de) Current indications show that German firms are considerably hesitant and eventually reluctant to engage themselves in the Kaesung Economic Special Zone.

Thus, it is not a coincidence, and further, a positive signal for future cooperation between both countries that the Munich-based MMI-Munich International Trade Fairs Pte, Ltd hosted the first International Technology and Infrastructure Exhibition (Pyongyang ITIE 2002). The Final Report of this exhibition said that 70 firms from 10 countries participated in this event focusing on transportation and logistics, IT, electronics, health and medical care as well as medical, hospital technology and equipment. (Park, 2004)

To conclude this segment of the article, the author wants to stress that the contribution by East Germans to development of IT industry in North Korea should not be overestimated. In the meantime, some authors such as Hayes (2003), Kim (2004), Park (2007), Noland (2008) etc. have indicated that for the beginning stage of IT development in North Korea, a combination of external support from India, UN, etc. and endogenous initiatives were instrumental.

2. Korea Computer Centre Europe (KCCE) as a Window for the West

Jan Holtermann, a German entrepreneur enabled the North Korean government and its institutions to accede to the internet. The website of the North Korean government is Naenara (our country).

Jan Holtermann, running Korea Computer Centre Europe located in Berlin went to North Korea for the first time in 2000. During his trip, he found North Korea has no internet access. He was motivated to help North Korea. His motivation was not simply to help North Koreans and eventually the Korean dictator, but to utilize the great manpower potential in software development (with at least 6000 software experts).

In 2003 he established Korea Computer Centre Europe in Berlin. One year later he expanded his business with 15 employees playing an exclusive representation of Korea Computer Centre of North Korea for Europe.

Opinions over availability of 'intelligence' in North Korea seem to be shared by most experts who worked in and with North Korea. This might have attracted a 'globetrotter' like Jan Holtermann who came to help North Korea in establishing internet service. He is convinced that North Korea will be following India in the near future thanks to 'high intelligence' of North Koreans. (http://www.golem.de retrieved March 15, 2006)

Holtermann's KCC Europe offers the following services: (http://www.kccp-europe.de/index.cfm?defnav=produkte&content=prod..; retrieved March 16, 2006.; Tjia, 2006)

1. internet access with the following details - planning for infrastructure and necessary resources suitable for local conditions; negotiations with German and international interest groups; installing internet access to Germany from Pyongyang; completion of ISP structure; construction of all infrastructures in

Germany and North Korea; broadened internal tests; functions test; construction of control centre; test operation of control centre synchronized with that of Pyongyang

2. individual authentication, bio-signal steering, bio-metric system - furthering research activities in the field of use of fingerprint software, for instance, bank automatic cash corner etc.

3. office automation, office communication - diverse softwares available for digitalization and archiving of data and information, maps, architectural designs, etc. and further, 'cyber friend' software for video-conference system.

KCC Europe has two functions: first, it enables North Korea to have internet access which is allegedly the first network between the closed North Korea and the global market; Second, it works as an intermediary to create contact with important institutions and business partners in the global market and to marketize North Korean software products. (Banks, 2005)

In this respect, a very important address is CARNEA Group GmbH known for providing full-fletched wireless service and integrated software systems, cost control and time-to-market consultancy, etc. To be more concrete, CARNEA specialized in the following: ATM based global network, transport of broadcasting signals between Europe and America, feed in and out stations at Moscow, Berlin Cologne, London, Paris, etc., 24×7 second line support, fault tolerance minimized to switch times lower than 1 ms, etc.; technical data base expertise - DWDM, SDH/PDH, ATM. TCP/IP, Voice. VoIP, Data Base, Unix, FreeBSD, Windows, Citrix, Novell. (http://www.kccp-europe.de/index.cfm?defnav= produkte&content=Partner, retrieved March 12, 2006; retrieved March 13, 2006)

How important this contact can be in the long run for the North Korean IT industry should be evidenced by prominent partners of CARNEA Group such as C4 Marketing Service Bundesdruckerei GmbH, Carrierline, IP-VPN and Security Data Centres, CBN Unify GmbH, HessNatur GmbH, International IP-VPN, mcs IT-Services GmbH, etc. (http://www.carnea.de/reference/reference.htm retrieved March 11, 2006)

Carnea Group is active in three main expertise fields:

-Information techniques,

-Telecommunication and Radio Broadcasting techniques

-providing consultancy and assistance in software and hardware.

This company has been known for having close business contact with many global operating firms such as Cisco Systems, Nortel Networks, Juniper Systems, Rad, Dell, HP/Compaq, IBM, SUN, Microsoft, Network Appliance, Oracle, etc.

Before KCC Europe's internet access was installed, the limited user circle (Kim Jong Il, high ranking politicians, researchers and research institutions) of North Korea has been privileged to enjoy internet access through the Ministry of Posts and Telecommunications presumably since long in order to collect outside information and data. Thanks to this kind of possibilities CSTIA (Central Scientific and Technical Information Agency) in North Korea could offer encyclopaedias, databases, journals, theses and other data on CD-Rom in 1999. Kim Il Sung University's team (under Prof. Hwang Tok-Man) succeeded to compile huge database by using IBM S-series computer and data from the Protein Database of the US Dept. of Energy's Brookhaven National Library. It is said that the Hwang-Team further used the Align, Clustal V, and FASTA programmes for comparing sequences of amino acid and exploiting overseas protein sequence database. (Mercado, 2004, url, retrieved March 11, 2006)

It looks that for North Korea, there is practically no difficulty to accede to overseas databases and information. One important source is Korean Association of Science and Technology (KAST) which made North Korean researchers accede to the National Diet Library, Patent Office and university libraries in Japan.

Mercado (2003) refers to accessibility of data within North Korea, since the Grand People's Study House (GPSH) is playing a role as a centre of data collection annexed by the Aeguk Reading Room with more than 0,5 million materials donation from overseas Koreans. Nowadays, one does not need to travel to Pyongyang for data collection. The intranet service Kwangmyong is now in a situation to offer all data of the GPSH, CSTIA, Kim Il Sung University and other institutions.

Korea Computer Centre Europe as an intensive cooperation partner of KCC and its Samilpho Information Centre in North Korea has been encouraging western firms and institutions to enter into cooperation with North Korean software developers in terms of providing project assignments and orders. (KCC/Samilpho Information Centre, 2008) This means KCCE is playing a mediating role.

Even though it is impossible for the time-being to note quantative business results between KCCE and North Korean firms, it seems interesting to see how and what range of offers and completed projects and, furthermore, which cooperation partners have been in foreign countries.

Online games (http://www.wickedoggames.com)

.3D Mahjong

.Top Majang

.3D Chess

-Mobile Games

.'Defend the Base' (in Japan)

.Species of Mobile being served: Nokia, Motorolla,Sony, Panasonic, Samsung, LG, Au-Brew, Dokomo, Vadofone (Softbank), etc.

-Mobile games responsing to Brew, MIDP 2, WIPI, Mobile 3D and Mobile Flash Support

Office Softwares

.Integrated Office Processing 'Office'

.Handwriting Recognition, Spell Check

.Multilingual Electronic Dictionary 'Samhung'

.Online Handwriting Input programme 'Koyro Pen'

.Spell Check programme

.Portable Digital Assistant (PDA)

-Management Softwares

.'Enterprise Management Integration System'

.Passport Management System

.Personality Information Service System

.Training Affairs Management System

Balancing Accounts Management System

.Book Keeping Management System

Technologies

.Database Oracle Server, etc.

Of great interest are the performances by the Korea Computer Centre in providing softwares for Japanese firms and public institutions. Without mentioning detailed information, the KCC and Samilpho Information Centre are listing up the following services granted to Japan:

-Finance Management System in Osaka

-State Affairs Management System, Japanese government

-Gastom Management System, Japanese government

-Taxation Management System, Japanese government

-Loaning Management System, Japanese government

-Depreciation Management System, Japanese government

-Personal Affairs and Wages Management System, Japanese government

-Debt Management System, Japanese government

-Book Keeping Management system, the Japanese government

To conclude, it would be extremely interesting to look into motivations and strategies by Japanese firms and public institutions why their outsourcing to

North Korea gained such popularity, in other words, becoming'business normality' in Japan. Beside very usual economic factors, such as quality, business credibility, timely delivery, last but not least, low cost, much has been mentioned about communicability between North Koreans and Japanese: this concerns not only Japanese language easily learnt by North Koreans, but also a large affinity in mutual understanding and business mentality conditioned by similar cultural backgrounds.

3. Animation Industry

According to the Annual Report on Global Animation 2007-2008 of CCID Consulting, (url) - China's largest research, consulting and IT outsourcing service company - there is a noticeable trend toward shift of the global animation industry to the region of Asia in next 40 years which can be buttressed by the fact that actually 90% of all American TV animation come from the region of Asia. (Market Research.com, 2009)

How the animation industry's outsourcing is being carried out, is shown as follows:

First step: USA/other western headquarters pursuing

script preparation, story board, exposure sheets before giving orders.

Second step: outsourcing to Asia - prepared packages being sent to the region for production; Asian firms are doing: drawing, colouring by hand, inking, painting, camera work

Third step: sending back to USA/ western headquarters:

American firms get involved in film editing, colour timing , sound work, etc.

The commonly known reasons for the above-mentioned shift are:

1. Excellent infrastructures and equipments through investment by local government agencies and foreign/local investors

2. Surge in local creative talent and incentives for them

3. Extremely low level of labour costs

3. Long working time and stable labour relations

4. Learning necessary skills and encouraging ingenious ideas

The development of animation industry seems to have affinity with the path of industrialization. To use Carmel's taxonomy of software exporting (see appendix 1), it can be expected that those countries ranging at lower development tiers would climb up successively to higher tiers. Out of those countries showing a promising perspective in the region of Asia-Pacific, North Korea is believed to be aligning with the top category of animation industry nations. Quite a number of animation experts who visited North Korea voiced out unisono the animation industry of North Korea would be promising: Staff of the American Walt Disney Corporation described "the country as one of the most talented centres of animation in the world." (Reuters: The Financial Express, August 11. 2005; Spero News, February 12, 2007)

Paul Tjia, a Dutch consultant (his company: GPI Consultancy based at Rotterdam) specialized in IT outsourcing especially to India and China released his travel report on North Korea in 2006.

In the following, the author cites some information from his report.

Mr Tjia's travel to North Korea aimed to find to which extent this country can be regarded as an upcoming outsourcing partner for IT. As regards locations for IT outsourcing, he was mentioning a shift from India to China, especially to North Korea, because prices of outsourcing in India surged very rapidly where Dutch firms such as ANB, Amro Bank, KLM, Philips, Heineken etc, have been working with Indian firms. Mr. Tjia was convinced that the quality of softwares in North Korea has already sufficiently evidenced by means of ISO9001, CMMl, Six Sigma, etc. He further pointed out the fact that Samsung has been using a great amount of softwares from North Korea. Noteworthy is the fact that North Korean firms have been able to pursue Business Process Outsourcing comprising detailed administration and office works. Especially interesting is to provide back-office services for western companies, in particular, Japanese companies which is much easier due to the language command by North Koreans.

Mr. Tjia is telling about his experiences at Dakor Company established in 1996 in connection with a Swiss firm. The author cites from his Report: "It (Dakor) works for European research companies, and it receives from them scanned survey forms electronically on a daily basis. It processes these papers and returns the results within 48 hours to their clients. The company is also conducting data-entry work for international organisations such as the United Nations and the International Red Cross. Their data, which is stored on paper only, is being made available for use online. Dakor is also offering additional Photo: data-entry at Dakor services, such as producing 2D and 3D designs for architectural firms, and it is also Programming websites." (Tjia , 2006)

According to Tjia's report, the SEK Studio with 1600 employees has been subcontracted to work for several European producers of children films. A new company Tin Ming Alan CG Studio set up in early 2006 has been focusing on

Computer Graphics, and 2D and 3D animation based on latest hardware and software.

In the recent time, an intensive cooperation between China and North Korea has been gaining importance: for instance, some of the staffs of Tin Ming Alan speak Chinese and the company has a marketing office in China. They are hired by Chinese advertisement companies to make the animation for TV-commercials. It also works on animation to be included in computer games. Gwangmyong IT Centre, a spin-off from Korea Computer Centre is specialized in network software and security, and it produces anti-virus, data encryption, data recovery, and fingerprint software. This firm is internationally active as well; it also has an office in China and some financial institutions in Japan support this company.

What are North Korea's specific advantages?

The local labour costs are extremely low. This is one of the most significant reasons for western firms' outsourcing to North Korea. It is naturally based on the condition that North Korea has advanced technical facilities, technology level and manpower skills. Yoon and Malecki (2009) regard this factor as the main reason for why AKOM, the biggest animation film company of South Korea is pursuing much of its outsourcing to North Korea. Again this fact enables western firms to undertake research and development in North Korea as well (for instance from Linux to parallel processing).

It has been said that the North Korean Government as well as North Korean IT-firms have been showing high commitment and extremely reliable business relations with Western firms which implies that smaller or medium sized western software companies can have an offshore production option. (Tjia, 2006; Spero News, February 12, 2007)

Yoon and Malecki (2009) argued very recently that North Korea which could catch up in technology of computer graphic imagery (CGI) production is now in a position to receive orders from US firms. This means that Chinese firms are now faced with competition from firms in North Korea. (Yoon and Malecki, 2009, p.15; http://icc.oxfordjournals.org/cgi/content/full/dtp040)

The differentiation made by Tjia as regards business behaviour of North Koreans is very interesting. One speaks generally of the closeness of North Korean personality and its reluctance to come into contact with others, especially with foreigners. Tjia's said: "My communication with them, both formal and informal, was pleasant. Communication with North Koreans is less difficult than with Japanese".

As regards quality of outsourced animation films, one can learn from European businessmen's experiences with North Koreans.

Dominique Boischot, president of the film production company Les Films de la Perrine and the French-Canadian animation expert Guy Delisle as well as the German Mil Thierig have been convinced of high quality of North Korean animation films. Especially Boischot with experiences in business with Chile, South Korea and China, came to say, "North Korea is much better. In terms of the relations between the quality and the price it is one of the best in the world". (Le Monde of 2007, April 4. 26) Very recently, the president of the Italian Mondo TV spoke even of "the best one in the world," saying "I could hardly believe my eyes when I saw the artistic skills of the painters. Cartoon films they (North Koreans) produced were all wonders." The proof for high quality of North Korean animation films has been in the meantime well-known in the business of animation industry. Above all, the cooperation with the following firms, such as Cobol, C, Visual Studio .Net, Visual C/C++, Visual Basic, Java, JBuilder, Powerbuilder, Delphi, Flash, XML, Ajax, PHP, Perl, Oracle, SQL Server, MySQL, Samsung, Sony, etc. seems to be a clear evidence.

4. Nosotek Joint Venture Company in North Korea

It is no wonder that the highly lauded animation industry and great potential of softwares in North Korea attracted Western businessmen. One of those pioneers is a German. Mr. Eloesser who at first glance appears to be a don quichotte like Jan Holtermann, seems to be convinced of his business success in North Korea.

Mr. Volker Eloesser founded a joint venture for R/D-oriented outsourcing in Pyongyang in 2005. The main task of his business is as follows:

-tailor-made e-Business solutions
-integrated content management solutions
-application management
-research development
-special component based software development
-video game development

Product Performance: The firm has been heavily involved in producing scientific softwares, video games, web applications, embedded softwares and 3D virtualization tools for foreign firms, as has been emphasized by the vice-president of Nosotek, Mr. Yu Jong Chul, a North Korean expert.

Intellectual Property: He stressed advantages of a dictatorship à la North Korea as regards protection of intellectual property rights as follows: "Our country is well known to have strong laws to protect secrets and we respect the value of IPs. And unlike what is common in other countries like China, there is only very little fluctuation of the workforce. Like in Japanese companies, our employees usually enter the company after university and stay their entire business life with the high personal motivation. This does not only help to keep trade secrets, it also helps to keep the experienced persons, who are needed for long-term partnership." (North Korean Economy Watch, Interview with Mr. Yu Jong Chul, vice-president of Nosotek)

Talent: Other advantages of Nosotek concerning qualification of North Korean engineers are: "software engineers are selected from the mathematics elite and learn Programming from the ground-up, such as assembler to C#, but also Linux kernel and Visual Basic macros.

Among them, Nosotek has attracted the cream of local talent as the only company in Pyongyang offering western working conditions and Internet access." (cf. Nosotek's Homepage)

Nevertheless, the author thinks a personal statement about his motivation to go to North Korea may be interesting. Therefore, he cites his interview at its full length as follows. (See Interview Blog)

“Klaus-Martin Meyer: Mr. Eloesser, you recently became the President of Nosotek Joint Venture Company in Pyongyang, the capital of North Korea. In which field of business is Nosotek operating?

Volker Eloesser: We do general IT outsourcing. This includes data base applications, 3D technology development as well as games production. Nosotek’s customers come from all over the world and some of our products are even used in the US.

Klaus-Martin Meyer: According to your CV, before you were heading to North Korea, you’ve been the general manager of Elocom, a subsidiary of a German Joint Venture between News Corporation (NWS.A) and Verisign (VRSN). It’s quite unusual for a high-ranking manager of a US based public company to move to North Korea.

Volker Eloesser: That is true. But I do not see my job as a political mission. At Elocom, I was managing a company producing mobile phone software technology. Neither my old job nor my new one is a political one.

Klaus-Martin Meyer: What's your opinion about the demolition of the nuclear cooling tower in Yongbyon and the announcement of the US President George W. Bush to remove the country from the terrorism blacklist?

Volker Eloesser: This was great news. I think that both parties, the Korean and US government, took wise decisions which hopefully help giving peace a chance through diplomacy. For our business, lifting the sanctions will have a very positive impact, as well as for the People in the DPRK. North Korean Companies, domestic and foreign-invested, were suffering a lot under the sanctions. Foreign trade was very difficult and many potential customers feared to get trouble when making business with the DPRK.

Klaus-Martin Meyer: When did you first get interested into the DPRK? Did you already do active business with North Koreans before?

Volker Eloesser: Of course I did. In the beginning of 2005, I held lectures at the Pyongyang Business School. The Korean participants of my lectures were great people really interested in international business.

Klaus-Martin Meyer: Who are the shareholders of Nosotek? Is it a state-run company?

Volker Eloesser: Nosotek is a joint-venture between a European owned private holding company and the General Federation of Science and Technology of DPRK, a non-government organisation.

Klaus-Martin Meyer: Along being the president of Nosotek, you are Chairman of the Supervisory Board of Next Generation Entertainment N.V. (NGE), a Dutch public company. Are there any links between NGE and North Korea?

Volker Eloesser: NGE's management is highly interested in investing into the DPRK software industry. The CEO Dr. Stefan Heinemann believes that the DPRK will become a very important sourcing market in the near future, which has many advantages over China and India. Having this in mind, it makes a lot of sense for NGE to have a board member with experience in dealing with North Koreans.

Klaus-Martin Meyer: How would you describe the difference of outsourcing software in the DPRK compared to China or India?

Volker Eloesser: The DPRK's software industry is already very well developed, but only for the demands of the domestic market. Although the skill level of the engineers is as high as the skill level in China or India, most DPRK software companies never made successful international business in large scale. The Korean engineers usually have no experience with western culture, habits and taste. But of course you'll experience the same, when working with some small Indian or Chinese companies. One major advantage of the Korean engineers is that they do not move to a new job frequently, like the Chinese. In this matter, you can compare the Koreans with Japanese staff, who usually never leave the company to move to another job. The result is obvious: the experience and knowledge stays within the company and there is no risk of IP leak.

Klaus-Martin Meyer: Are you personally living in North Korea or can you do your job remotely?

Volker Eloesser: It's definitely required to have western management in a company dealing with western customers. Every attempt of people trying to do this remotely has failed. I'm planning to live in Pyongyang most of the year. I have a nice apartment in the city centre.

Klaus-Martin Meyer: Living in Pyongyang sounds hard. How are the living conditions for foreigners in Pyongyang? What about your family?

Volker Eloesser: Well, it's not as hard as western readers may think. Of course the hardest thing is to live separated from my wife, but she promised to visit me frequently. Generally, the living conditions for westerners in Pyongyang are good: The air is totally clean, there is no risk of becoming a crime victim, there is a lot of green in the city and the Korean people are generally very friendly.

Klaus-Martin Meyer: Usually, western media has almost no idea about the real working and living conditions of the people in North Korea. Can you tell us something about the working conditions of your local staff?

Volker Eloesser: One of my goals is to achieve working conditions according to German standard. The staff is equipped with the latest computer hardware and enjoys a lot of incentives from the company to make their live comfortable. For example, the company is providing free lunch for the whole staff, which is delicious and nutritious. I myself have lunch together with my engineers every day, and I like it very much. Additionally to the large number of public holidays, the company even sponsors a one-week holiday trip. This is the way we appreciate the performance on the job.

Klaus-Martin Meyer: What are the most difficult obstacles, western managers are facing in the DPRK? Do you stuffer from political pressure?

Volker Eloesser: I've not yet experienced any political pressure, but of course you need to get used to the local security regulations and bureaucracy. When you behave politely, do not do derogative statements about politics and respect the Korean culture, you will not face any serious problems. The most difficult obstacle is the absence of international experience of the software engineers, combined with the cultural differences typical to Asian countries.

Klaus-Martin Meyer: How many European business people like you have discovered the DPRK as tomorrow's sourcing market?

Volker Eloesser: Actually, not many so far. The European community in Pyongyang is very small. After a few weeks, you know every foreigner. Most Europeans who do business in the DPRK are organized in the European Business Association. But I feel that the community is growing since business managers are more and more recognizing that doing business in and with the DPRK is of course working with a frontier framework but also with a great potential of highly-skilled people with an impressive work ethic and an attractive cost-performance ratio –and also an emerging domestic market.

Klaus-Martin Meyer: What drives you personally to go there and build up an internationally operating company?

Volker Eloesser: Leading a foreign invested company in North Korea is a great challenge for me. During my lectures at the Pyongyang Business School, I realized that the skilled North Korean IT engineers have a huge potential for successful software development. This potential is almost unrecognized in the world and therefore unused. I like to be the pioneer who builds up this new outsourcing destination. I believe that economic progress will lead to a general improvement of the people's living conditions and IT business is a key to economic progress. If you ask me, I would tell you that my work will have a greater impact on improving the North Korean living conditions then just sending bags of rice.

Klaus-Martin Meyer: Do you experience economic progress or political changes in North Korea?

Volker Eloesser: The question about political changes should better be answered by the politicians. But indeed you can see economic progress: Compared to my first visit in 2005, there are now much more cars in the street and the number of foreign investment seem to have significantly grown. A group from Hong Kong is building a large shopping and business area along the Taedonggang River and Orascom from Egypt is continuing the Ryugyong Hotel construction as well as investing into a modern mobile phone network. And recently the German-based Prettl Group (Automotive industry) announced that it will be the first foreign non-Korean company to build a factory in Kaesong.

Klaus-Martin Meyer: Nosotek is located in Pyongyang. Do you think things could be easier for companies operating out of the Kaesong free trade zone?

Volker Eloesser: I've never been in Kaesong myself. From what I've heard, the free trade zone, which has been build with ROK investment, is a modern factory area, mostly targeted to low-cost production of shoes or textile. I do not know of any software development in Kaesong. Pyongyang, being the economic and cultural centre of the DPRK with large universities, offers a huge number of qualified engineers.

Klaus-Martin Meyer: What are your plans for Nosotek's future? How do you see your company in five years? What is your strategy?

Volker Eloesser: My plan for Nosotek is a constant growth. First of course, everybody in Nosotek has to understand the demands of our customers; not only the technical demands but also the usual communication style and habits of the western world. At the moment, we're only fifty people and I'm starting to build up a powerful middle management, who knows their customer's expectations. After this has been done, we can begin scaling the business volume.

Klaus-Martin Meyer: Are there other western IT companies having operations in the DPRK?

Volker Eloesser: Nosotek still is the only one. But according to Paul Tjia of GPI Consultancy who organizes business missions to the DPRK, the number of people interested into software development in the DPRK is constantly growing. I hope that Paul will bring more people here to operate software companies. With other Foreigners here, working in the same or similar field of business we together can help strengthening the DPRK to become better known source for software development. Bangalore is still far, but I'm sure the quality delivered by the Korean IT engineers will be convincing, not only to grow Nosotek, but also to grow the country itself as an outsourcing destination."

It is plausible that NOSOTEK engaged in the European Business Association in North Korea is actively working together with Pyongyang Business School (see details in the article by Mr. Hur Joon-young in this book) where NOSOTEK's president is committed to teaching. The Pyongyang Business School was founded by Swiss people in 2004 with an inaugural lecture by the Director General of the Swiss Agency for Development and Cooperation (SDC). It takes the form of a Public Private Partnership (PPP) with Peninsula Partners Ltd., an enterprise representing a number of renowned international companies and investors based in the Democratic People's Republic of Korea (DPRK) and in charge of concept, promotion and implementation of the Business School. The Korean partners are the Flood Damage Rehabilitation Committee (under the auspices of the Cabinet), the Ministry of Foreign Affairs and the Ministry of Light Industries.

5. North Korea as ICT Outsourcing Outpost

One has recently observed an increasing trend in the software and animation industry towards shift, to use the taxonomy by Erran Carmel (2003; see Appendix 2), from the so-called Tier 1, 2 and 3 countries such as OECD countries, India and China, South Korea, Hungary Czech, etc. to Tier 4 so called infant stage of software exporting countries (Cuba, El Salvador, Jordan, Egypt, Vietnam, Indonesia, Iran etc.) and non-competing countries, the so-called least developed countries such as North Korea. (See Figure 13.1)

For Paul Tjia it is an interesting question: who will be succeeding to India in ICT? His answer is differentiated by categorizing IT activities into IT-outsourcing services (software development. etc.) and IT-enabled services (business process outsourcing); in this category the manual data entry is interesting for outsourcing to India. Contact centre services, especially call centre services are transferred to India, Kenya, Mexico and Philippines; labour-intensive Animation film production can be offshored to North Korea producing actually for Spanish, French, Italian and German film and TV companies. (Tjia, 2009)

Figure 13.1 IT outsourcing services and IT enabling services

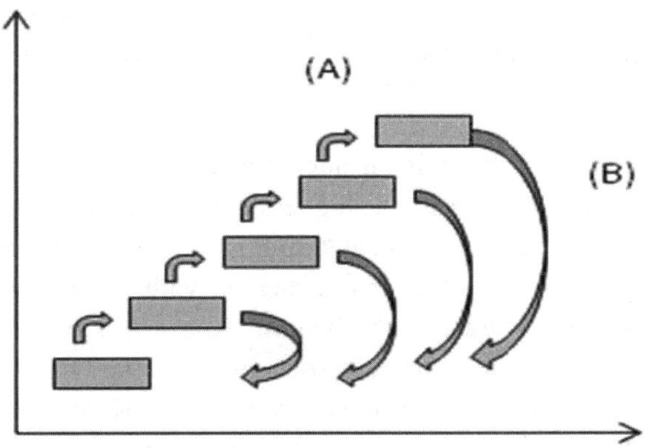

Tier 1
Major software exporting countries
Tier 2:
Transition software exporting countries
Tier 3:
Emerging software exporting countries
Tier 4:

Infant stage software exporting countries non-competing:
Least developed countries

The move from the bottom to above tiers (marked here with (A) depends on many factors Carmel mentioned in his Oval Model, such as active government vision and policy, human capital, quality of life, capital, technological infrastructure, the industry (cluster, branding etc.), linkages and last but not least, wages. South Korea belonging to the Tier 3 according to Carmel requires several factors to be fulfilled in order to gain the fame of being a 'strong IT nation'.

In case of North Korea, Carmel (2003(1)), different from Tjia, is pessimistic about its perspective, even though this country has allegedly wage advantage, as can be shown in the following table:

Table 13.3 International Comparison of software engineers (annual, unit: US $)

USA 63000	Japan 44000
Russia 7500	Philippines 65-10000
China 5000-8000	China 5000-9000
Indonesia 5000	Ukraine 5000 median for software engineer
Vietnam 1400-6000	North Korea 500?????

Source: Carmel (2003-1), p.6; 500 US $ for North Korea assessed by the author

In the wage structure, there is an international stringently comparable wage hierarchy. The higher the Tier is, the higher the wage level seems to be the case. That is the reason why countries located in higher Tier groups tend to seek suppliers operating at lower cost which is marked with (B) in the table. Carmel terms this phenomenon a 'race to the bottom'. (Carmel, 2003, p 6). Carmel further mentions similarity in industrial production with software development in location advantage determined by lower wage. North Korea's advantage seems to be, above all, in lower wage, whilst it has no technological capacity of specialization and differentiation. However, North Korea as a new comer seems to have, beyond the low wage advantage, other strengths such as quality, credibility in transaction, and 'lowest risk in intellectual property' which is the reason why India and China facing the rapid surge of wage level tend to extent increasingly more project assignments to North Korea. (Lee and Hwang, 2004; Yoon and Malecki, 2009) At any rate, judging from Carmel's 'Offshore Visibility Index', North Korea is better known for having nuclear weapons, not for being strong in software development, and from 'Offshore Attractiveness Index' it is further known that this country has very poor communication infrastructure and relatively low level of IT education output. For this reason, it is hardly thinkable for North Korea to meet the criteria 'maturity', 'critical mass' and 'a certain level of export revenue' in a foreseeable future.

The EU-initiative of 2007 to pursue matchmaking for North Korean companies with European and other companies affords a particular global attention. The officially termed project "Route to the Democratic People's Republic of Korea (DPRK) for European Companies" created in the framework of "Asia-Invest Programme" of EU started in 2007. The project aims to "foster links between European small and medium-sized enterprises and North Korean companies in a selected range of industries." (http://www.routetodprk.org/site/project.htm)

Industrial fields being taken into account are agriculture, fisheries and forestry, construction, trading, information technology, infrastructure, light industry and textiles, logistics and transportation, machine tools and mining and metalworking (cf. the list in appendix), where in every sector one or more companies on the North Korean side has been 'recommended' to a European partner.

The chosen North Korean firms in IT for matchmaking are the following:

Table 13.4 List of North Korean IT firms for matchmaking for EU-DPRK workshop March 28-29, 2007

Name of company	cooperation field specified
Korea Computer Centre (KCC)	localization, outsourcing, joint development of software
SEK Studios	Subcontracting, JV Production, Financing and Training in Animation
Korea Undok Group	IT Programmes Outsourcing, Drawing Machines
Korea Myohyang Group	IT Programmes Outsourcing Sending IT experts abroad
Korea Myohyang Group	IT Programmes Outsourcing Sending IT experts aboard
Korea Unha General Trading Corporation	Production of Multimedia and Cartoons

source: http://routetodprk.org/site/dprks_companies.htm

Projects are to be funded by the EU to be managed by the (North) Korean-Italian-Belgian partnership:

The main organizer is Foreign Trade Office of Piemonde Chambers of Commerce, Turin supported by the European Union-(North) Korean Industrial Cooperation Agency, Piemontese Consortium for Training in Foreign Trade, Turin and the Association for Promotion of International Economic and Technical Change, Pyongyang.

How the cooperation between North Korean Firms and European ones come to reach cooperation can be described in concreto with an example of Korea Computer Centre's Application for a European partner (the Application document downloadable).

The Case of Korea Computer Centre (KCC):

The Korea Computer Centre (KCC) with various 2,500 computers and main development centres which got ISO-9001 Certification under KCC is seeking a partner in IT production and distribution. Out of five countries such as China, Japan, Germany, Russia, and South Korea a partner may come.

KCC describes very extensively its activities and strengths as follows:

> KCC as the largest software enterprise of DPRK has 10 software development centres on various Sectors in Pyongyang, 1 IT centre in each province (total of 11) and 1 IT college and 1 IT training centre. KCC is leading the software industry of DPRK
>
> Main activities of KCC are :
>
> – Research, development, distribution and service software like operating system, Network communication, office software, games and embedded software.
>
> – Education and training of software specialists
>
> – Operation of the main portal website [naenara] in DPRK
>
> – Import and selling of hardware related IT
>
> – Consulting for government and IT company in setting-up of IT-policy and rational management of IT Resources.

The following list shows a great variety of main products by KCC which has been made public very rarely in this form:

> 1. Korean Linux Distribution: Linux Operating system
> 2. Real time Linux system: Real time OS Linux
> 3. Embedded Database Management System: Embedded software, DBMS
> 4. Korean Song Collection (including over 8,500 Korean songs): music processing software
> 5. Music Notation editor : music processing software, music notation edition
> 6. Cardio & Cerebral Vascular Disease Diagnosis System: medical diagnosis system
> 7. Human body classification system based on fingerprint: Human body classification, traditional medicine
> 8. Computer go software: intelligent game software, computer Go
> 9. Network security system: network security
> 10. Video Conference System based on PC: Video Conference System, media stream service
> 11. Biometric system (finger print, face, voice): individual verification system, personal identification
> 12. e-dictionary (English-Korean, Chinese-Korean, Japanese-Korean, Russian-Korean, German- Korean) e-dictionary.
> 13. Machine translation software (English-Korean, Chinese-Korean,

Japanese-Korean)
14. Multi User PC System: Multi User PC, PC Sharing

KCC's performances in international cooperation are noted as follows, by showing its customers relations with firms in China, South Korea and Japan, and through its education and training activities. Furthermore, KCC seems to have a great ambition to have a partner which has financial, production and distribution capability in IT. It is also greatly interested to have entry into the EU market in terms of training marketing specialists and receiving orders from European customers, and developing softwares jointly with cooperation partners working especially on Linux-based projects. However, there is no doubt that KCC's priority is placed on technical cooperation ranging from cooperation in R/D through joint production and subcontracting to patent/license purchase.

The Application Document was signed in the year of 2007. However, it is unknown what came out of it. Nevertheless, one can constate that the North Korean side must have reacted in an exceptionally positive way toward the initiative by EU and has shown readiness to make relatively confidential data public regarding main products. This is also the case with the other Application Document by Korea Ponghwa General Corporation, downloadable from the internet. This corporation consists of 7 producing and trading companies specializing in producing garments and some others and exports their products to China, Japan and South Korea. It is seeking a joint venture partner for production and trading, providing professional sellers in garments, shoes, etc. and specialists in training and transfer of processing technology and investment of equipment for shoes, garments, etc. (see Asia-Invest II Project "Route to DPRK for European Countries." company profile & cooperation projects)

Since the EU-DPRK Workshop in March 2007, there seems to be no indication for concrete business cooperation and transaction between North Korean firms and European ones. The author himself does not possess any other information.

6. Conclusion

Undoubtedly, the EU, European governments and firms have less scruple in contact with North Korea and North Korean firms than governments and firms from other regions. Above all, they have been sticking to the principle of division between humanitarian aid (humanitarianism) and business, and further between development aid and inacceptable attitude towards the nuclear issue.

Nevertheless, as regards this issue, one cannot see any indication for change of the official EU policy.

It seems, however, that the EU has been taking the 2002 Country Strategy Paper as the orientation point for cooperation with North Korea. The main points of this paper are:

-Institutional support and capacity building

-Sustainable development and use of natural resources including access to sustainable energy sources

-Reliable and sustainable transport sector and rural development.

Since then, the EU continued technical, institutional and financial assistance for North Korea, even though the volume of the assistance has not been huge. The focus was especially placed on support of economic and structural reforms of North Korea as well as its opening policy. In this framework, there have been various cooperation schemes, out of which the author discussed projects in private sector. To which extent these projects can be evaluated as epoch-making landmarks for the promising perspective is uncertain. In the long run, it is questionable whether it will reach a sustainable development based on low wage level (Carmel, 2003), ideology and nuclear weapons (Berkofsky, 2009).

References

Bank, Stacey (2005, Fall). North Korean Telecommunications: on Hold, *North Korean review*, 88-94.

Carmel, Erran (2003). Taxonomy of New Software Exporting Nations, *EJISDC*, 13 (1), 1-6.

Carmel, Erran (2003). The New Software Exporting Nations: Success Factors, *EJISDC*, 13 (4), 1-12.

Carmel, Erran & Tjia, Paul (2005). *Offshoring Information Technology. Sourcing and Outsourcing to a Global Workforce*, Cambridge University Press

Hayes, Peter (2003). *DPRK Information Technology - Doest it Exist?*, Ch. 4, url (retrieved 2009=10-14).

KCC.Samilpo Information Centre (2008).

Kim,Yoo Hyang (2004). North Korea's Cyberpath, *Asian Perspective*, 28 (3), 191-209.

Lee, Heejin & Hwang, Jaeho (2004). ICT Development in North Korea: Changes and Challenges, *Information Technologies and International Development*, 2 (1), 75-87.

Market Research.com (2009). Global Animation Industry: Strategies, Trends, and Opportunities, Digital Victor. Nosotek Interview blog, url.

Mercado, Stephen (2003). Hermit Surfers of Pyongyang, US Intelligence Agency, Centre for the Study of Intelligence, *Unclassidied Studies*, 48/1, 2004.

Noland, Marcus (2008). *Telecommunications in North Korea: Has Orascom made the Connection?*

Park, sung-jo (1991). *Technology Transfer from East Germany to North Korea, Berlin* (in Korean).

Park, Sung-jo (2004). Renovation of Humanitariaism or Global Capitalism? Technology/Science Transfer from Germany to North Korea. Oh Yean-Chean et al (Ed.), *The Unification Research and Strategy in Korea and Germany*, Hakrimsa, 205-219.

Park, Sung-jo (2007). IT-Industry Development in System Transformation: the Case of North Korea, Mica Jovanovic et al (Ed.), *System Transformation in Comparative Perspective,* LIT Berlin, 387-412.

Tjia, Paul (2006). North Korea: an Upcoming Software Destination (retrieved 2009-10-14).

Berkofsky, Axel (2009, March). The European Union in North Korea: Player or only Payer? *ISPI Policy Brief*, no.123.

Tjia, Paul (2009, June). The next India: Outsourcing IT: Challenges and Opportunities, *The Broker Issue 14*, 21-23.

Yoon, Hyejin & Malecki, Edward J. (2009, September, 7). Cartoon planet: World of Production and global production networks in the animation industry, *Industrial and Corporate Change, ICC Advance Access published online*.

Appendix 1

The 4-tier taxonomy of the world's software exporting nations

Tier 1 major software exporting nations : mostly OECD nations: USA< Canada, UK, Germany, Japan..... Includes entrants the 1990s: Ireland, Israel, and India

Tier 2 transition software exporting nations: only Russia and China

Tier 3 emerging software exporting nations: Brazil, Costa Rica, Mexico....... South Korea....Hungary....

Tier 4 Infant Stage software exporting nations: Cuba, El Salvador, Jordan, Bangladesh, Vietnam...

Non-Competing: Most of the smaller, least developed countries (North Korea)

Source: Carmel 2003

Appendix 2

List of North Korean companies seeking European partners prepared for the EU-DPRK Workshop March 28-29, 2007, Torino organized by EUKICA and Centro Estero in connection with EU Asia-Invest II.

This list was prepared in advance by the North Korean side and presented to the above-mentioned workshop which served as matchmaking.

This matchmaking event is multi-sectoral and industries represented hereunder are based on each DPRK company's cooperation projects:

Agriculture, Fisheries & Forestry Sector:

1.Korea Daehung General Trading Company (Marine Products : sales, training & equipments)

2.Organic Agriculture Development Association (OADA) (Organic feed additives, bio-diesel, milk)

3.Pyongyang Solgyong Trading Corporation (Eggs, Chicken, Ducks & Soybean Oil Products)

4.Samilpo Foods Company (Korea Foodstuff Industry Trading Corporation) (Food processing equipments & raw materials, joint-venture development)

5.Korea Daesim Trading Corporation (JV in upgrading production techniques of pulp & paper, JV for processing of wood for furniture)

Construction Sector:

6.Korea Rungrado General Trading Corporation (Overseas Construction)

General Trading :

7.Korea Daesong Trading General Corporation (trading with European countries in all fields)

Information Technologies Sector :

8.Korea Computer Centre (Localization, outsourcing, joint development of software, training in IT marketing)

9.SEK Studios (Subcontracting, JV Production, Financing & Training in Animation Films)

10.Korea Undok Group (IT Programmes Outsourcing / Drawing Machines)

11.Korea Myohyang Group (IT Programmes Outsourcing / Sending IT Experts abroad)

12.Korea Unha General Trading corporation (Production of Multimedia & Cartoon Products)

Infrastructures Sector :

13. Korea Yonghung Trading Corporation

(Railways rolling stock, Used Rails, Passenger / Freight Cars, Locomotives)

Light Industry & Textile Sector :

14.Korea Daesong Jei (Number 2) Trading Corporation (purchase of 1500 sewing machines / Garment processing contracts)

15.Korea Daily Necessities Industry Trading Corporation (joint production of bottles for cosmetics, of plastic wares, PVC flooring, enamel ware, stainless steel goods, processing on commission of watches)

16. Korea Ponghwa General Corporation (investment, training & technology transfer for production of Shoes, Garments and Gum)

17. Korea Rungrado General Trading Corporation (equipments for Cosmetics & Soap processing, Garment processing, health food production)

18.Korea Shoes Trading Corporation (EVA Injection Shoemaking Machine, joint production of Shoes)

19.Korea Unha General Trading corporation (Garment Processing, R&D)

20.Korea Undok Group (Garment Processing)

Logistics & Transportation Sector:

21.Korea Myohyang Group (Ship Repair / Sending Skilled Workers abroad / Train Seamen / Build Sea Dock / Operate Liner) Machine Tools Sector :

22. Korea General Machinery Trading Corporation (Precision Machinery for production of Machine Tools)

Mining & Metalworking Sector :

23. Korea Kwangop Trading Corporation (Zinc & Copper Mining / Mines Rehabilitation & Development)

24.Korea Undok Group (Mining of Zirconium, Lead & Electrolytic Zinc, JV production of Nb / Ta / Zr)
25.Korea Unha General Trading corporation (Molybdenum Trading)

15

From Communist Cadres into Capitalistic Managers?: The Case of Western Business Schools - Pyongyang and Rajin-Sonbong

Joon-Young Hur

Contents

I. Say good-bye to Cadre Elite of Socialism?
II. Theoretical Background: Elite in North Korea
1. Cadre: Elite in Socialist Countries
2. Elite in North Korea: the New Species Cadre?
III. Capacity Development Programme for North Korean Elites
1. Overview
2. Business Institute and Centre in Rajin/Sonbong
3. Swiss MBA Programme in Pyongyang
IV. Concluding Remarks: The Juche Ethic and the Spirit of Capitalism?

I. Say goodbye to Cadre Elite of Socialism?

"What they head up, what they have, what they belong to, who they really are"

C. Right Mills (1956: 366)

North Korea has long had a socialized, centrally planned command economy isolated from the rest of the world. Traditionally, poor domestic economic performance was offset with infusions of Soviet aid. But after the collapse of the Soviet Union in 1991, the aid stopped and the economy was adversely affected.[1]

To make matters worse, the death of Kim Il Sung in July 1994 and the following natural disaster in the middle of nineties drove North Korean regime in imminent peril. It was not a wonder that many scholars expected that North Korea would collapse soon. However until now no extreme change has happened there. It has shown apparently its political stability so far and it is said that the power of North Korea derived from the extremely strong cohesion of elites, with ideology and loyalty to their labour party and the person Kim Jong-il.[2]

Confronting those situations, even stubborn North Korea with 'Juche ideology', which stresses on self-reliance,[3] could not help begging for worldwide foreign aids and it was the initial stage of opening the country to western capitalistic countries.[4] Furthermore with the continuing stagnation, these aids have been continuously increased at least till 2004 under the strict control of North Korea. Its behaviour could be well understood in that foreign capitalistic influence to ordinary people could be menacing factor to hamper its own system stability. Therefore it seems to be inevitable to North Korea that the more aids are welcome and needed to enhance the economy but only if it is absolutely under the control.

Starting with humanitarian aids, as time goes on, the highlight on the form of the aids has been moved to capacity building, which inevitably assumes direct contacts between teachers and students during the education. It is derived from both sides' needs: Foreign agencies such as UN and NGOs as well as individual investors have realized from their more than ten-year experience that their aids have changed North Korea a lot and they have worked. Also the North Korean government knows well that even if it preserves its regime, there is nothing to gain if there is no economic booming. Moreover, it acknowledges that it is the matter of know-how to catch fish rather than just of fish itself. The matter of

[1]The means of production, which are largely obsolete, are owned by the state through state-run enterprises or collectivized farms. Prices, wages, trade, budget, and banking are under strict government control (Library of congress - Federal Research Division, 2007, p. 8).

[2] Other communist countries usually collapsed due to the bottom-up revolution or gradually changed by introduction of new elites from outside of existing power block. However, until now it seems to be hard to find a considerable protest and opposition group in North Korea.

[3] 'Juche ideology' came from the saying of Kim Il Sung. It has been reinforced through the propaganda to preserve the North Korean regime after abolishing the communist countries such as GDR, Soviet Union, and former east European communist countries.

[4] The direct reason why there was a sudden opening is told to be due to the tremendous famine derived from devastating flood in 1995. There were also trades among communist countries such as Eastern Germany, Soviet Union, und China before 1990's. However those trades were hardly ever done in the form of capitalistic way but provided as aids to North Korea under the solidarity.

primary concern to him is making the shock from capitalistic wave as weak as possible.

Those capacity building programmes include educations and practices about capitalism. It seems to be very paradoxical that elite in North Korea should learn against their socialist belief, which makes their tight unity. Especially in the case of recent Swiss Business School in Pyongyang, it would be regarded as the avant-garde of the capitalism in that it aims to raise a high ranking entrepreneur who runs a private enterprise and inspirits other employees in his firm with the spirit of capitalism.

The interesting point here is that the entrepreneur himself is the very enemy, whom cadre elite in socialism should demolish in order to build communist country. The communist cadre has a crucial mission that they are supposed to destroy bourgeois through a proletariat revolution.[5] However, in North Korea, they are to be trained for an entrepreneur, who is a typical example of bourgeois. How can we understand this? Does this mean that North Korea would say good bye to communist cadre? Is it possible to suspect, that there may be a rivalry against North Korean regime after that? Those are research questions of this paper.

For this purpose, at first, we will look into the communist elite, so called cadre elite in socialism, and a trend of elite in North Korea as a theoretical background. Then, as a case study, we will consider the recent capacity development programme focused on the western business schools and apply to a previous theoretical perspective.

II. Theoretical Background: Elite in North Korea

Contrary to its rigid political image, which is notorious as an Axis of Evil, outpost of tyranny and Rogue state, North Korea has been shown many promising signs of changes in economic field. For example, on 1st of July 2002 some of the economic improvement measures were taken, such as partial opening of the market and lots of special economic zone, and so on. Considering these facts, North Korea seems to be already in the low level of economic transition through the open-policy, even though it is still restricted.

---

[5] The ideological borrowing of the word "cadre" is taken from military jargon. According to the orthodox socialist definition, members of cadre are persons grounded in political and technical knowledge and commissioned by the state to guide collectives of workers engaged in the realization of social objectives and tasks, or, as scientifically trained specialists, to contribute toward this realization (Ehlert et al, 1973; König, 1993, p. 386)

In the processes of transition from command to market economy as well as in the ordinary life in socialist country, it is the elites, not ordinary people who maintain its system and shape these processes. Thus, studies of elites in the context of institutional changes are absolutely crucial to the understanding of regime transitions. (Szablowski / Derlien, 1993, p. 304)

1. Cadre: Elite in Socialist Countries

In the western classical theories, Elites are usually regarded as the people who are leading executives of the most important institutions and organisations at the national as well as regional level. They execute their power beyond their ordinary position inside their individual organisation by regularly influencing and participating in key decisions in political- and social fields as well as economical fields for the society as a whole (Boyer, 1999, p. 12; Steger / Lang, 2003, p. 169). Unlike the western democracies, in the socialist countries, the existence of elites, so called cadre elite, itself was peculiar and a coherent recruitment policy existed under the cadre policy tradition (von Beyme, 1999, p. 411).

Cadre elites were the leading groups in communist countries. The ideal Cadre was supposed to come from working classes and tied with them (Boyer, 1999, p. 28). The ideal Cadre used to be the combination of Marxist-Leninist education and political loyalty on the one hand and the technical-administrative competence on the other hand. Indeed the "professional" and the "political-ideological" dimensions can be hardly fully separated from each other. Therefore, both were often closely linked duality of demands. However, the basic qualification of the cadre elites was political-ideological suitability.[6] It applied even for the administrative cadre elite, who would be assumed to be ready to serve any political party in power with their own profession under the neutrality like western civil officers (König, 1992, p. 235; König, 1993, p. 386-387). Furthermore, the know-how necessary for the planned economy was not "neutral" but "political" knowledge (Boyer, 1999, p. 12).

The forming of cadre was not a "natural" process. It was a process, which was not only motivated through power interest but also pursued with ideological guidelines. Moreover, the cadres that this process aimed at were not expected to

[6] It was after 1960s, when specific technical qualifications were introduced in the definition and a role description of the cadre, and in response, new educational institutions were established by offering courses and studies in state sciences to meet the increasing demand for state functionaries. This development, however, did not give the cadre its own professional expertise (König, 1992, p. 235; König, 1993, p. 386-387).

be functionally specialized but rather to be homogeneous to be put into every area, such as economy, public and politics (Wagner, 1999, p. 54-56).[7]

The power which controlled the cadre was the party: The cadre was made by the party to internalize an external control and be subjected to it. The ideal model of professional and – or just for this reason – unbureaucratic as well as folks-friendly cadre had little to do with the reality; the identity of those ruling and those ruled was not able to be brought about through the recruiting of worker cadres (Boyer, 1999, p. 12-13).[8]

In sum, educational systems in the ex-communist regimes were conservative and old fashioned as a whole and the opportunity structures were distorted as well. Those regimes did not bring forth the kind of professionals and managers, who are needed for a changing economy. Instead, they contributed to the existing distortion of status ascription. The opportunities for younger aspiring elites were declining correspondingly with their higher qualifications (Haller / Kolosi / Robert, 1990, p. 69).[9]

2. Elite in North Korea: the New Species Cadre?

Officially, North Korea is a communist state, in which the party is the central coordinator of administrative and economic activities at the national and local levels, under the one-man leadership of Kim Jong Il. Therefore it could be assumed that the general characteristic of North Korean cadre elite would be similar to that of communist countries.[10]

According to Hassig (2004, III-5-6), number of North Korean elite is anywhere from thousand to two million, depending upon how one defines them. Whatever their number, as a class, they share the characteristics of the typical communist privileged group so called "nomenklatura". Needless to say, it is

---

[7] Cadre policy was an extensive and detailed one, which based on a long-term strategy that recruited, supported, trained, supervised and controlled the staffs for policy and administration. The cadre did not know of the "civic" separation telling public from private as well as private from intimate sphere (Boyer, 1999, p. 12-13).

[8] According to Stalin's opinion, the "maintenance" of cadre is the golden fund of the communist party, in the sense that an individual becomes at least in principal a disposable quantity for a "benevolent despotism", where care and guardianship become blurred due to socialist moral (Boyer, 1999, p. 12-13)

[9] The growth of the tertiary economic sectors of services was blocked by the communist regimes still burdened with a powerful bias in favour of the heavy manufacturing sector. The value of services was not even included in the calculations of the national domestic product.

[10] He is chairman of the National Defence Commission which is the nation's highest administrative authority as well as supreme commander of the Korean People's Army (KPA) and general secretary of the Korean Workers' Party (KWP). (Country Profile, 1993, p. 14)

natural that one should be a member of the "loyal" class in order to become a bureaucrat or official.[11]

The recruitment and training of cadre elites have long been the primary concern of North Korean leadership. Those demands are very high especially for the party cadre elites, in that the party penetrates all aspects of life, namely all government and economic agencies. Therefore, it is natural, that North Korean cadre elites in party are those officials placed in key positions in party organisations, ranging from the Political Bureau to the village party committees; in government agencies; in economic enterprises; in military and internal security units; in educational institutions; and in mass organisations.[12]

The duties of cadres are to educate and lead party and non-party members of society and to ensure that party policies and directives are carried out faithfully. Without exception, key government positions are filled by party loyalties, most of who are trained in the North Korean system, which emphasizes ideology and practical expertise. (Library of Congress or Kim, 1993 - Savada) Furthermore, since the collapse of socialism in some countries, Kim Jong-Il has stressed the motto "to serve the people", the importance of reinforcing the party's ideological unity and cohesion, and elucidated tasks that would strengthen education in the principle of Juche, revolutionary traditional education, and socialist and patriotic education (Hassig, 2004: III.-5).[13]

In sum, as we have seen before, the characteristic of North Korean Elite is not quite different from that of communist elite. First, in the perspective of ideology, it is the most important element in both sides. However, the big difference is that, the loyalty in North Korea means just to Kim Jong-Il and the personal background as a loyal family is important to be elite. Second, the technical and professional capacity is required to both of them, in that it takes a role as a symbol of origin based on working classes.[14] It is interesting that it has been hardly

---

[11] The security Organisations classify people according to their presumed loyalty to the regime, with classification based primarily on family history going back several generations. These classifications may be reviewed whenever an individual is considered for occupational promotion. (Hassig, 2004: III-5-6)

[12] Associations and guidance committees exist at all levels of society, with a local party cadre serving as a key member of each committee (Savada, 1993:).

[13] The elite are proud to have been chosen to serve Kim, and they enjoy the power and privileges that come with the job. At the same time, they realize that their positions depend entirely on pleasing Kim, and this puts a lot of pressure on them because the alternative to working for Kim may be working in a labour camp. All in all, however, they probably find the benefits of their positions to exceed the costs (Hassig, 2004: III.-5).

[14] The "Mosquito net" strategy was established by Kim Il Sung. He would like to accept trade with other countries but under the primary condition which blocks the capitalism. Therefore, like a mosquito net, capitalism should be filtered beforehand.

ever reported that former typical socialist countries such as GDR, Soviet Union und former east socialist countries allowed them to give a chance to learn capitalism. However, at least since 1997, North Korea seemed to struggle in economic development and accepted western helps with capitalism education. It is very ironic that capitalism has been so long time considered as an evil spirit. Then, we should look more carefully what the capitalism education in the name of the capacity building programmes in North Korea is like. We can assume that their appearance seems to be capitalistic but the contents might be not. Or, if they really show capitalistic educations, then we should acknowledge that the elites in North Korea go different track from other communist cadre.

III. Capacity Development Programme for North Korean Elites

To ensure the economic transformation and the sustainable development of North Korea, the importance of human resource development cannot be overemphasized.[15]

1. Overview

The highlight of foreign aides to North Korea has been changed gradually from humanitarian aid such as food and medicine to more long-term development interventions, namely capacity building programme.[16] Among the various capacity building programmes, here I focus on economics-related programme because it is inevitably linked directly to the capitalism education.

According to the recent study of Park & Jung (2007) ninety-one Economics-related Capacity Development Programme (ECDP) were undertaken during the recent decade (1997-2006). As depicted in Table 14.1, the year 2001 was a clear turning point for the trend of ECDP. This change might be influenced by Kim Jong-Il's successive visits to China - to Beijing in May 2000 and to Shanghai's

[15] Economic transition also calls for a process of retraining many professionals to enable them to work in the market environment (Kolodko, 2000).

[16] Instead of the word "Capacity Building Program", "Knowledge partnership" (Park & Jung, 2007) and "Knowledge Sharing" (Ireson, 2007) is also used in other articles. Here I assume that those words are not apparently different from each other in that they are designating a wide range of capacity-building projects in less-developed countries for meeting their sustainable development goals and economic transition needs by sharing knowledge and building partnerships.

Pudong district in January 2001 - as well as the historic inter-Korean summit in Pyongyang in June 2000.[17]

Table 14.1 ECDP Projects by year 1997 – 2006

	97	98	99	00	01	02	03	04	05	06	To tal
Num ber	4	5	4	5	16	13	10	20	9	5	91

Source: Park & Jung (2007, p. 80)

However, after the boom period by 2004, the number of projects decreased tremendously and returned to pre-2001 levels. It could be well explained by the North Korean nuclear issue as following. In February 2005 North Korea officially claimed nuclear deterrent capability and in October 2006 it went ahead with a nuclear test as well. However, as the geopolitical environment after the provocation is likely to be better than previous years, the prospects for ECDP are somewhat positive (Park & Jung, 2007, pp. 79-80).

2. Business Institute and Centre in Rajin/Sonbong

The Rajin Business Institute (RBI) is the first Western-style business school built in 1998 which is operating in North Korea to train prospective businessmen needed for settling down and maintaining the capitalist market system. As depicted in Figure 1, the Rajin Business Institute is a body affiliated to Rajin University which consists of five departments such as Maritime Transportation Department, Finance Department, Economic Management Department, RBI, and a night school.

[17] The most important reason why the figures rose in 2004 is the third visit of Kim Jong Il to China, which took place in April 2004 (Park & Jung, 2007, p. 80).

Figure 14.1 Outline of Rajin Business Institute

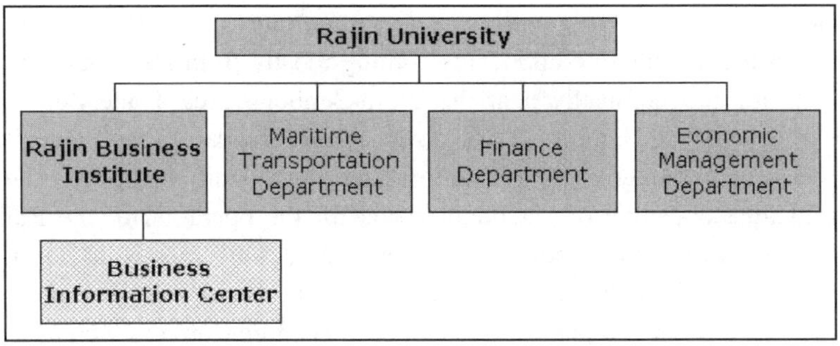

Source: North Korea Times

According to Kim, Gwang Yon who is the President of RBI, this institute was built in order to train those who are able to work at local restaurants, shops and hotels which deal with foreigners in Rajin/Sonbong special economic area.[18] Pyongyang has been experimenting within the Rajin-Sonbong free trade zone.

Regarding the fund and support, mainly U.N. Development Programme (UNDP) and U.N. Industrial Development organisation (UNIDO) have been supporting since 1996. Besides, some overseas Koreans donated teaching materials for this project. It is a joint project between the DPRK government and UNDP.

1) Facilities and Courses

The institute teaches 11 practical business subjects needed to understand the market economy.[19] Special emphasis was put on computer science and foreign languages such as English, Chinese, and Japanese. The period of school terms depends on majors which students choose and the school courses of five years

[18] Among such agencies are the External Economies Research Institute, affiliated with the Trade Ministry's Research Bureau, the International Affairs Research Institute and Kim Il Sung University's Department of Politics and Economics. The Rajin Business Institute thus plays the role of collecting foreign documents required for studying a limited opening of the North's market to the outside world.

[19] Subjects are business finance and accounting, banking and project finance, inventory control, services and tourism management, business administration, marketing, international trade, tax laws and business laws(Chosun Ilbo, 2001)

and six months are offered.[20] Foreign scholars from Singapore and Thailand were invited for lecture.[21]

2) Student profile and career path after the graduation

Students in the institute are applicants coming mostly from Hamgyang provinces which are geographically near the Rajin-Sonbong Free Trade Zone and some are from across the country. To be a successful candidate, a favorable family and ideological backgrounds are required as a precondition. In accordance with the institute objective of personnel needs for the operation of the Rajin-Sonbong Trade Zone, the institute's graduates find jobs mostly at foreign-invested firms operating in the Rajin-Sonbong Zone.[22] After graduation they work in famous foreign companies in that special economic area as well as governmental agencies. Graduates from the institute are generally well regarded as hard workers.

3) Functions and Roles

This institute has a significant meaning in that it is the first western business school in North Korea and that it tried to combine with the existing normal education institute. In that sense, North Korean authorities seemed to think that they could raise local elites as workers, who have a language and computer skill, in Rajin-Sonbong Free Trade Zone.

Along with the institute, the Rajin Business Information Centre is aimed at integrating and systematizing a subject-wise information structure concerning the Rajin-Sonbong economic zone, and offering convenience to foreign investors as well as domestic researchers and students.

3. Swiss MBA Programme in Pyongyang

The Pyongyang International Business School was established in 2004. A need for further education and training in business management and administration tools was noted by the DPRK government which resulted in discussions

---

[20] The institute offered only a six-month course at its inauguration, but now runs one- and two-year courses. With a quorum of 50 students per course, the institute has produced a total of 350 graduates from the 1998 second-term to the 2001 second term.

[21] The faculty originally consisted of professionals hailing from Singapore and Thailand and about a score of North Koreans who had undergone a five-month business administration course at Nanjing University in Singapore. Some ethic Koreans born in China and the United States have subsequently joined the faculty.

[22] For example, employing the largest numbers of them are the world-renowned Royal Dutch Shell Group that has set up crude oil refining facilities near the port of Rajin, the Thailand-based Rocksley Group, taking charge of communications in the free trade zone, and Hong Kong-based Emperor Group that runs the Hwanggwan Hotel. Graduates are also hired by the Rason City People's Committee, which administers the Rajin-Sonbong Free Trade Zone (Chosun Ilbo).

about parameters for a business programme with the DRPK authorities and the Swiss Development Cooperation.[23] Under Swiss sponsorship, the school enjoys the advisory support of the European Business Association.[24]

1) Facilities and Courses

A programme includes 12 three-day seminars per year sanctioned by examinations. The programme covers a broad range of themes relevant to business management and administration like western MBA. According to the theme programme, lectures were categorized as follows: (1) New Markets and Marketing, (2) Major Export Markets for North Korean companies, (3) organisational Behaviour and Human Resource Management, (4) Legal issues in International Business, (5) other Management Issues.

Furthermore, Lecturers are top managers from leading European corporations, who count among the world's experts in their particular industrial or commercial field, as well as renowned academics from European and Asian Universities.[25]

2) Student profile and career path after graduation

The students attending the seminars are already senior professionals. They belong to companies, ministries and institutions as senior officers as well as company executives. With the graduation, they have more possibility to access leading cadre elite group in Pyongyang.

3) Functions and Roles

It is clear that the institute functions as a training base for economic bureaucrats demanded when Pyongyang adopts a partially-open market system. Furthermore it plays a role as a hub to spread capitalism. The school also publishes

[23] In a context of severely restricted financial resources, one very cost effective training and appropriate exposure to its activities. Indeed, there is a need for Korean management staff to be trained in international state of the art practices to meet the requirements of foreign investors and contribute to more foreign investment as another important hard-currency earner for the national economy. Dealing with foreign investors also requires the ability for policy makers and officials to develop a legal framework to promote an attractive investment terrain in the North Korea.

[24] According to SDC Cooperation Program in North Korea (2006), the object of this program is to contribute to the North Korea's efforts for internal reforms which improve the performance of individuals, Organisations, networks and institutions by increasing their respective potential to deal with reforms.

[25] According to Felix Abt, director of this school, "most of the lecturers have been coming from Hong Kong Management Association. They have an academic teaching background and, in addition, international management experience of 20 years on average. A further asset they have, and that's another reason why I have chosen them, is that most of them also built up subsidiary companies in mainland China on behalf of Western companies. Thus, they not only have teaching knowledge acquired from books but also a lot of highly useful hands-on experience and are also well aware of the different business worlds and of the very different economic, cultural and political aspects in East and West, which is essential to know when interacting with businesses of other countries. Needless to say, they can understand and empathize with North Korea better than European and other Western lecturers who would have to overcome much more than just a wide geographical distance." (Interview in Blog)

its lectures and associated texts for dissemination to North Korean firms, universities, ministries and institutions. The lectures and other materials are published in Korean and English for dissemination to ministries, firms, universities and posted on the North Korean intranet as well.

IV. Concluding Remarks: The Juche Ethic and the Spirit of Capitalism?

Under the condition of the restricted data, we have reviewed two western business schools. It is sure that they are meaningful and somewhat far forward actions toward open-economy under the critical economic situation. As we have seen, the structure and function of two business schools have not big differences from that of other business schools in western countries. However, we need more data on the perspective of a receiver, namely students in order to evaluate how those actions influence them.

Here is one interesting episode at Swiss MBA in Pyongyang. One day, during the class of strategy about SWOT-Analysis, which is a strategic planning method used to evaluate the Strengths, Weaknesses, Opportunities, and Threats involved in a project or in a business venture, all the students chose socialism not as a Threat factor but as an Opportunity factor.

For them, capitalism seems to be just a tool in order to save their country from significant economic situation. It meets the intention of Kim Jong-Il, because he supposes to introduce capitalism to his elites gradually under the Juche ideology as an instrument for his people's relief. For him, the spirit of Capitalism seems to be based on the Juche ideology. However, it sounds very familiar to us, if we exchange the word "Juche" to "Protestantism". Max Weber explains that the origin of capitalism in West is from Calvin tradition as a personal relief to god.

As Mills (1956, p. 366) correctly points out, whatever the elites do, it is their belonging that their identity and existence ordain. North Korean cadre elites would also try to accept the capitalism as an instrument for the time being, to which they could show their loyalty and get a personal relief to the indisputable ruler. It is not clear whether we could find 'elective affinity' here; at least in my point of view, it just looks like 'artificial affinity'. However, the one thing that is clear is that the spirit of capitalism seems to be holy at first, but as times goes on, it would reveal its real face and push elites into the jungle of struggling for money. Who knows, maybe this could be a good condition to encourage a faction in North Korea?[26]

---

[26] As the North Korean economy has deteriorated, many elites have opened trading companies to earn foreign currency. This in turn has led to increasing corruption and weakening of the cohesion of the

References

Boyer, Christoph (1999). Kaperpolitik und zentrale Planbürokratie in der SBZ/DDR (1945-1961), in: Stefan Hornbostel (.), *Sozialistische Eliten : horizontale und vertikale Differenzierungsmuster in der DDR* (pp.11-30) Opladen : Leske und Budrich.

Carlin, Robert L. and Wit, Joel S. (2006). North Korean reform : politics, economics and security, Abingdon, Oxon : Routledge for the International Institute for Strategic Studies.

Ehlert, Willi et al. (1973). Wörterbuch der Ékönomie: Sozialismus. Berlin (Ost).

Gause, Kenneth. (2004). The North Korean Leadership: System Dynamics and Fault Lines. In *North Korean Policy Elites*, Kongdan Oh Hassig et al. Institute for Defence Analyses.

Hassig, Kongdan Oh, et al. (2004, June)North Korean Policy Elites. Institute for Defence Analyses.

Hassig, Ralph C. (2004). The Well-Informed Cadre. In *North Korean Policy Elites*, Kongdan Oh Hassig et al. Institute for Defence Analyses.

Hornbostel, Stefan (Ed.). *Sozialistische Eliten : horizontale und vertikale Differenzierungsmuster in der DDR*. Opladen : Leske und Budrich, 1999.

Hübner, Peter (Ed.). (1999). Eliten im Sozialismus : Beiträge zur Sozialgeschichte der DDR . Köln/Weimar/Wien: Böhlau.

Ireson, Randall. The Knowledge Sharing Experience in Agriculture, Presented at the Conference, Ten Prospects for International Cooperation in Knowledge Sharing in the Service of Economic Development in the DPRK, Seoul, November 2007 from www.ncnk.org/resources/publications/Ireson_KS_paper_Nov_07.doc

Kolodko, Grzegorz W (2000, June). Globalization and Catching-up: From Recession to Growth in Transition Economies. International Monetary Fund (IMF) Working Paper No. 00/100.

König, Klaus (1993). Bureaucratic Integration by Elite Transfer: The Case of the Former GDR. *Governance,* 6 (3). Blackwell Publishers, Cambridge

Mills, C. Wright (1956). *The power Elite*, New York.

Park, Jin and Jung, Seung-Ho (2007). Ten Years of Knowledge Partnership with North Korea, Asian Perspective, 31 (2). 75-93.

---

privileged class. Since the North Korean system is based on "feudal service nobility," where loyalty is ensured through privilege, if the regime loses its ability to placate the elite through goods and services, there is a real chance of the creation of factions. At first, these factions will compete with each other for the ever-declining privileges; if the situation persists, this factionalism could transform itself into centres of opposition to the regime (Gause, 2004, II-43).

Savada, Andrea Matles (Ed.). (1993). North Korea: A Country Study. Washington: GPO for the Library of Congress, 1993. From http://countrystudies.us/north-korea/61.htm

Wagner, Matthias. (1999). Das Kadernomenklatursystem - Ausdruck der führenden Rolle der SED, in: Stefan Hornbostel (Ed.). *Sozialistische Eliten : horizontale und vertikale Differenzierungsmuster in der DDR*. (pp.45-48). Opladen : Leske und Budrich.

Internet websites:

Swiss Development Cooperation
Pyongyang Business School
North Korea Times
Chosun Ilbo

Index

1

1994 Agreed Framework · 55

A

Acculturation strategies · 150
ADRA · 63
African Development Bank (afdb) · 231
Altruism · 62, 63
ASEAN plus 3 · 211, 220, 221, 222
Asia Invest · 16, 189
Asian Economic Cooperation · 231
Asian Monetary Fund · 237
Asia-Pacific Economic Cooperation · 281
Authoritarianism · 48

B

Bank of Korea · 185
Barcelona Traction Co · 78, 89, 92
Bavaria · 188, 206, 281
Berlin Congress of 1878 · 178
Berlin Wall · 169
Bernd Schaefer · 141
Bernhard Seliger · 13, 175, 225
Bretton Woods · 229
Bundestag · 108, 142
Busan Declaration · 236

C

Campus für Christus · 63, 65, 66, 67, 70
Capacity-building for North Korea · 239
Capitalism · 302, 307, 309, 313, 317, 318
Central and Eastern European states · 212, 220, 233
Chairman of the German-Korean Parliamentary Group · 13
Cheongjin · 251, 252, 258
China
  Cell phone companies · 48
  Economic transition · 50, 104, 309
  Trade with North Korea · 13, 191
  WTO membership · 212
Christian Social Union · 188
Chuncheon · 195, 210
Cold War · 10, 25, 57, 60, 74, 143, 144, 230, 231, 235
Colmberg · 206
Communism · 30, 170
Communist cadre · 17, 129, 307, 309, 313
Community-building · 34
Constructivism · 32, 36, 37, 40
Convention for the Protection of Human Rights and Fundamental Freedoms · 86
Copenhagen criteria · 219
Council of Europe · 24

D

Daean-Meccamidi (TM) joint-venture Company · 262
Daedong Credit Bank · 228
Dae-Jung Kim · 33, 216
Dae-Soon Kim · 77
Defectors
  Cognitive dissonance · 149, 156, 157
  Cultural integration · 164
  Culture shock · 153, 155, 166
Democratic People's Republic of Korea · 83, 84, 141, 180, 197, 294
Denuclearization · 13, 21, 22, 54
Development and Relief Agency · 64
DMZ · 197, 200, 254

Donghae · 195, 196
Draft articles on Diplomatic Protection · 79
Duck-Woo Nam · 236

E

East Asia
  Regionalism · 35
  Security cooperation · 35
ECHO · 23, 27, 176, 181
Einigungsvertrag · 105, 106
Etatism · 113
EU
  Accession of the eight Central and Eastern European countries · 219
  As a theory · 32
  As role model · 32
  Business in North Korea · 191
  Commercial policy · 33
  Common Foreign and Security Policy (CFSP) · 26
  Country Strategy Paper 2001-2004 · 30
  Dialogue with China · 180
  Dialogue with third countries · 28
  EU's 2007-2010 Food Security Thematic Programme · 31
  EU-DPRK cooperation · 26
  EU-DPRK trade capacity project · 182
  Europeanization · 36
  Food security Programmeme · 23, 181
  Humanitarian Aid Department · 23
  Integration · 28
  Investment in North Korea · 263
  Lessons from · 35
  National Indicative Programme (NIP) · 180
  Official Development Aid · 176, 178, 241
  Policy of engagement in North Korea · 27
  Policy on human rights · 28
  Relation with North Korea · 37, 60, 177, 297
  Relation with South East Asia · 190
  Support for inter-Korean reconciliation · 29
EU-Korea Industrial Cooperation Agency (EUKICA) · 191
Eurasian Development Bank (EDB) · 233, 234
European Bank of Reconstruction and Development (EBRD) · 232
European Business Association · 293, 294, 317
European Commission · 23, 27, 29, 265
European Council · 29
European Parliament · 26, 29
European Union Project Support · 14

F

Fascism · 167
Federation of German Industries · 281
Financial crisis · 226, 233, 237
Francois Mitterand · 232
Free trade agreement · 220, 222, 253
Freedom House · 29
Füssen · 205

G

Gangneung · 195, 196, 207
Gangwon · 16, 195, 196, 203, 209
  Education · 210
  Population · 196
  Potential tourism · 203
Geneva Agreement · 21
Geojin · 197
George Woods · 230
German Academic Exchange Service · 47, 280
German Agro Action · 61, 64, 67, 69, 176
German Cancer Research Institute · 280
German Cultural Institute · 61, 190
German diplomats in Pyongyang · 147
German Institute for Development Policy (Deutsches Institut für Entwicklungspolitik) · 69

German media · 146, 182
German Ostasiatischer Verein · 281
German unification · 142
German-Korean Friendship Society · 281
Germany
Constituional Amendments · 103
Constituional Courts · 122
Constitutional Amendments · 113, 116, 117
Constitutional law · 106, 117
Federal Republic of Germany · 103, 114, 142, 143, 230
GDR-FRG relations · 146
Inter-German Treaties · 103
IT Development in NK · 273
Labour costs in East and West · 152
Parliament · 108
Penal prosecution · 110, 111, 130, 134
Political parties · 82
Rehabilitation · 109, 176
Romantic road · 205
Unification · 71, 141, 149, 157, 188, 277
Geumgangsan · 186, 197, 216, 217, 219, 265
Goseong · 195, 196, 197, 203, 204, 205, 208, 209
Grundgesetz · 102
Gwang-Yon Kim · 315

H

Habermas on modernization and industrialization · 62
Hanns Seidel Foundation · 74, 175, 177, 182, 186, 188, 190
Hartmut Koschyk · 13
Heidelberg University Report on NK IT · 280
Helsinki Final Act (HFA) · 25
Hoengseong · 195, 196
Human rights
1948 Universal Declaration of Human Rights · 80
1966 Human Rights Covenants · 80
Human rights violation · 24, 80
International Covenant on Economic, Social and Cultural Rights. · 80
Human Rights without Frontiers · 29
Humanitarian Intervention · 92
Hwacheon · 195, 196
Hyundai Conglomerate · 217

I

Incheon · 204, 256, 264
Inje · 195, 196
Inter-American Development Bank · 231, 243
Inter-Korea
Dialogues · 144, 266
Institution-building · 30
Reconciliation · 21
Trade · 214
International Bank for Reconstruction and Development (IBRD) · 229, 230
International Commission on Intervention and State Sovereignty · 96
International Development Association (IDA) · 230
International financial institutions (IFI) · 237
International Financial Institutions (IFI) · 50, 51, 52, 188, 228, 237
International humanitarian law · 90, 93
International Monetary Fund (IMF) · 50, 229
Investment of Netherlands to NK · 269

J

Jacques Attali · 232
Jan Holtermann · 282, 289
Japan (Relation with NK) · 54
Japan External Trade Organisation (JETRO) · 54
Jeongseon · 195, 196
Joint Declaration of South and North · 144
Joon-Young Hur · 10, 294, 307

Juche · 145, 150, 211, 212, 213, 215, 219, 222, 307, 308, 318
Junichiro Koizumi · 81

K

Kaesong Special Economic Zone (SEZ) · 54, 186, 197, 211, 219
Kantian Dilemma · 60
Kim Chaek University of Technology · 259, 272
Kim Il Sung · 143, 145, 148, 308
Kim Il Sung University · 284
Kim Jong Il · 59, 284, 311, 314
Klaus-Martin Meyer · 290
Kofi Annan · 96
Kolja Naumann · 101
Korea
  Liability of a unified Korea · 124
  Principle of Equality · 134
  Proposed constitutional amendments · 137
Korea Asset Management Corporation · 226
Korea Computer Centre · 271, 273, 277, 282, 284, 285, 288, 298
Korea Computer Centre Europe · 277, 282
Korea-EU FTA · 265
Korean Association of Science and Technology (KAST) · 284
Korean European Technology and Economic Services (KETES) · 188
Korean peninsula · 147, 179, 181, 218
  Integration · 219
  Nuclear crisis · 32, 189
  Reconciliation · 37, 132, 191
  Unification · 34, 71, 112, 121, 147
Korean Peninsula Energy Development Organisation (KEDO) · 21, 23, 26
Korean Research Institute for Human Settlements (KRIHS) · 198
Korean summit · 21, 216, 314
Korean War · 81
Korean-European Cooperation Coordinating Agency (KECCA) · 189
Korea-US FTA · 266
Kyungdong University · 203, 207

L

Lee Hu-rak · 145
Lee Myung-Bak · 183
Linking Relief, Rehabilitation and Development (LRRD) · 31
Lisbon Treaty · 33
London club · 240
Lotus case · 86, 88

M

Maastricht Treaty · 33
Marcus Noland · 64
Market system · 48, 314, 317
Marxism-Leninism · 213
Mavrommatis Palestine Concessions case · 78
Max Planck Institute · 280
Max Weber · 318
Mercy Corps · 55, 73
Myoung-Kyu Park · 13, 21

N

Nampo · 249, 250, 253, 255, 256, 257, 259, 262, 264
Nampo-Pyongyang Corridor · 259, 265
Namyang · 253
NGO · 14, 46, 176
  Activities and operation in North Korea · 15, 60, 64, 72, 193
  European ngos · 14, 23, 59, 60, 65, 74, 227
  Humanitarian aid · 59, 300
Non-proliferation · 25, 177
North
  Relation with international fianancial institutions · 50

North Atlantic Treaty Organisation (NATO) · 29, 94
North Korea
Asylum to foreign terrorists · 82
Companies seeking European partners · 303
Concept of nation · 143
Conflict with China · 216
Constitution · 82, 98
Debt and financial system · 183, 228, 239, 241
Diplomat training · 55
Economy · 44, 125, 182, 185, 281
Energy · 49
Famine (1990s) · 14, 227
Financial sanction · 238
Foreign investments · 89, 221, 263
Future foundation · 28
Government, leadership and politics · 56, 144
Humanitarian assistance · 13, 14, 23, 27, 29, 72, 177, 178
Illicit trade · 227
Imports · 227
Industries · 251, 252, 253, 254, 255, 262, 294
Inflation · 185
Intellectual property right · 290
International trade · 211, 214, 221, 242
IT · 269
Japanese abductions · 81
Market · 175
Military · 213, 221
Monetary policy · 185
Nuclear policy · 26
People's traits · 71
Policies · 183
Power plant · 49
Problem on bank membership · 236
Proposed Constituional Amendments for North Korea · 136
Relatioinship with China · 211, 227, 253
Relation with the US · 14
Relations with the EU · 14, 55, 263
Rural development · 66, 67
Spillover effect · 34
Tourism · 203
Transition · 51
Transportation · 260
UNDP presence · 51, 235
Workers' Party · 120
WTO membership · 220
North Koreans
Reunification · 124
Training in China and EU countries · 184
Northeast Asia · 184, 225, 237
Northeast Asia Economic Forum · 235, 236
Northeast Asian Commercial Bank (NACB) · 237
Northeast Asian Development Bank · 16, 225, 236
Northeast Asian Development Bank (NADB) · 228, 235
Nosotek Joint Venture · 289
Nuremberg · 206

O

Oil price shock · 231
Organisation of American States (OAS) · 231
Organisation of Petroleum Exporting Companies (OPEC) · 231
Ostpolitik · 142

P

Paris club · 240, 241
Park Chung-hee · 145
Paul Tjia · 269
Peter Jurczek · 16, 195
Peter M. Beck · 15, 43
Pyongyang
Energy consumption · 261
EU Troika delegations' visit · 24

Private Voluntary Organisation Consortium (PVOC) · 73
Pyongyang International Information Centre for new Technology and Economy (PIINTEC) · 190
Pyongyang's strategy of snubbing the EU on security issues · 180
University of Science and Technology · 187
Pyongyang International Business School · 316

R

Rajin Business Institute (RBI) · 314
Rajin/Sunbong special economic zone · 215, 216, 244, 253, 254, 315, 316
Ralph M. Wrobel · 211
Resolution 1674 · 96
Resolution 62/167 · 83
Responsibility to protect · 92
Robert mcnamara · 230
Romantic Franconia · 206
Royal Institute of Technology (Sweden) · 227
Russia debt · 241
Russian financial crisis · 241

S

S. Stanley Katz · 236
Samcheok · 195, 196
Security · 25
Sinuiju · 216, 252, 253, 258
Sinuiju Special Administrative Region (SAR) · 253
Six party talks · 27, 177, 178, 226
Socialism · 61, 307, 309, 312, 318
Socialist Unity Party · 142
Sokcho · 195, 196, 207
Somalia · 95
Songun · 188
Soon-Hyung Yi · 149
South Korea
Chaebol · 54
Constituional amendments · 115
Constitutional law · 118, 121
Human rights · 116
Investments to North korea · 49
Military strength · 144
National assembly · 117
Politics · 118
Relatioin with NK · 115, 189
Self-perception · 143
Technical aid to NK · 53
Unification policy · 71
Soviet Union · 102, 112
Stalinism · 167
Stanislas Roussin · 249
Sung-Jo Park · 13, 277
Sunshine policy · 71
Swiss Aid · 187

T

Taebaek · 195, 196
Terrorism · 35, 53, 245, 291
Tin Ming Alan · 287
Totalitarian regime · 98, 125
Tumen River Development Project · 236

U

United Nations · 51, 143, 243
Charter · 85
Children's Fund (UNICEF) · 50
Covenant of the League of Nations · 85
Development Programmeme (UNDP) · 50, 315
Economic Commission for Asia and the Far East · 231
Educational, Scientific and Cultural Organisation (UNESCO) · 51
Food and Agriculture Organisation (FAO) · 51
Human Rights Commission · 22
Industrial Development Organisation (UNIDO) · 51, 315

Institute for Training and Research (UNITAR) · 52
International Law Commission · 79
Role in North Korea · 51
Role in Vietnam · 51
Sanctions to NK · 226
UN Security Council · 97
UN summit 2005 · 178
World Food Programmeme (WFP) · 23, 50, 238
United States
And the Korean War · 144
Sanctions to North Korea · 226

V

Vienna Convention on the Law of Treaties · 85, 86, 88
Vietnam economic transition · 186, 242
Volker Eloesser · 290, 291, 292, 293
Volkskammerwahlen · 103

W

W. Thess · 278
Wahlvertrag · 106
Weimar Republic · 141
Wonju · 195, 196
Wonsan · 207
World Bank · 52, 53, 55, 229, 230, 232, 236
World Health Organisation · 213
World Summit of 2005 · 96
World Trade Organisation · 211, 220
World War II · 77, 79, 92, 103, 141, 150, 229
Worldwide debt crisis · 240
Würzburg · 205

Y

Yang Bin · 216
Yanggu · 195, 196
Yangyang · 195, 196, 204, 207